Red String™

story and art by
Gina Biggs

Dark Horse Books™

Publisher
Mike Richardson

Art Director
Lia Ribacchi

Designer
Heidi Fainza

Editor
Mike Carriglitto

Editorial Assistants
Ryan Jorgensen and Samantha Robertson

Published by
Dark Horse Books
A division of
Dark Horse Comics, Inc.
10956 SE Main Street
Milwaukie, OR 97222

To find a comics shop in your area,
call the Comic Shop Locator Service toll-free at
1-888-266-4226

First edition: December 2006
ISBN-10: 1-59307-624-X
ISBN-13: 978-1-59307-624-5

10 9 8 7 6 5 4 3 2 1

Printed in U.S.A.

Contents

Foreword

As an author, I find that if something interests me, I want to write about it. I have to write about it. The story just begs to be set free one way or another. I started *Red String* for that very reason. There was a story that was begging to be brought to life and I had no choice, but to comply. Thus, a webcomic was born.

People often ask me at conventions a question I am sure many writers receive: "So what's this story about?" In the beginning I would simply answer that it's a story about romance and arranged marriage. However, as my one-shot story ballooned into a full-blown series I have come to realize it is much more than that. It is a story about discovering who you are. It's about growing up.

Those awkward years leading to adulthood are a universal event, even if for some of us they exist as just a vague memory. Adults who remember might discover a sense of nostalgia within these pages and those going through them now will find they are not alone. That's what I feel is special about this story. Anyone can find someone to identify with in *Red String*. My hope is that you do.

I thank you for your support of *Red String*.

You can continue reading at the website.
http://redstring.strawberrycomics.com/

—Gina

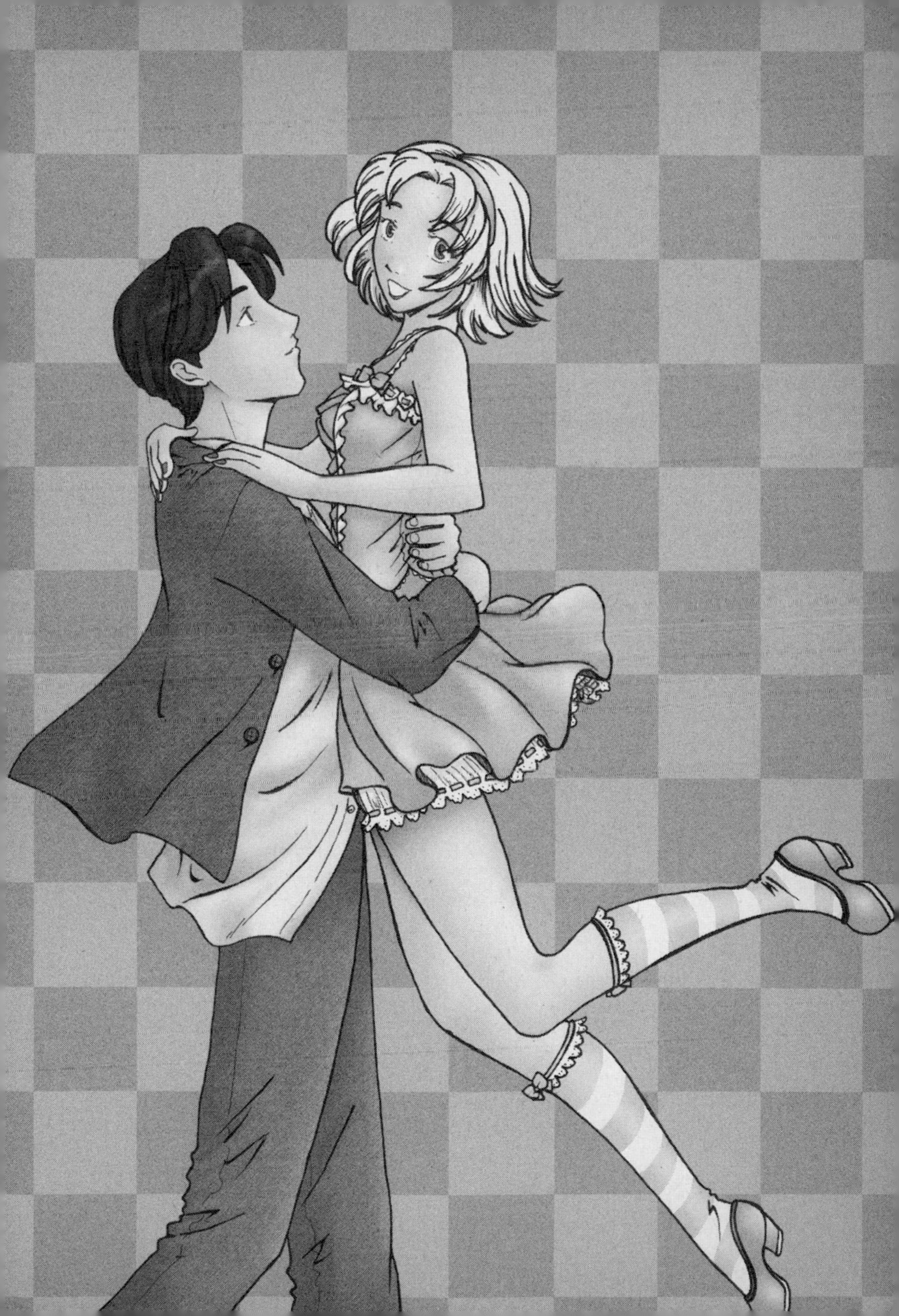

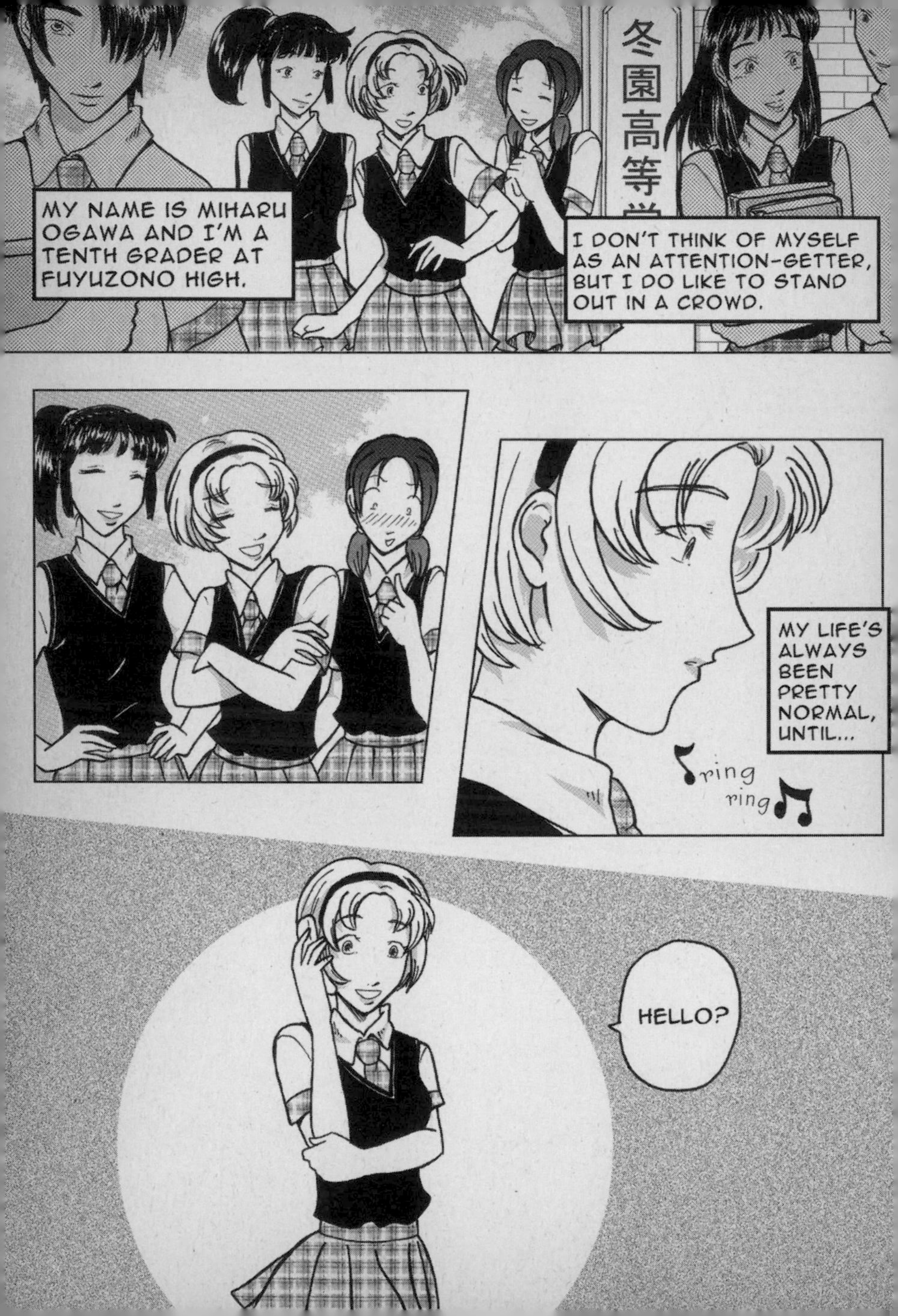

冬園高等学
MY NAME IS MIHARU OGAWA AND I'M A TENTH GRADER AT FUYUZONO HIGH.
I DON'T THINK OF MYSELF AS AN ATTENTION-GETTER, BUT I DO LIKE TO STAND OUT IN A CROWD.
MY LIFE'S ALWAYS BEEN PRETTY NORMAL, UNTIL...
ring ring
HELLO?

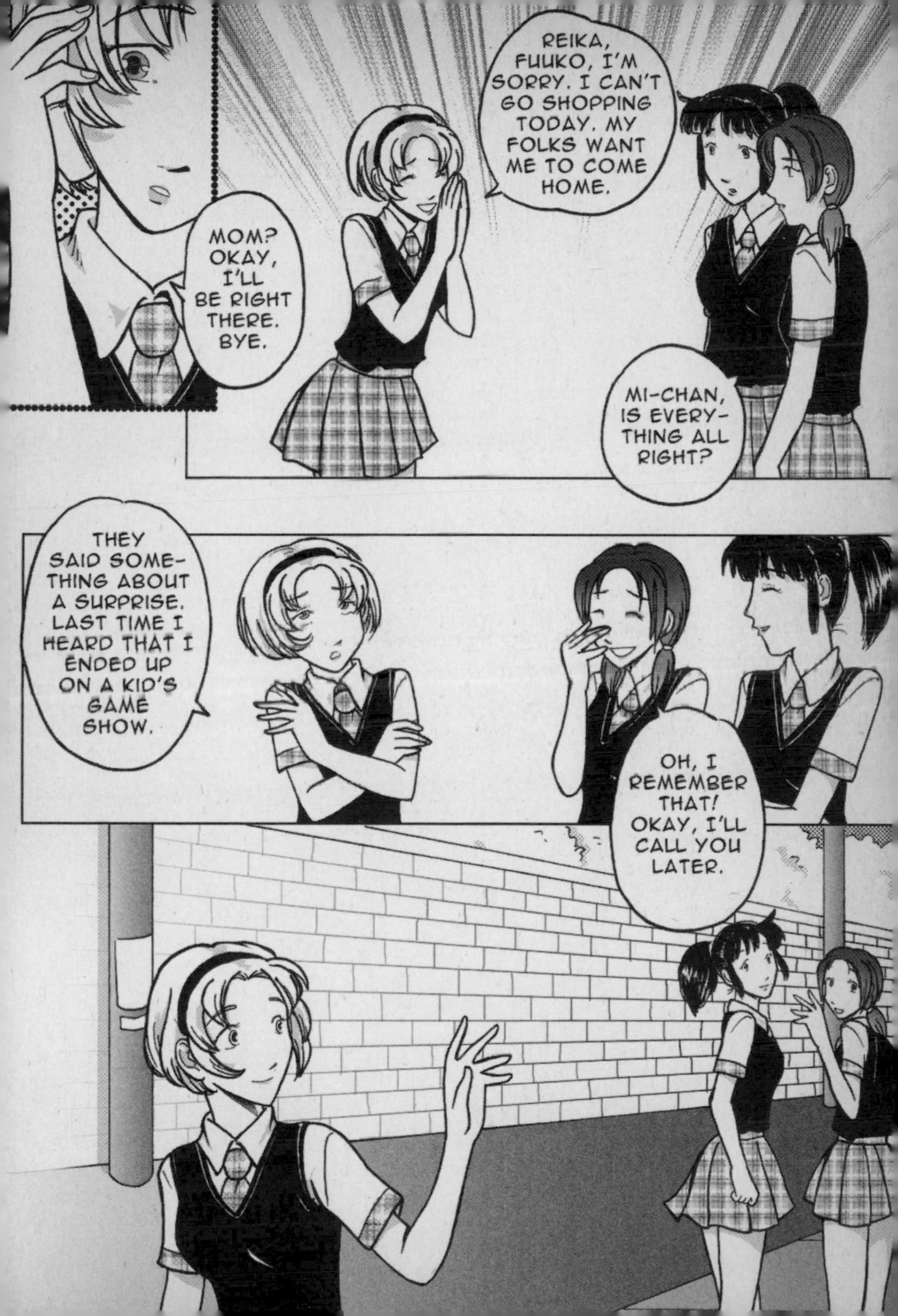
MOM? OKAY, I'LL BE RIGHT THERE. BYE.
REIKA, FUUKO, I'M SORRY. I CAN'T GO SHOPPING TODAY. MY FOLKS WANT ME TO COME HOME.
MI-CHAN, IS EVERYTHING ALL RIGHT?
THEY SAID SOMETHING ABOUT A SURPRISE. LAST TIME I HEARD THAT I ENDED UP ON A KID'S GAME SHOW.
OH, I REMEMBER THAT! OKAY, I'LL CALL YOU LATER.

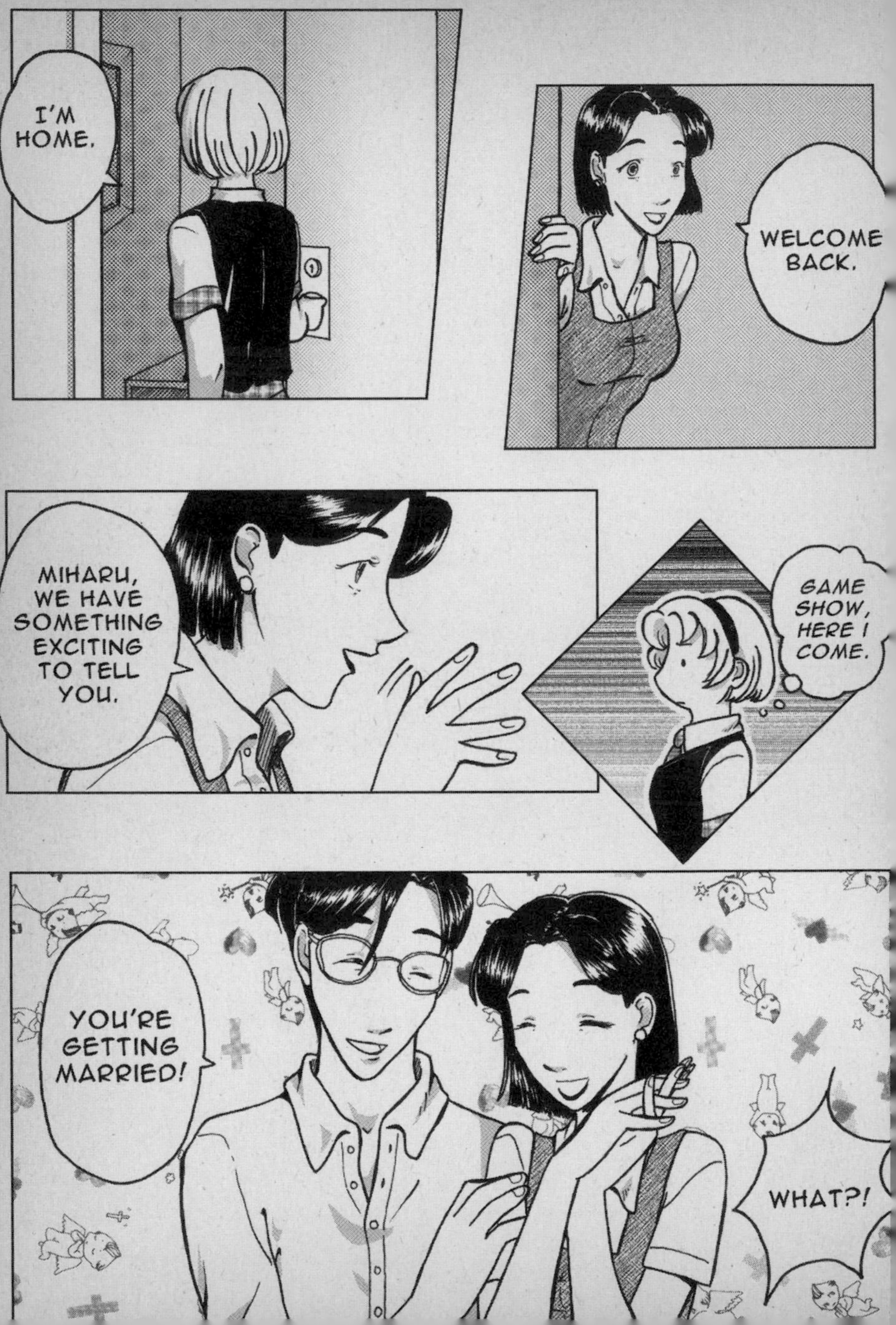

I'M HOME.
WELCOME BACK.
MIHARU, WE HAVE SOMETHING EXCITING TO TELL YOU.
GAME SHOW, HERE I COME.
YOU'RE GETTING MARRIED!
WHAT?!

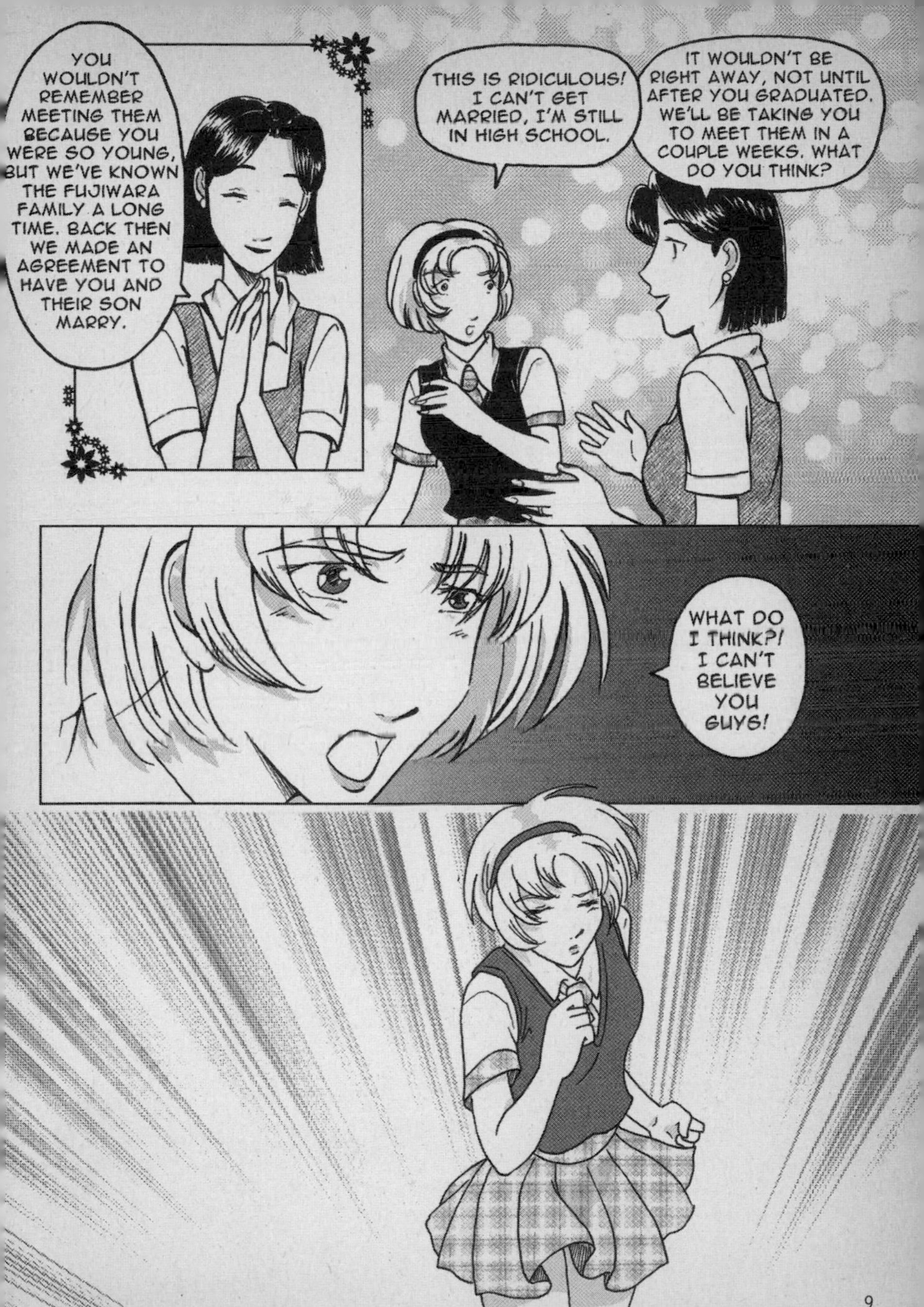
YOU WOULDN'T REMEMBER MEETING THEM BECAUSE YOU WERE SO YOUNG, BUT WE'VE KNOWN THE FUJIWARA FAMILY A LONG TIME. BACK THEN WE MADE AN AGREEMENT TO HAVE YOU AND THEIR SON MARRY.
THIS IS RIDICULOUS! I CAN'T GET MARRIED, I'M STILL IN HIGH SCHOOL.
IT WOULDN'T BE RIGHT AWAY, NOT UNTIL AFTER YOU GRADUATED. WE'LL BE TAKING YOU TO MEET THEM IN A COUPLE WEEKS. WHAT DO YOU THINK?
WHAT DO I THINK?! I CAN'T BELIEVE YOU GUYS!

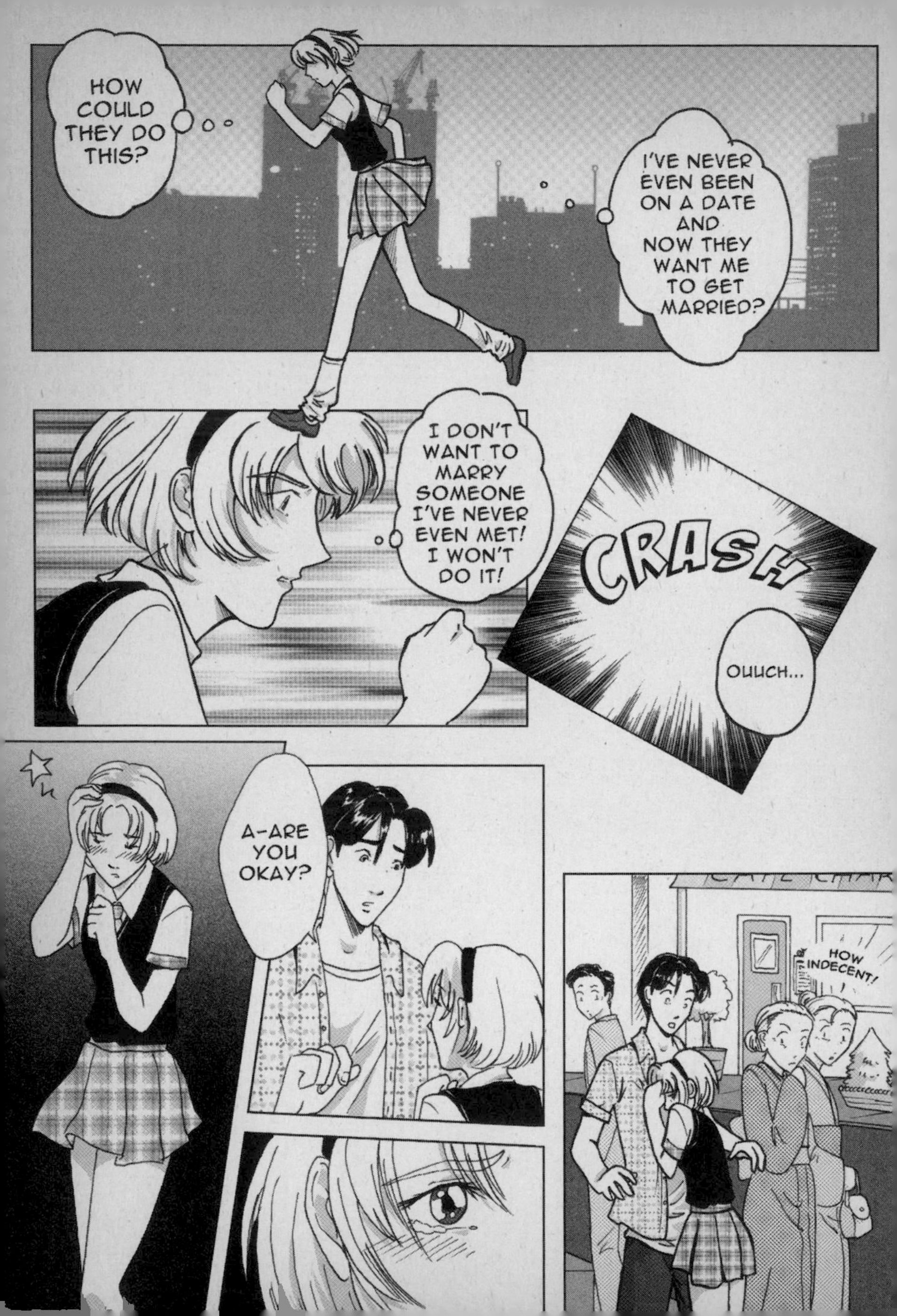
HOW COULD THEY DO THIS?
I'VE NEVER EVEN BEEN ON A DATE AND NOW THEY WANT ME TO GET MARRIED?
I DON'T WANT TO MARRY SOMEONE I'VE NEVER EVEN MET! I WON'T DO IT!
CRASH
OUUCH...
A-ARE YOU OKAY?
HOW INDECENT!

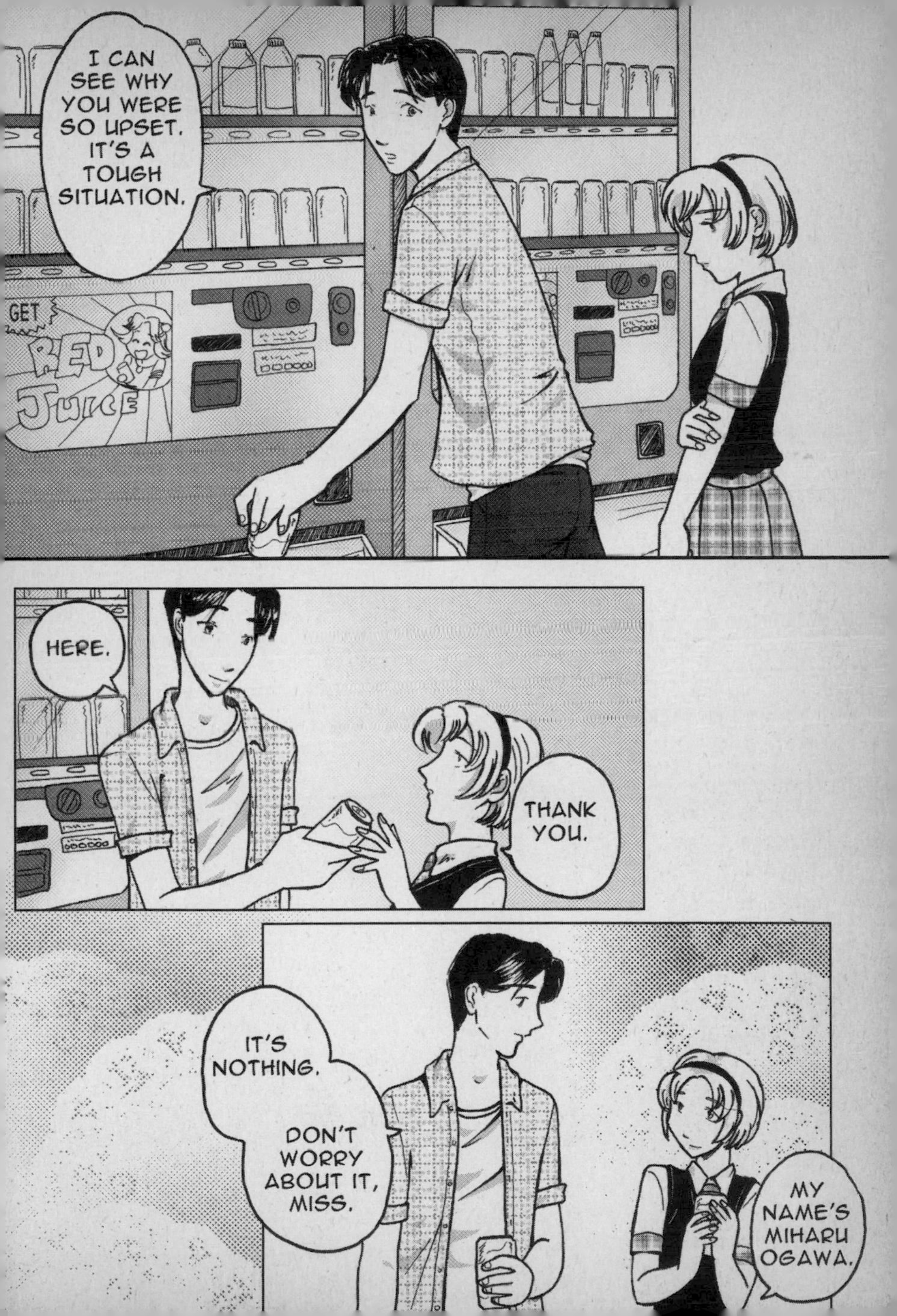
I CAN SEE WHY YOU WERE SO UPSET. IT'S A TOUGH SITUATION.
GET RED JUICE
HERE.
THANK YOU.
IT'S NOTHING.
DON'T WORRY ABOUT IT, MISS.
MY NAME'S MIHARU OGAWA.

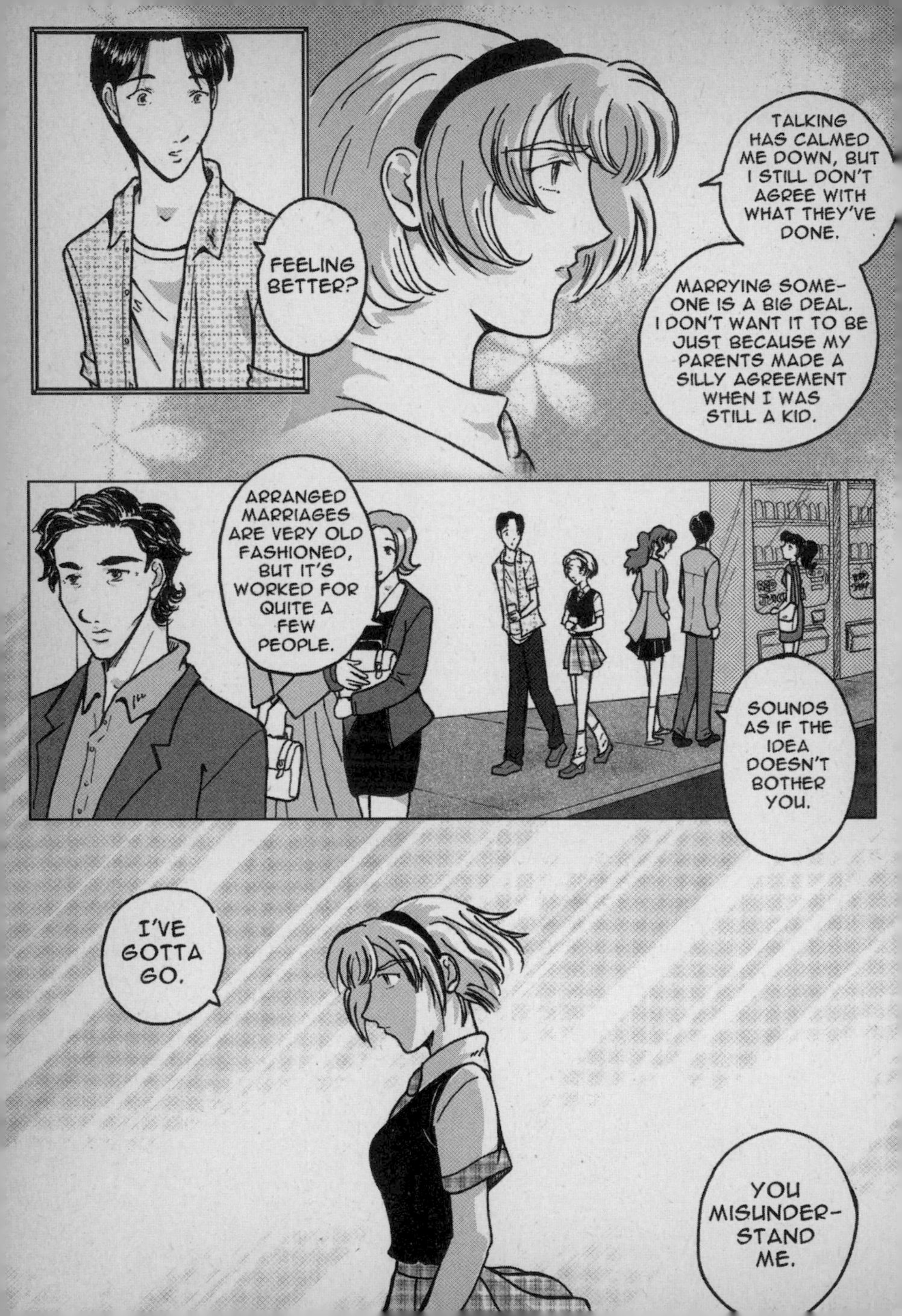
FEELING BETTER?
TALKING HAS CALMED ME DOWN, BUT I STILL DON'T AGREE WITH WHAT THEY'VE DONE.
MARRYING SOME-ONE IS A BIG DEAL. I DON'T WANT IT TO BE JUST BECAUSE MY PARENTS MADE A SILLY AGREEMENT WHEN I WAS STILL A KID.
ARRANGED MARRIAGES ARE VERY OLD FASHIONED, BUT IT'S WORKED FOR QUITE A FEW PEOPLE.
SOUNDS AS IF THE IDEA DOESN'T BOTHER YOU.
I'VE GOTTA GO.
YOU MISUNDER-STAND ME.

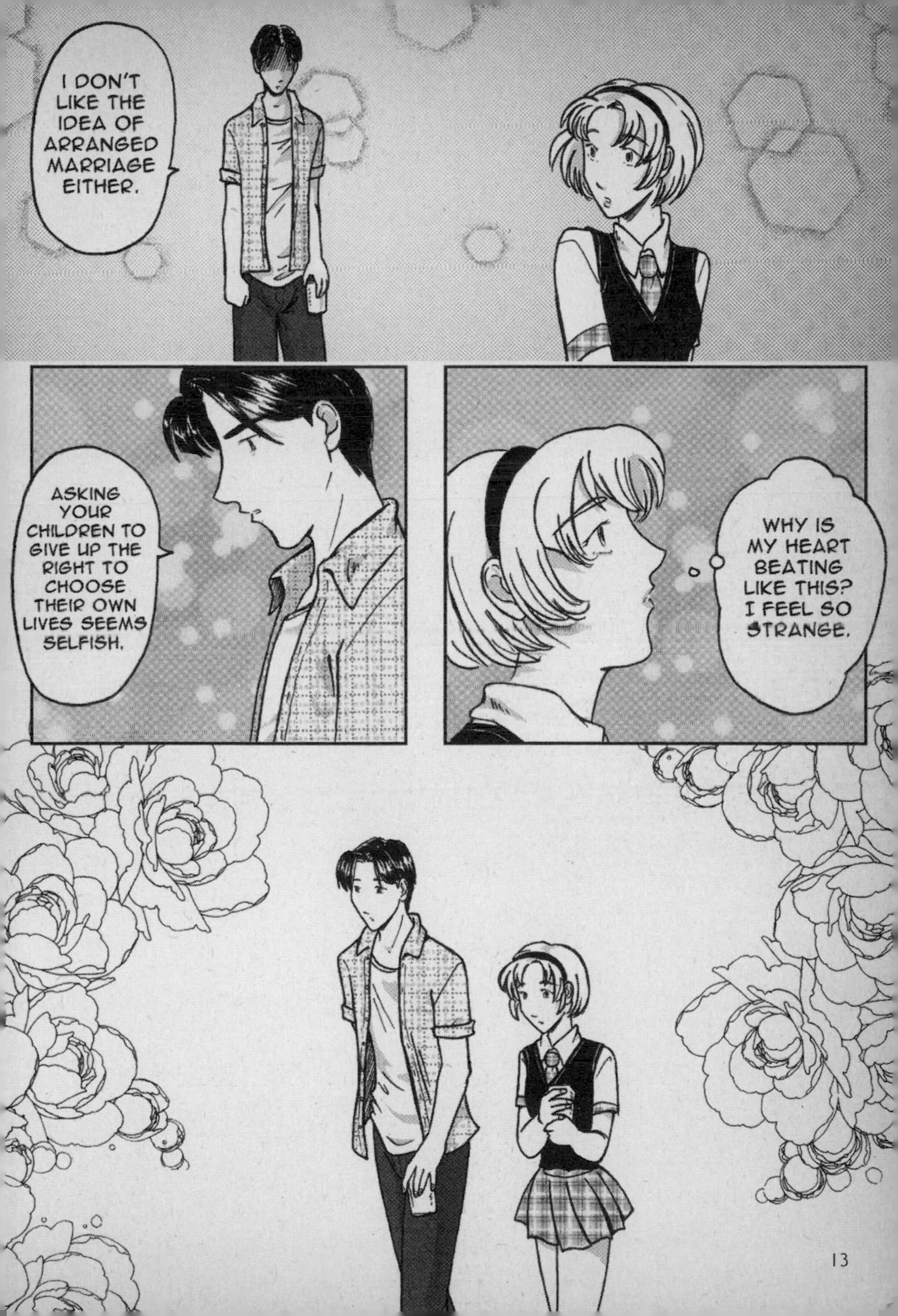
I DON'T LIKE THE IDEA OF ARRANGED MARRIAGE EITHER.
ASKING YOUR CHILDREN TO GIVE UP THE RIGHT TO CHOOSE THEIR OWN LIVES SEEMS SELFISH.
WHY IS MY HEART BEATING LIKE THIS? I FEEL SO STRANGE.

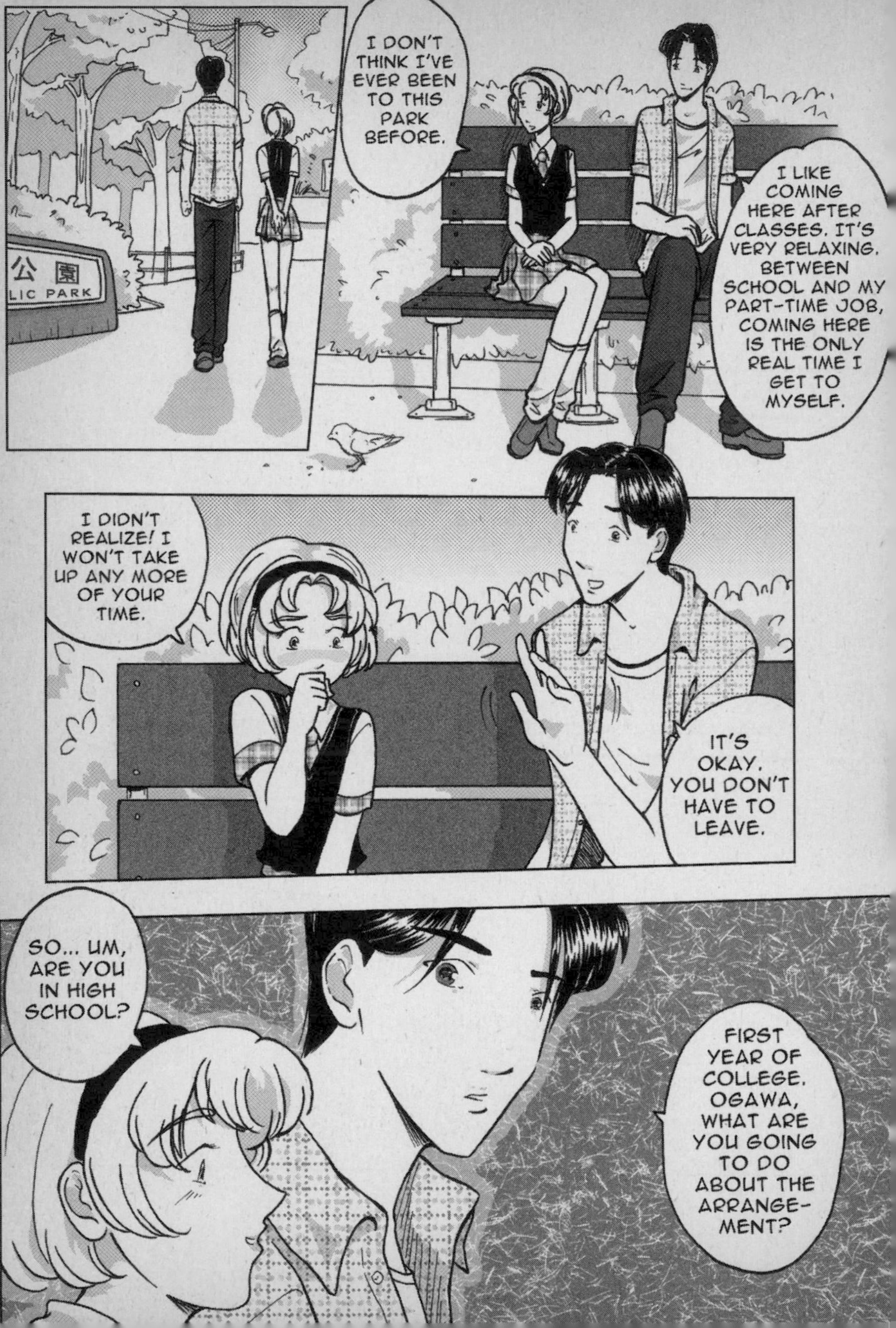
公園
LIC PARK
I DON'T THINK I'VE EVER BEEN TO THIS PARK BEFORE.
I LIKE COMING HERE AFTER CLASSES. IT'S VERY RELAXING. BETWEEN SCHOOL AND MY PART-TIME JOB, COMING HERE IS THE ONLY REAL TIME I GET TO MYSELF.
I DIDN'T REALIZE! I WON'T TAKE UP ANY MORE OF YOUR TIME.
IT'S OKAY. YOU DON'T HAVE TO LEAVE.
SO... UM, ARE YOU IN HIGH SCHOOL?
FIRST YEAR OF COLLEGE. OGAWA, WHAT ARE YOU GOING TO DO ABOUT THE ARRANGE-MENT?

I DON'T KNOW.
MOM SAYS THAT TWO PEOPLE DESTINED FOR EACH OTHER ARE TIED TOGETHER BY A RED STRING. HOW AM I SUPPOSED TO FIND THAT PERSON IF THEY ARRANGE A MARRIAGE WITH SOMEONE I'VE NEVER MET?

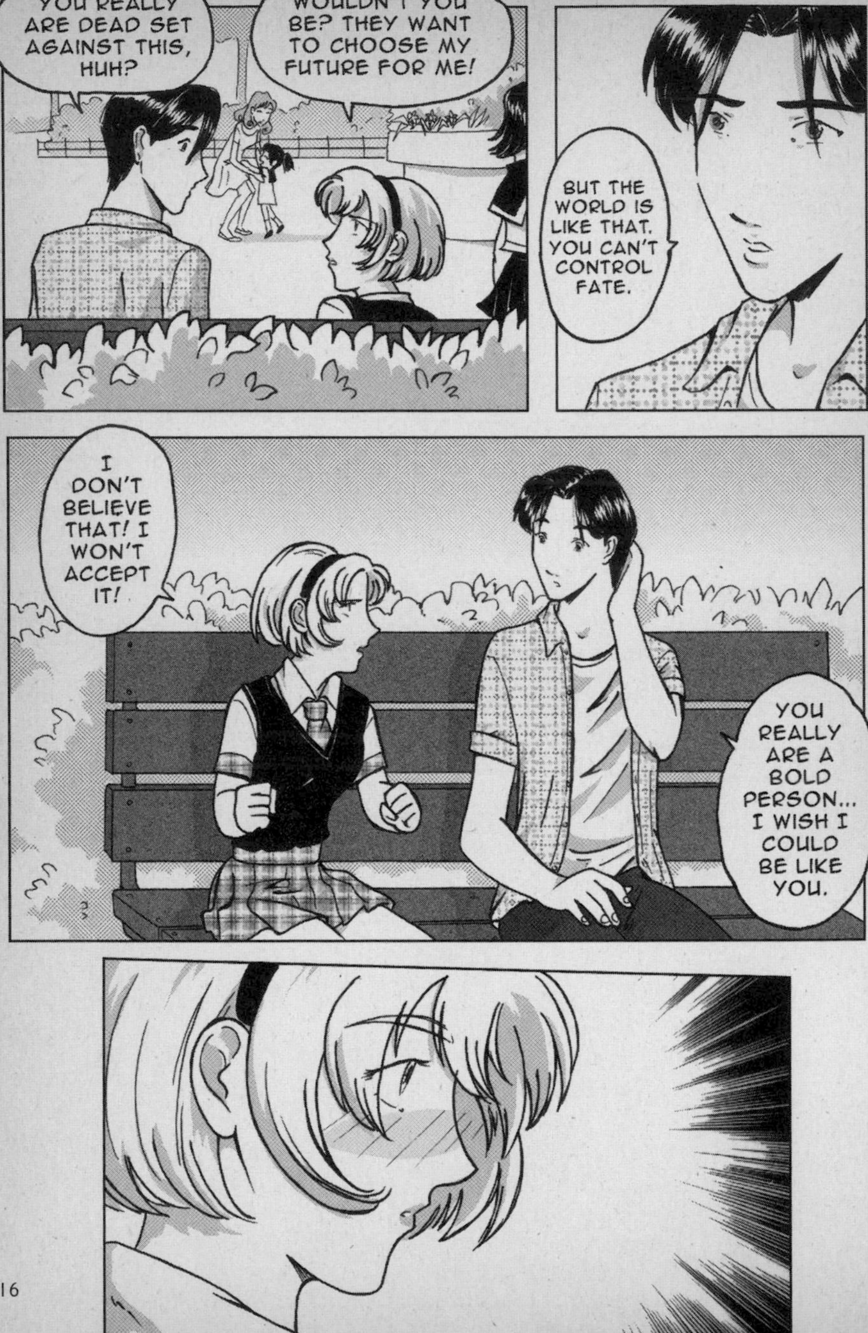
YOU REALLY ARE DEAD SET AGAINST THIS, HUH?
WOULDN'T YOU BE? THEY WANT TO CHOOSE MY FUTURE FOR ME!
BUT THE WORLD IS LIKE THAT. YOU CAN'T CONTROL FATE.
I DON'T BELIEVE THAT! I WON'T ACCEPT IT!
YOU REALLY ARE A BOLD PERSON... I WISH I COULD BE LIKE YOU.

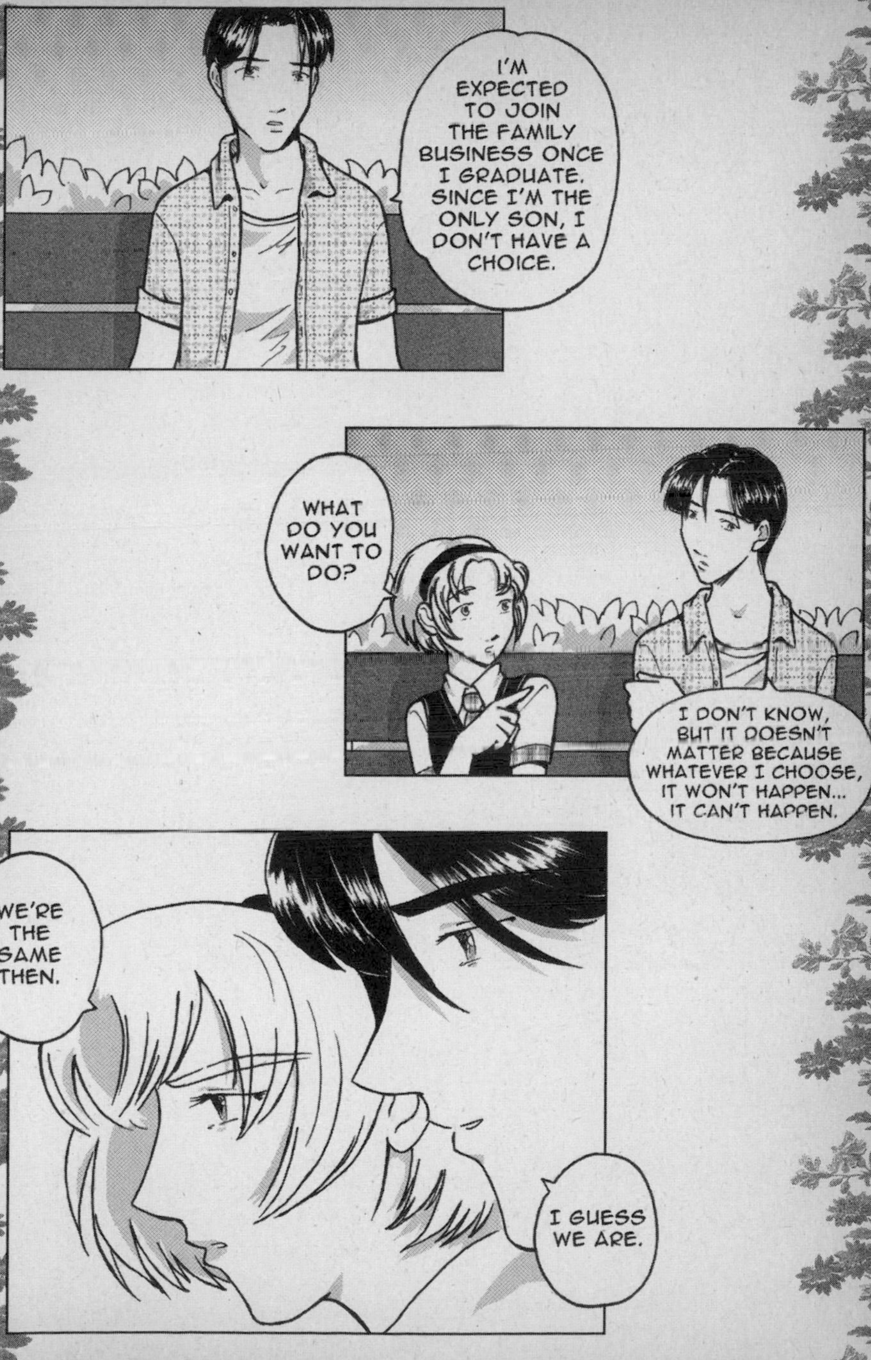
I'M EXPECTED TO JOIN THE FAMILY BUSINESS ONCE I GRADUATE. SINCE I'M THE ONLY SON, I DON'T HAVE A CHOICE.
WHAT DO YOU WANT TO DO?
I DON'T KNOW, BUT IT DOESN'T MATTER BECAUSE WHATEVER I CHOOSE, IT WON'T HAPPEN... IT CAN'T HAPPEN.
WE'RE THE SAME THEN.
I GUESS WE ARE.

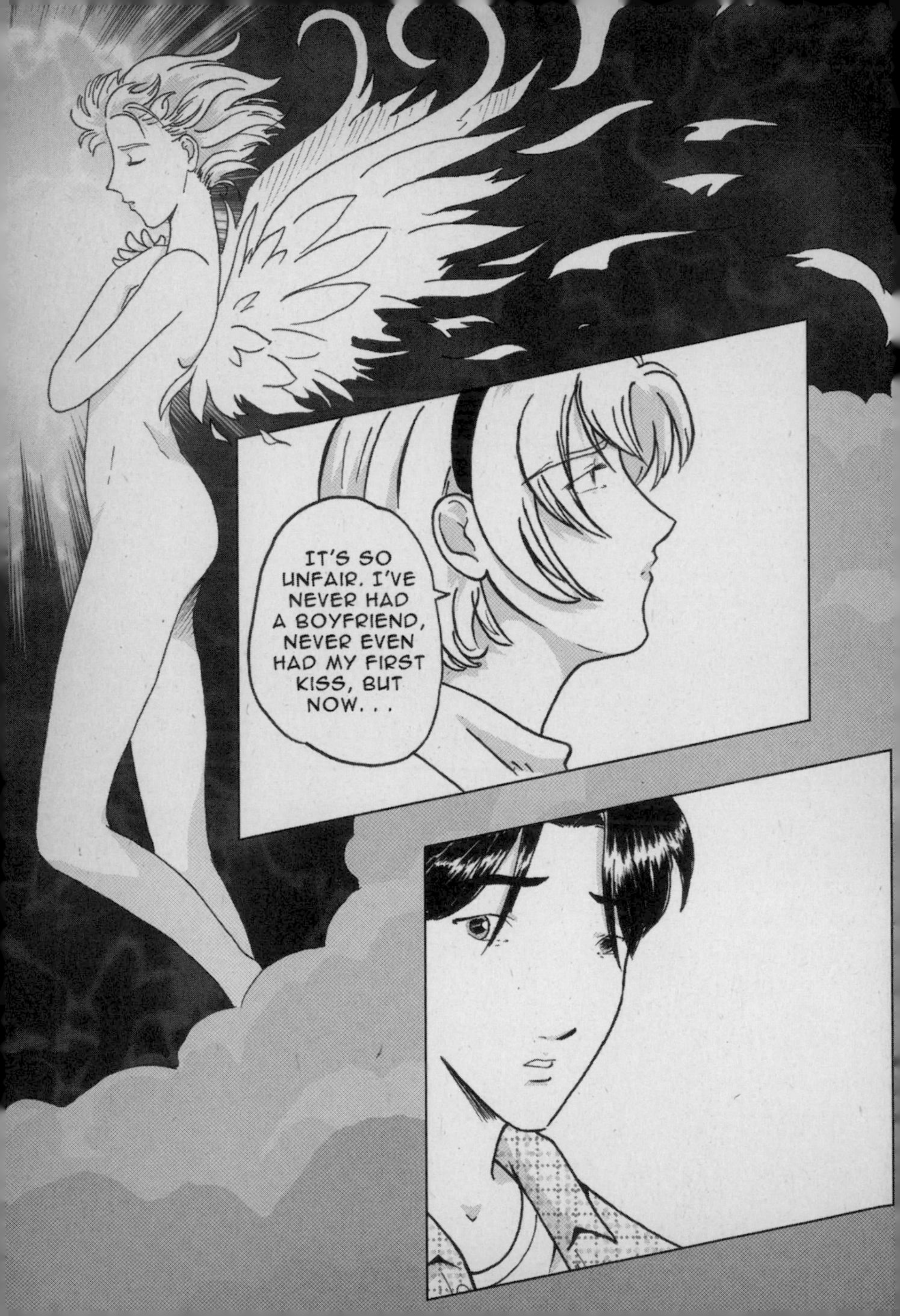
IT'S SO UNFAIR. I'VE NEVER HAD A BOYFRIEND, NEVER EVEN HAD MY FIRST KISS, BUT NOW. . .

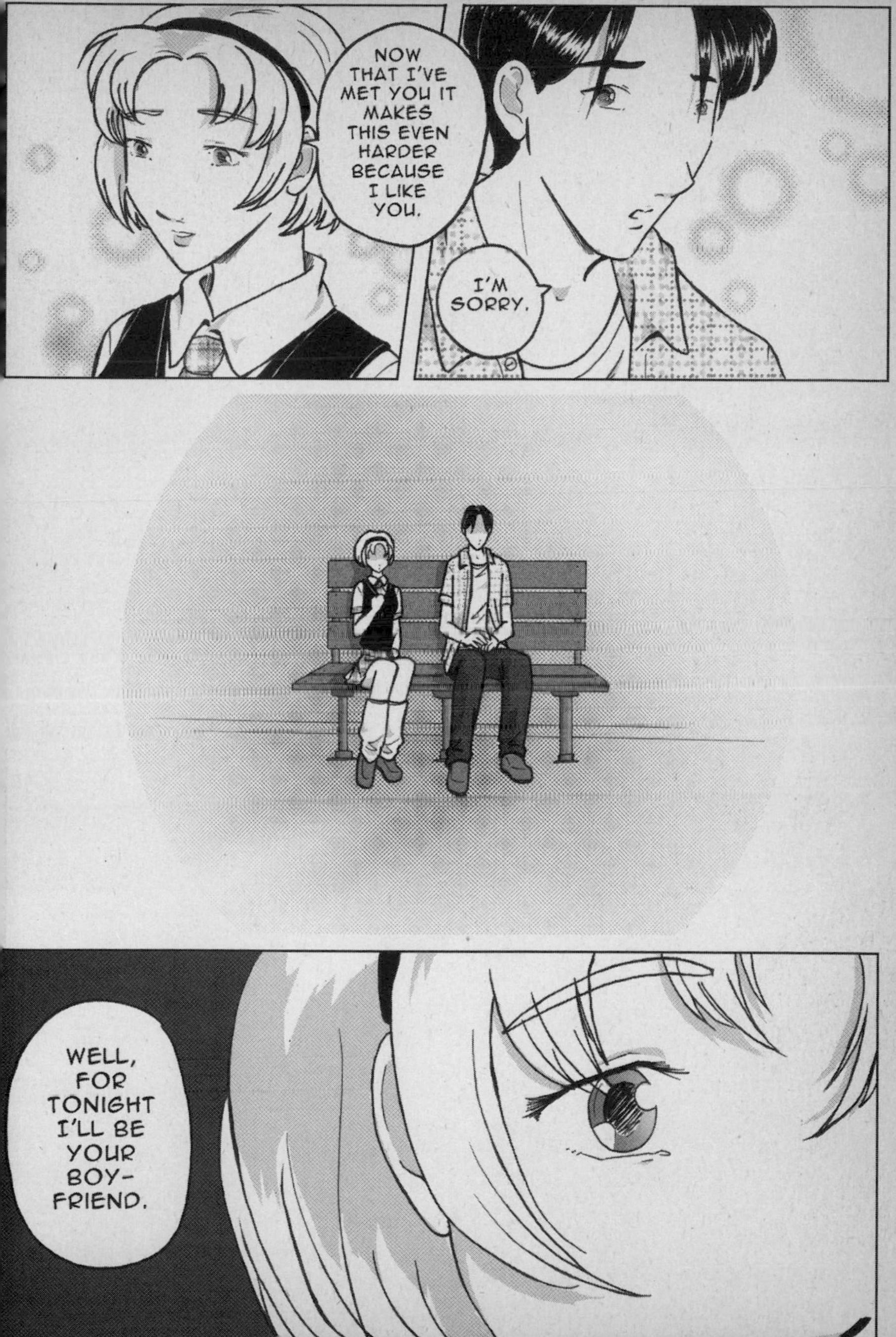
NOW THAT I'VE MET YOU IT MAKES THIS EVEN HARDER BECAUSE I LIKE YOU.
I'M SORRY.
WELL, FOR TONIGHT I'LL BE YOUR BOY-FRIEND.

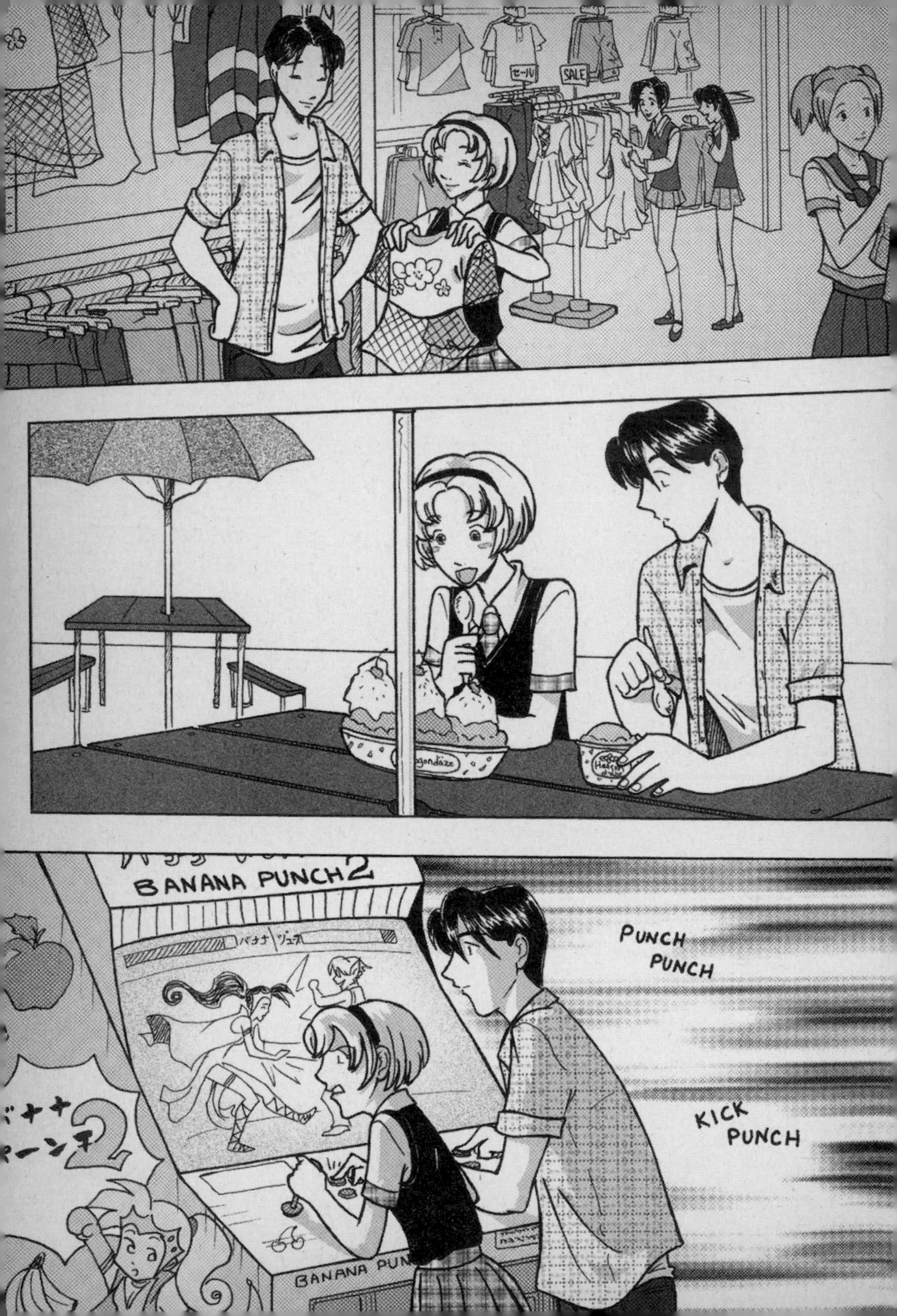
セール
SALE
BANANA PUNCH2
PUNCH
PUNCH
KICK
PUNCH
BANANA PUN

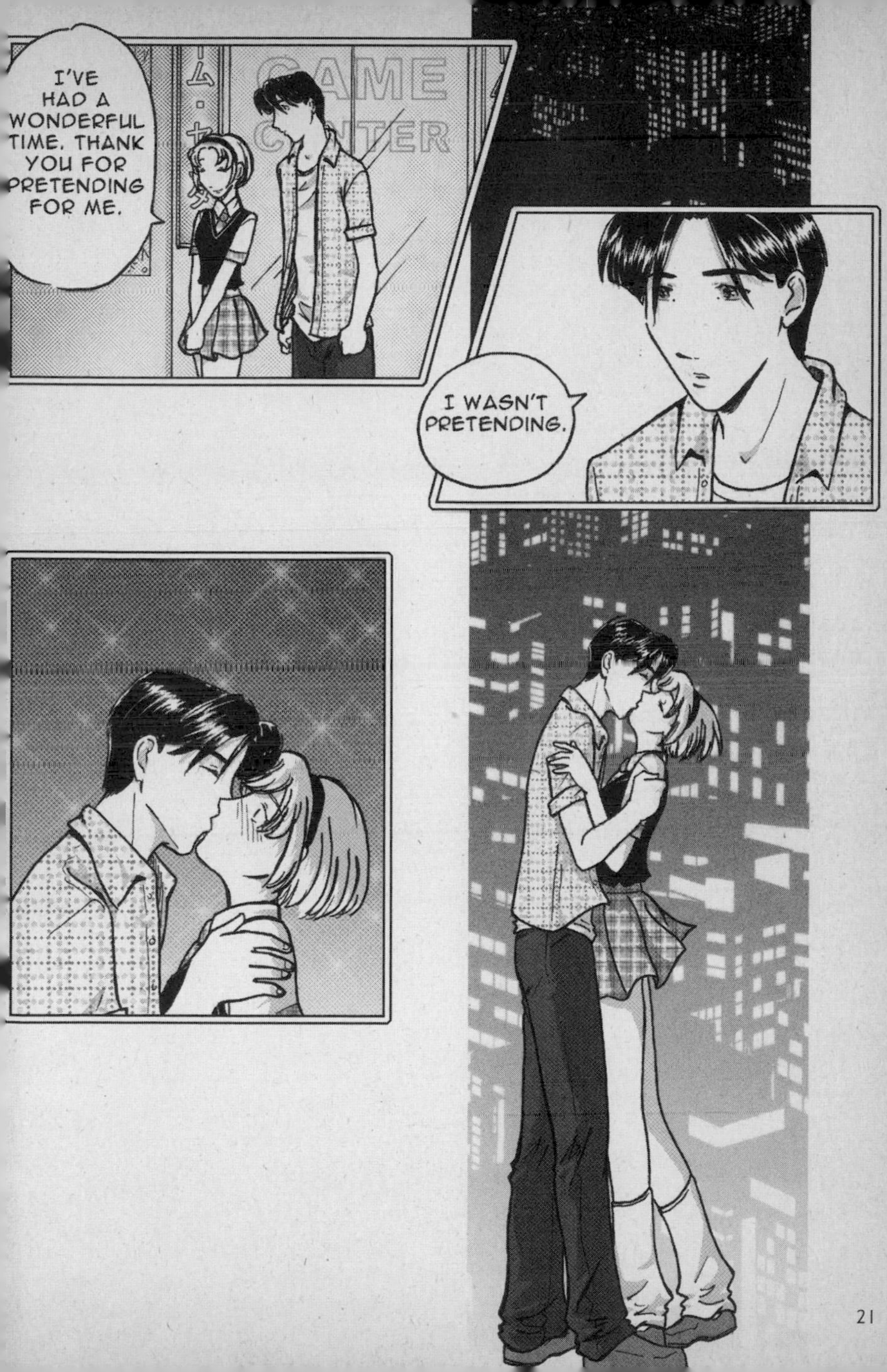
GAME CENTER
I'VE HAD A WONDERFUL TIME. THANK YOU FOR PRETENDING FOR ME.
I WASN'T PRETENDING.

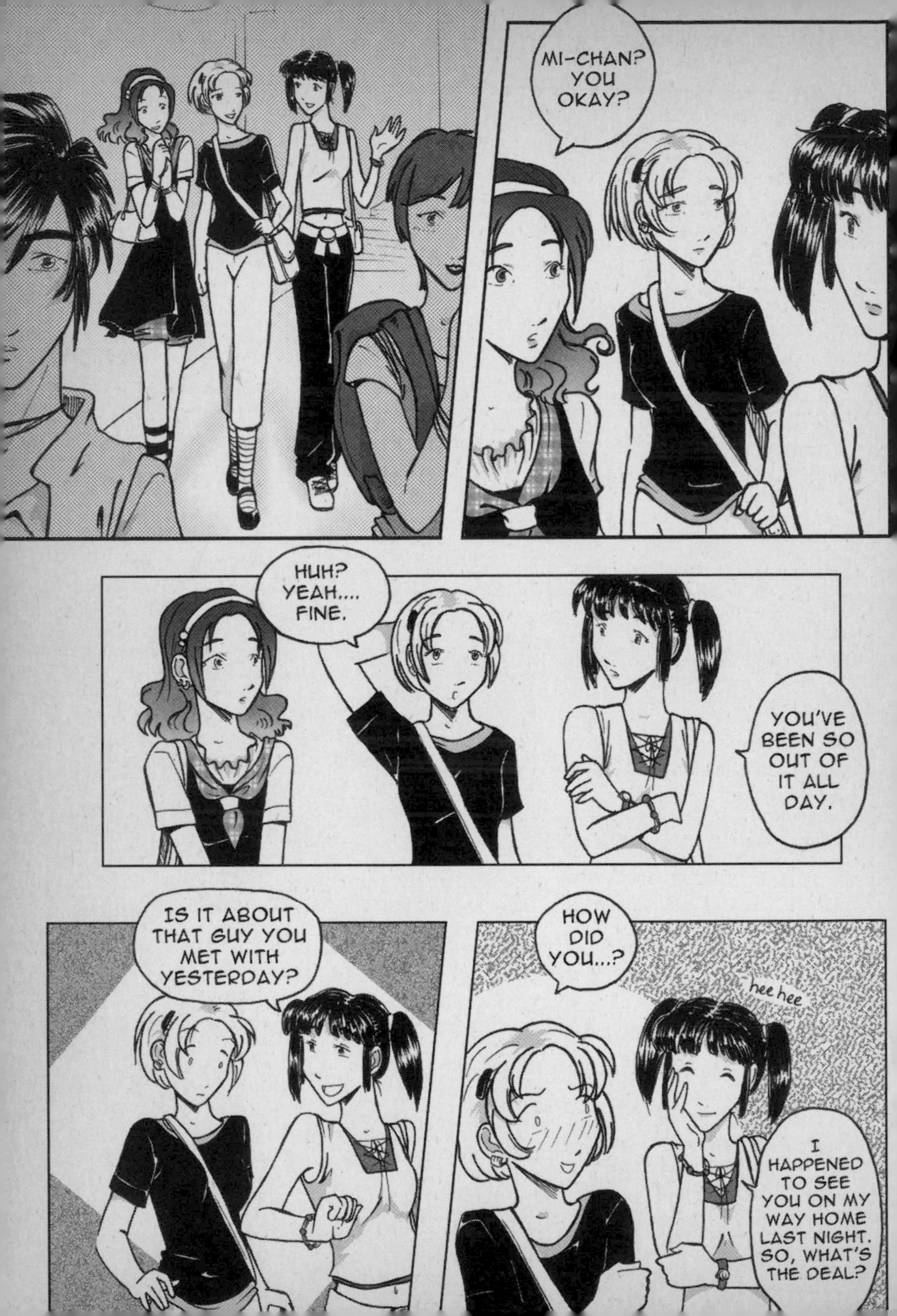
MI-CHAN? YOU OKAY?
HUH? YEAH.... FINE.
YOU'VE BEEN SO OUT OF IT ALL DAY.
IS IT ABOUT THAT GUY YOU MET WITH YESTERDAY?
HOW DID YOU...?
hee hee
I HAPPENED TO SEE YOU ON MY WAY HOME LAST NIGHT. SO, WHAT'S THE DEAL?

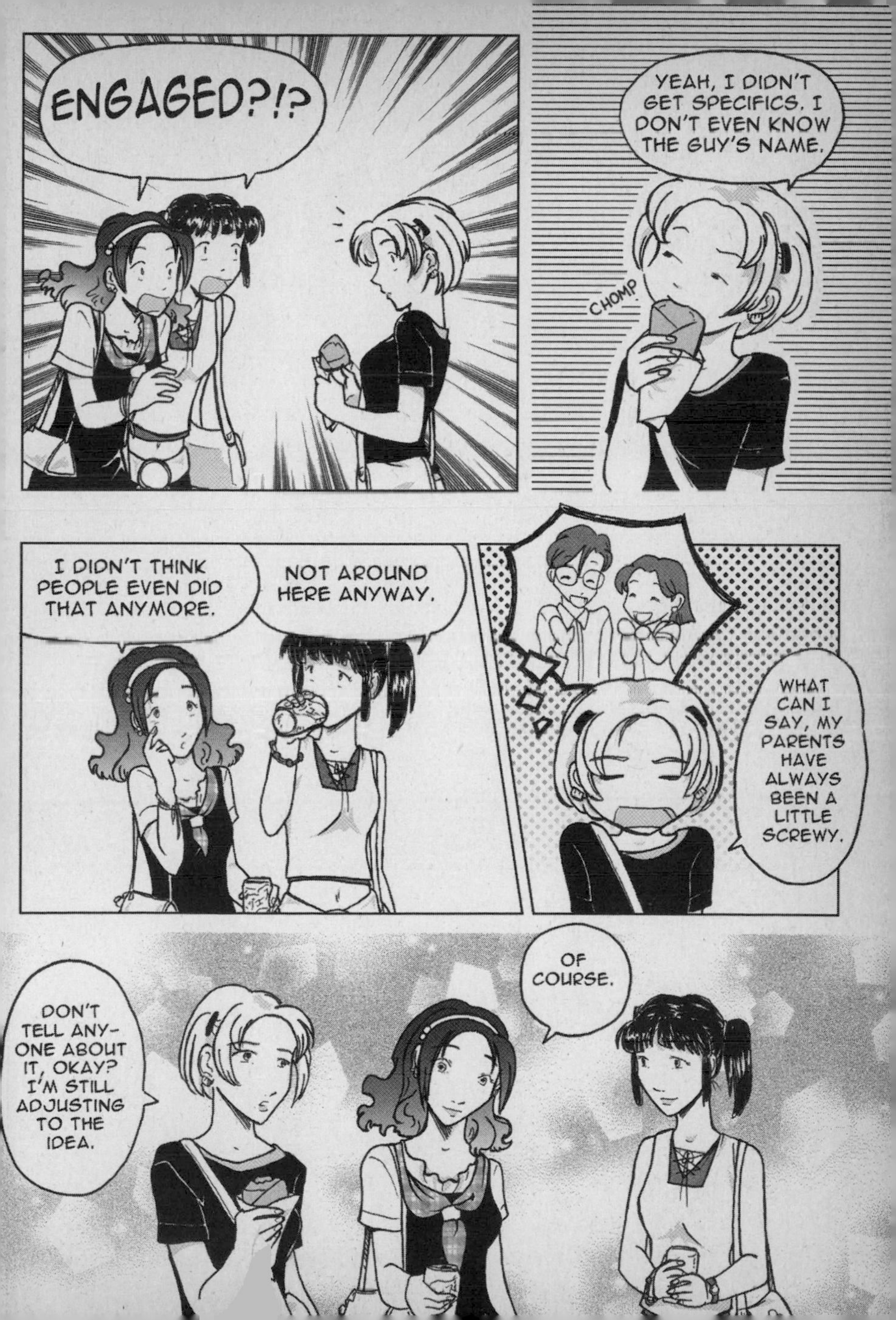
ENGAGED?!?
YEAH, I DIDN'T GET SPECIFICS. I DON'T EVEN KNOW THE GUY'S NAME.
CHOMP
I DIDN'T THINK PEOPLE EVEN DID THAT ANYMORE.
NOT AROUND HERE ANYWAY.
WHAT CAN I SAY, MY PARENTS HAVE ALWAYS BEEN A LITTLE SCREWY.
DON'T TELL ANY-ONE ABOUT IT, OKAY? I'M STILL ADJUSTING TO THE IDEA.
OF COURSE.

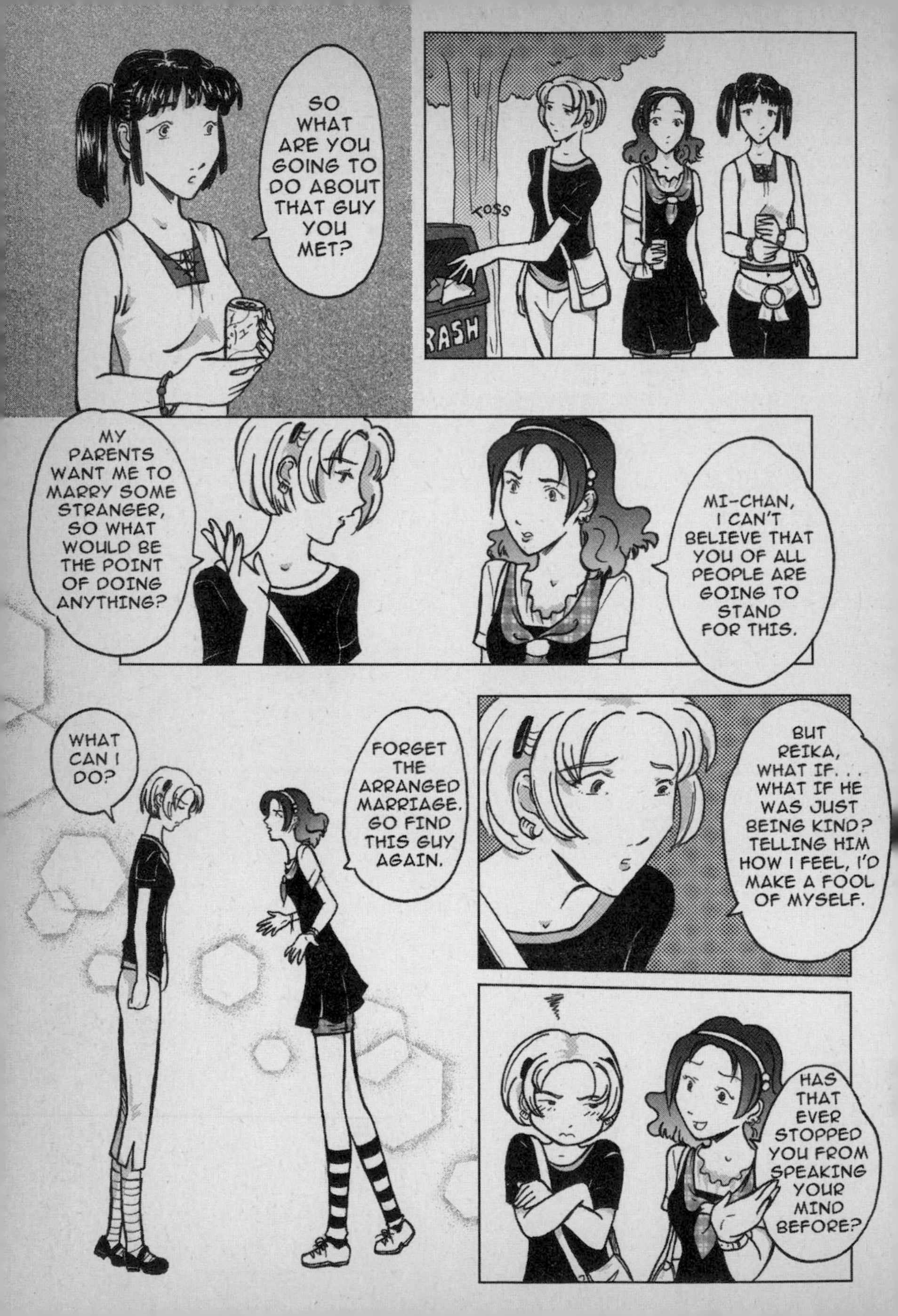
SO WHAT ARE YOU GOING TO DO ABOUT THAT GUY YOU MET?
TOSS
RASH
MY PARENTS WANT ME TO MARRY SOME STRANGER, SO WHAT WOULD BE THE POINT OF DOING ANYTHING?
MI-CHAN, I CAN'T BELIEVE THAT YOU OF ALL PEOPLE ARE GOING TO STAND FOR THIS.
WHAT CAN I DO?
FORGET THE ARRANGED MARRIAGE. GO FIND THIS GUY AGAIN.
BUT REIKA, WHAT IF. . . WHAT IF HE WAS JUST BEING KIND? TELLING HIM HOW I FEEL, I'D MAKE A FOOL OF MYSELF.
HAS THAT EVER STOPPED YOU FROM SPEAKING YOUR MIND BEFORE?

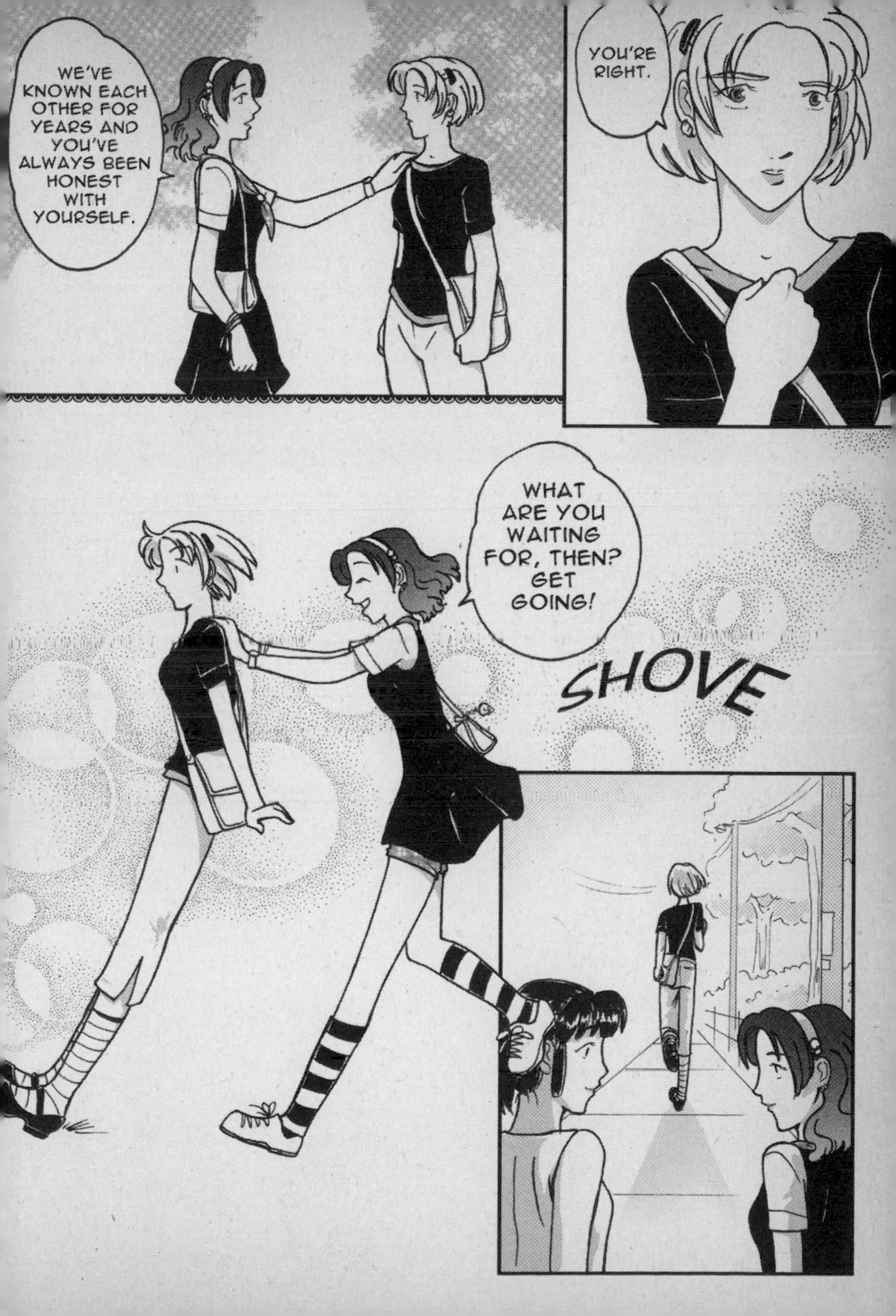
WE'VE KNOWN EACH OTHER FOR YEARS AND YOU'VE ALWAYS BEEN HONEST WITH YOURSELF.
YOU'RE RIGHT.
WHAT ARE YOU WAITING FOR, THEN? GET GOING!
SHOVE

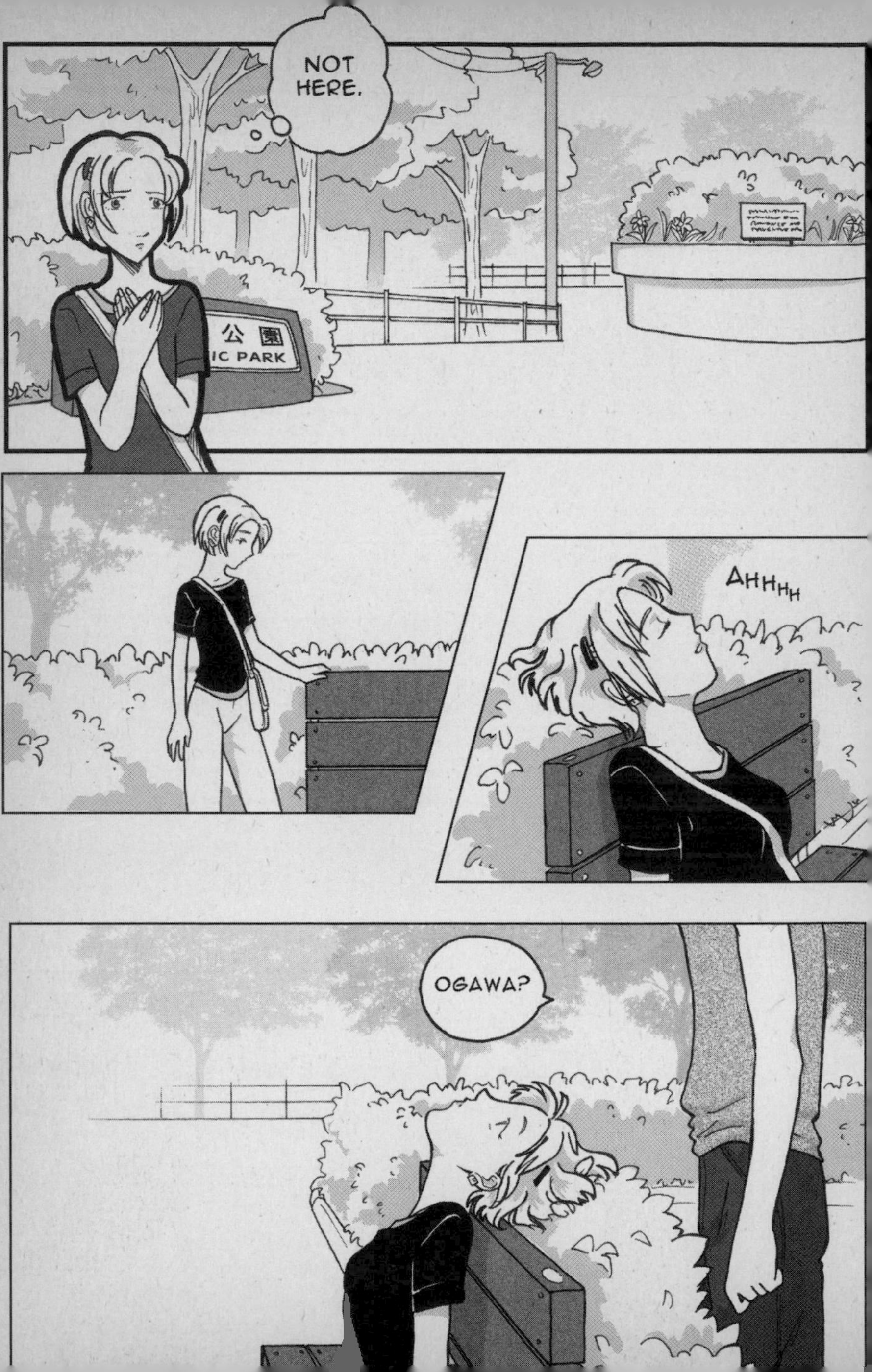
NOT HERE.
公園
IC PARK
AHHHH
OGAWA?

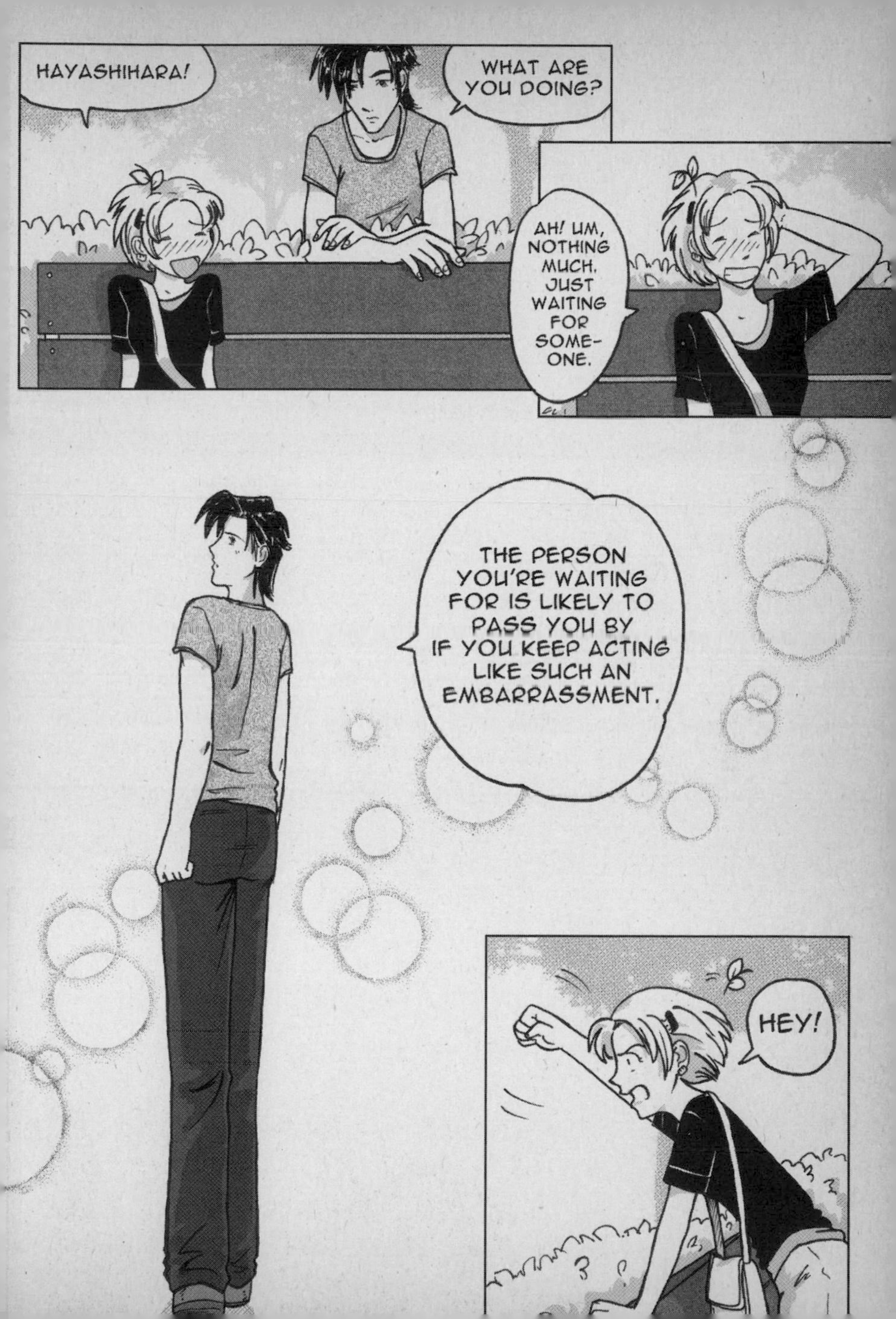
HAYASHIHARA!
WHAT ARE YOU DOING?
AH! UM, NOTHING MUCH. JUST WAITING FOR SOME-ONE.
THE PERSON YOU'RE WAITING FOR IS LIKELY TO PASS YOU BY IF YOU KEEP ACTING LIKE SUCH AN EMBARRASSMENT.
HEY!

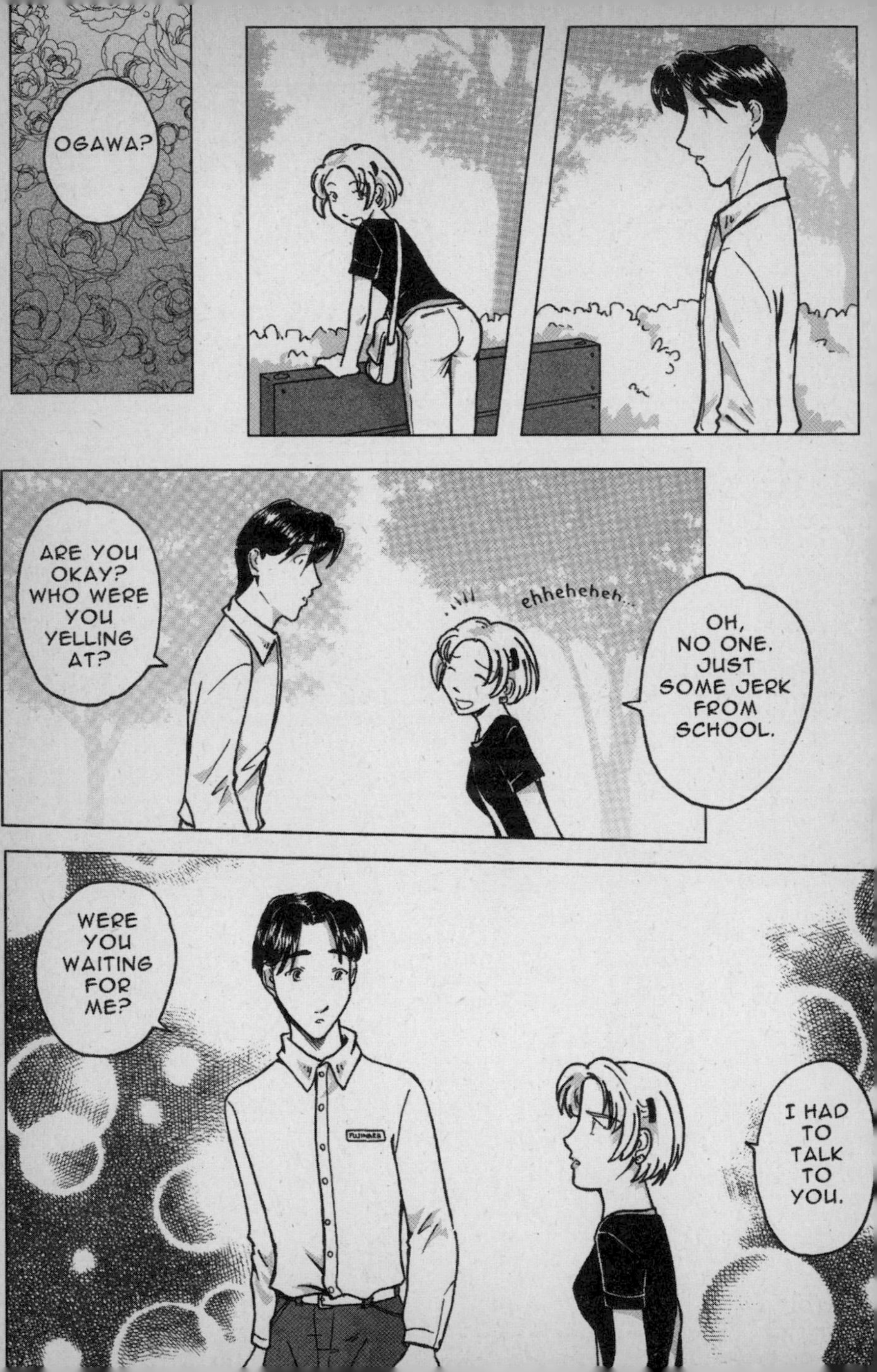

OGAWA?
ARE YOU OKAY? WHO WERE YOU YELLING AT?
ehheheheh...
OH, NO ONE. JUST SOME JERK FROM SCHOOL.
WERE YOU WAITING FOR ME?
I HAD TO TALK TO YOU.

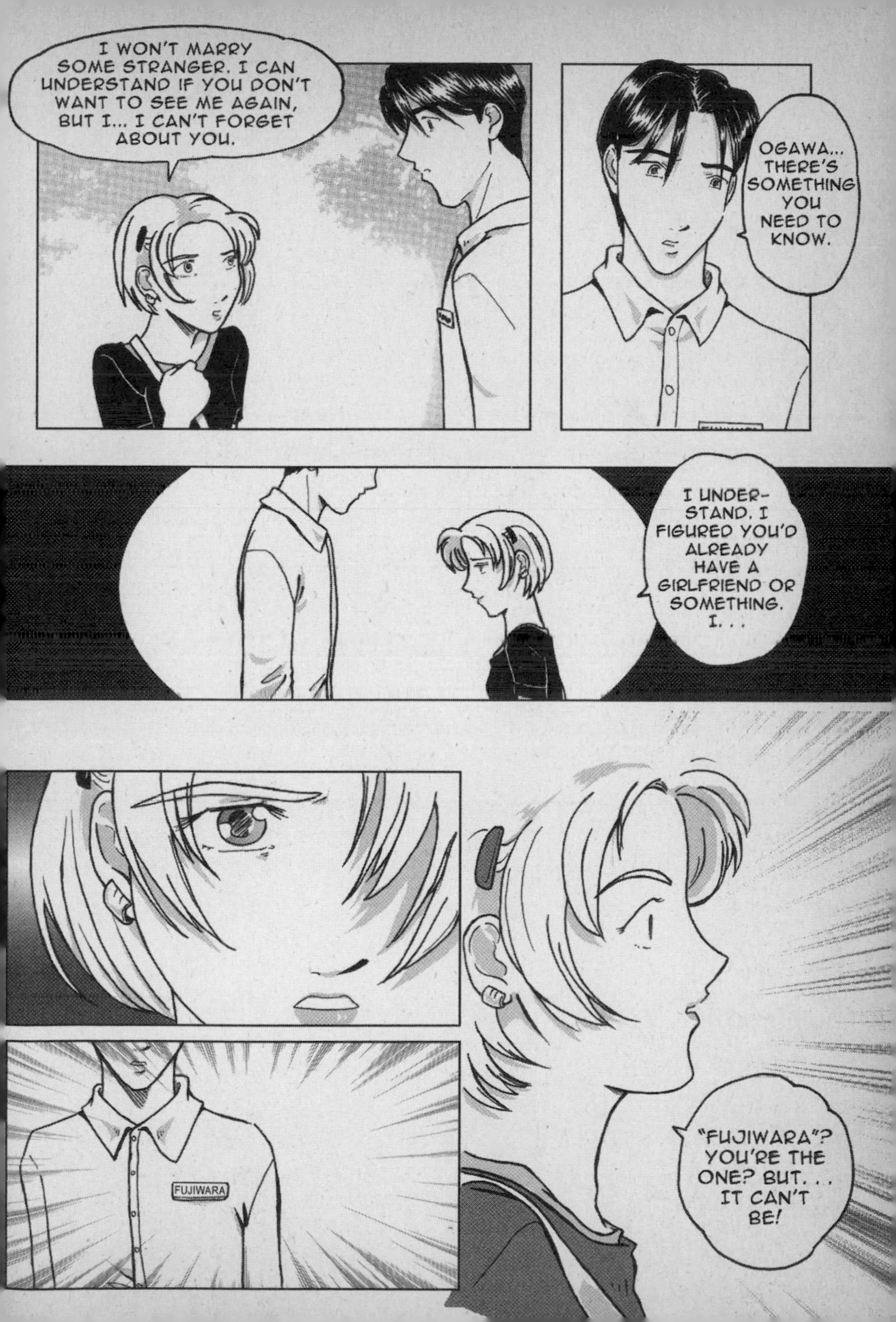
I WON'T MARRY SOME STRANGER. I CAN UNDERSTAND IF YOU DON'T WANT TO SEE ME AGAIN, BUT I... I CAN'T FORGET ABOUT YOU.
OGAWA... THERE'S SOMETHING YOU NEED TO KNOW.
I UNDER-STAND. I FIGURED YOU'D ALREADY HAVE A GIRLFRIEND OR SOMETHING. I. . .
FUJIWARA
"FUJIWARA"? YOU'RE THE ONE? BUT. . . IT CAN'T BE!

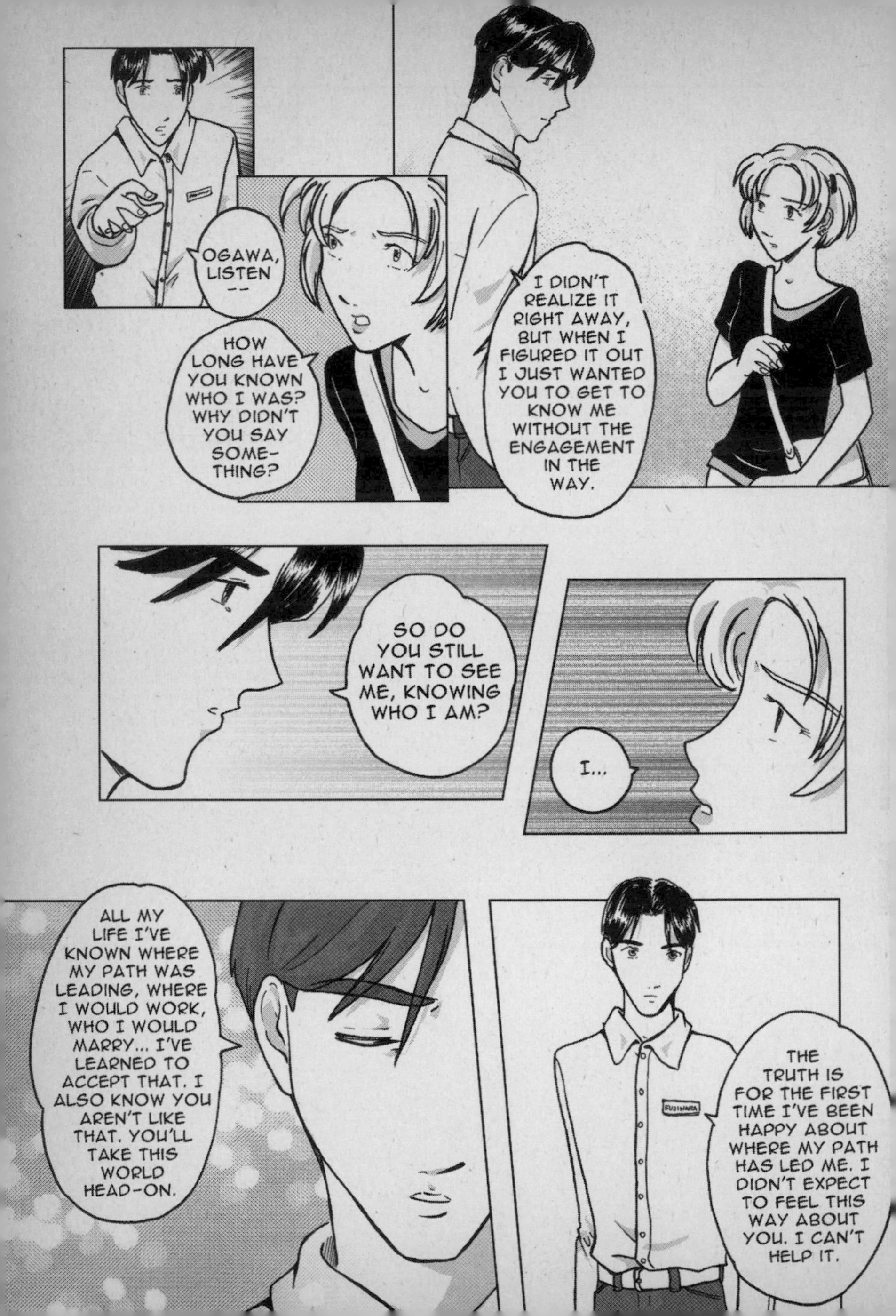
OGAWA, LISTEN --
HOW LONG HAVE YOU KNOWN WHO I WAS? WHY DIDN'T YOU SAY SOME-THING?
I DIDN'T REALIZE IT RIGHT AWAY, BUT WHEN I FIGURED IT OUT I JUST WANTED YOU TO GET TO KNOW ME WITHOUT THE ENGAGEMENT IN THE WAY.
SO DO YOU STILL WANT TO SEE ME, KNOWING WHO I AM?
I...
ALL MY LIFE I'VE KNOWN WHERE MY PATH WAS LEADING, WHERE I WOULD WORK, WHO I WOULD MARRY... I'VE LEARNED TO ACCEPT THAT. I ALSO KNOW YOU AREN'T LIKE THAT. YOU'LL TAKE THIS WORLD HEAD-ON.
FUJIWARA
THE TRUTH IS FOR THE FIRST TIME I'VE BEEN HAPPY ABOUT WHERE MY PATH HAS LED ME. I DIDN'T EXPECT TO FEEL THIS WAY ABOUT YOU. I CAN'T HELP IT.

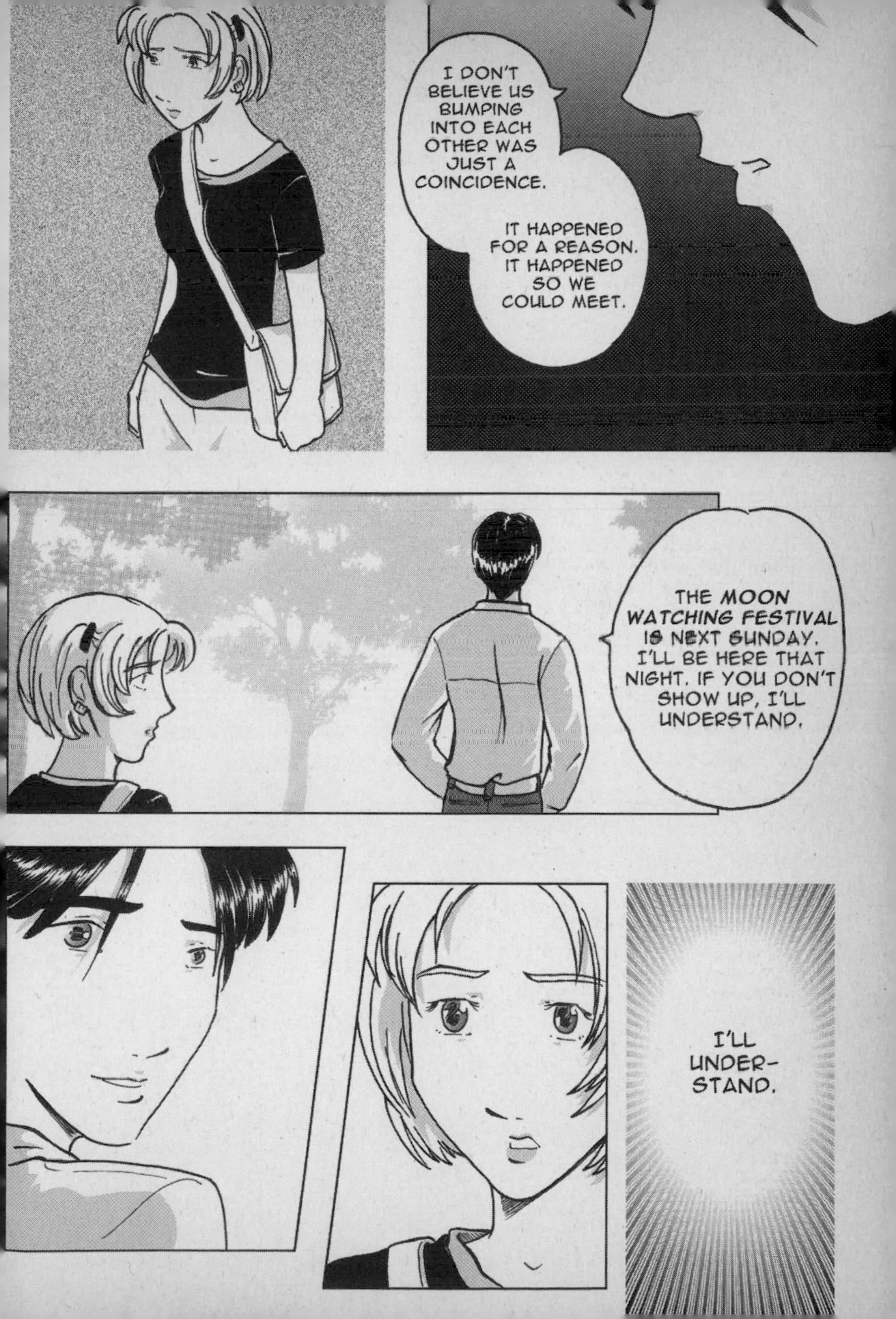
I DON'T BELIEVE US BUMPING INTO EACH OTHER WAS JUST A COINCIDENCE.
IT HAPPENED FOR A REASON. IT HAPPENED SO WE COULD MEET.
THE MOON WATCHING FESTIVAL IS NEXT SUNDAY. I'LL BE HERE THAT NIGHT. IF YOU DON'T SHOW UP, I'LL UNDERSTAND.
I'LL UNDER-STAND.

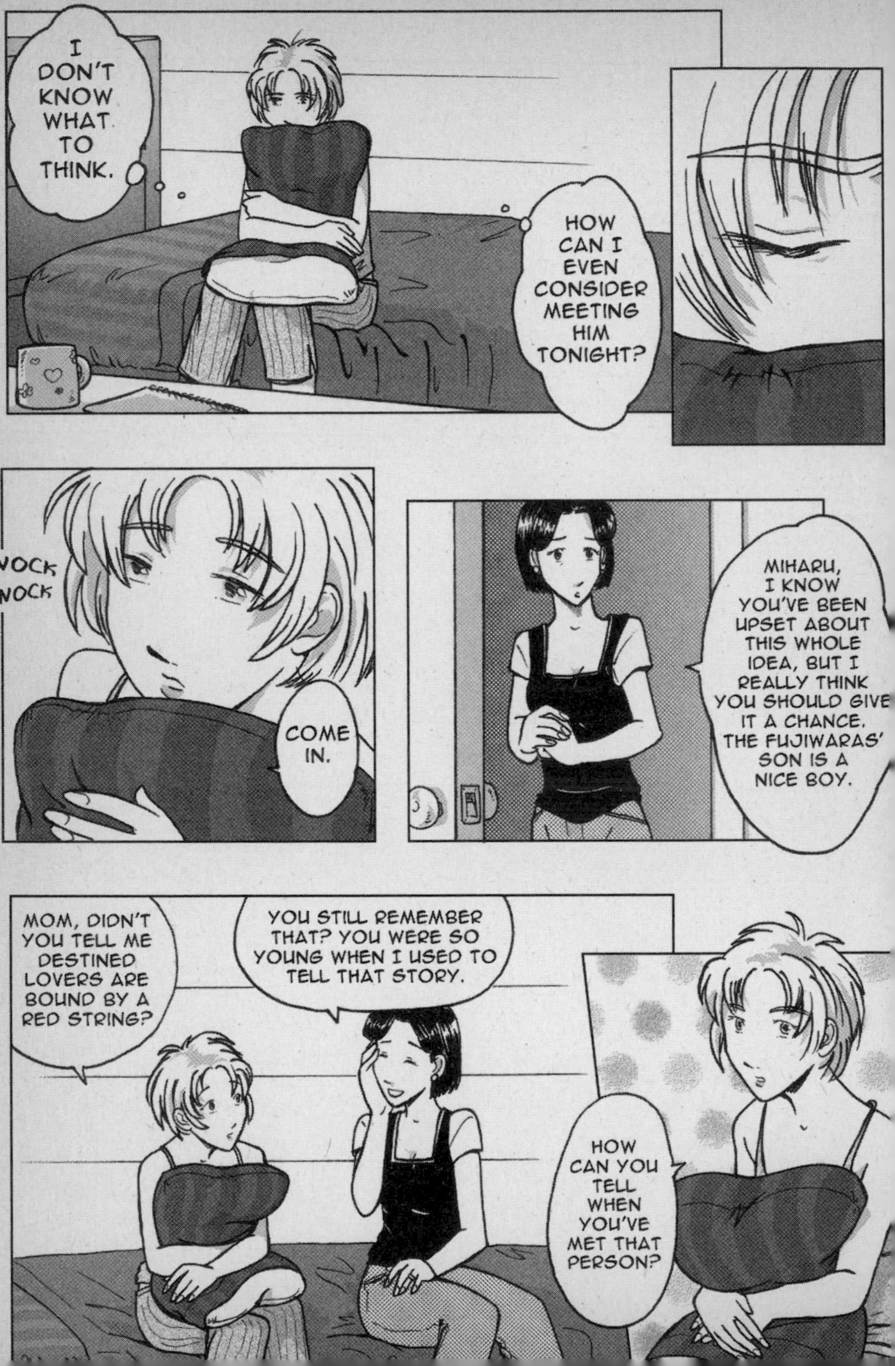
I DON'T KNOW WHAT TO THINK.
HOW CAN I EVEN CONSIDER MEETING HIM TONIGHT?
KNOCK KNOCK
COME IN.
MIHARU, I KNOW YOU'VE BEEN UPSET ABOUT THIS WHOLE IDEA, BUT I REALLY THINK YOU SHOULD GIVE IT A CHANCE. THE FUJIWARAS' SON IS A NICE BOY.
MOM, DIDN'T YOU TELL ME DESTINED LOVERS ARE BOUND BY A RED STRING?
YOU STILL REMEMBER THAT? YOU WERE SO YOUNG WHEN I USED TO TELL THAT STORY.
HOW CAN YOU TELL WHEN YOU'VE MET THAT PERSON?

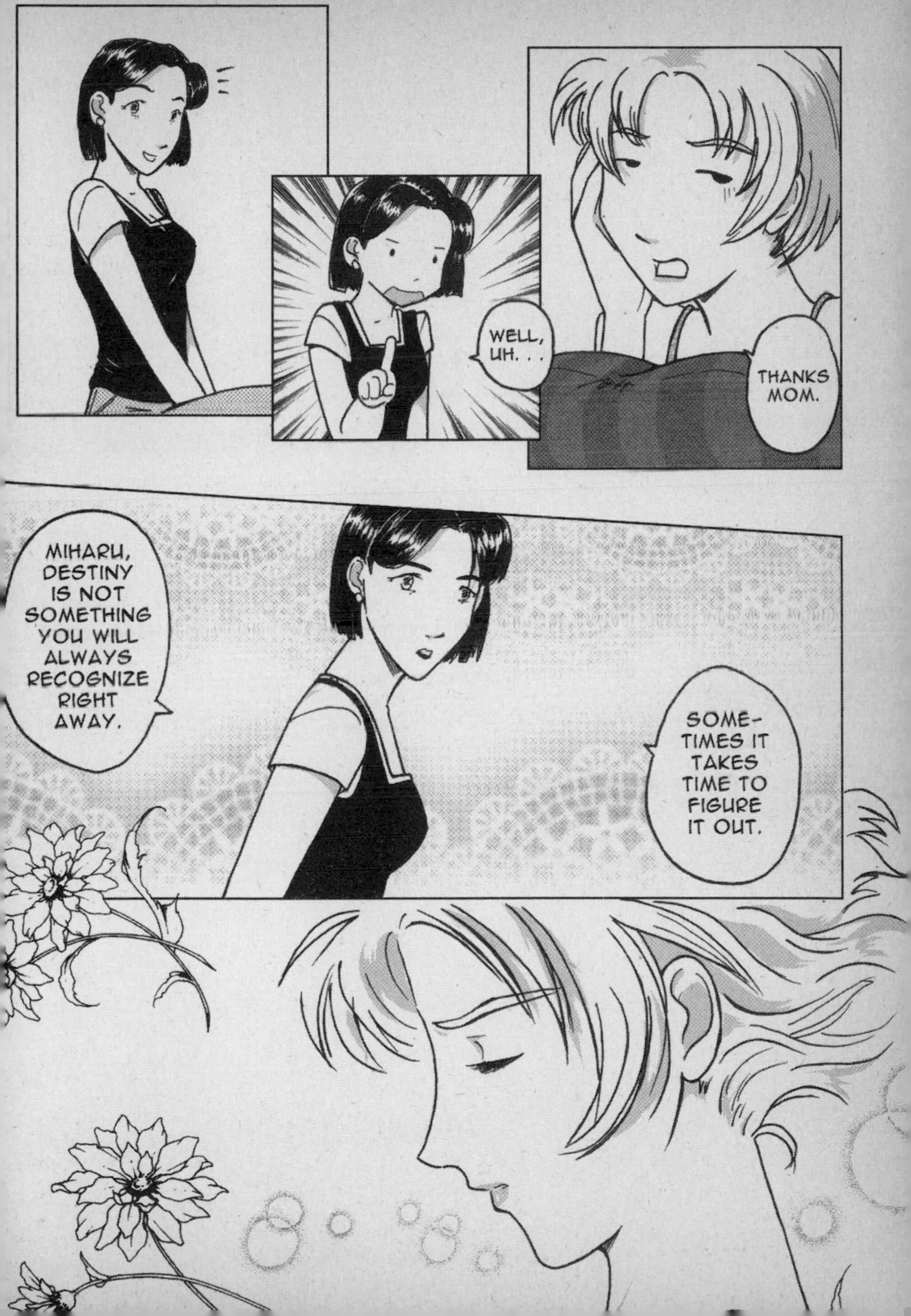

WELL, UH. . .
THANKS MOM.
MIHARU, DESTINY IS NOT SOMETHING YOU WILL ALWAYS RECOGNIZE RIGHT AWAY.
SOME-TIMES IT TAKES TIME TO FIGURE IT OUT.

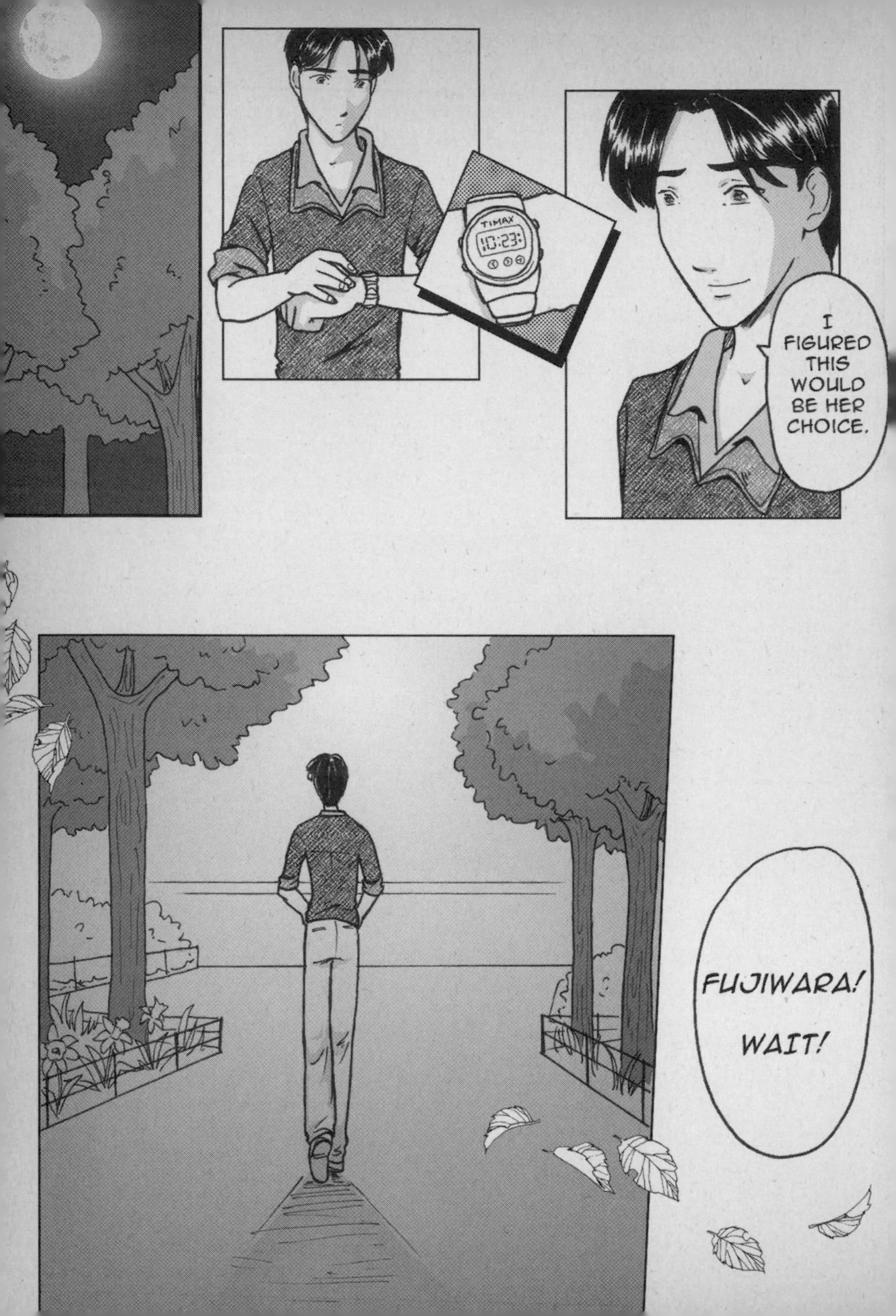
TIMAX
10:23
I FIGURED THIS WOULD BE HER CHOICE.
FUJIWARA! WAIT!

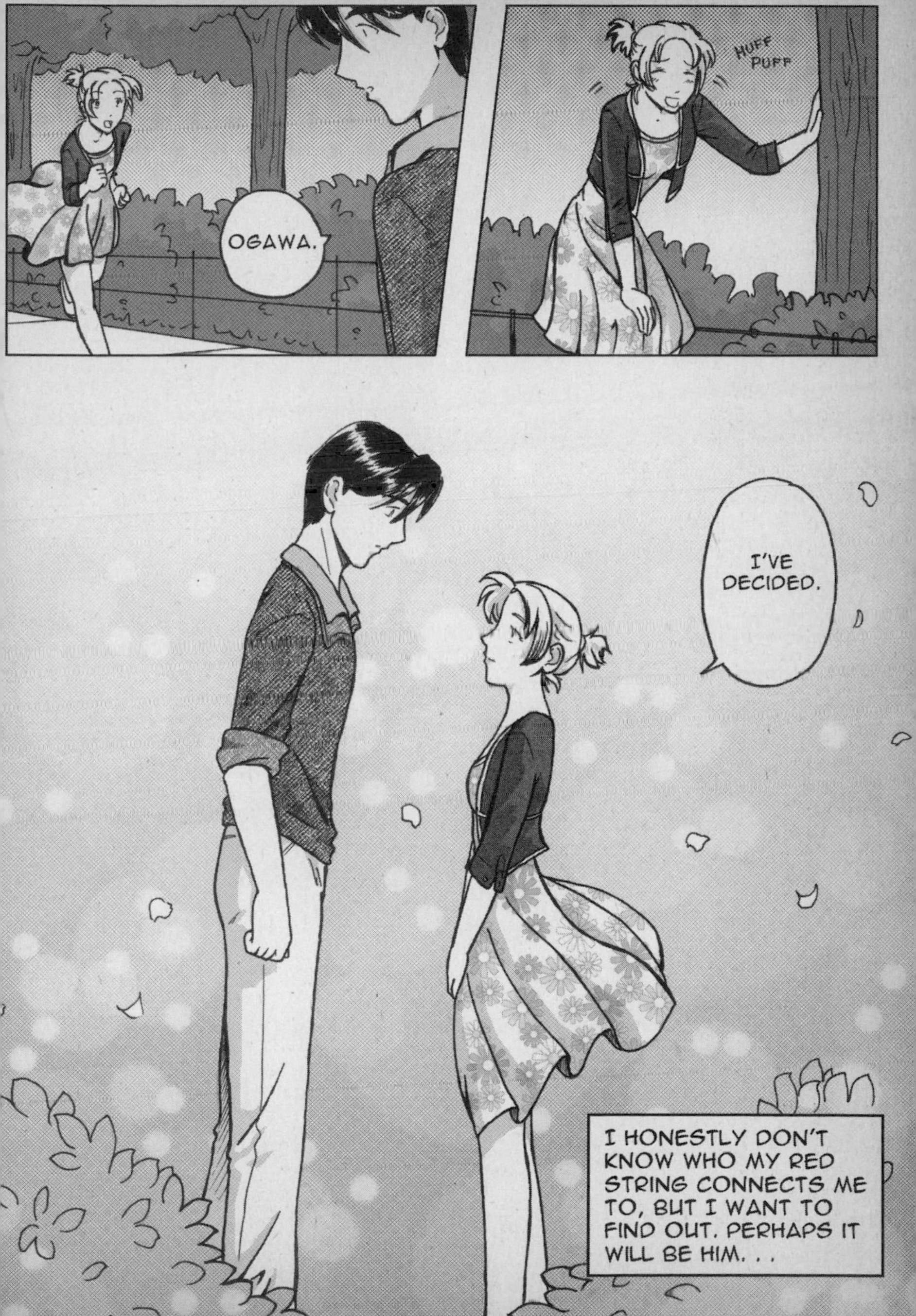
OGAWA.
HUFF PUFF
I'VE DECIDED.
I HONESTLY DON'T KNOW WHO MY RED STRING CONNECTS ME TO, BUT I WANT TO FIND OUT. PERHAPS IT WILL BE HIM. . .

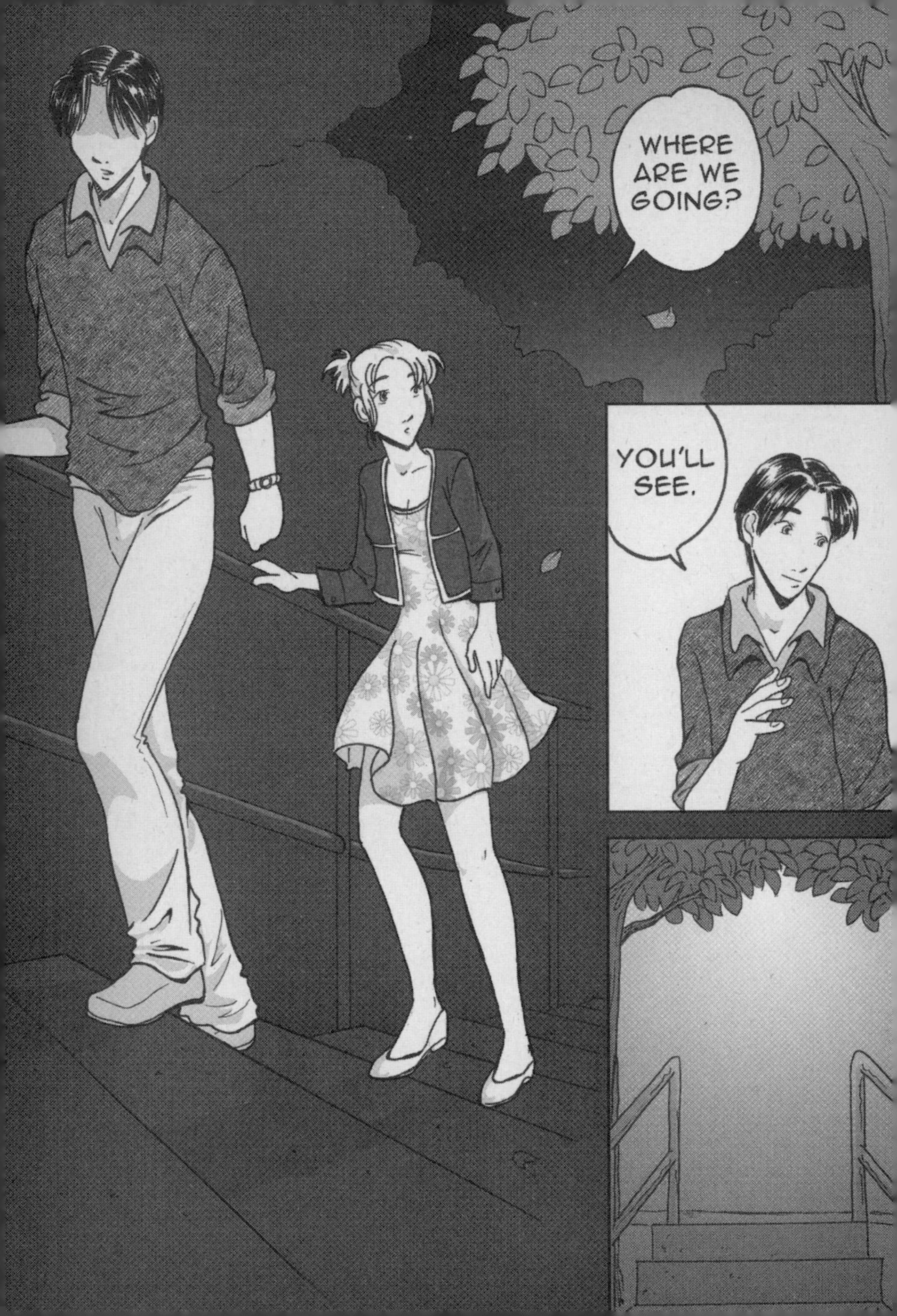
WHERE ARE WE GOING?
YOU'LL SEE.

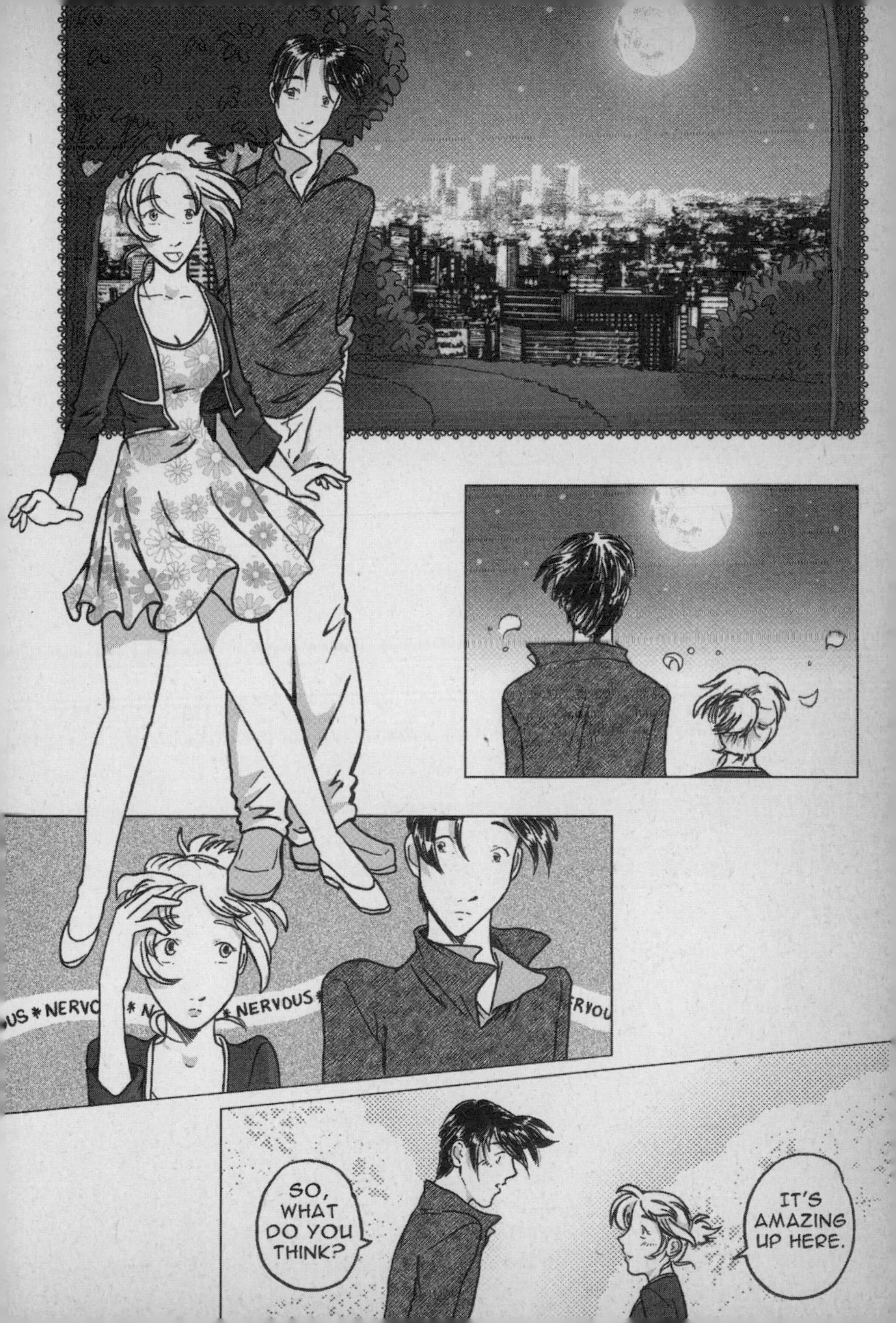

NERVOUS * NERVOUS * NERVOUS
IT'S AMAZING UP HERE.
SO, WHAT DO YOU THINK?

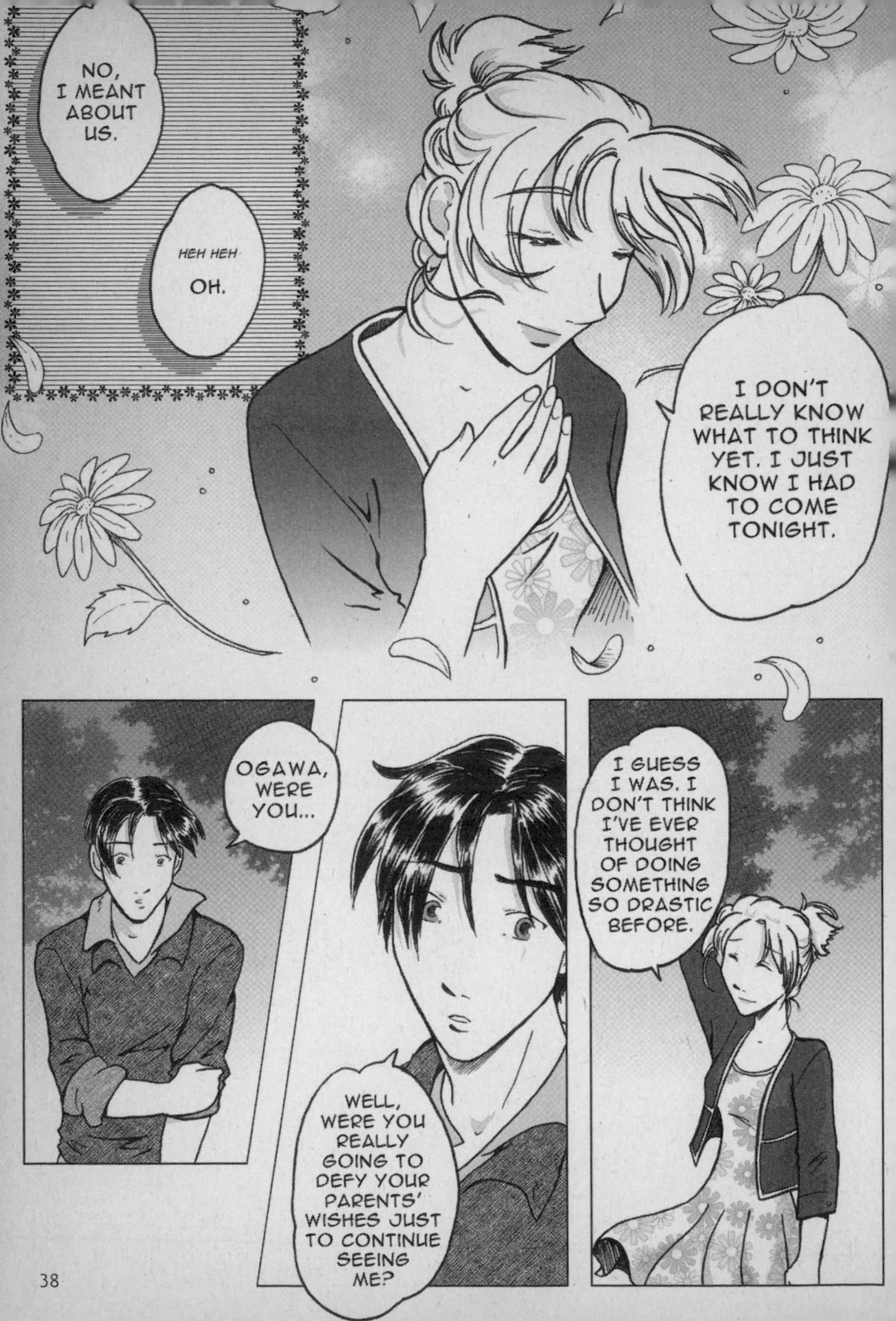
NO, I MEANT ABOUT US.
HEH HEH
OH.
I DON'T REALLY KNOW WHAT TO THINK YET. I JUST KNOW I HAD TO COME TONIGHT.
OGAWA, WERE YOU...
WELL, WERE YOU REALLY GOING TO DEFY YOUR PARENTS' WISHES JUST TO CONTINUE SEEING ME?
I GUESS I WAS. I DON'T THINK I'VE EVER THOUGHT OF DOING SOMETHING SO DRASTIC BEFORE.

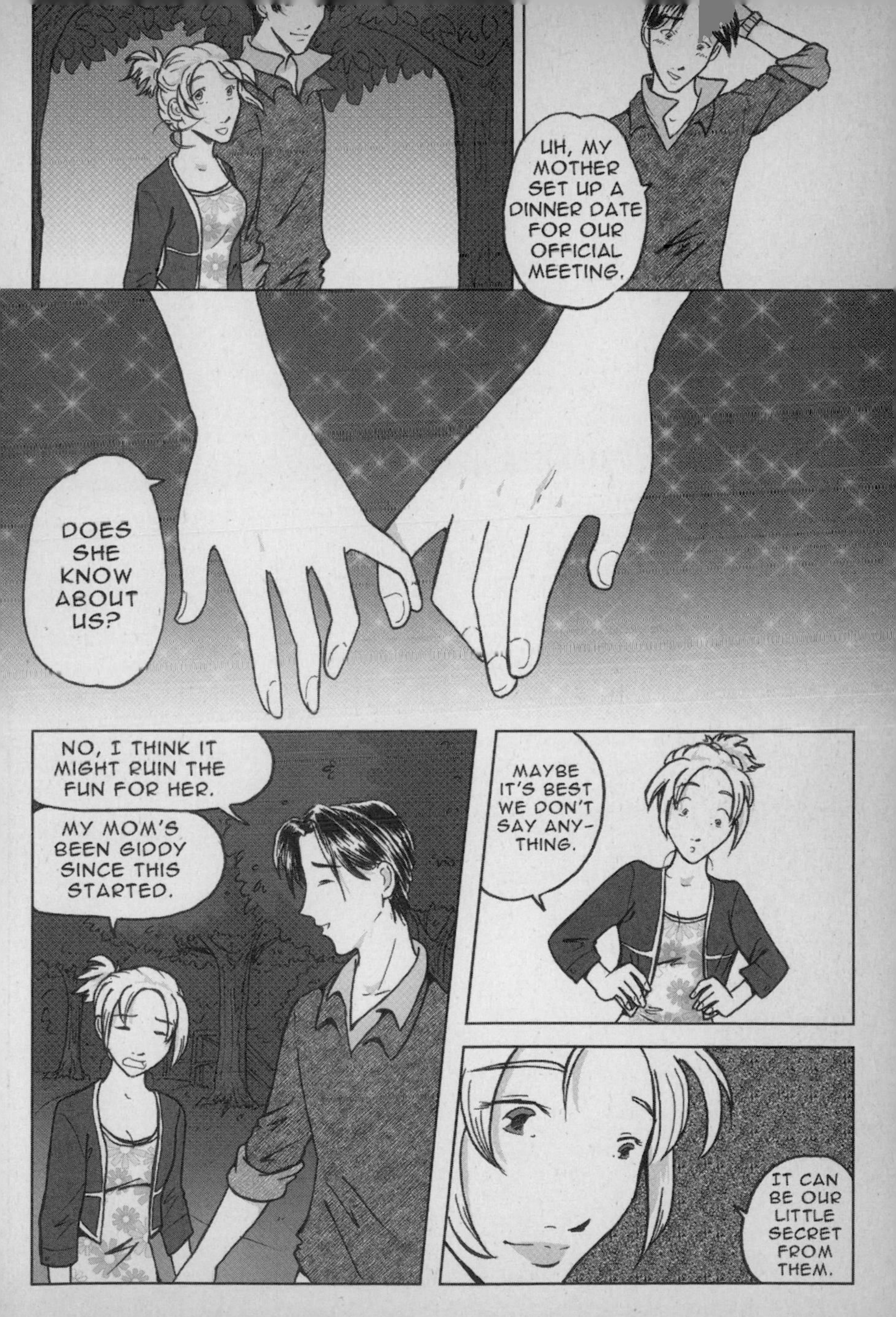
UH, MY MOTHER SET UP A DINNER DATE FOR OUR OFFICIAL MEETING.
DOES SHE KNOW ABOUT US?
NO, I THINK IT MIGHT RUIN THE FUN FOR HER.
MY MOM'S BEEN GIDDY SINCE THIS STARTED.
MAYBE IT'S BEST WE DON'T SAY ANY-THING.
IT CAN BE OUR LITTLE SECRET FROM THEM.

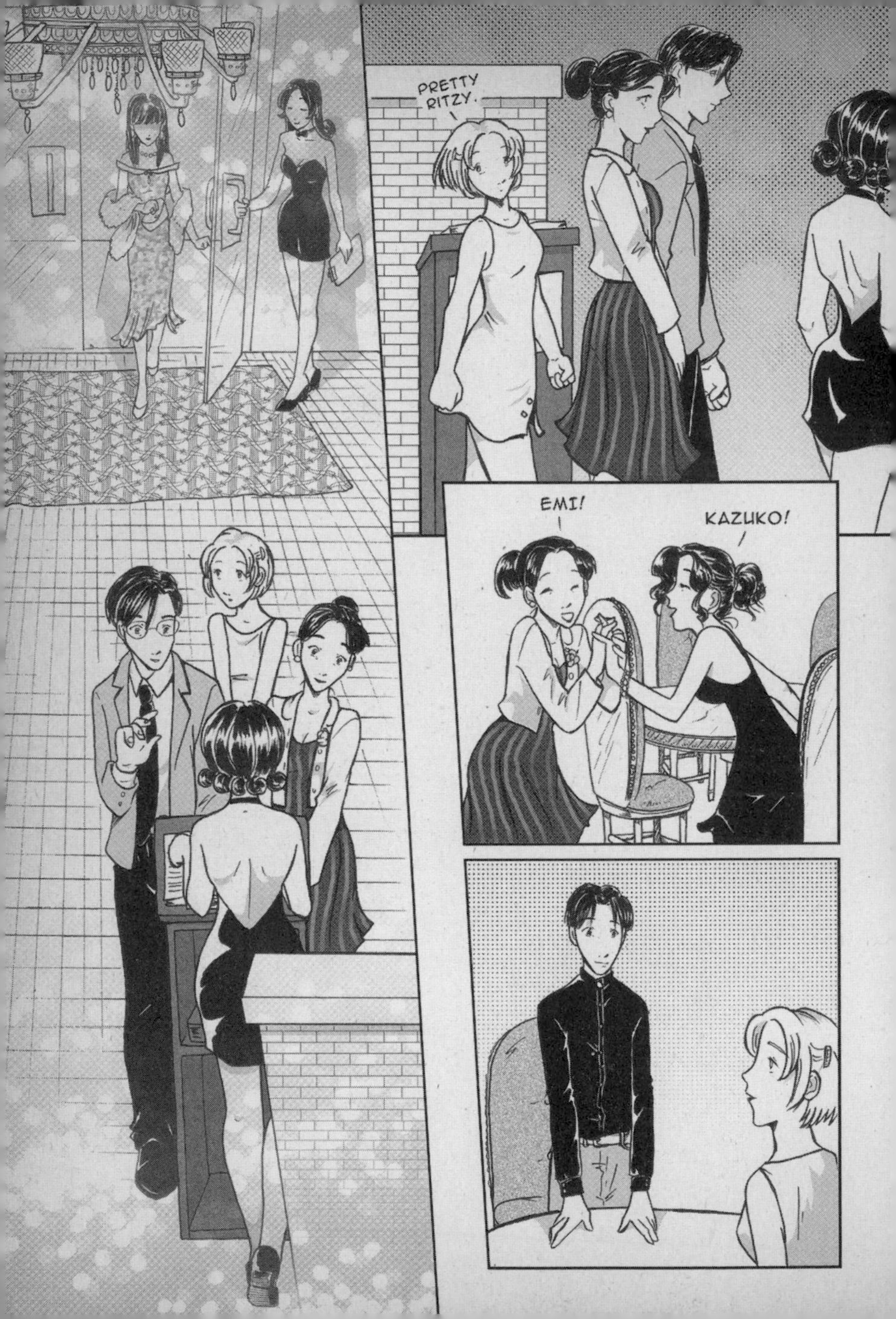
PRETTY RITZY.
KAZUKO!
EMI!

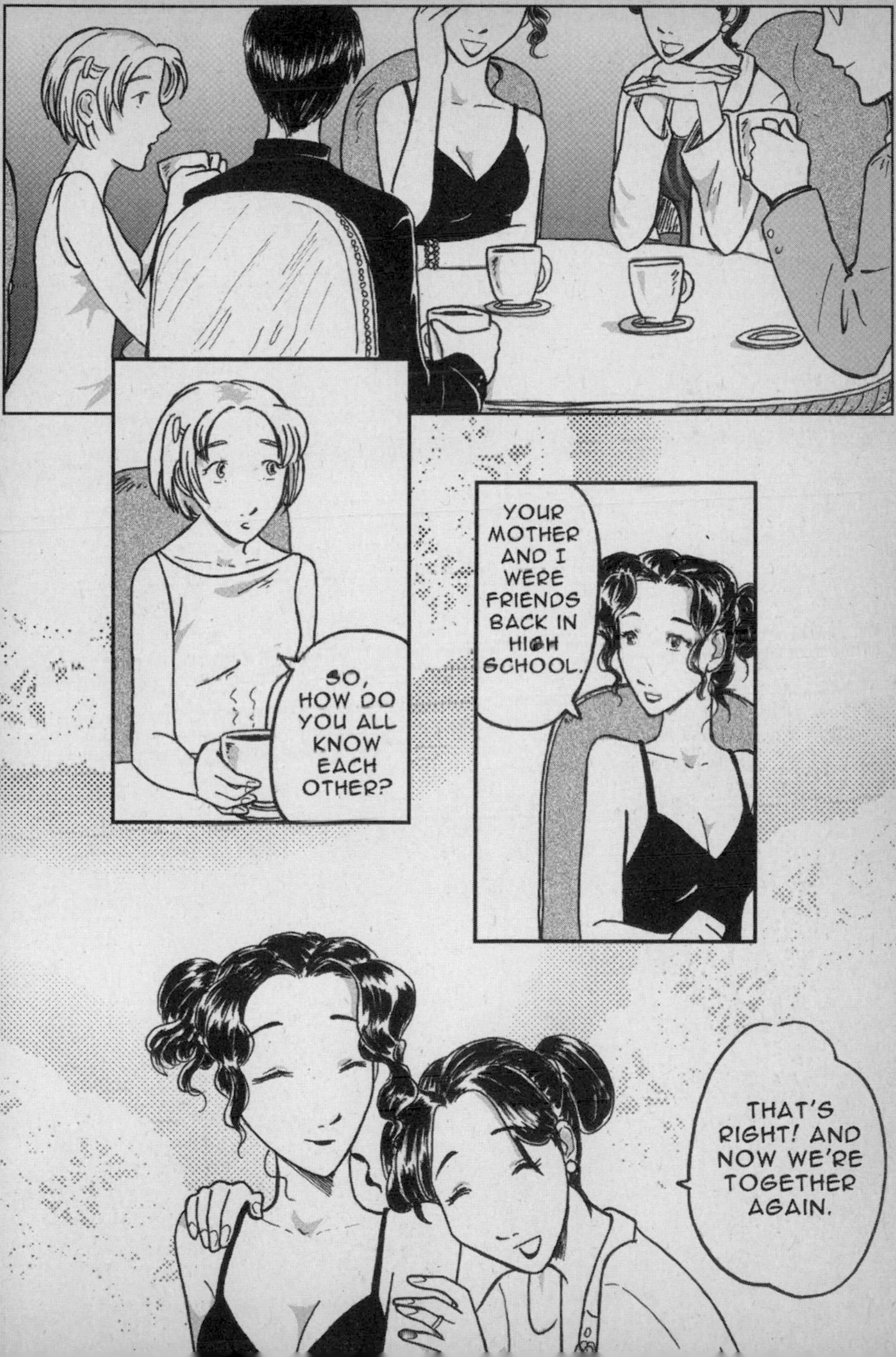
SO, HOW DO YOU ALL KNOW EACH OTHER?
YOUR MOTHER AND I WERE FRIENDS BACK IN HIGH SCHOOL.
THAT'S RIGHT! AND NOW WE'RE TOGETHER AGAIN.

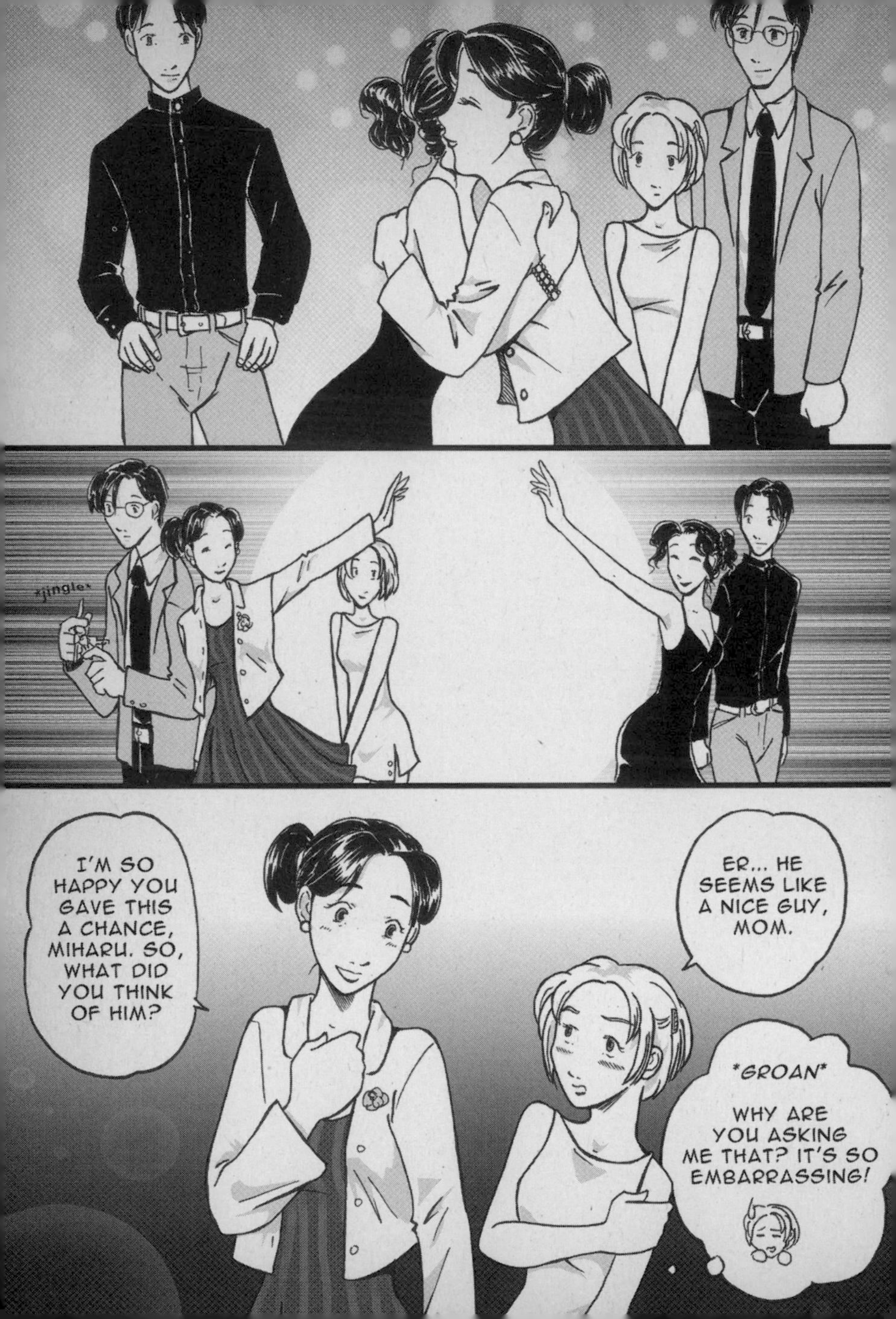
jingle
I'M SO HAPPY YOU GAVE THIS A CHANCE, MIHARU. SO, WHAT DID YOU THINK OF HIM?
ER... HE SEEMS LIKE A NICE GUY, MOM.
GROAN
WHY ARE YOU ASKING ME THAT? IT'S SO EMBARRASSING!

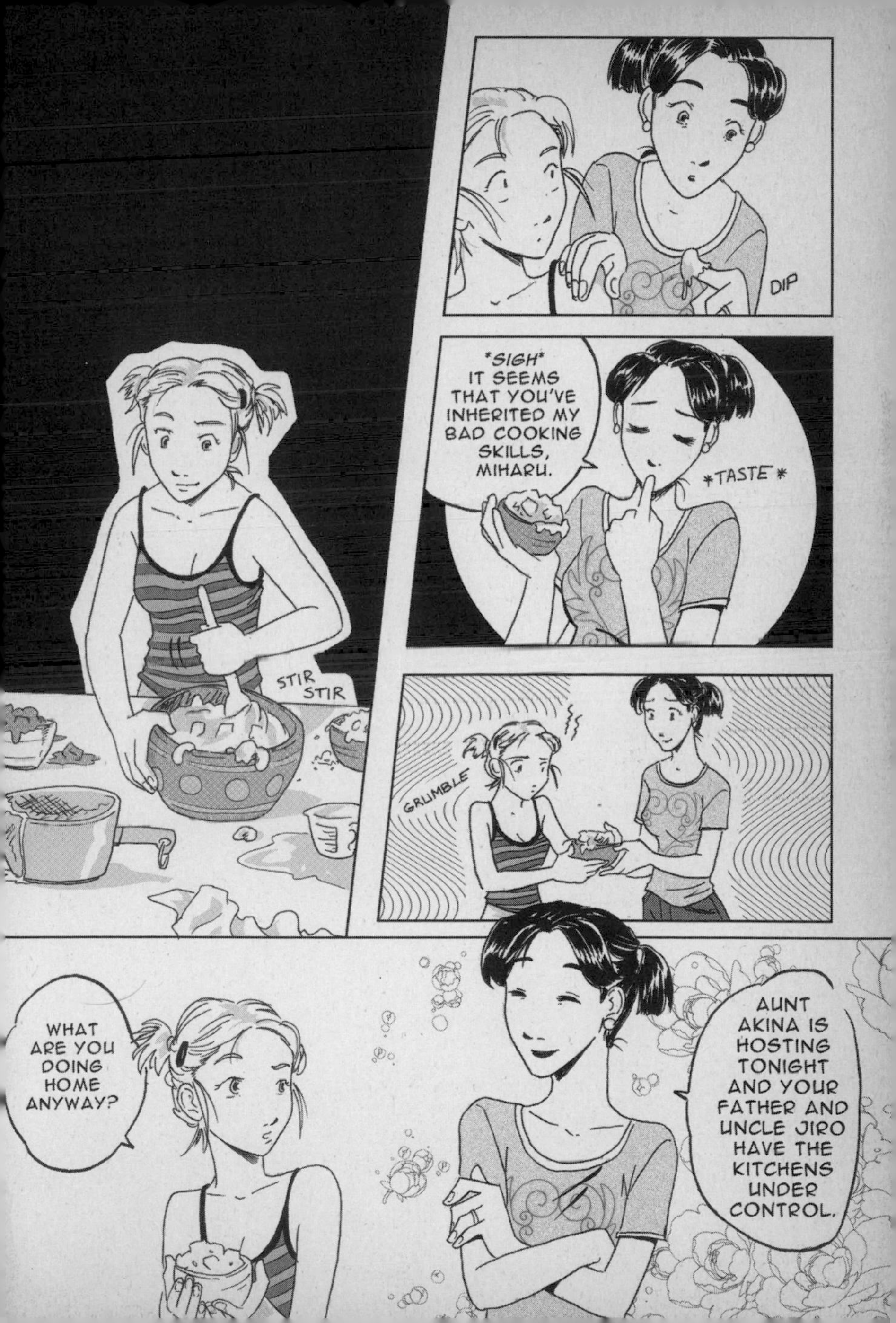
STIR STIR
DIP
SIGH IT SEEMS THAT YOU'VE INHERITED MY BAD COOKING SKILLS, MIHARU.
TASTE
GRUMBLE
WHAT ARE YOU DOING HOME ANYWAY?
AUNT AKINA IS HOSTING TONIGHT AND YOUR FATHER AND UNCLE JIRO HAVE THE KITCHENS UNDER CONTROL.

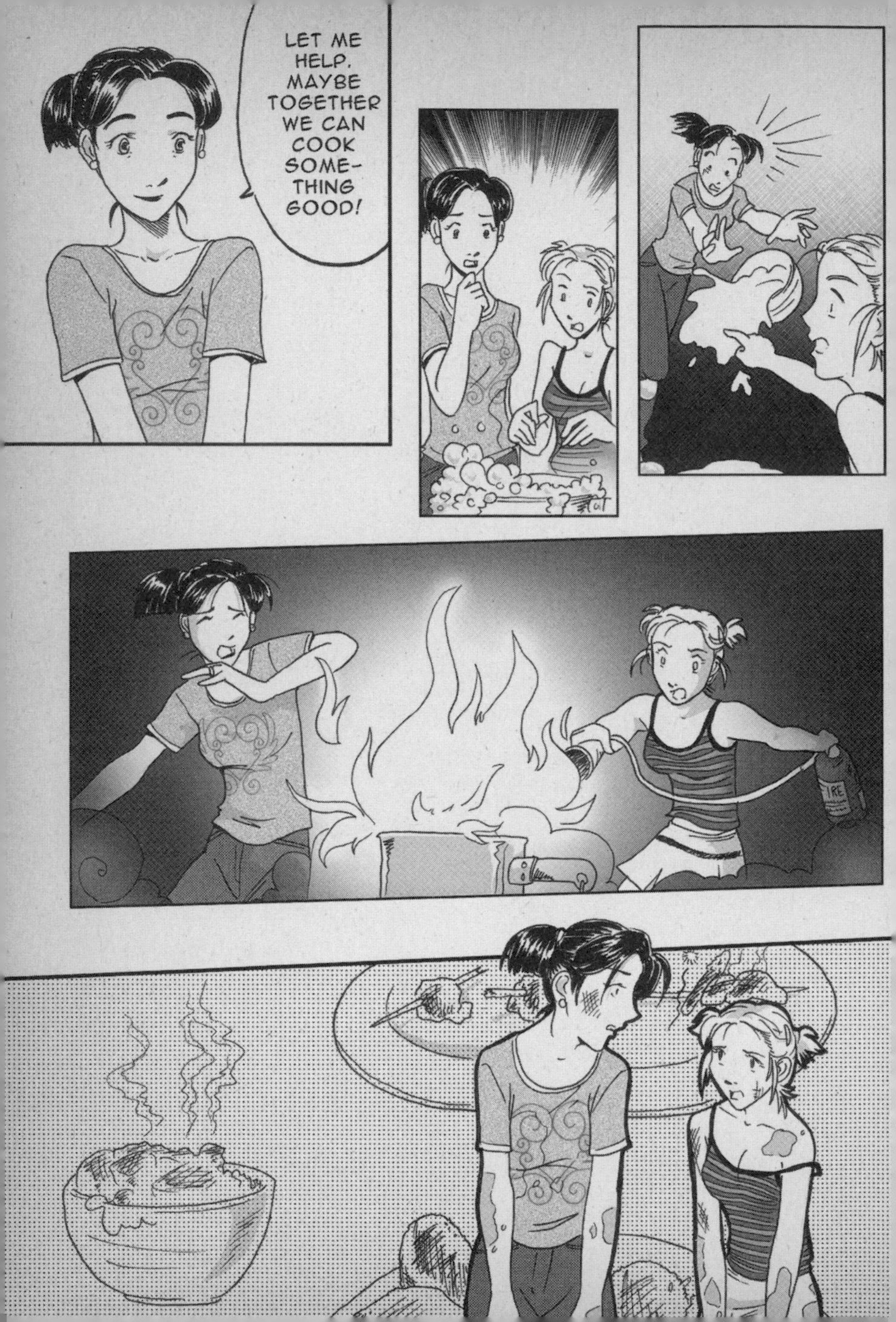
LET ME HELP. MAYBE TOGETHER WE CAN COOK SOME-THING GOOD!

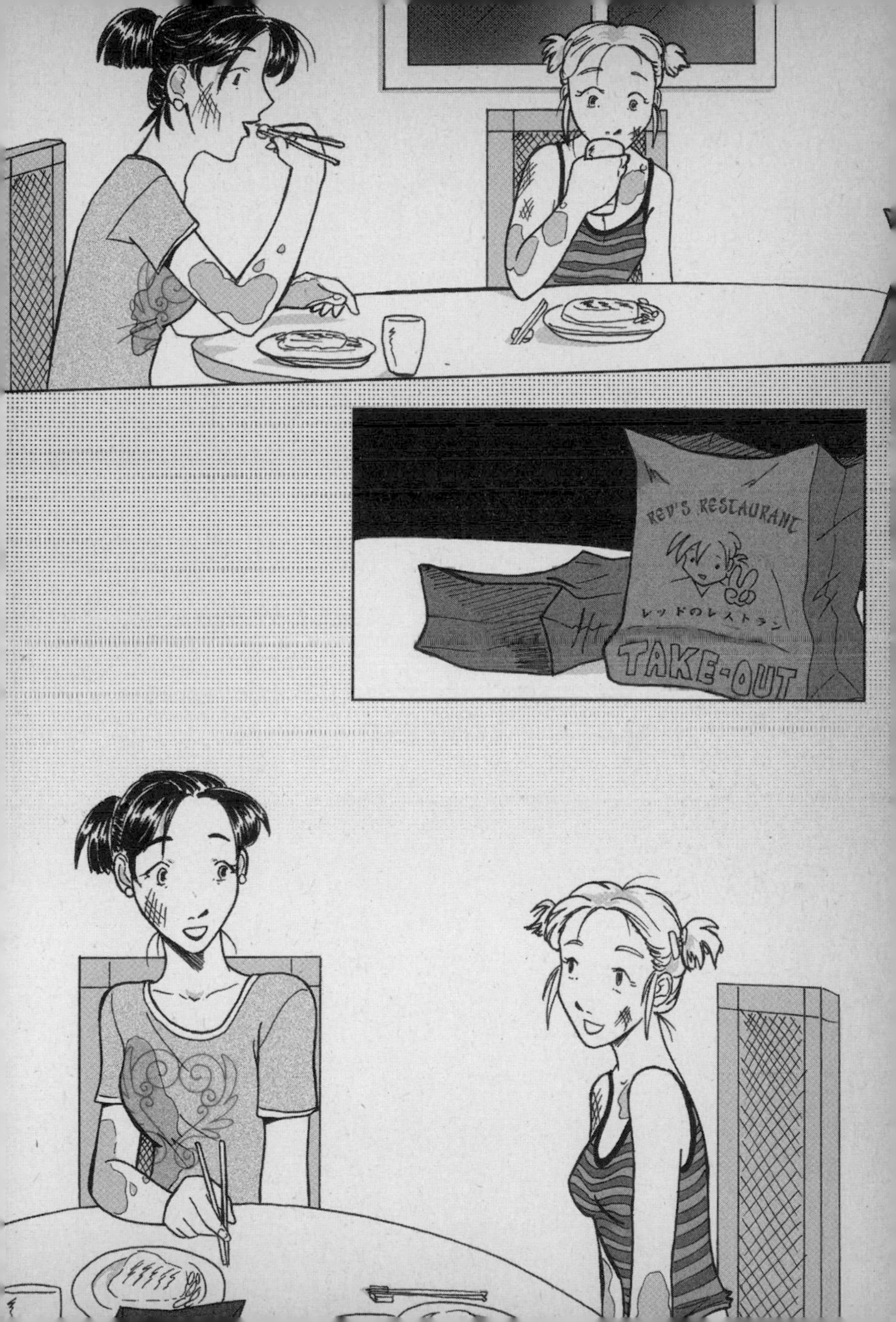
RED'S RESTAURANT
レッドのレストラン
TAKE-OUT

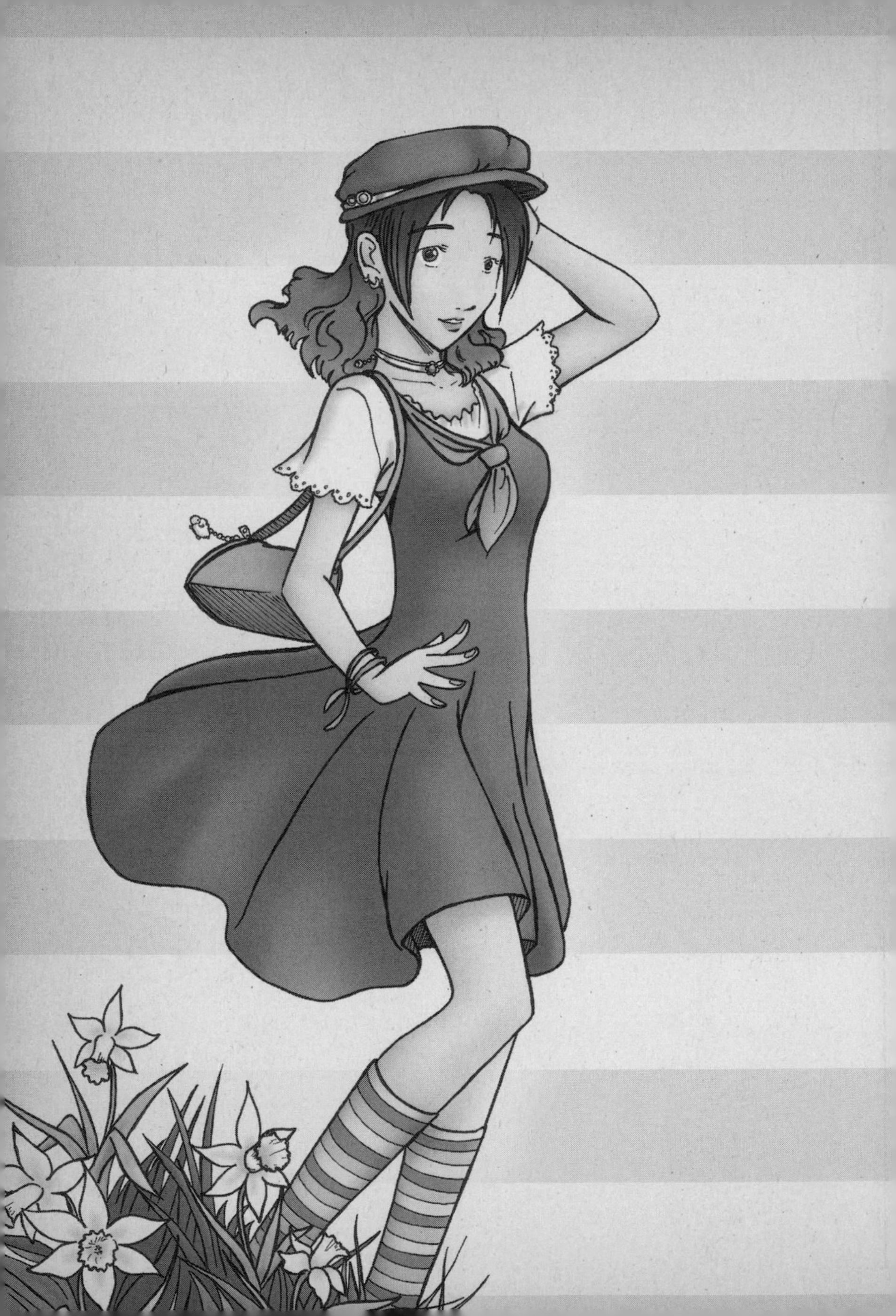

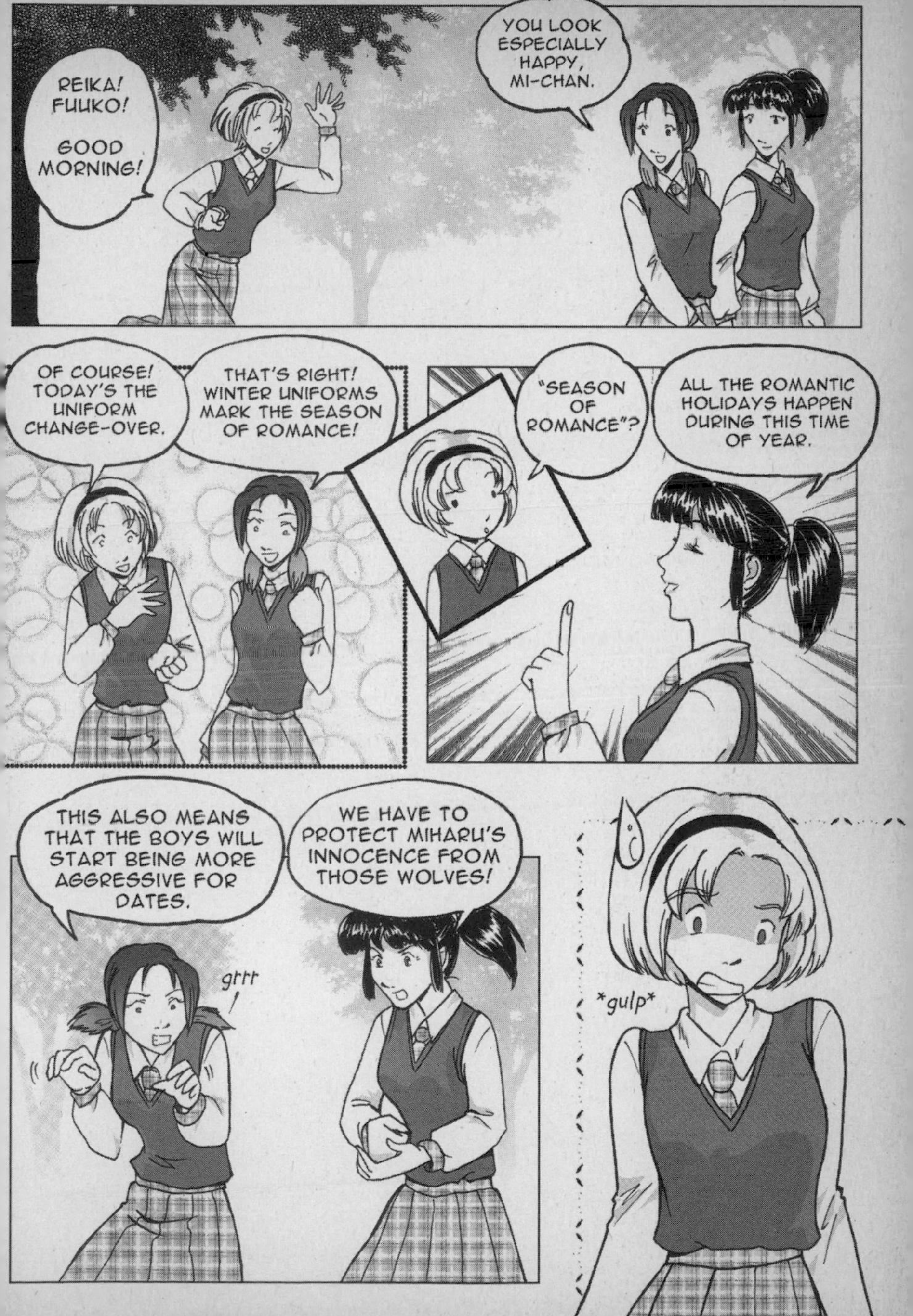

REIKA! FUUKO! GOOD MORNING!
YOU LOOK ESPECIALLY HAPPY, MI-CHAN.
OF COURSE! TODAY'S THE UNIFORM CHANGE-OVER.
THAT'S RIGHT! WINTER UNIFORMS MARK THE SEASON OF ROMANCE!
"SEASON OF ROMANCE"?
ALL THE ROMANTIC HOLIDAYS HAPPEN DURING THIS TIME OF YEAR.
THIS ALSO MEANS THAT THE BOYS WILL START BEING MORE AGGRESSIVE FOR DATES.
WE HAVE TO PROTECT MIHARU'S INNOCENCE FROM THOSE WOLVES!
grrr
gulp

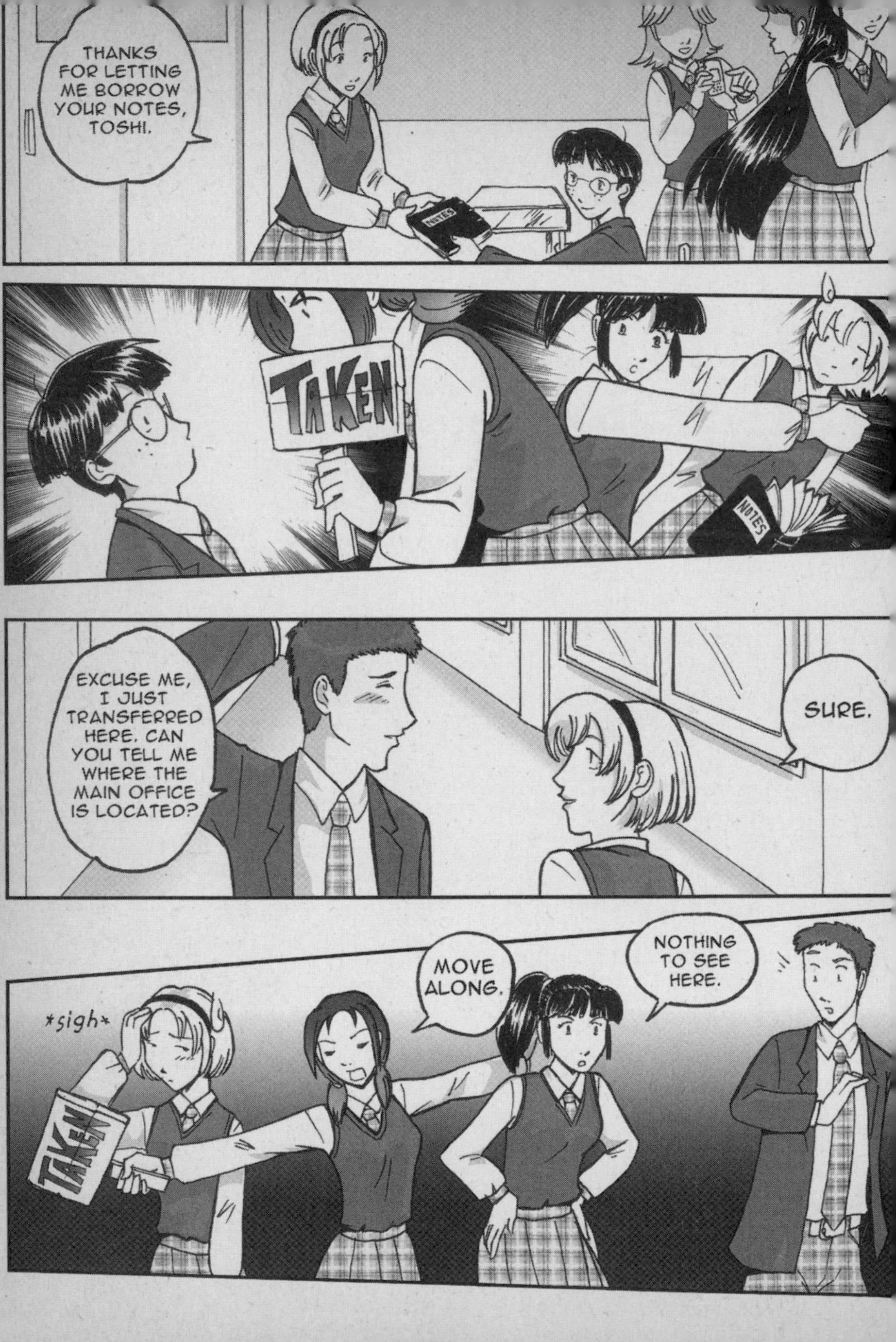
THANKS FOR LETTING ME BORROW YOUR NOTES, TOSHI.
NOTES
TAKEN
NOTES
EXCUSE ME, I JUST TRANSFERRED HERE. CAN YOU TELL ME WHERE THE MAIN OFFICE IS LOCATED?
SURE.
NOTHING TO SEE HERE.
MOVE ALONG.
sigh
TAKEN

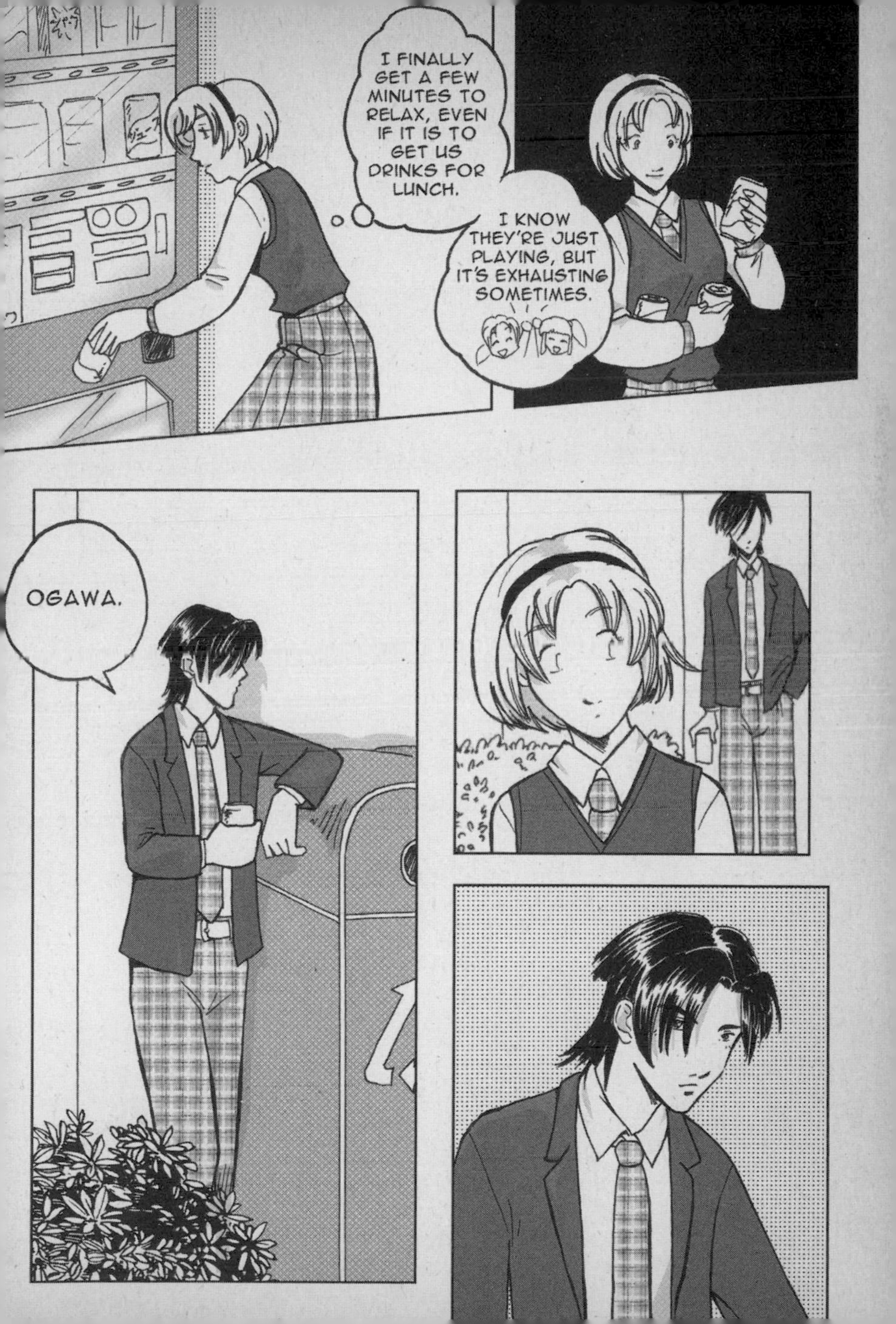
I FINALLY GET A FEW MINUTES TO RELAX, EVEN IF IT IS TO GET US DRINKS FOR LUNCH.
I KNOW THEY'RE JUST PLAYING, BUT IT'S EXHAUSTING SOMETIMES.
OGAWA.

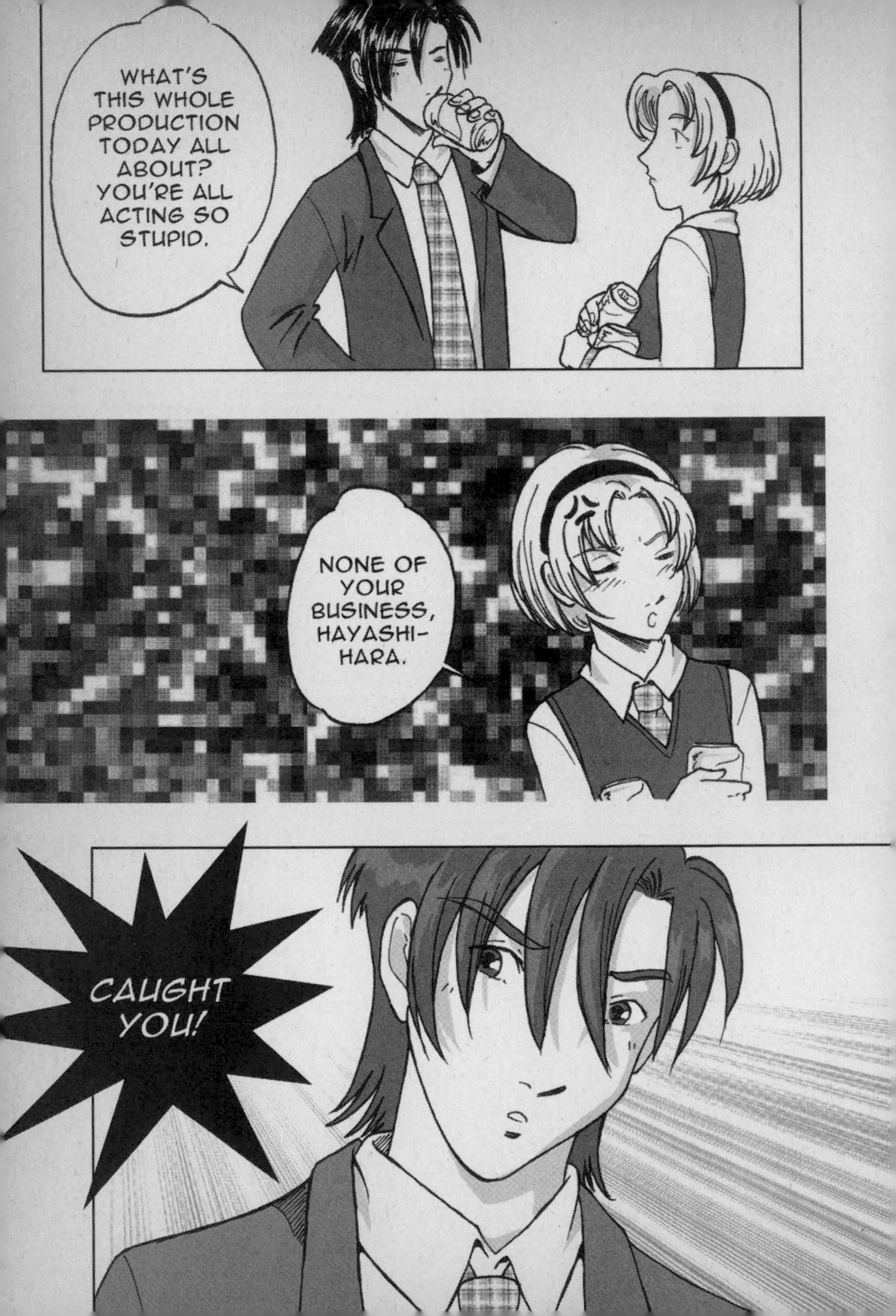
WHAT'S THIS WHOLE PRODUCTION TODAY ALL ABOUT? YOU'RE ALL ACTING SO STUPID.
NONE OF YOUR BUSINESS, HAYASHI-HARA.
CAUGHT YOU!

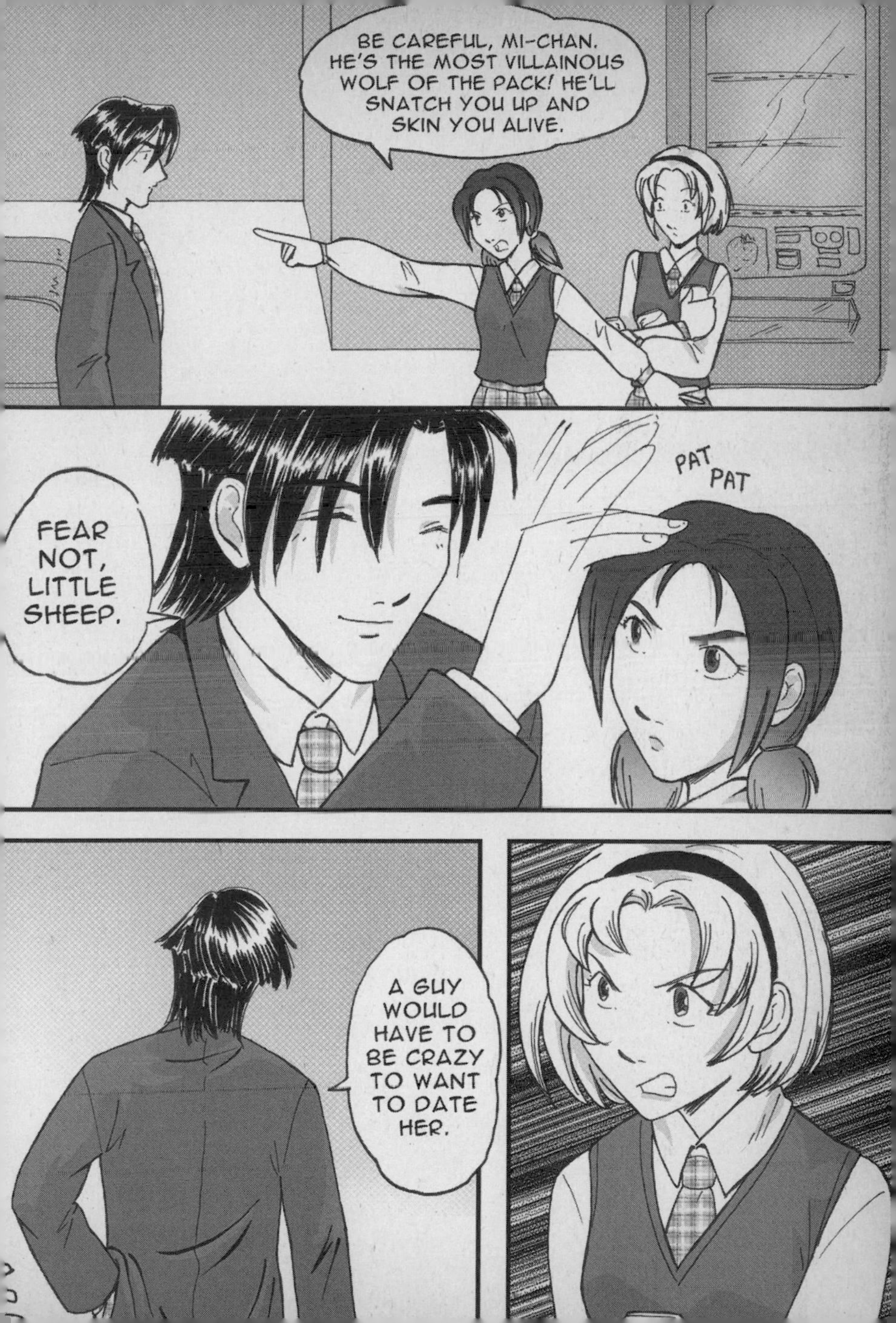
BE CAREFUL, MI-CHAN. HE'S THE MOST VILLAINOUS WOLF OF THE PACK! HE'LL SNATCH YOU UP AND SKIN YOU ALIVE.
FEAR NOT, LITTLE SHEEP.
PAT PAT
A GUY WOULD HAVE TO BE CRAZY TO WANT TO DATE HER.

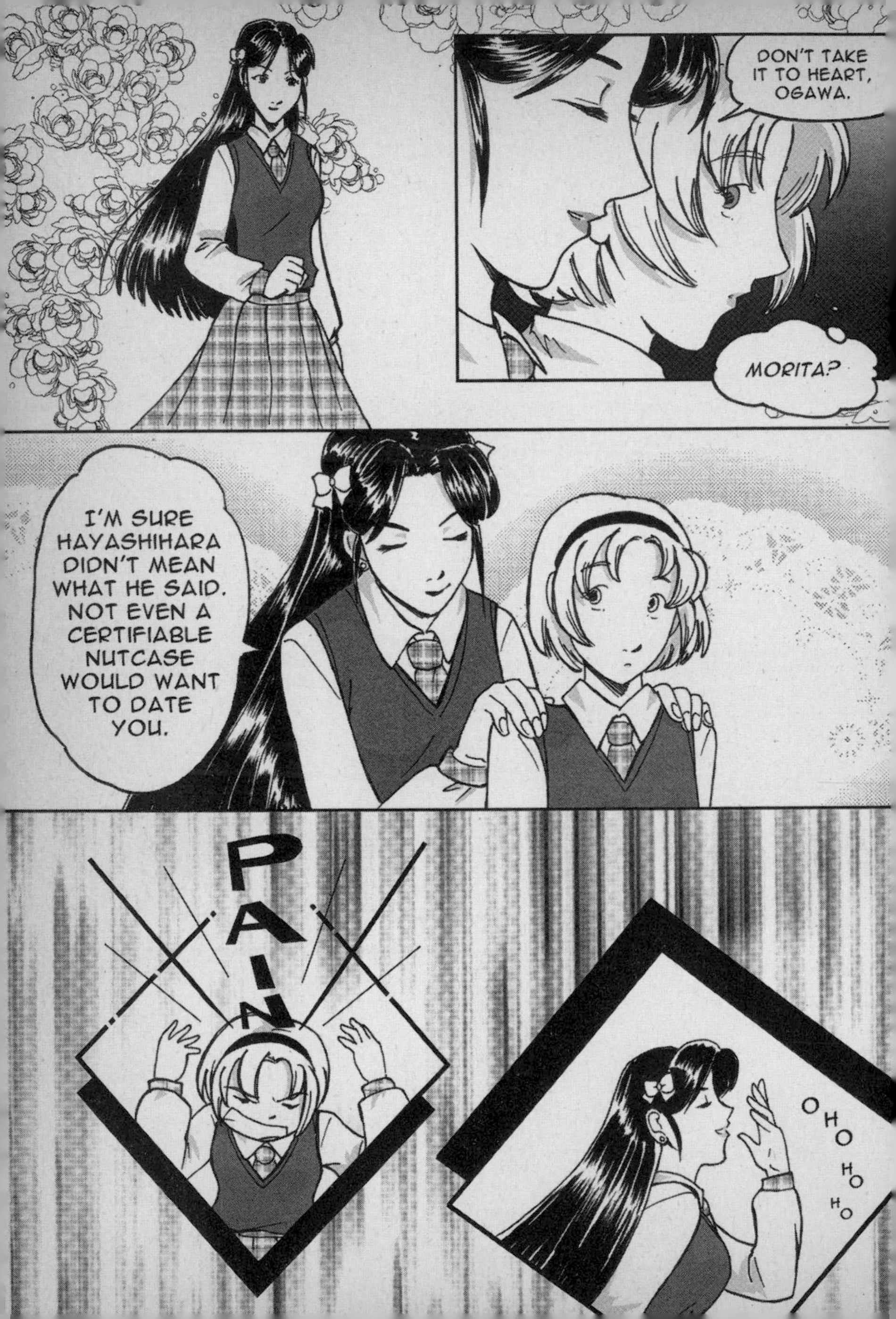

DON'T TAKE IT TO HEART, OGAWA.
MORITA?
I'M SURE HAYASHIHARA DIDN'T MEAN WHAT HE SAID. NOT EVEN A CERTIFIABLE NUTCASE WOULD WANT TO DATE YOU.
PAIN
OHO HO HO HO

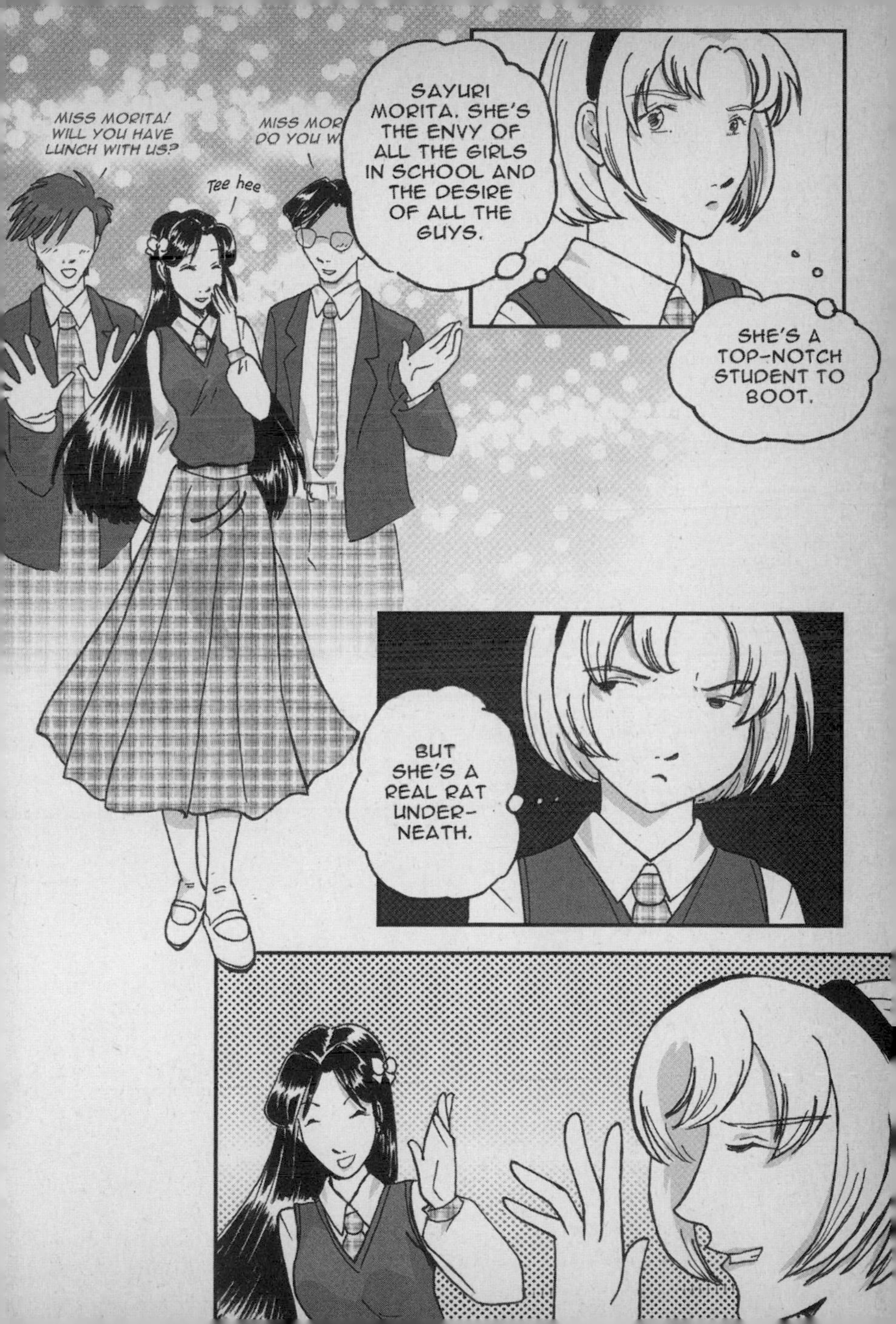
SAYURI MORITA. SHE'S THE ENVY OF ALL THE GIRLS IN SCHOOL AND THE DESIRE OF ALL THE GUYS.
MISS MORITA! WILL YOU HAVE LUNCH WITH US?
Tee hee
SHE'S A TOP-NOTCH STUDENT TO BOOT.
BUT SHE'S A REAL RAT UNDER-NEATH.

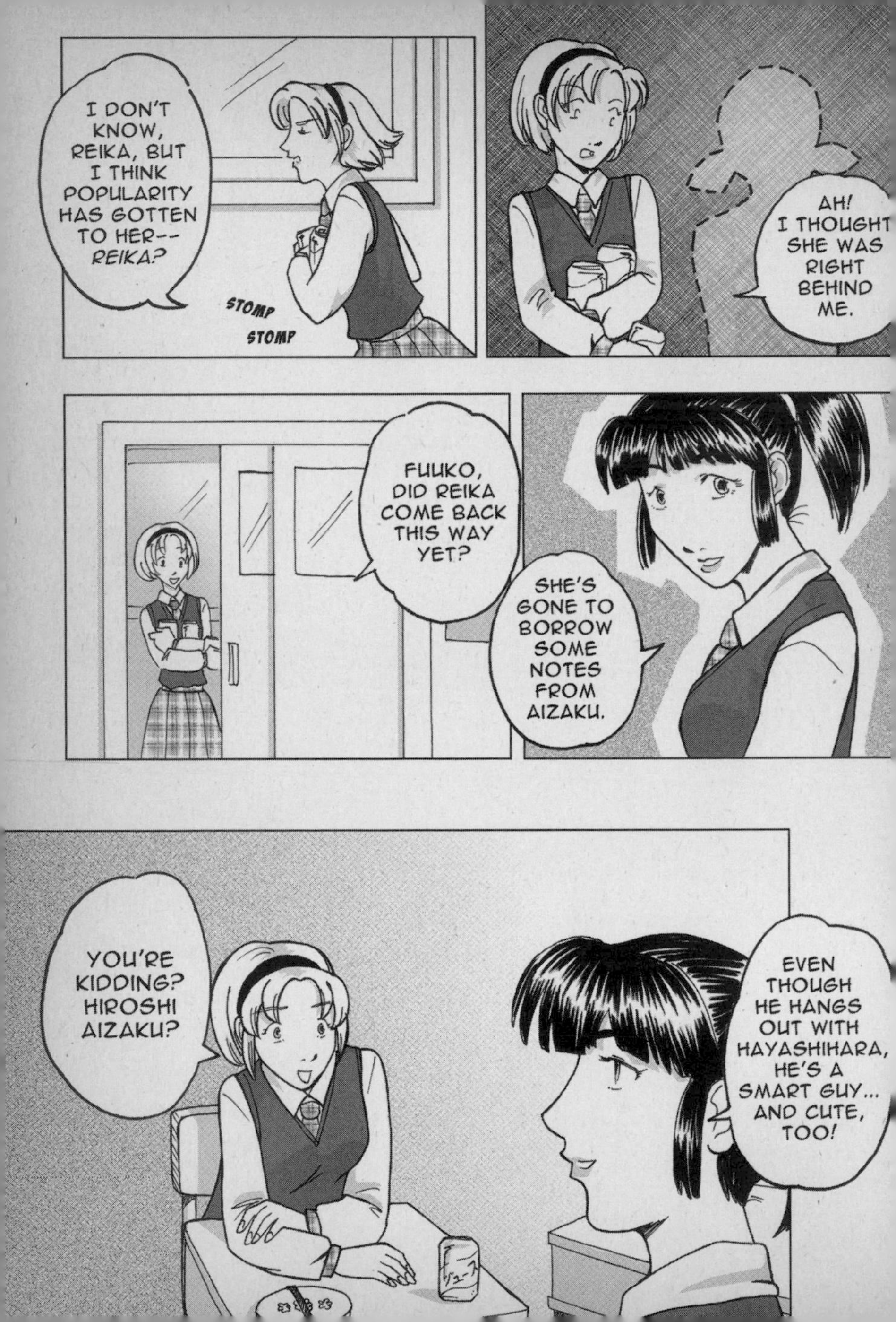
I DON'T KNOW, REIKA, BUT I THINK POPULARITY HAS GOTTEN TO HER-- REIKA?
STOMP
STOMP
AH! I THOUGHT SHE WAS RIGHT BEHIND ME.
FUUKO, DID REIKA COME BACK THIS WAY YET?
SHE'S GONE TO BORROW SOME NOTES FROM AIZAKU.
YOU'RE KIDDING? HIROSHI AIZAKU?
EVEN THOUGH HE HANGS OUT WITH HAYASHIHARA, HE'S A SMART GUY... AND CUTE, TOO!

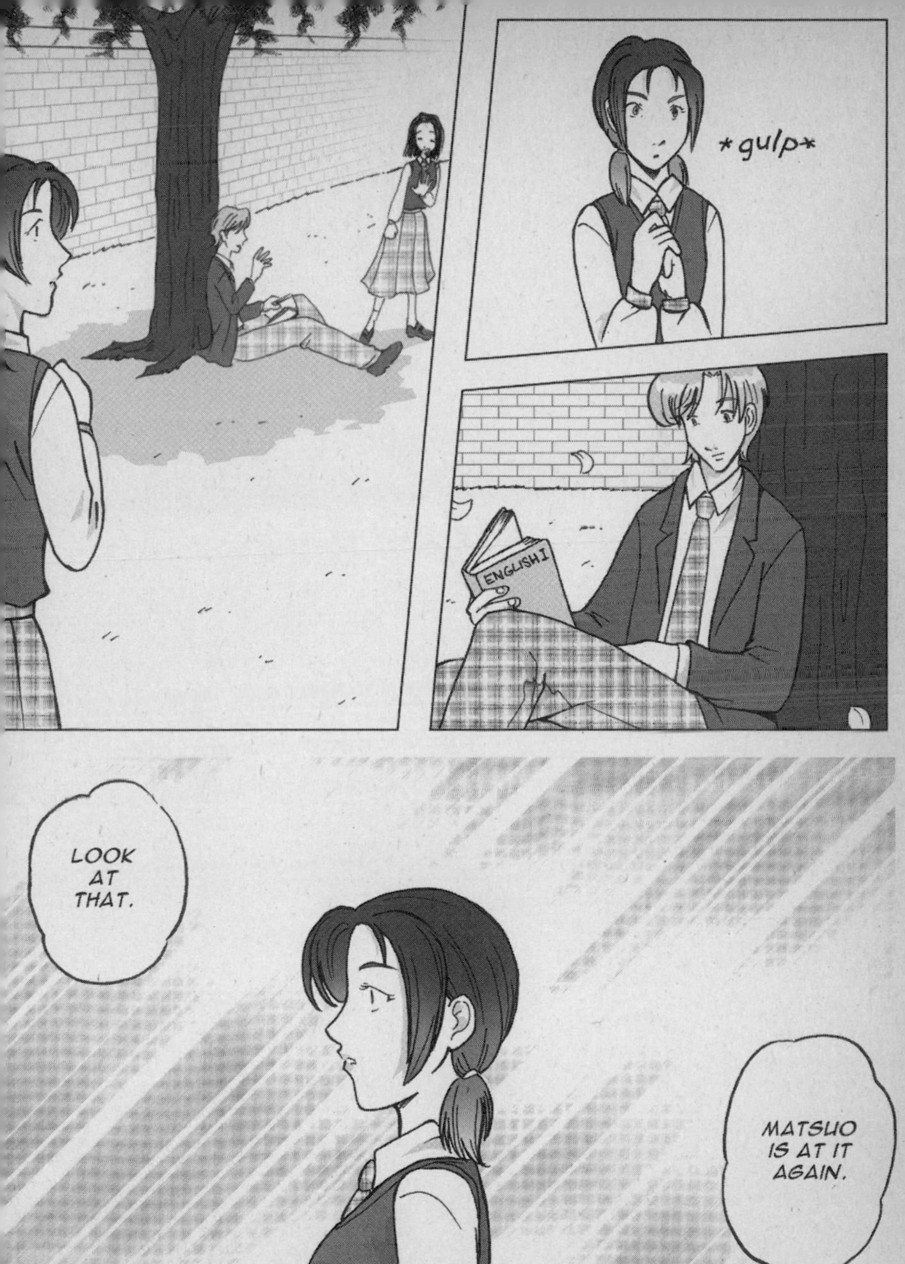
gulp
ENGLISH I
LOOK AT THAT.
MATSUO IS AT IT AGAIN.

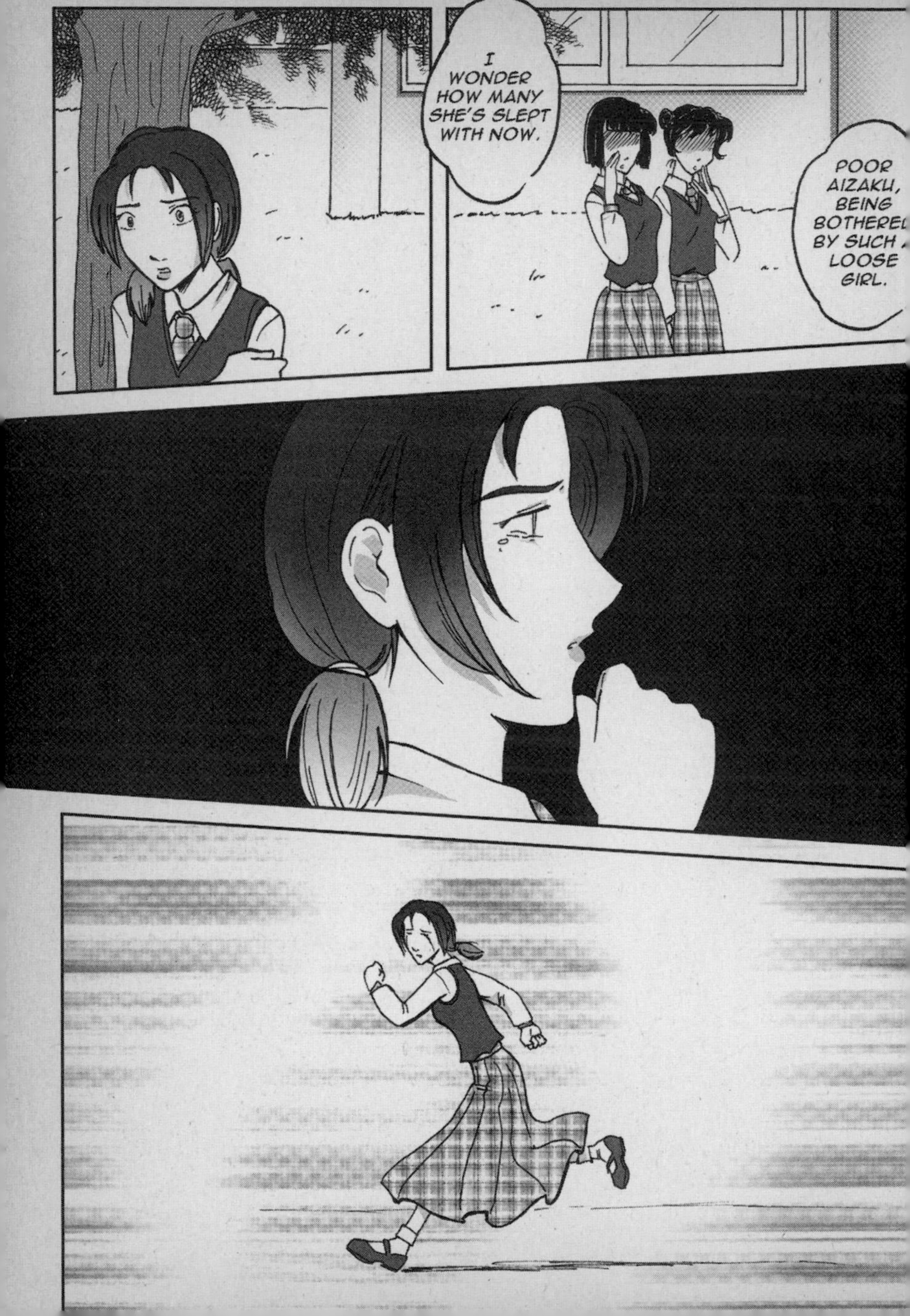
POOR AIZAKU, BEING BOTHERED BY SUCH A LOOSE GIRL.
I WONDER HOW MANY SHE'S SLEPT WITH NOW.

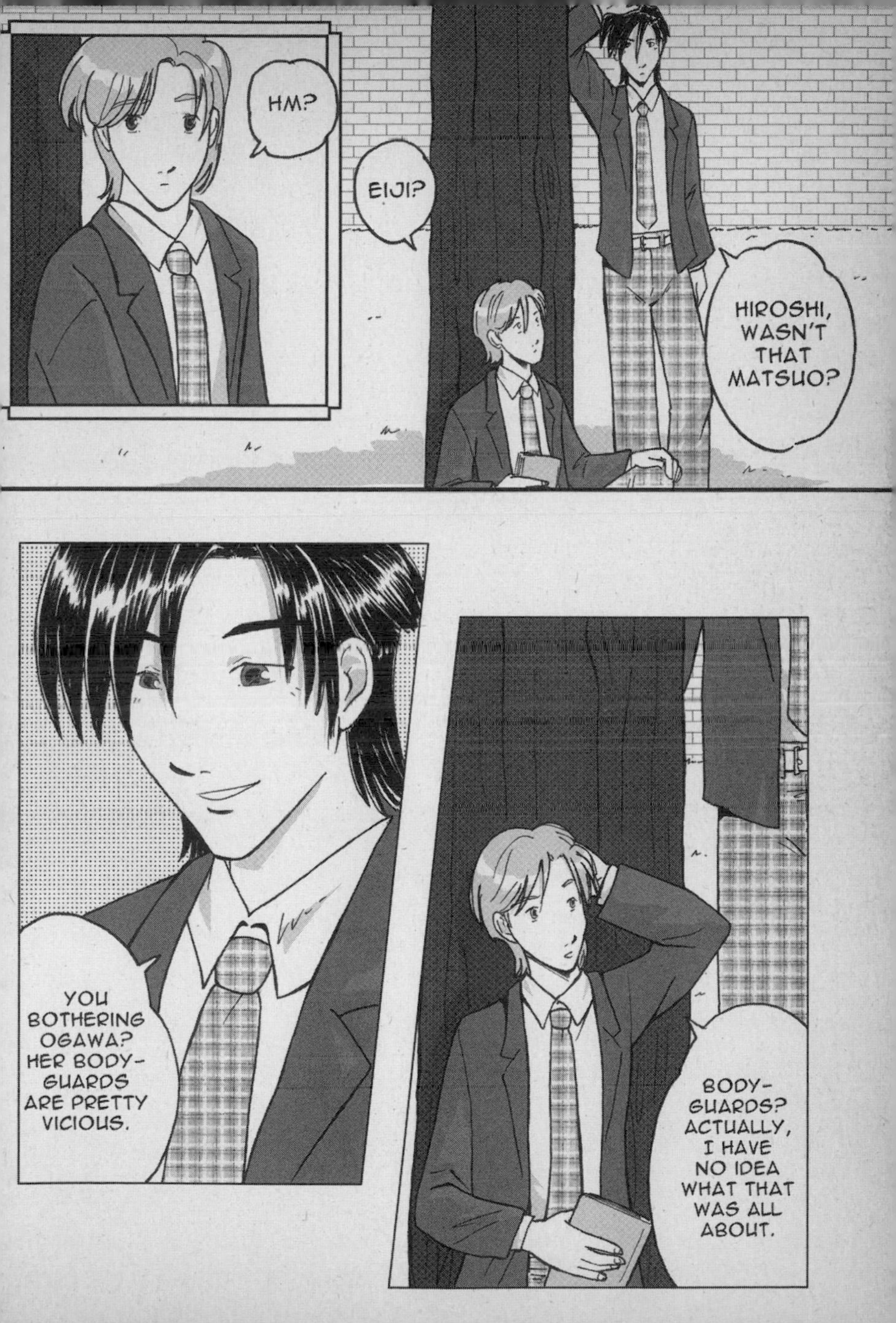
HM?
EIJI?
HIROSHI, WASN'T THAT MATSUO?
YOU BOTHERING OGAWA? HER BODY-GUARDS ARE PRETTY VICIOUS.
BODY-GUARDS? ACTUALLY, I HAVE NO IDEA WHAT THAT WAS ALL ABOUT.

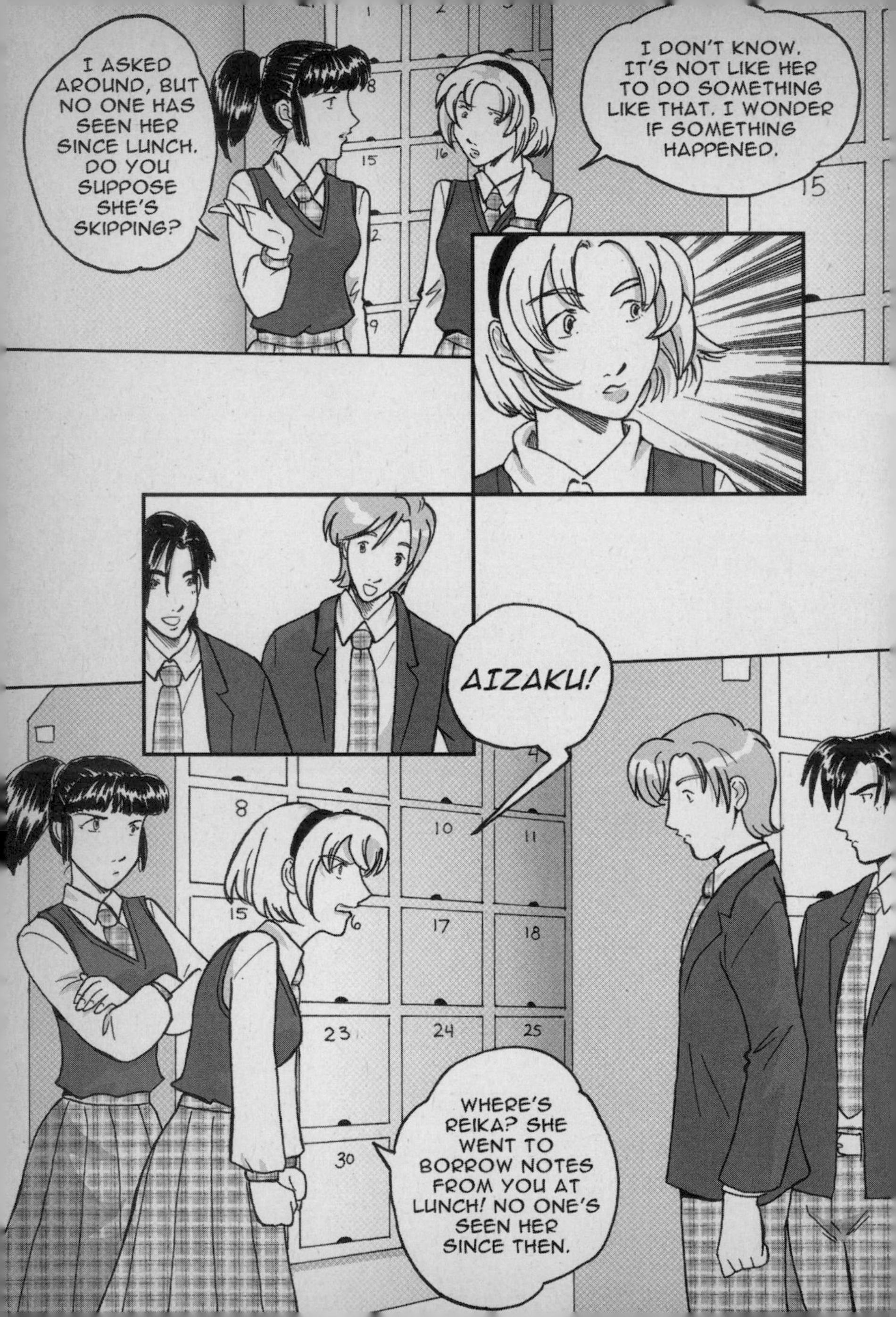
I ASKED AROUND, BUT NO ONE HAS SEEN HER SINCE LUNCH. DO YOU SUPPOSE SHE'S SKIPPING?
I DON'T KNOW. IT'S NOT LIKE HER TO DO SOMETHING LIKE THAT. I WONDER IF SOMETHING HAPPENED.
AIZAKU!
WHERE'S REIKA? SHE WENT TO BORROW NOTES FROM YOU AT LUNCH! NO ONE'S SEEN HER SINCE THEN.

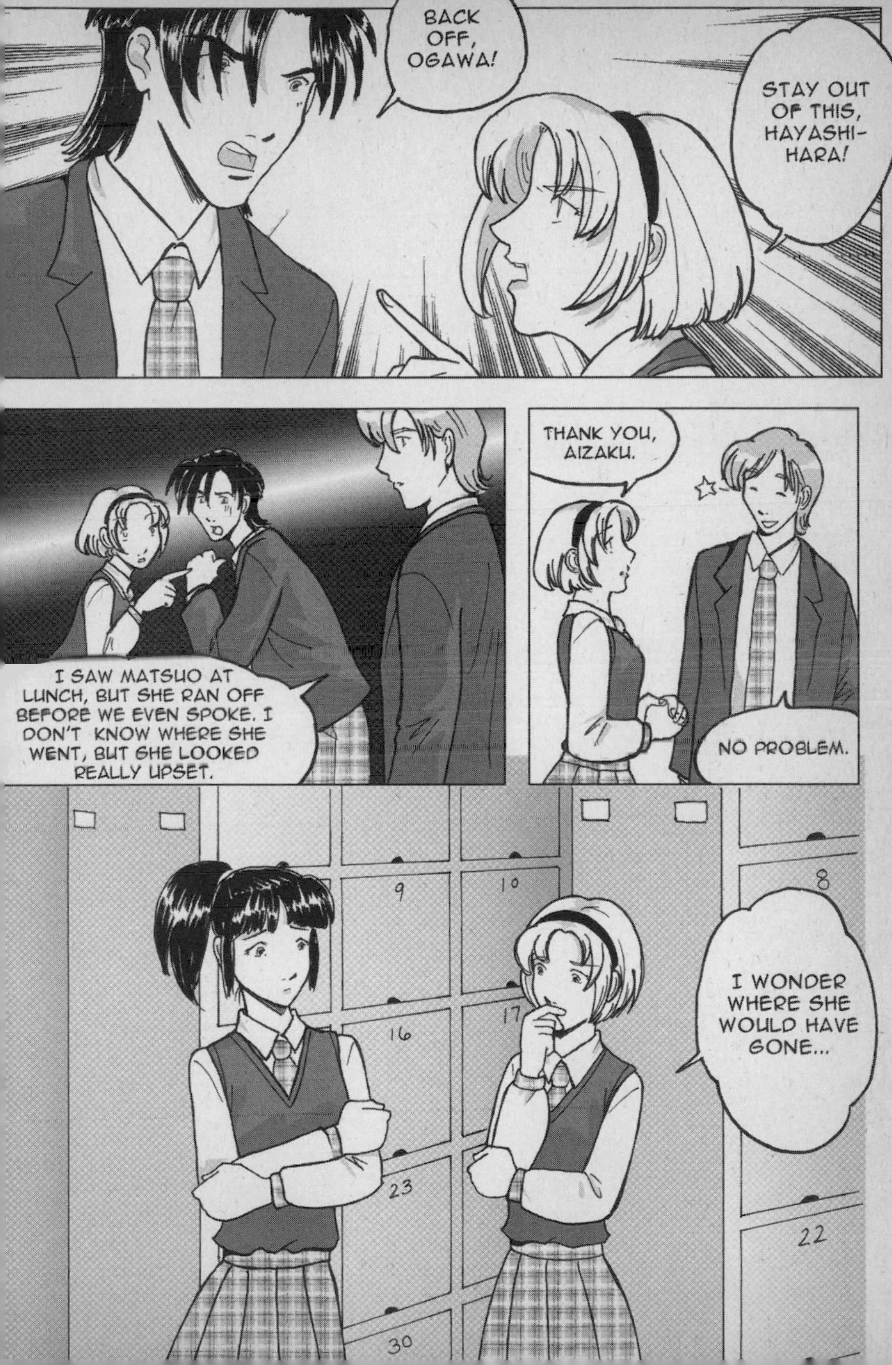
BACK OFF, OGAWA!
STAY OUT OF THIS, HAYASHI-HARA!
I SAW MATSUO AT LUNCH, BUT SHE RAN OFF BEFORE WE EVEN SPOKE. I DON'T KNOW WHERE SHE WENT, BUT SHE LOOKED REALLY UPSET.
THANK YOU, AIZAKU.
NO PROBLEM.
I WONDER WHERE SHE WOULD HAVE GONE...

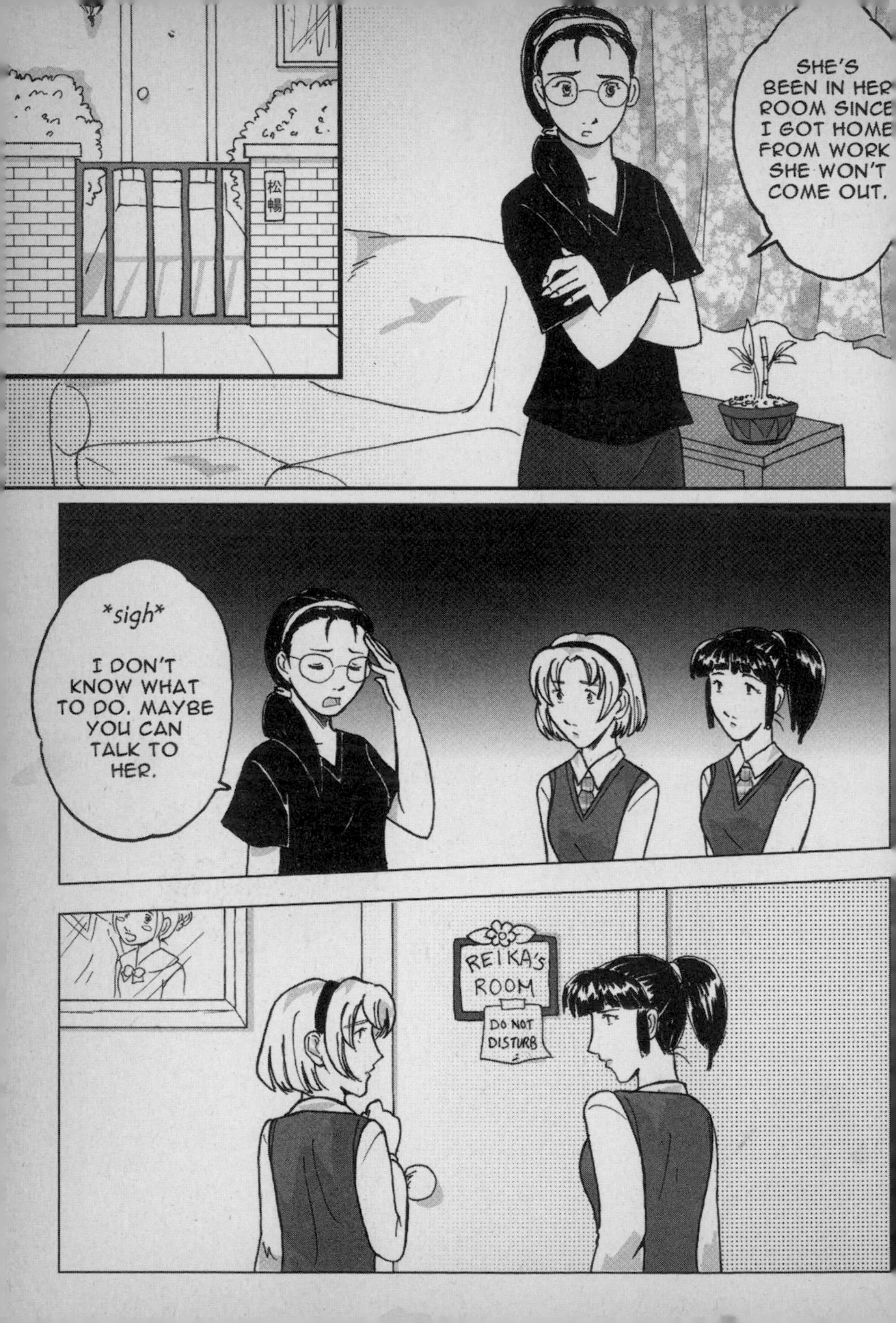
松暢
SHE'S BEEN IN HER ROOM SINCE I GOT HOME FROM WORK SHE WON'T COME OUT.
sigh
I DON'T KNOW WHAT TO DO. MAYBE YOU CAN TALK TO HER.
REIKA's ROOM
DO NOT DISTURB

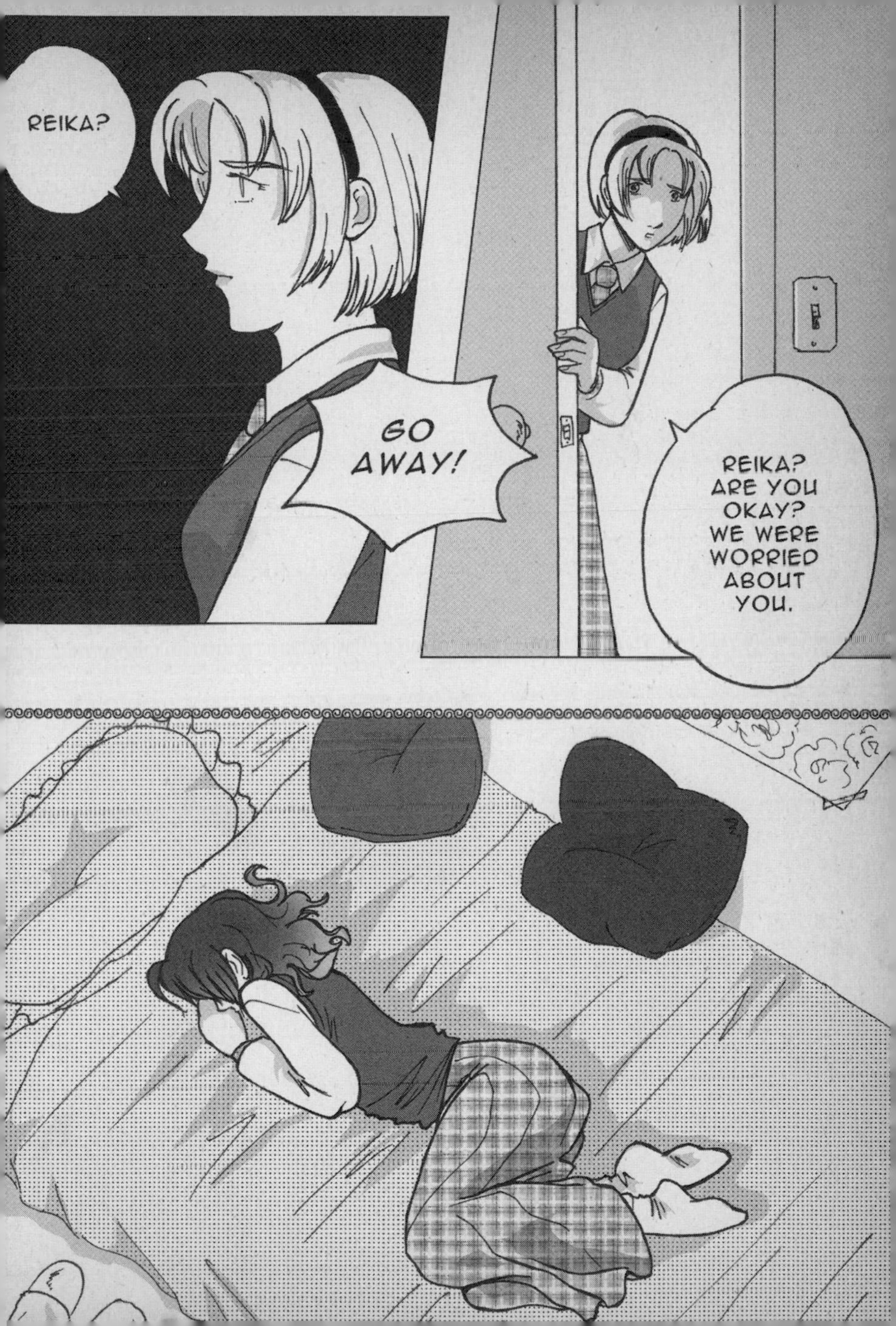
REIKA?
REIKA? ARE YOU OKAY? WE WERE WORRIED ABOUT YOU.
GO AWAY!

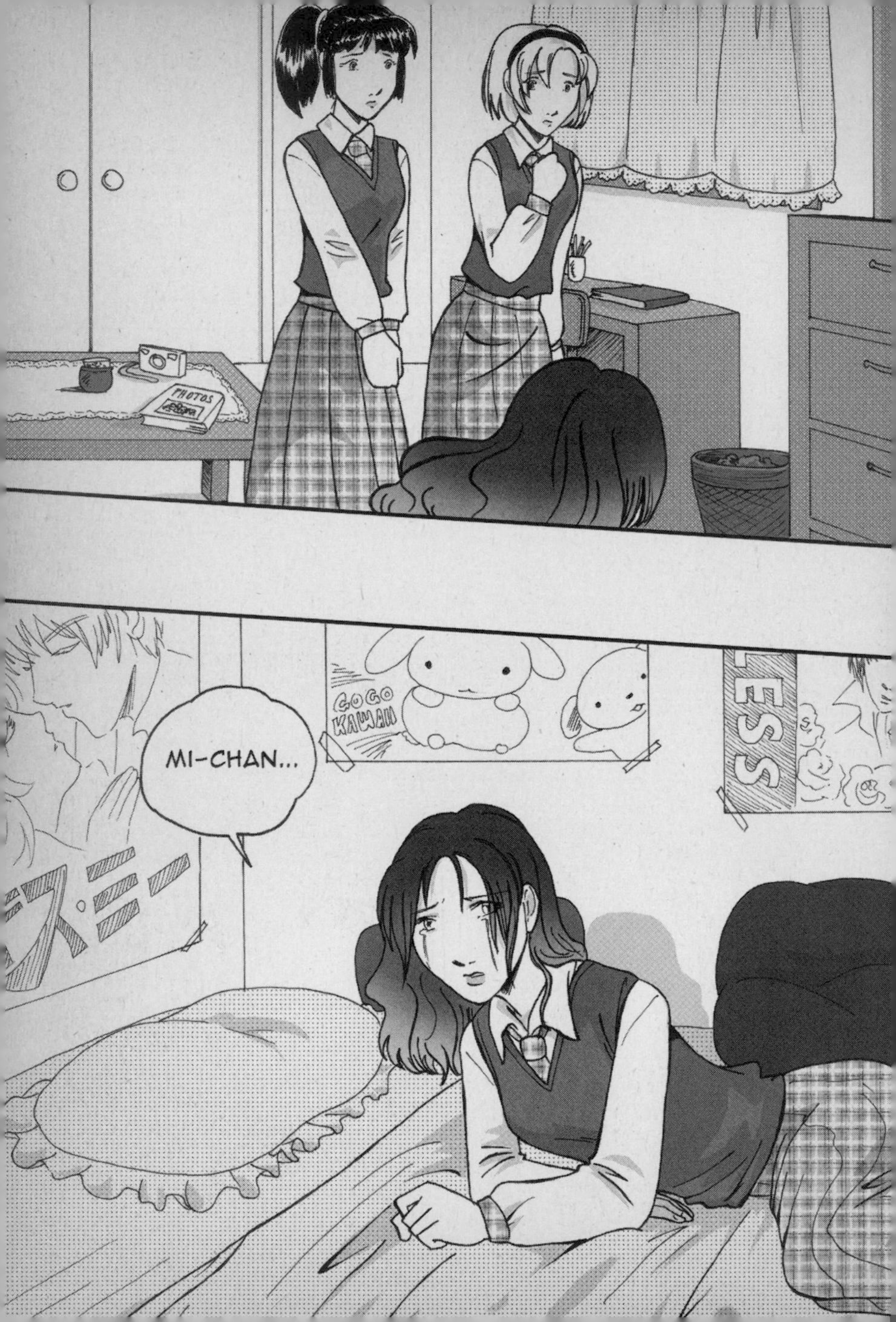
PHOTOS
GOGO KAWAII
MI-CHAN...

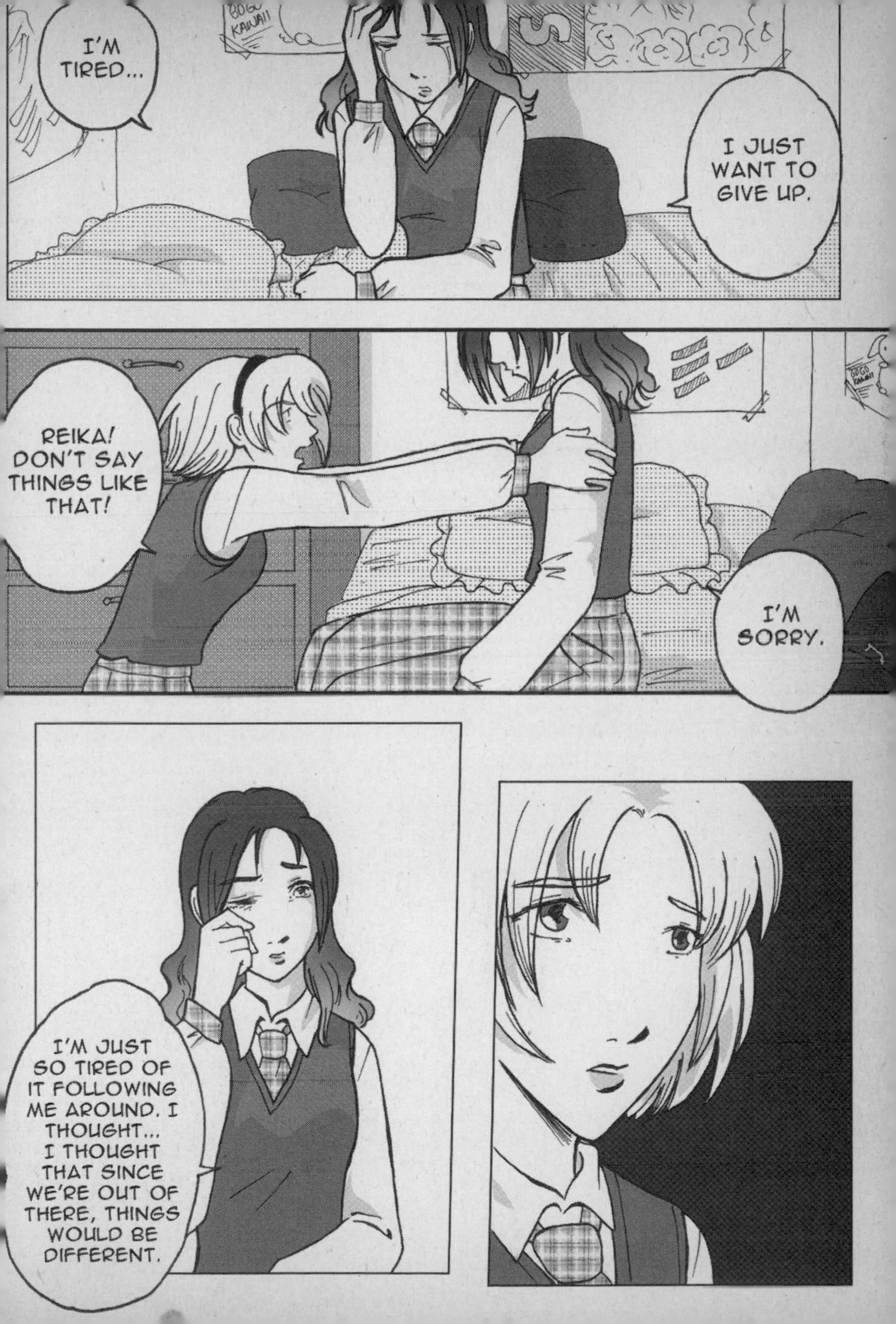

BOGO KAWAII
I'M TIRED...
I JUST WANT TO GIVE UP.
REIKA! DON'T SAY THINGS LIKE THAT!
I'M SORRY.
I'M JUST SO TIRED OF IT FOLLOWING ME AROUND. I THOUGHT... I THOUGHT THAT SINCE WE'RE OUT OF THERE, THINGS WOULD BE DIFFERENT.

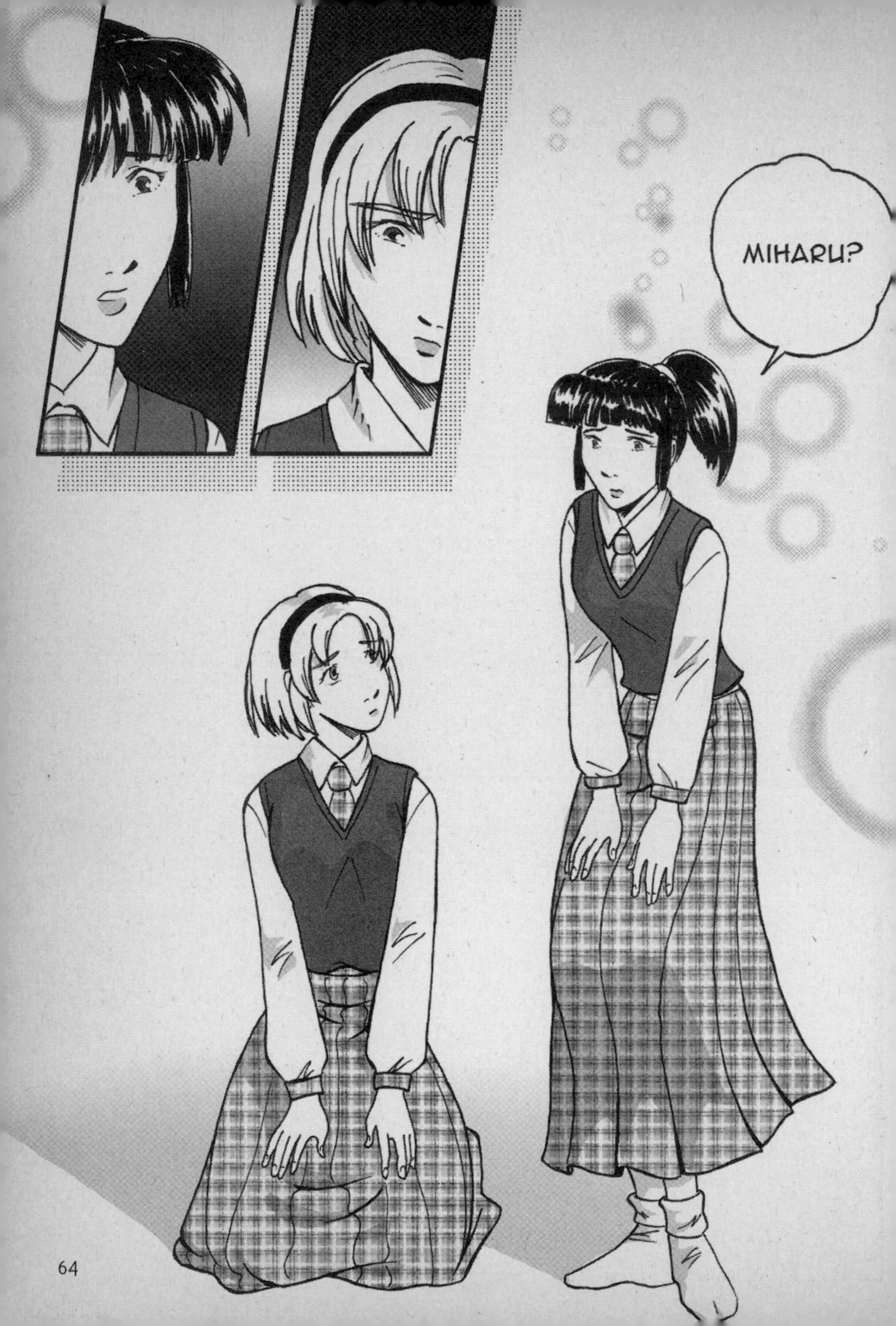
MIHARU?

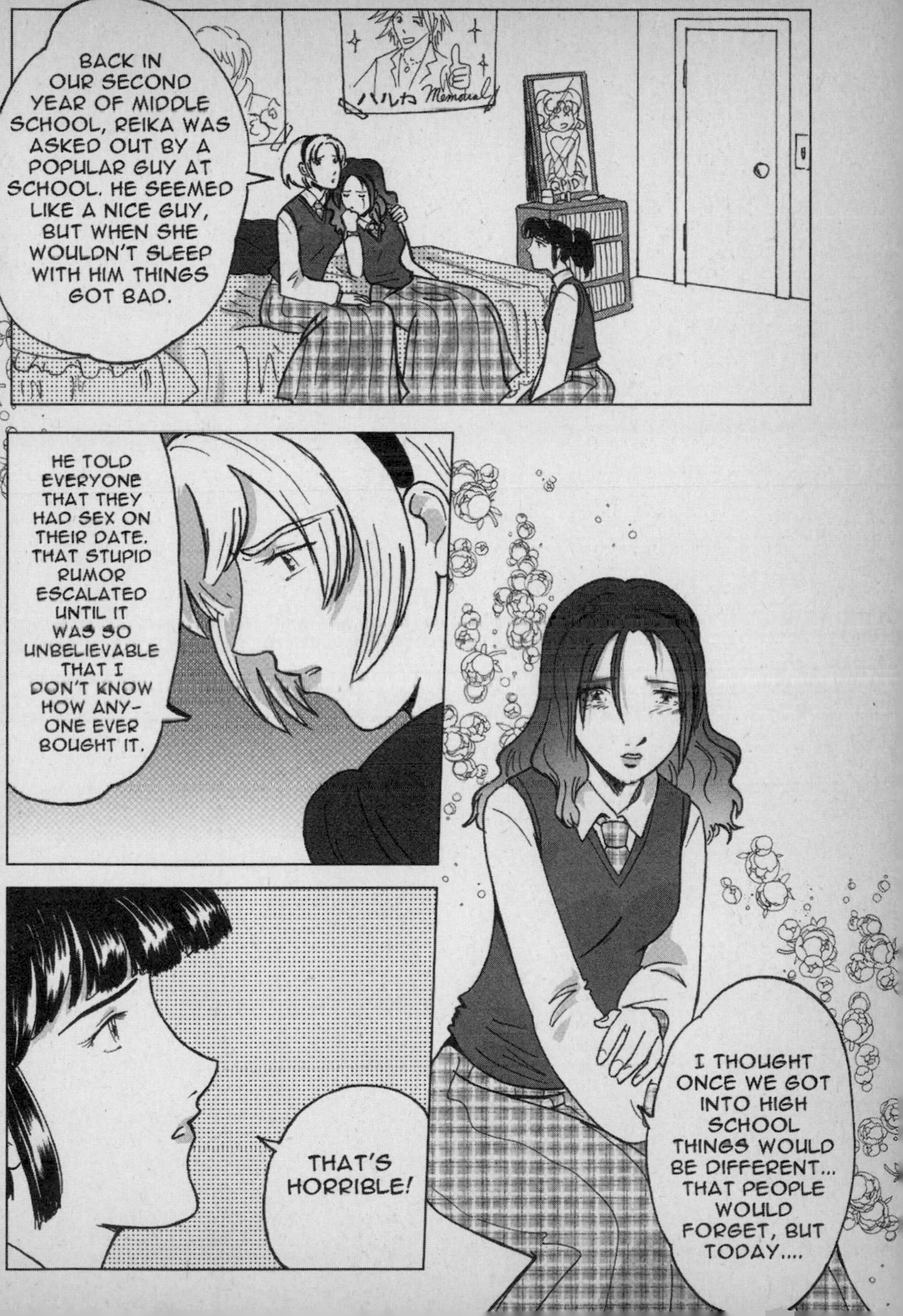
BACK IN OUR SECOND YEAR OF MIDDLE SCHOOL, REIKA WAS ASKED OUT BY A POPULAR GUY AT SCHOOL. HE SEEMED LIKE A NICE GUY, BUT WHEN SHE WOULDN'T SLEEP WITH HIM THINGS GOT BAD.
HE TOLD EVERYONE THAT THEY HAD SEX ON THEIR DATE. THAT STUPID RUMOR ESCALATED UNTIL IT WAS SO UNBELIEVABLE THAT I DON'T KNOW HOW ANY-ONE EVER BOUGHT IT.
THAT'S HORRIBLE!
I THOUGHT ONCE WE GOT INTO HIGH SCHOOL THINGS WOULD BE DIFFERENT... THAT PEOPLE WOULD FORGET, BUT TODAY....

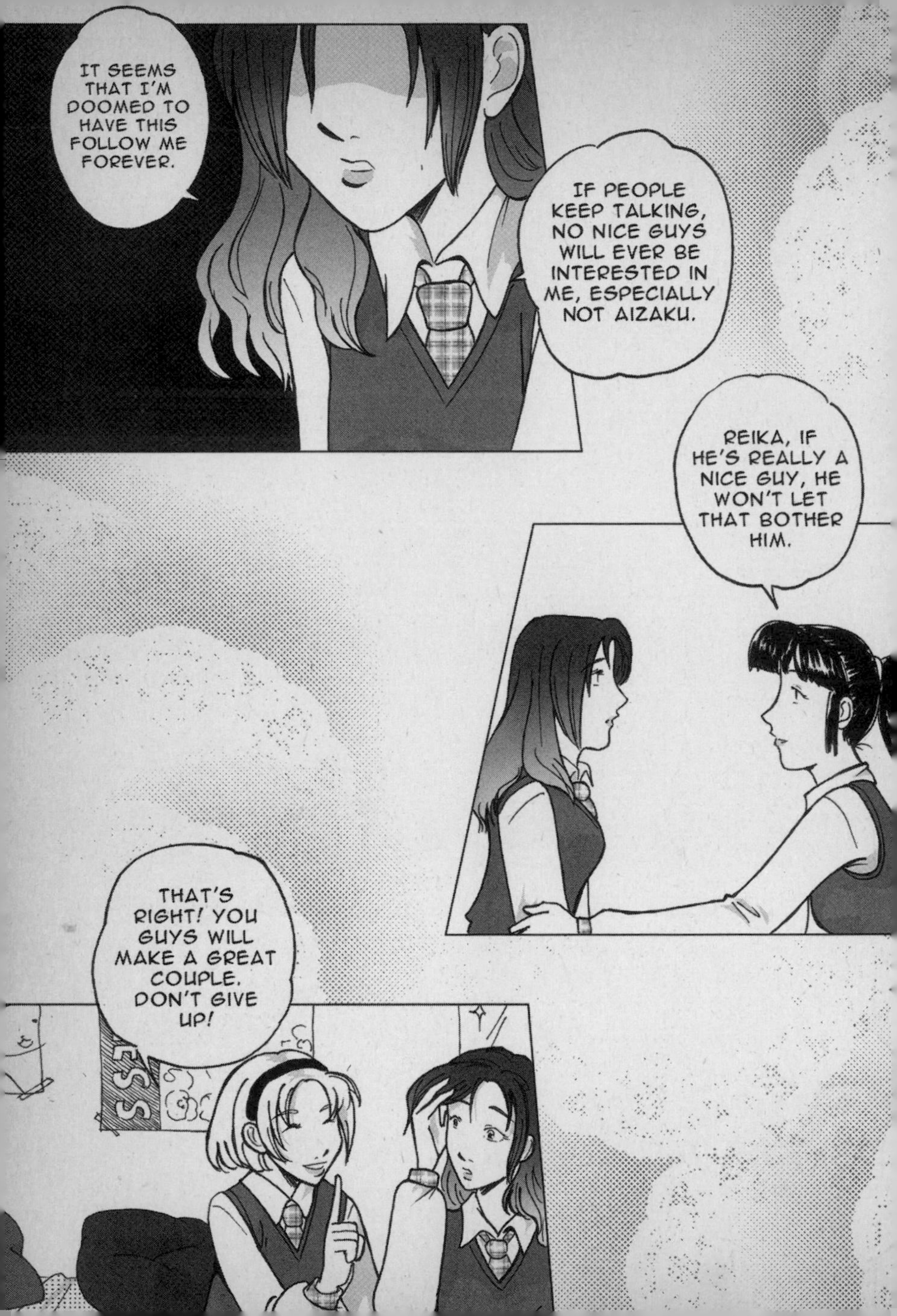
IT SEEMS THAT I'M DOOMED TO HAVE THIS FOLLOW ME FOREVER.
IF PEOPLE KEEP TALKING, NO NICE GUYS WILL EVER BE INTERESTED IN ME, ESPECIALLY NOT AIZAKU.
REIKA, IF HE'S REALLY A NICE GUY, HE WON'T LET THAT BOTHER HIM.
THAT'S RIGHT! YOU GUYS WILL MAKE A GREAT COUPLE. DON'T GIVE UP!

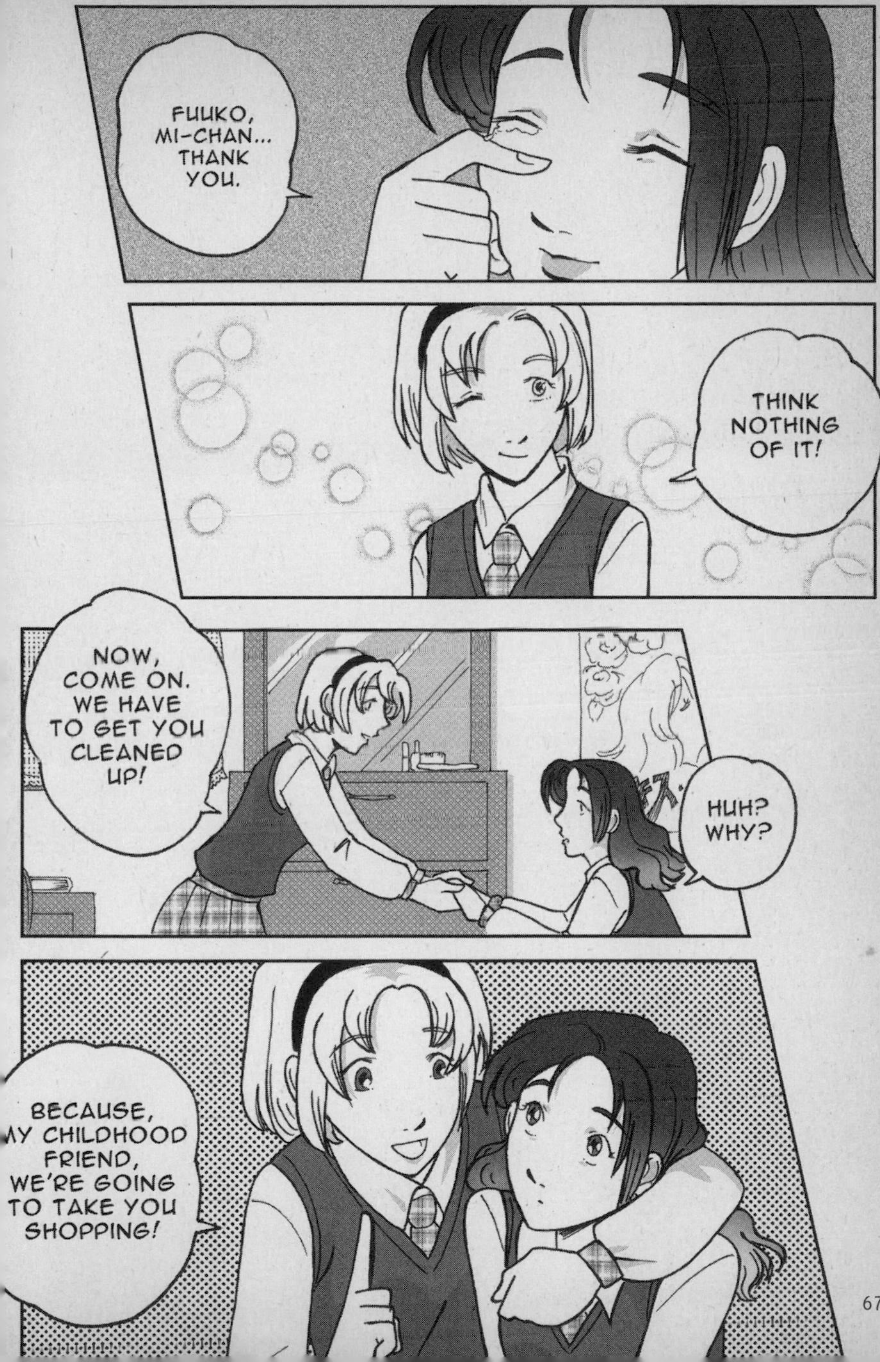
FUUKO, MI-CHAN... THANK YOU.
THINK NOTHING OF IT!
NOW, COME ON. WE HAVE TO GET YOU CLEANED UP!
HUH? WHY?
BECAUSE, MY CHILDHOOD FRIEND, WE'RE GOING TO TAKE YOU SHOPPING!

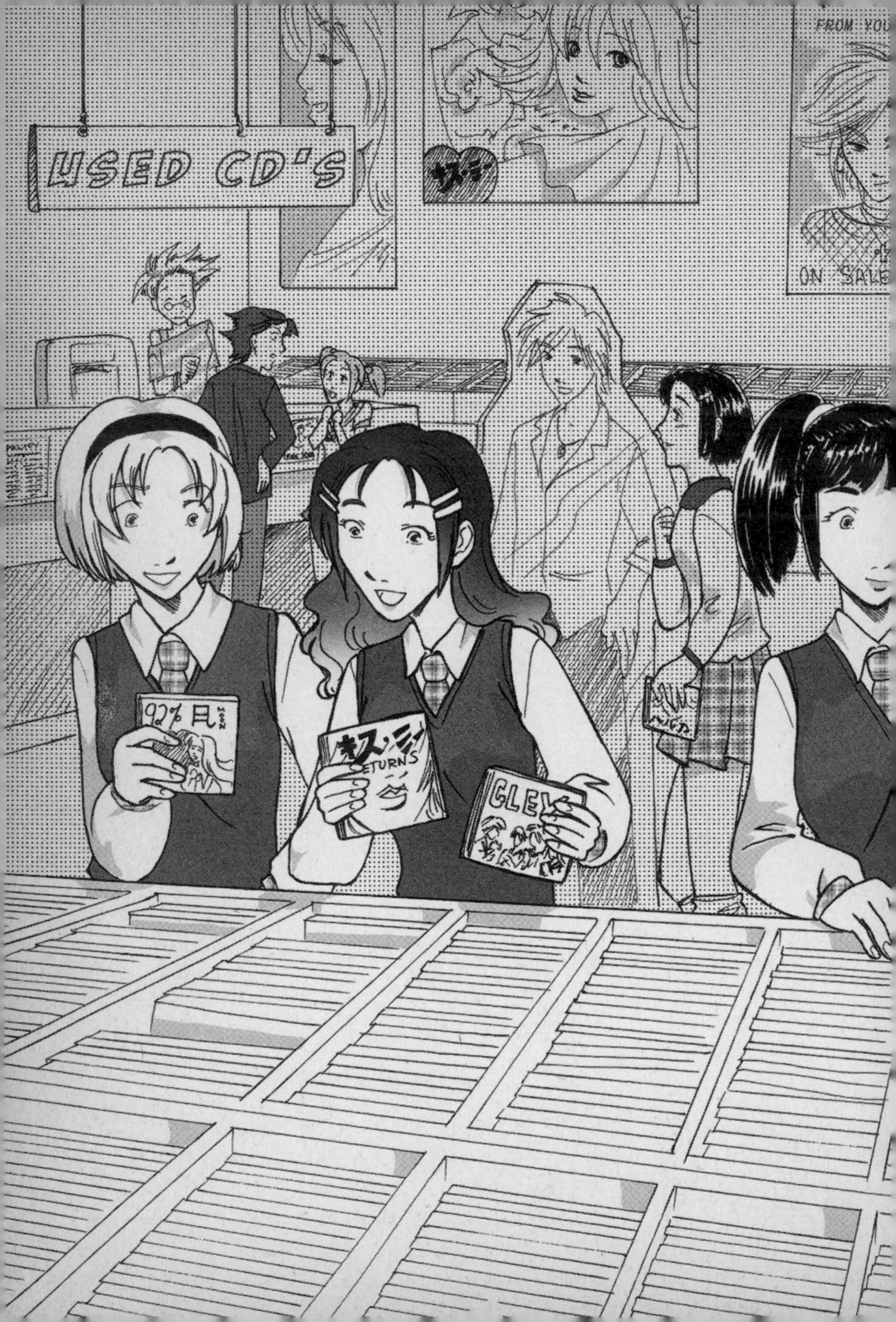
USED CD'S
FROM YOU
ON SALE
92% 月
CLEV

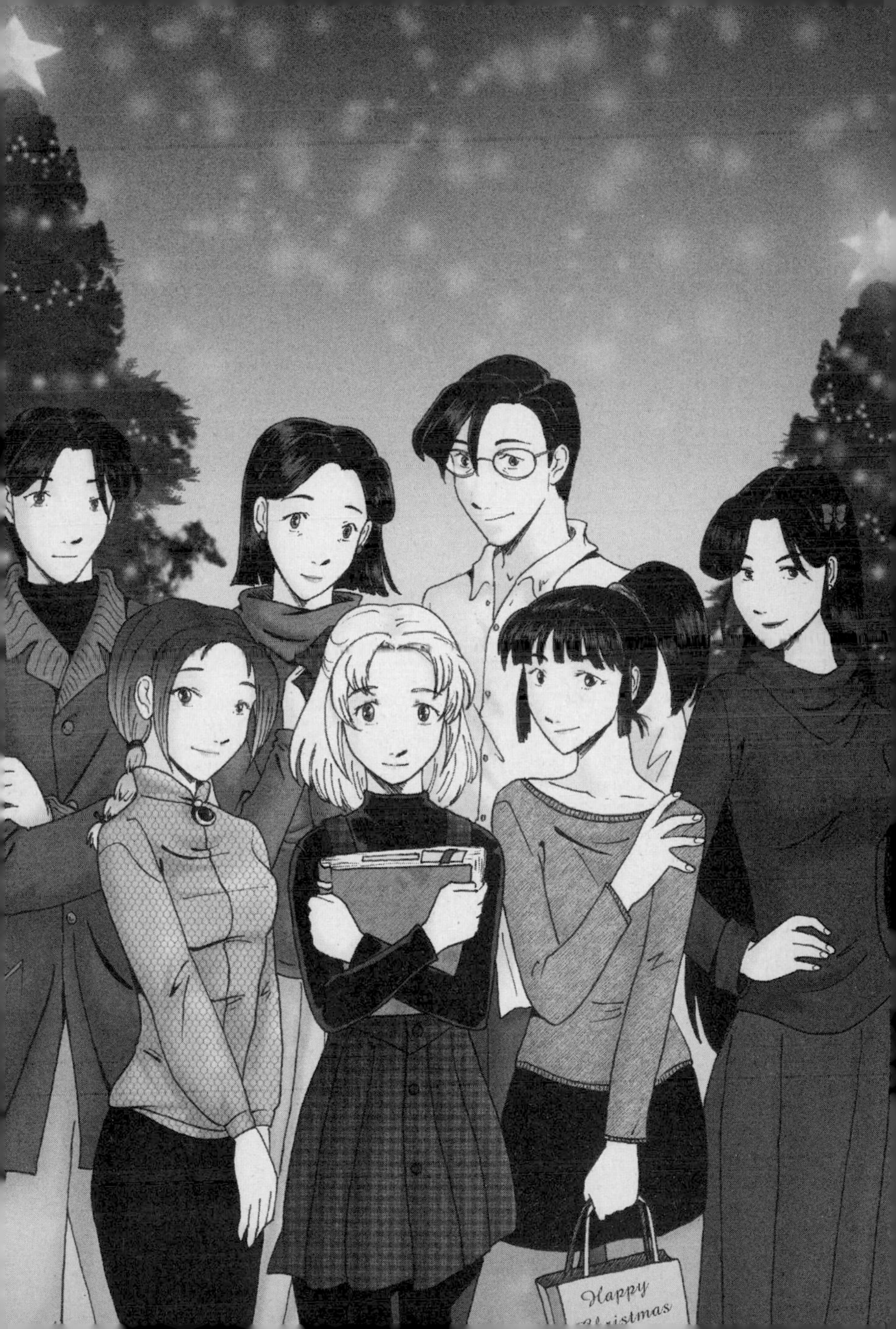
Happy

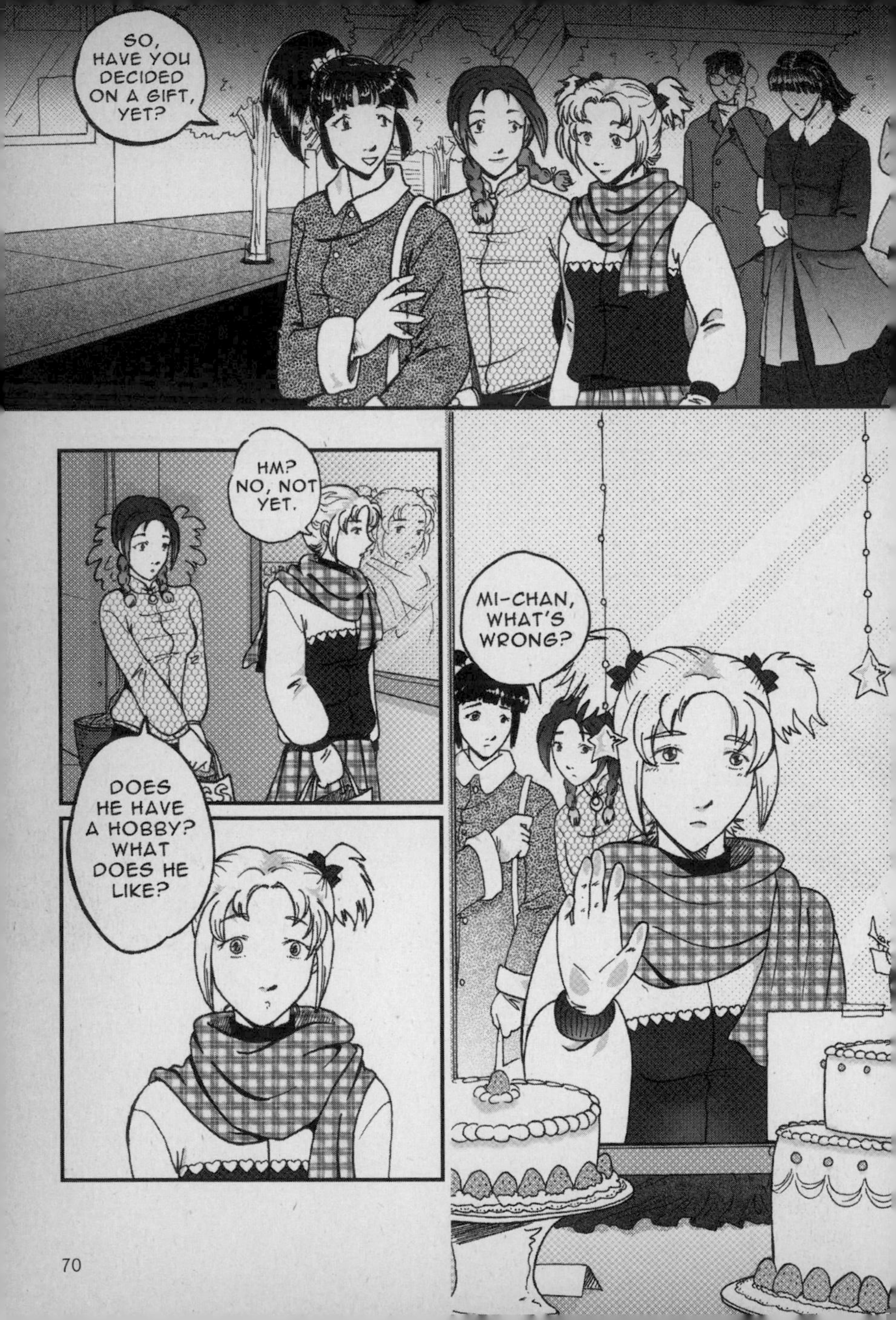
SO, HAVE YOU DECIDED ON A GIFT, YET?
HM? NO, NOT YET.
DOES HE HAVE A HOBBY? WHAT DOES HE LIKE?
MI-CHAN, WHAT'S WRONG?

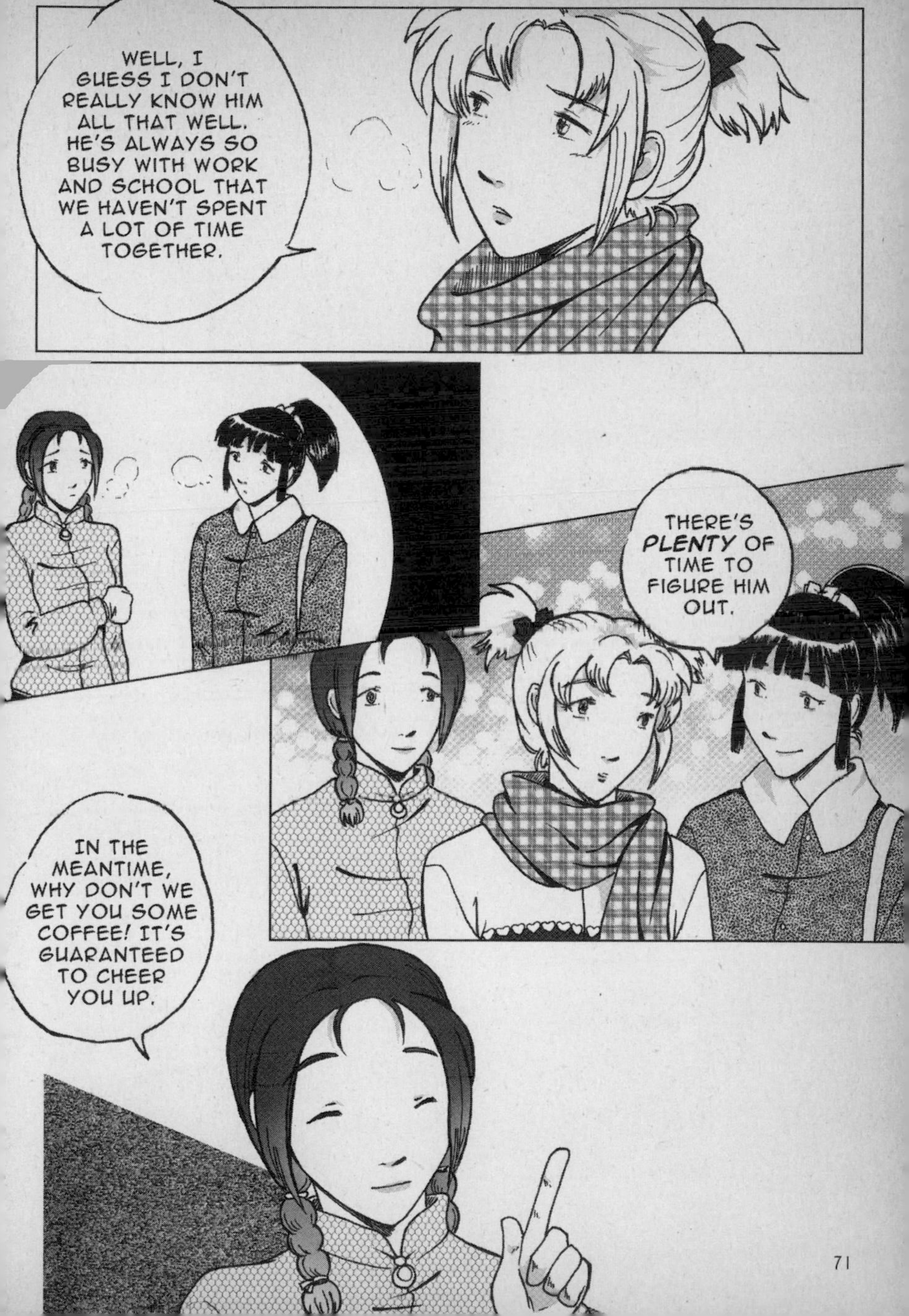
WELL, I GUESS I DON'T REALLY KNOW HIM ALL THAT WELL. HE'S ALWAYS SO BUSY WITH WORK AND SCHOOL THAT WE HAVEN'T SPENT A LOT OF TIME TOGETHER.
THERE'S *PLENTY* OF TIME TO FIGURE HIM OUT.
IN THE MEANTIME, WHY DON'T WE GET YOU SOME COFFEE! IT'S GUARANTEED TO CHEER YOU UP.

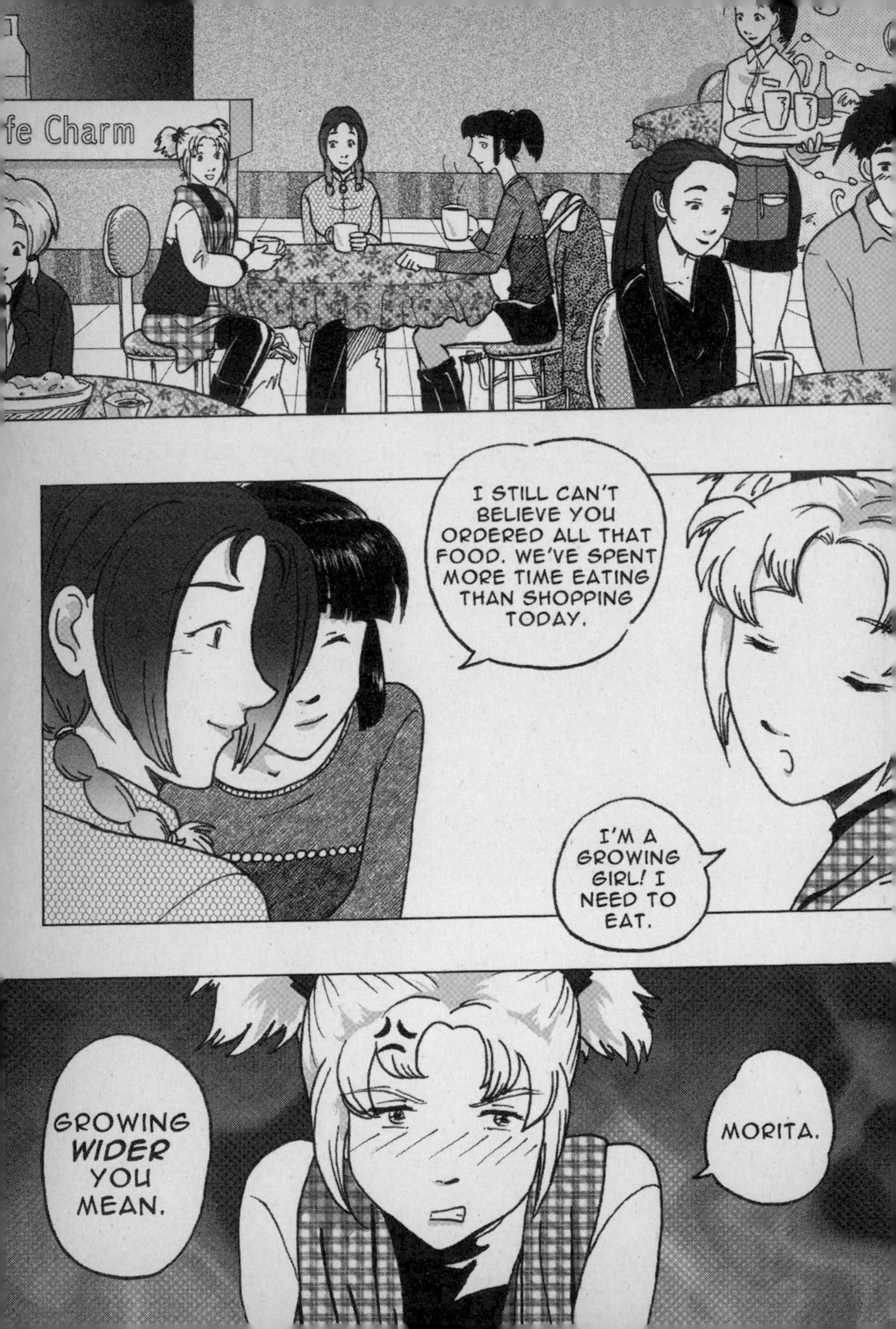
fe Charm
I STILL CAN'T BELIEVE YOU ORDERED ALL THAT FOOD. WE'VE SPENT MORE TIME EATING THAN SHOPPING TODAY.
I'M A GROWING GIRL! I NEED TO EAT.
MORITA.
GROWING WIDER YOU MEAN.

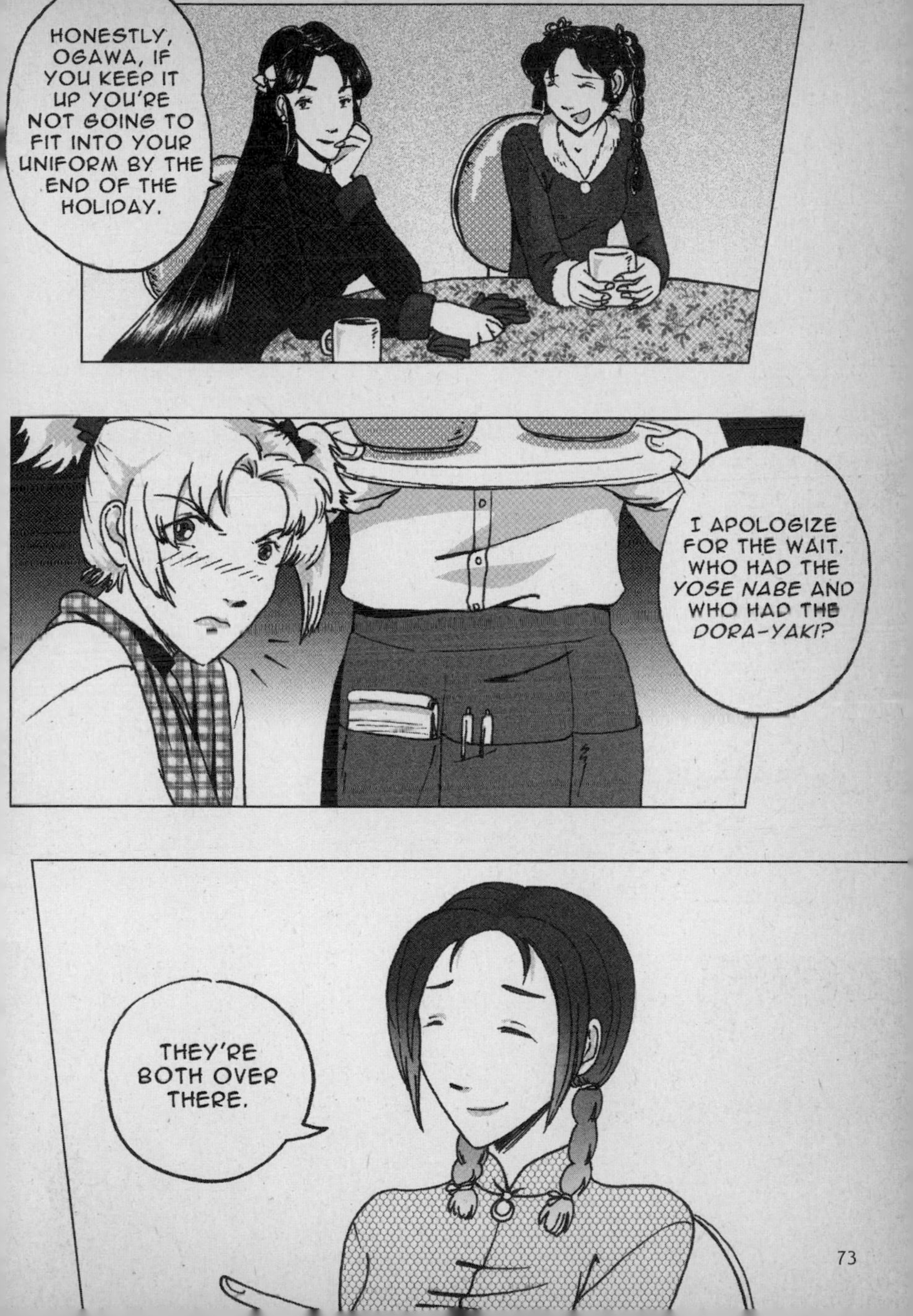
HONESTLY, OGAWA, IF YOU KEEP IT UP YOU'RE NOT GOING TO FIT INTO YOUR UNIFORM BY THE END OF THE HOLIDAY.
I APOLOGIZE FOR THE WAIT. WHO HAD THE *YOSE NABE* AND WHO HAD THE *DORA-YAKI*?
THEY'RE BOTH OVER THERE.

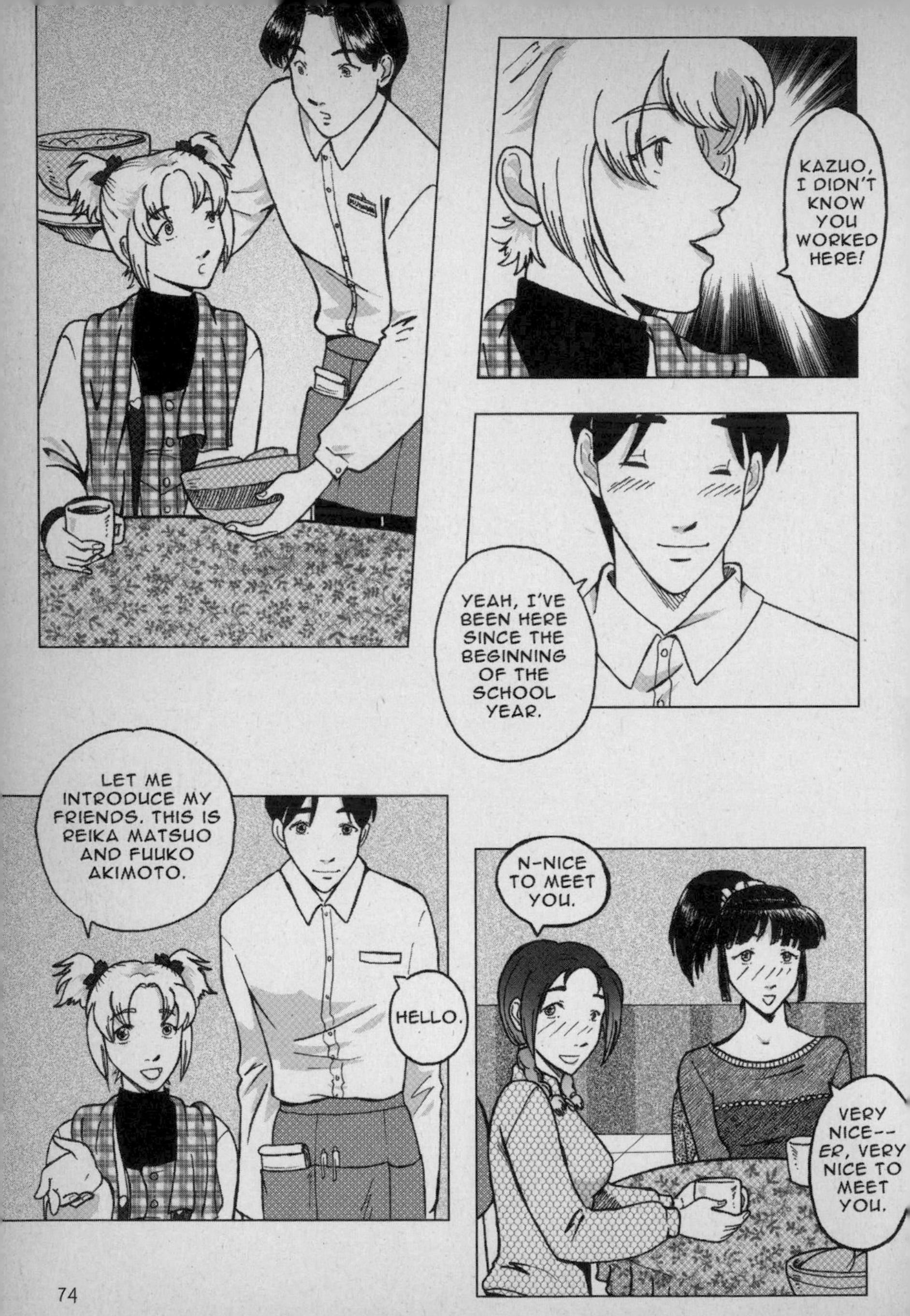
KAZUO, I DIDN'T KNOW YOU WORKED HERE!
YEAH, I'VE BEEN HERE SINCE THE BEGINNING OF THE SCHOOL YEAR.
LET ME INTRODUCE MY FRIENDS. THIS IS REIKA MATSUO AND FUUKO AKIMOTO.
HELLO.
N-NICE TO MEET YOU.
VERY NICE-- ER, VERY NICE TO MEET YOU.

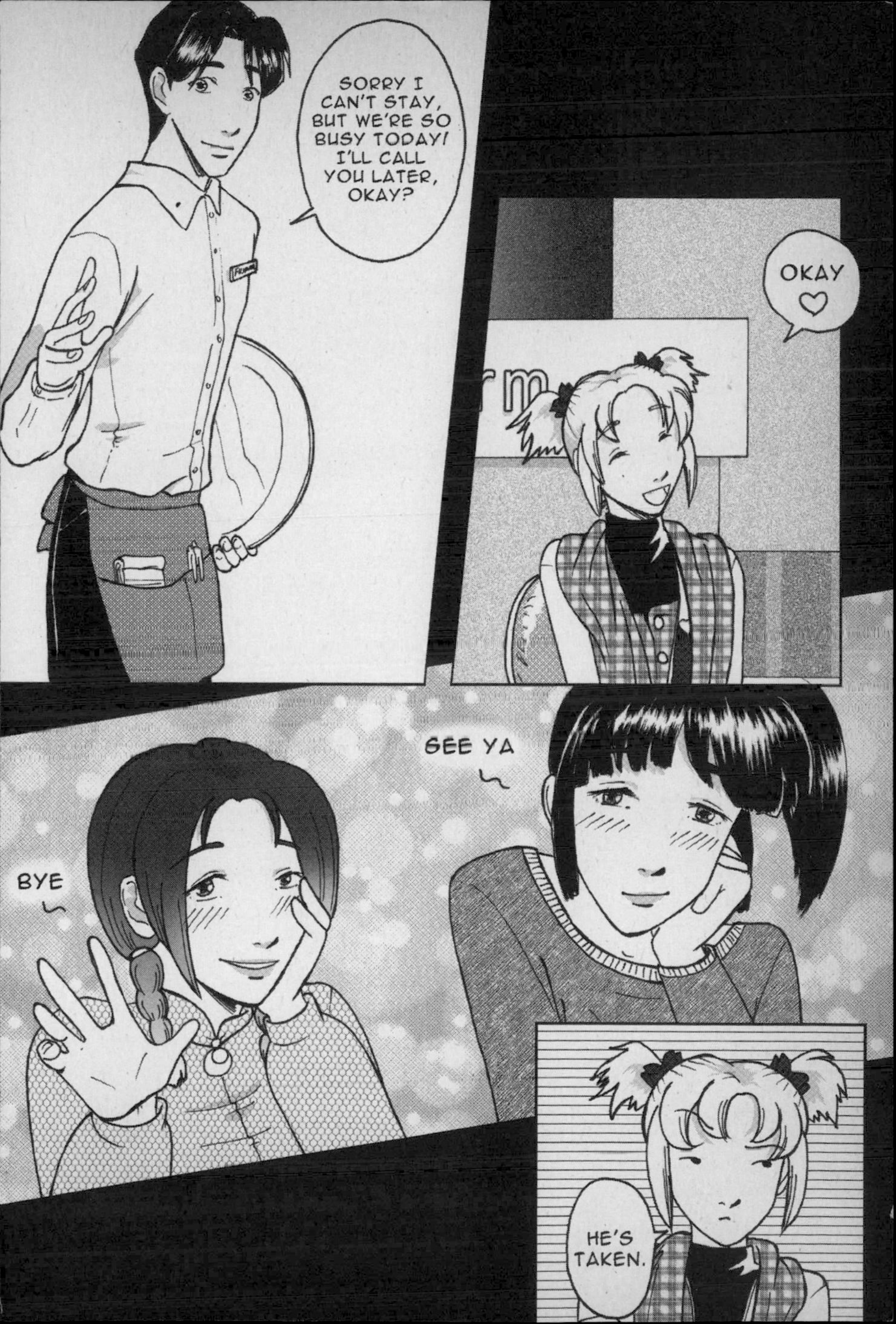
SORRY I CAN'T STAY, BUT WE'RE SO BUSY TODAY! I'LL CALL YOU LATER, OKAY?
OKAY ♡
SEE YA
BYE
HE'S TAKEN.

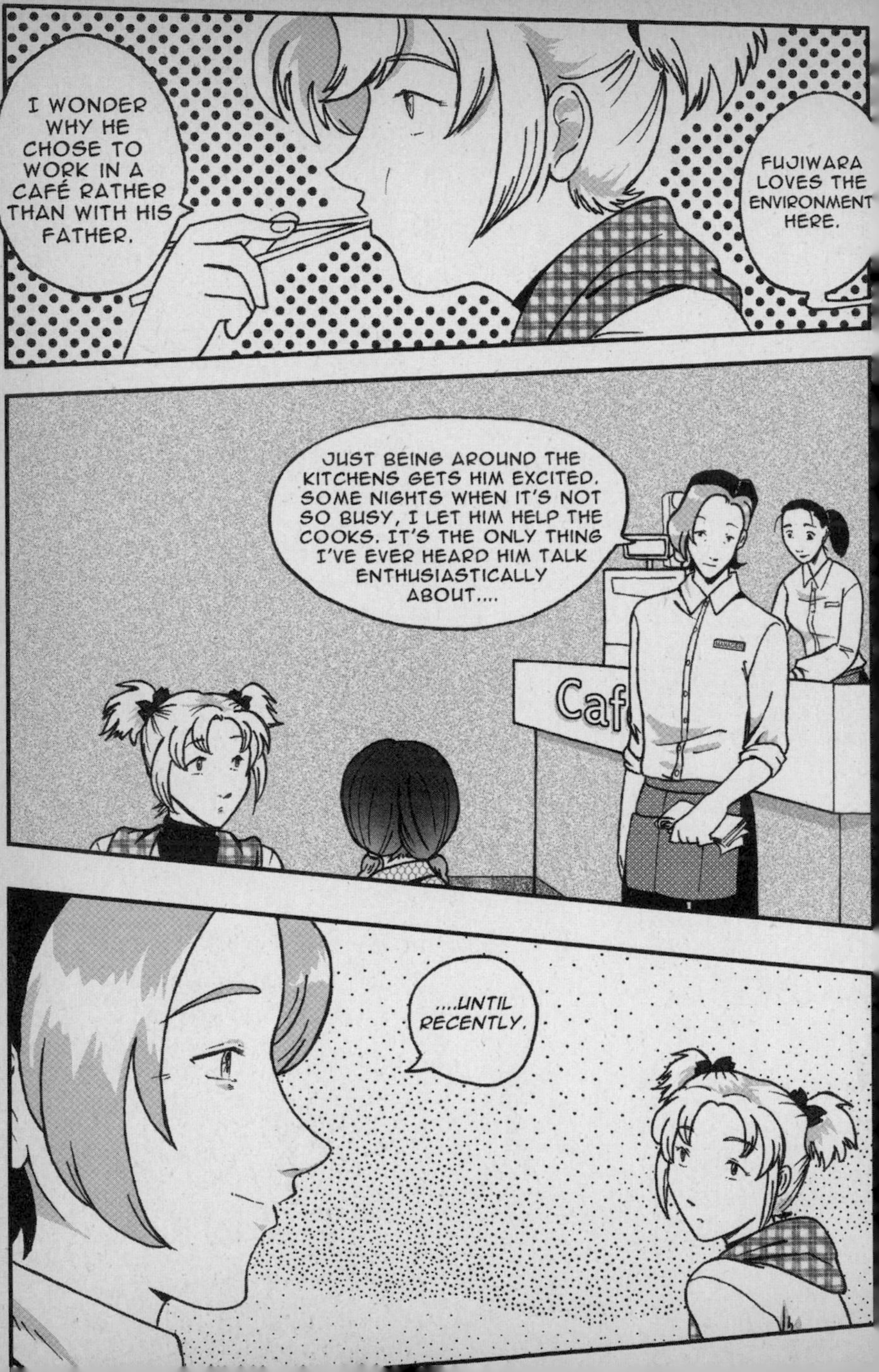
I WONDER WHY HE CHOSE TO WORK IN A CAFÉ RATHER THAN WITH HIS FATHER.
FUJIWARA LOVES THE ENVIRONMENT HERE.
JUST BEING AROUND THE KITCHENS GETS HIM EXCITED. SOME NIGHTS WHEN IT'S NOT SO BUSY, I LET HIM HELP THE COOKS. IT'S THE ONLY THING I'VE EVER HEARD HIM TALK ENTHUSIASTICALLY ABOUT....
Caf
....UNTIL RECENTLY.

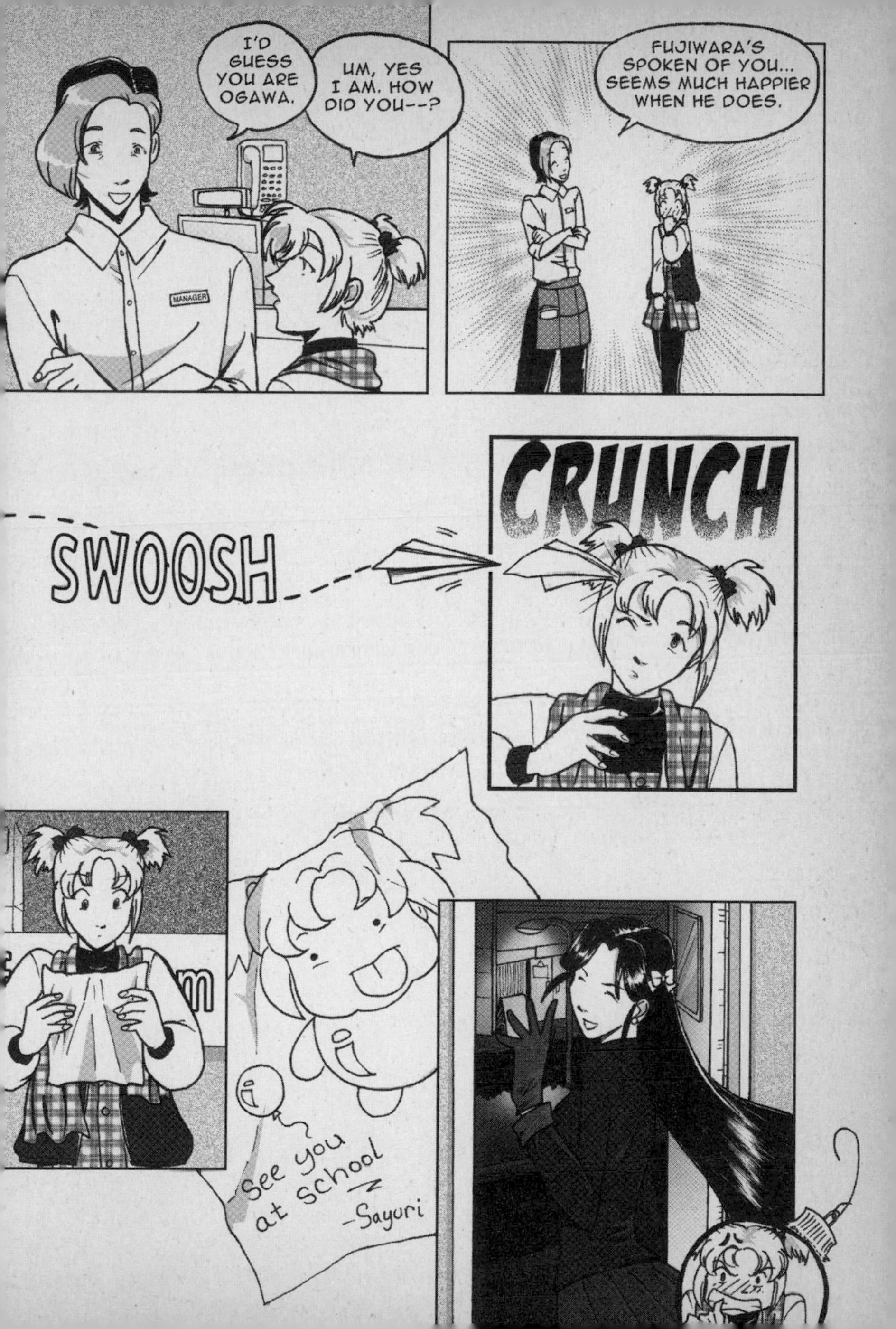
I'D GUESS YOU ARE OGAWA.
UM, YES I AM. HOW DID YOU--?
MANAGER
FUJIWARA'S SPOKEN OF YOU... SEEMS MUCH HAPPIER WHEN HE DOES.
SWOOSH
CRUNCH
See you at school
-Sayuri

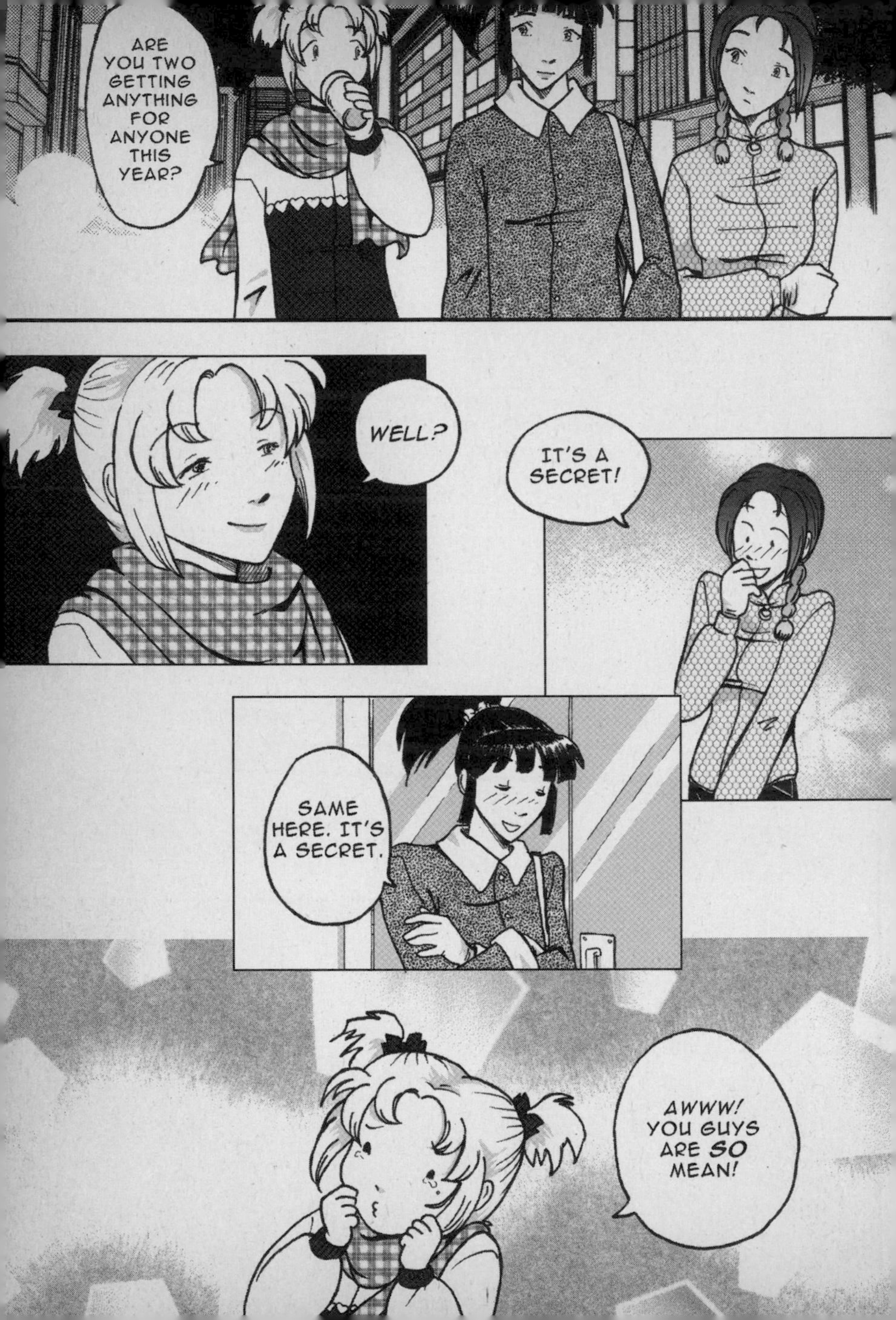
ARE YOU TWO GETTING ANYTHING FOR ANYONE THIS YEAR?
WELL?
IT'S A SECRET!
SAME HERE. IT'S A SECRET.
AWWW! YOU GUYS ARE SO MEAN!

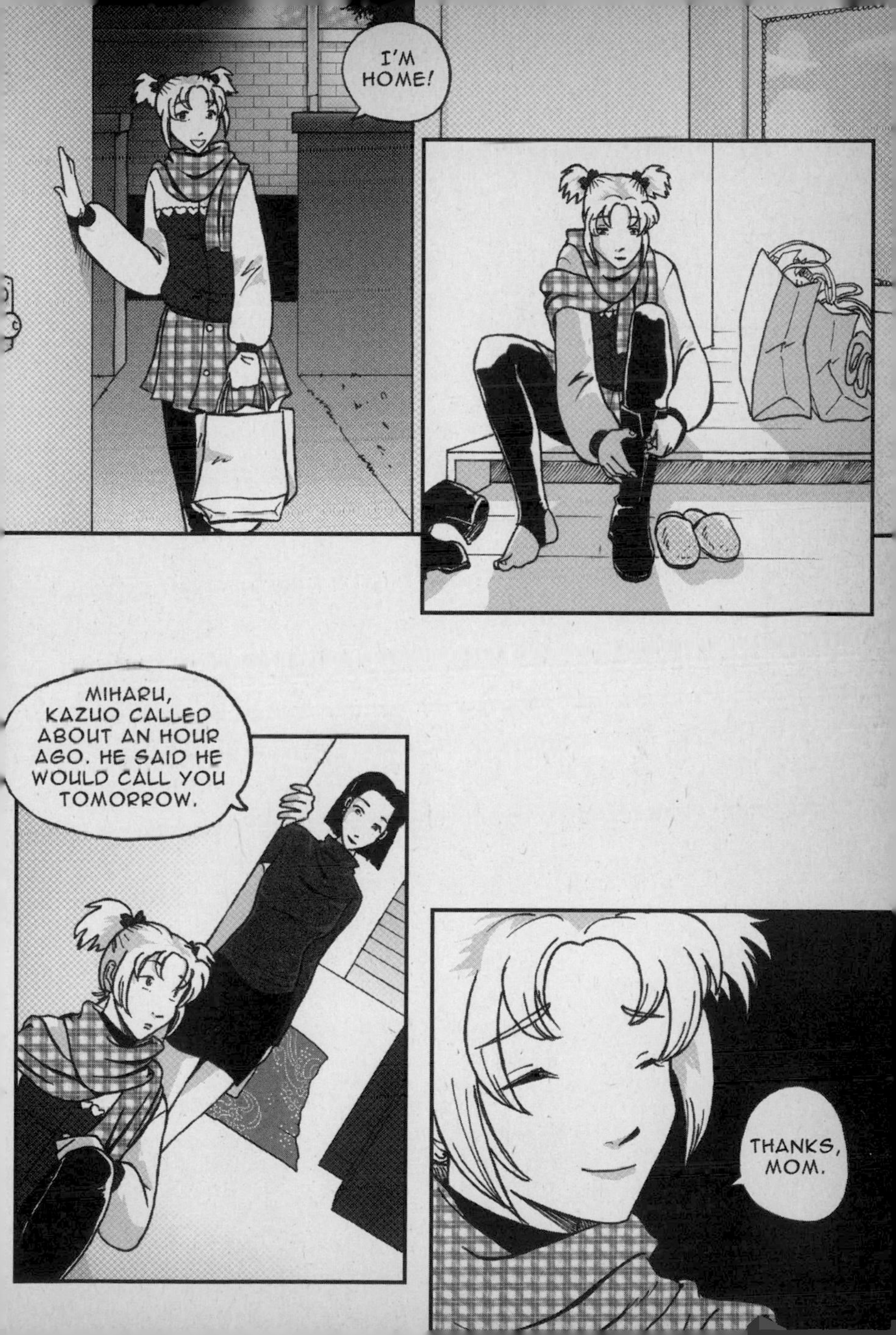
I'M HOME!
MIHARU, KAZUO CALLED ABOUT AN HOUR AGO. HE SAID HE WOULD CALL YOU TOMORROW.
THANKS, MOM.

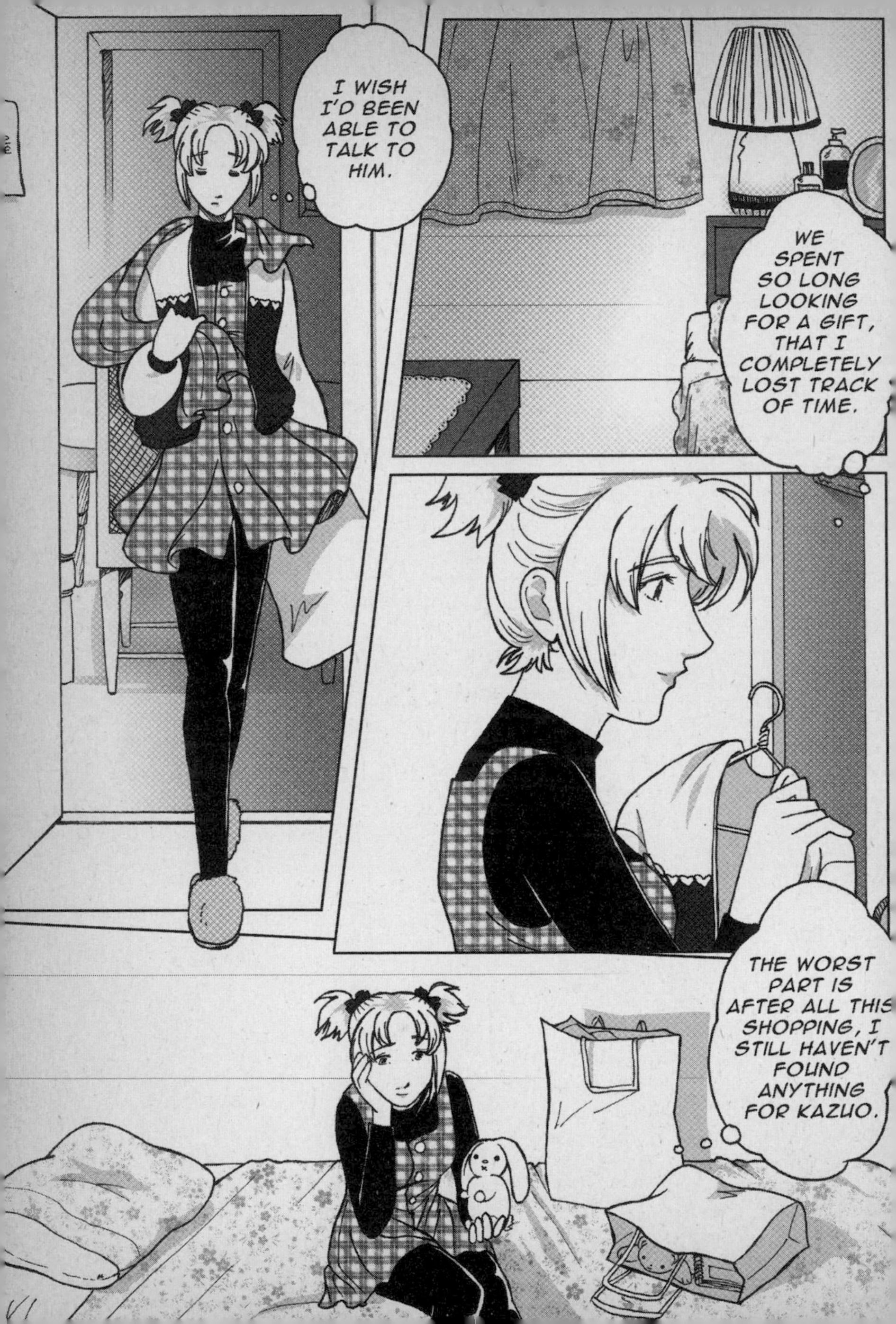
I WISH I'D BEEN ABLE TO TALK TO HIM.
WE SPENT SO LONG LOOKING FOR A GIFT, THAT I COMPLETELY LOST TRACK OF TIME.
THE WORST PART IS AFTER ALL THIS SHOPPING, I STILL HAVEN'T FOUND ANYTHING FOR KAZUO.

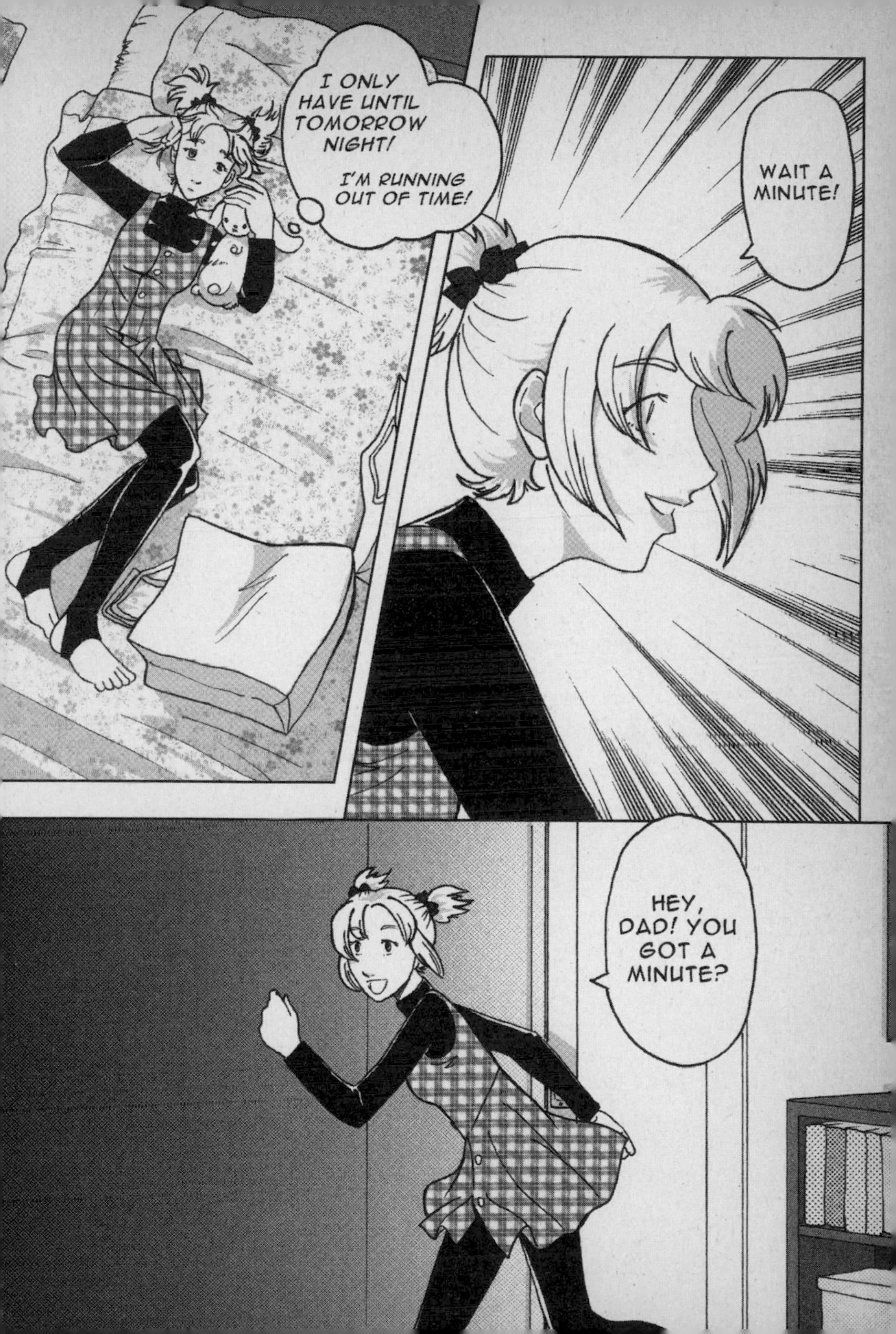
WAIT A MINUTE!
I ONLY HAVE UNTIL TOMORROW NIGHT!
I'M RUNNING OUT OF TIME!
HEY, DAD! YOU GOT A MINUTE?

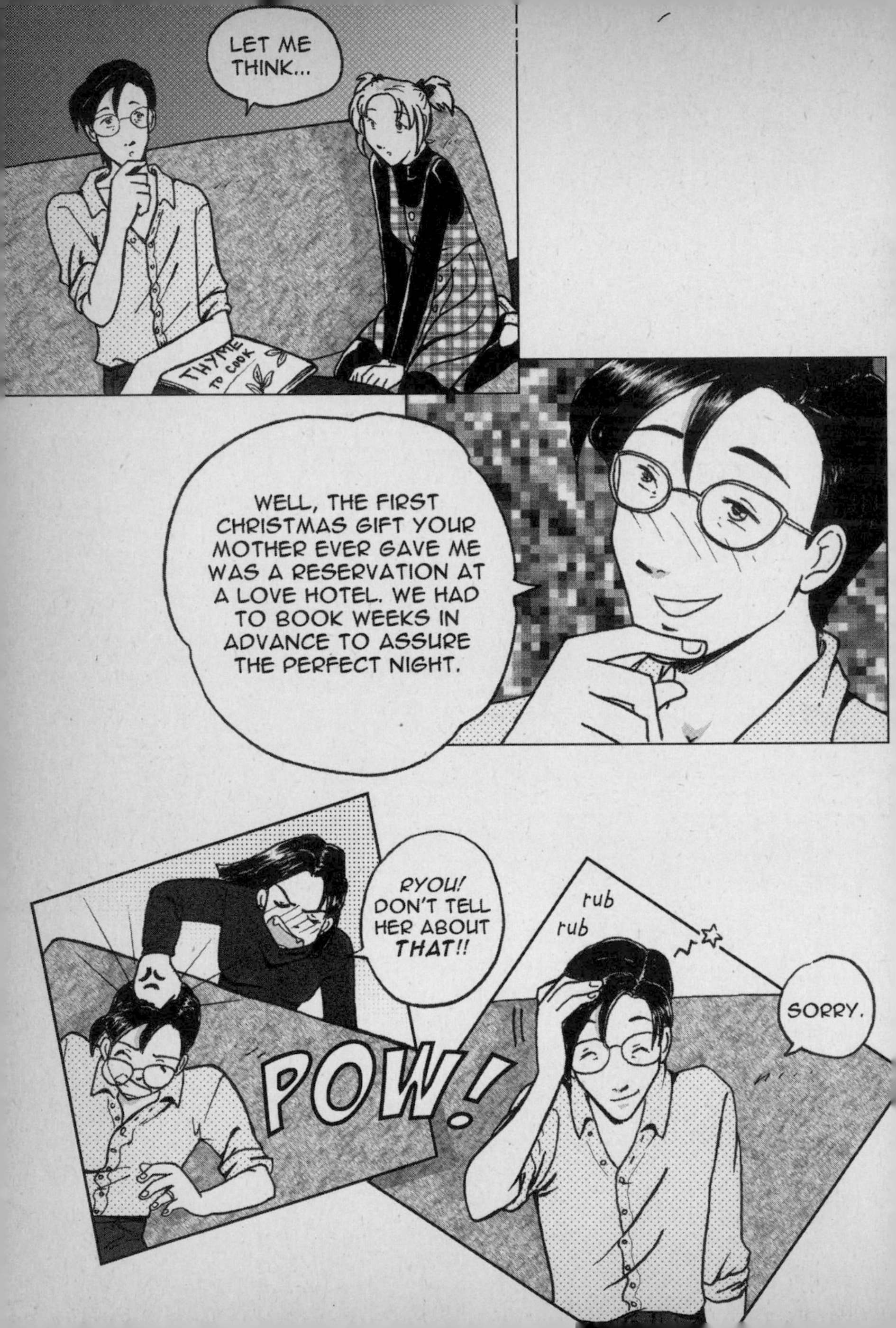
LET ME THINK...
THYME TO COOK
WELL, THE FIRST CHRISTMAS GIFT YOUR MOTHER EVER GAVE ME WAS A RESERVATION AT A LOVE HOTEL. WE HAD TO BOOK WEEKS IN ADVANCE TO ASSURE THE PERFECT NIGHT.
RYOU! DON'T TELL HER ABOUT THAT!!
POW!
rub
rub
SORRY.

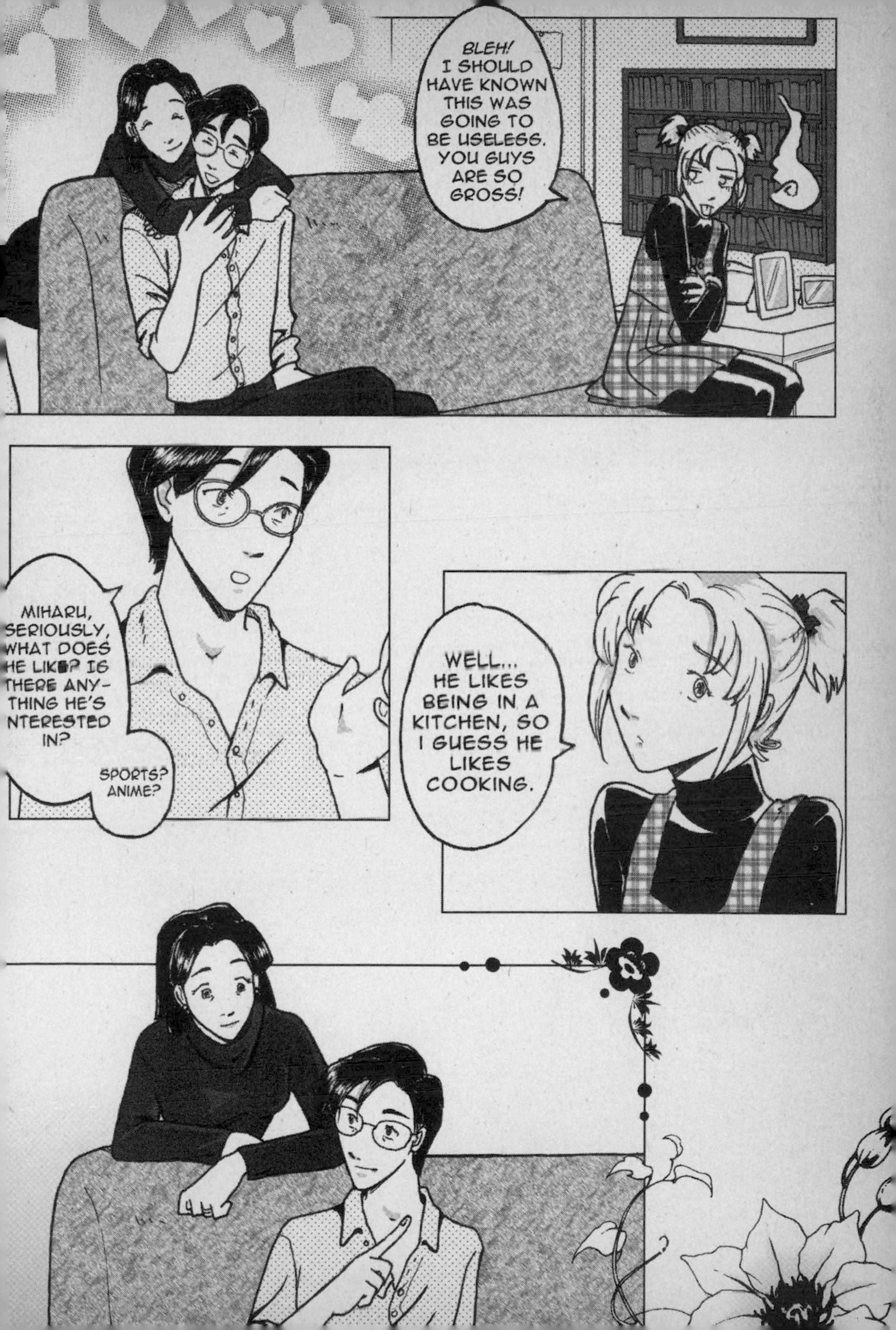
BLEH! I SHOULD HAVE KNOWN THIS WAS GOING TO BE USELESS. YOU GUYS ARE SO GROSS!
MIHARU, SERIOUSLY, WHAT DOES HE LIKE? IS THERE ANYTHING HE'S NTERESTED IN?
SPORTS? ANIME?
WELL... HE LIKES BEING IN A KITCHEN, SO I GUESS HE LIKES COOKING.

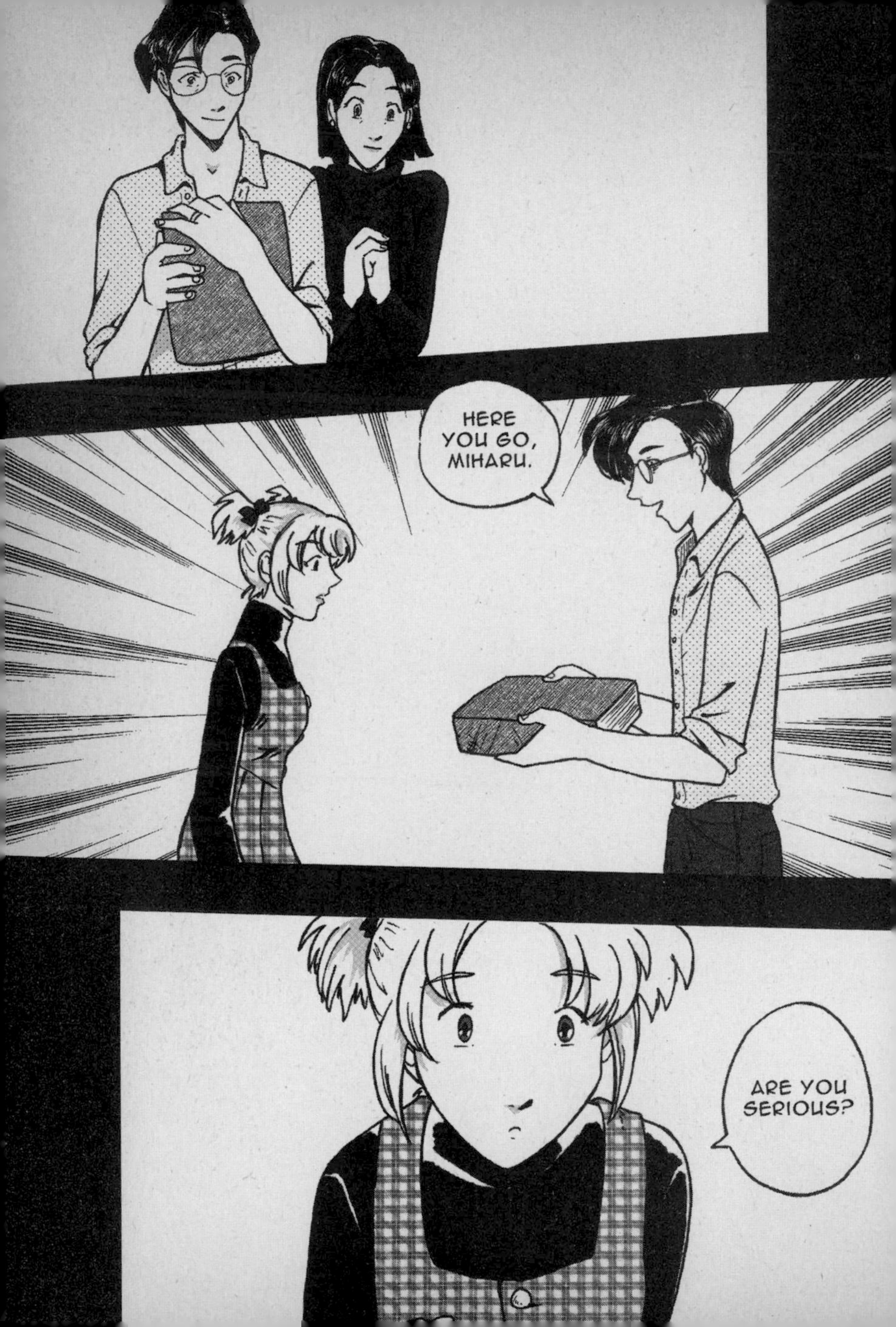
HERE YOU GO, MIHARU.
ARE YOU SERIOUS?

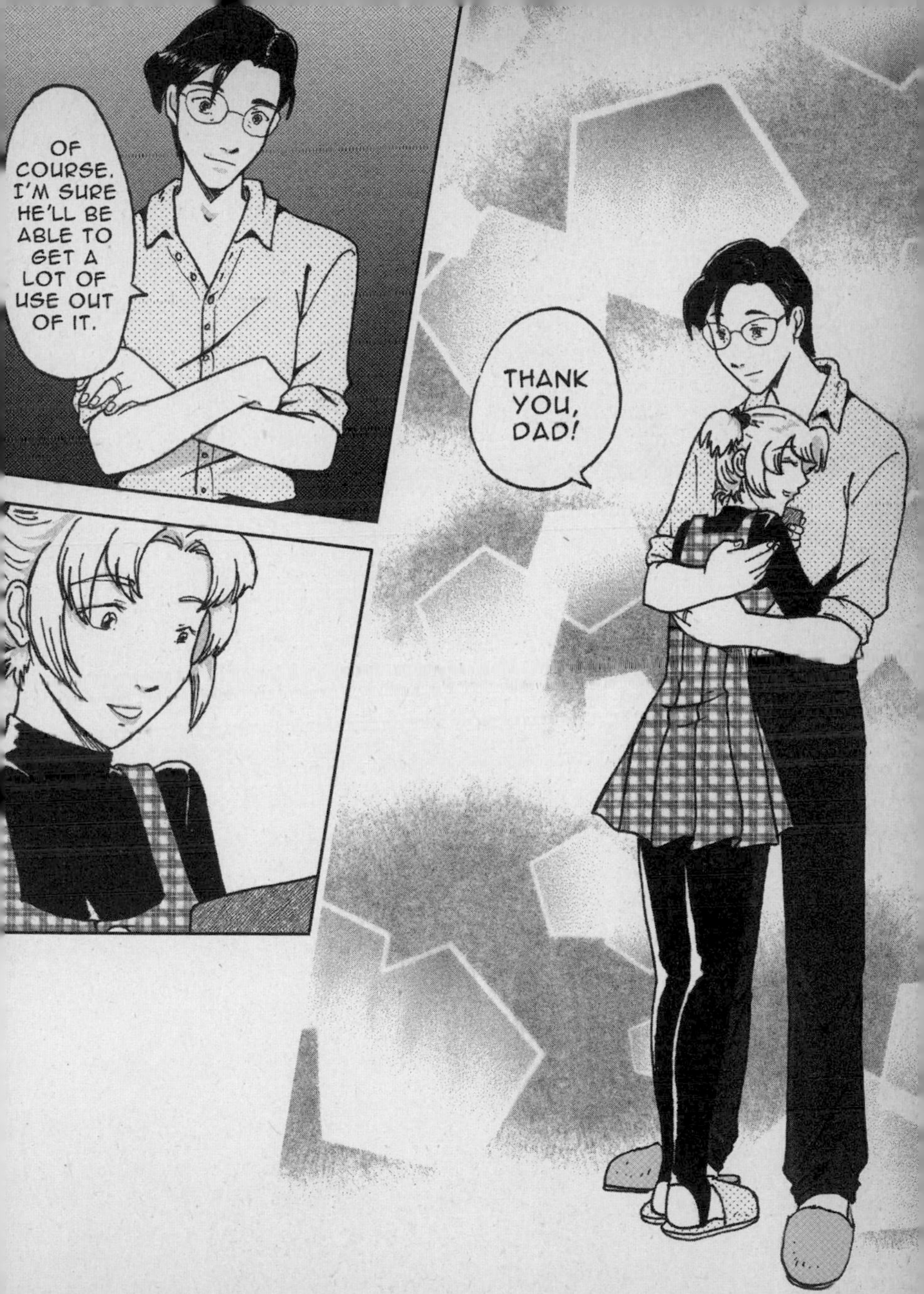
OF COURSE. I'M SURE HE'LL BE ABLE TO GET A LOT OF USE OUT OF IT.
THANK YOU, DAD!

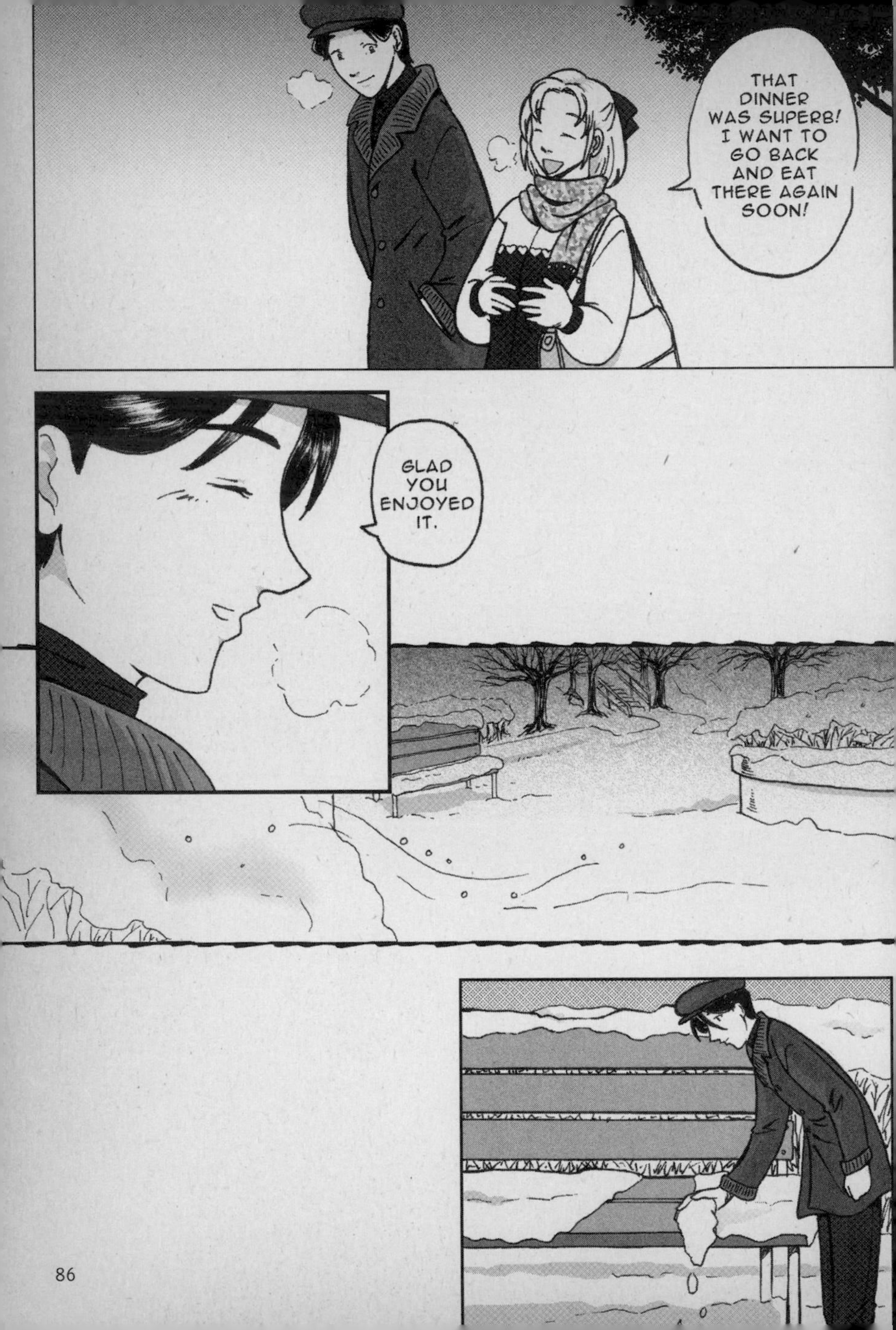
THAT DINNER WAS SUPERB! I WANT TO GO BACK AND EAT THERE AGAIN SOON!
GLAD YOU ENJOYED IT.

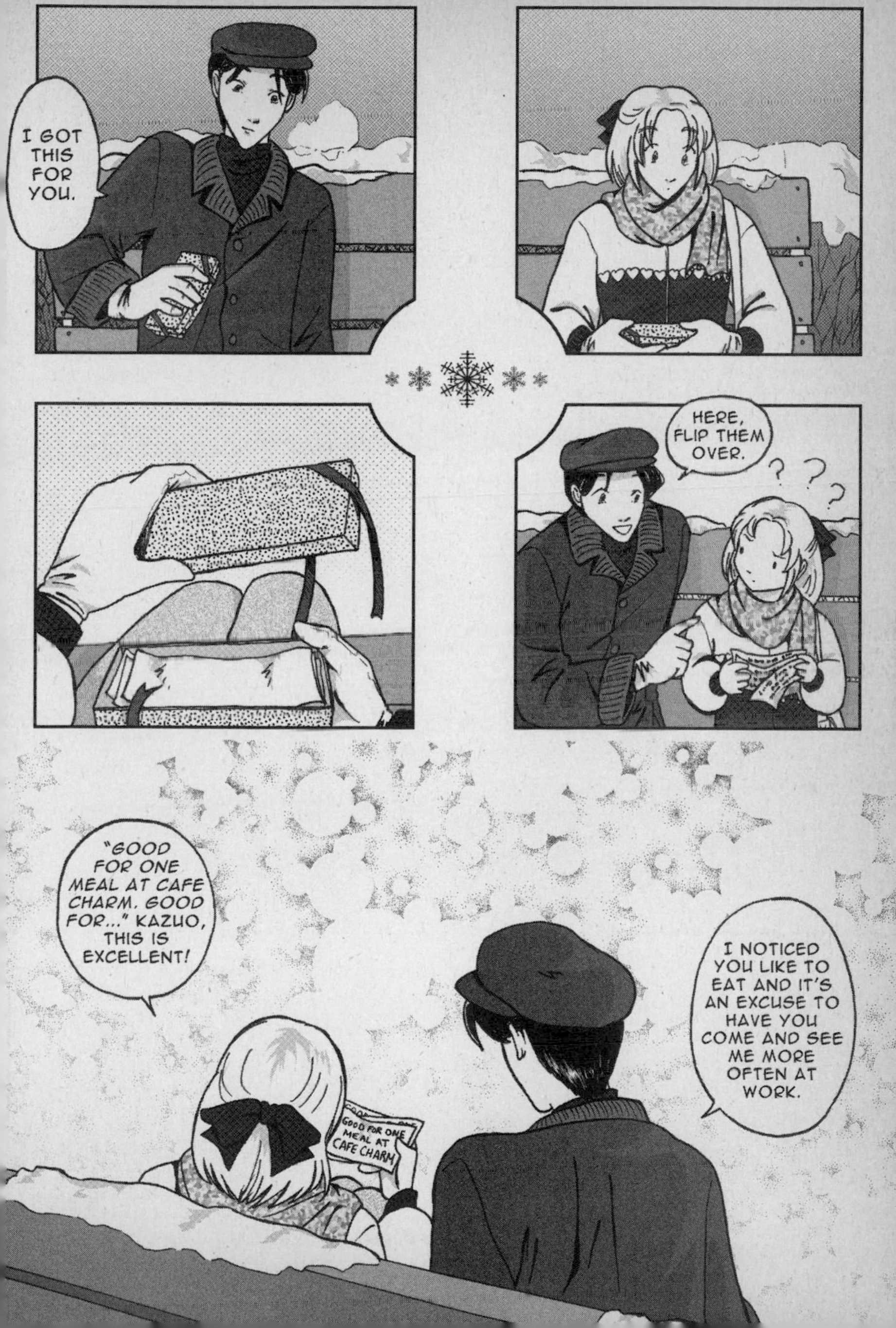

I GOT THIS FOR YOU.
HERE, FLIP THEM OVER.
?
?
?
"GOOD FOR ONE MEAL AT CAFE CHARM. GOOD FOR..." KAZUO, THIS IS EXCELLENT!
GOOD FOR ONE MEAL AT CAFE CHARM
I NOTICED YOU LIKE TO EAT AND IT'S AN EXCUSE TO HAVE YOU COME AND SEE ME MORE OFTEN AT WORK.

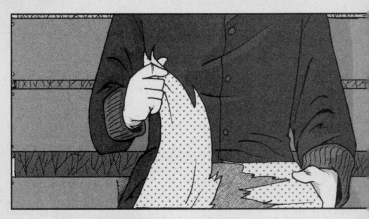

MIHARU...

IT WAS MY FATHER'S FIRST COOKBOOK. IT HELPED HIM BECOME A GREAT CHEF.

THE COOK'S FIRST STEPS

BY RIE ASAYAMA

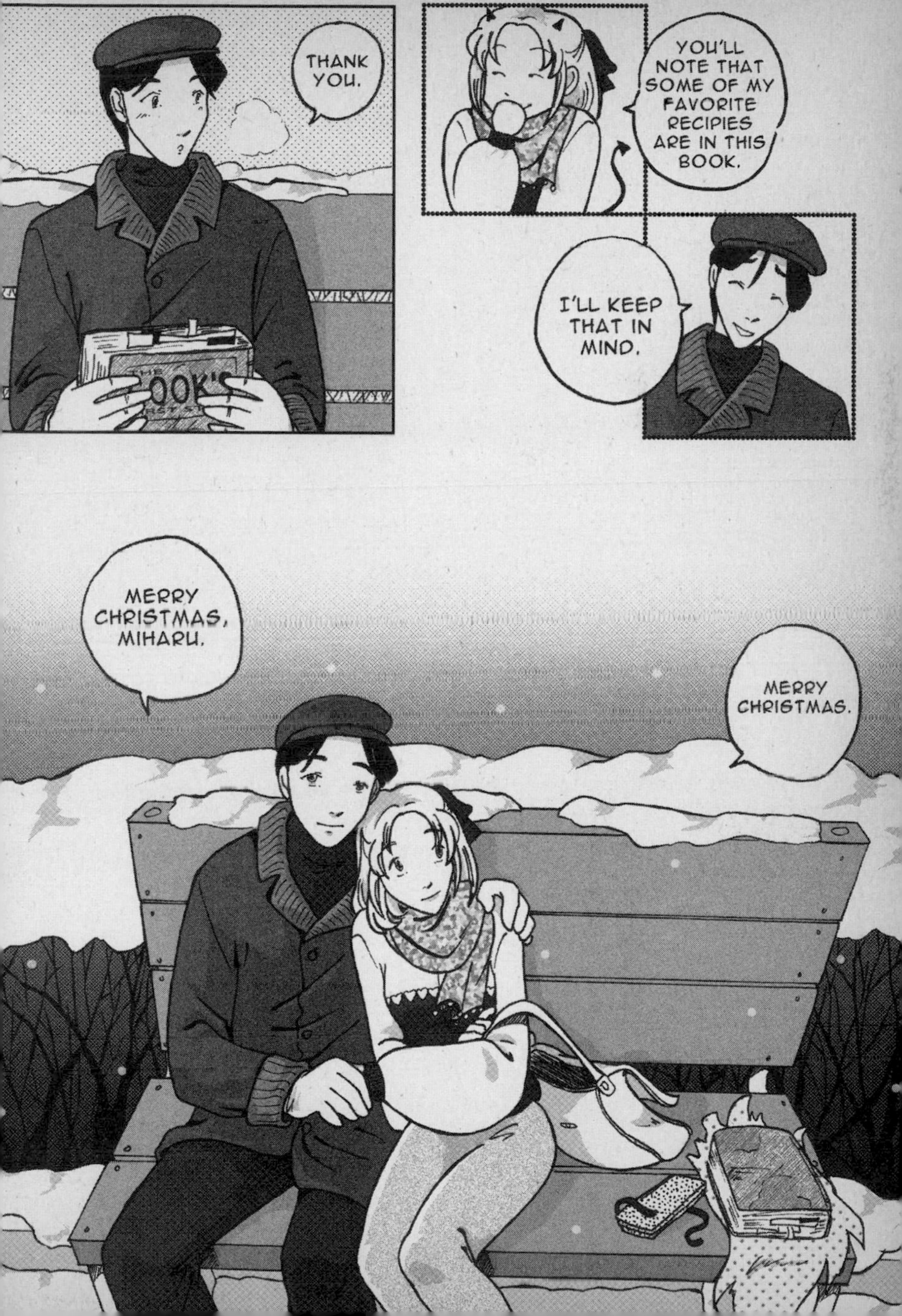
THANK YOU.
YOU'LL NOTE THAT SOME OF MY FAVORITE RECIPIES ARE IN THIS BOOK.
I'LL KEEP THAT IN MIND.
MERRY CHRISTMAS, MIHARU.
MERRY CHRISTMAS.

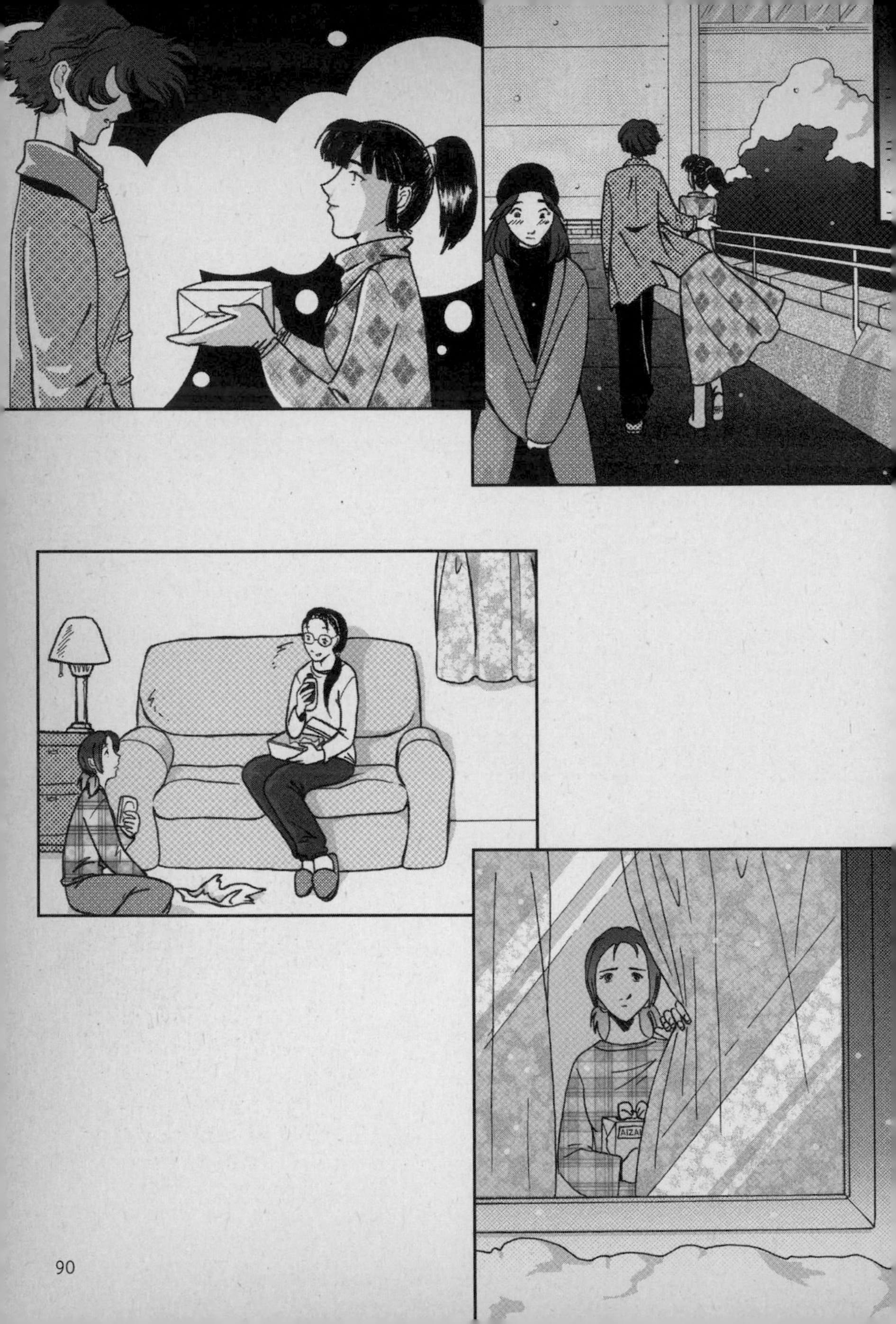

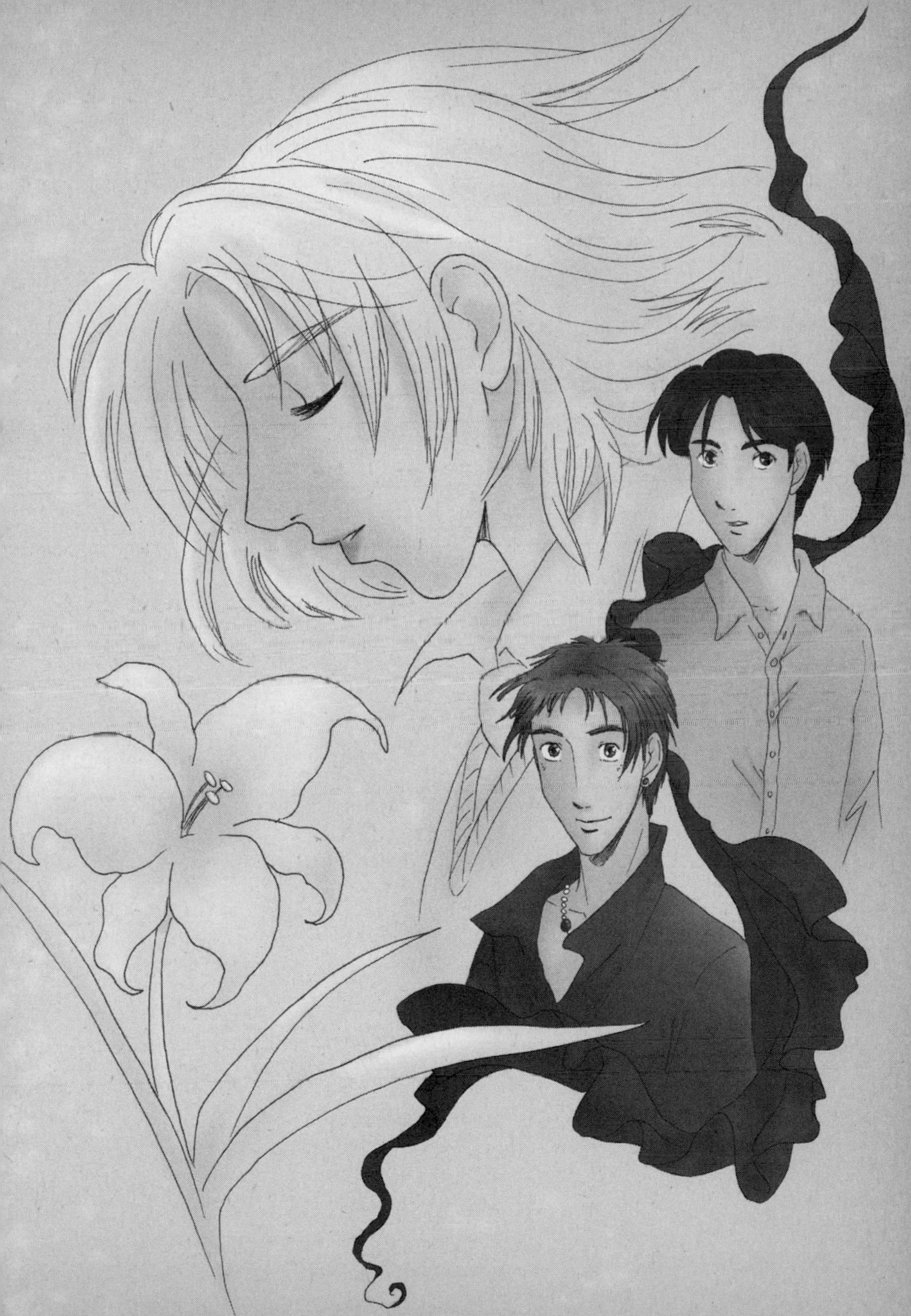

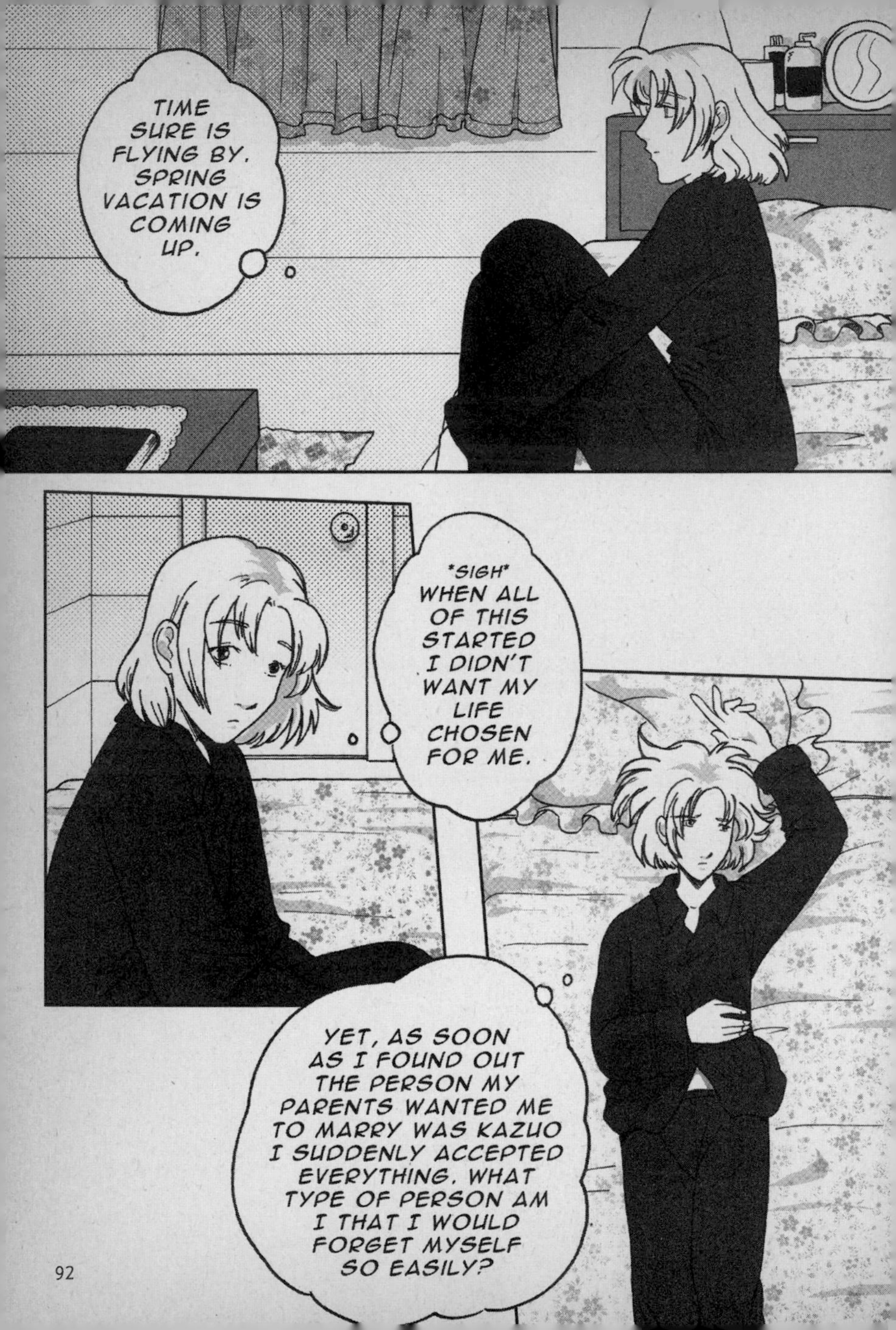
TIME SURE IS FLYING BY. SPRING VACATION IS COMING UP.
SIGH WHEN ALL OF THIS STARTED I DIDN'T WANT MY LIFE CHOSEN FOR ME.
YET, AS SOON AS I FOUND OUT THE PERSON MY PARENTS WANTED ME TO MARRY WAS KAZUO I SUDDENLY ACCEPTED EVERYTHING. WHAT TYPE OF PERSON AM I THAT I WOULD FORGET MYSELF SO EASILY?

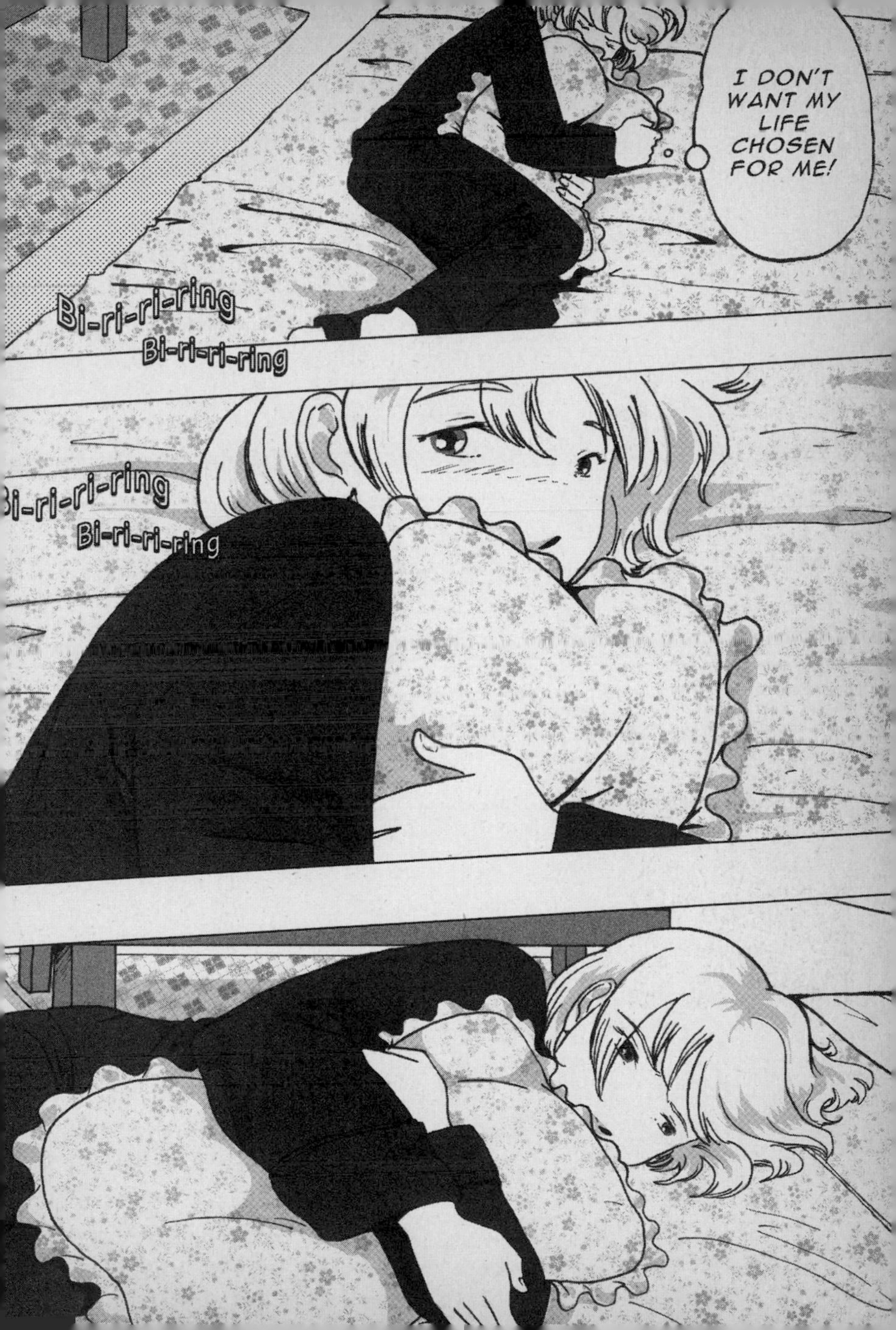
I DON'T WANT MY LIFE CHOSEN FOR ME!
Bi-ri-ri-ring
Bi-ri-ri-ring
Bi-ri-ri-ring
Bi-ri-ri-ring

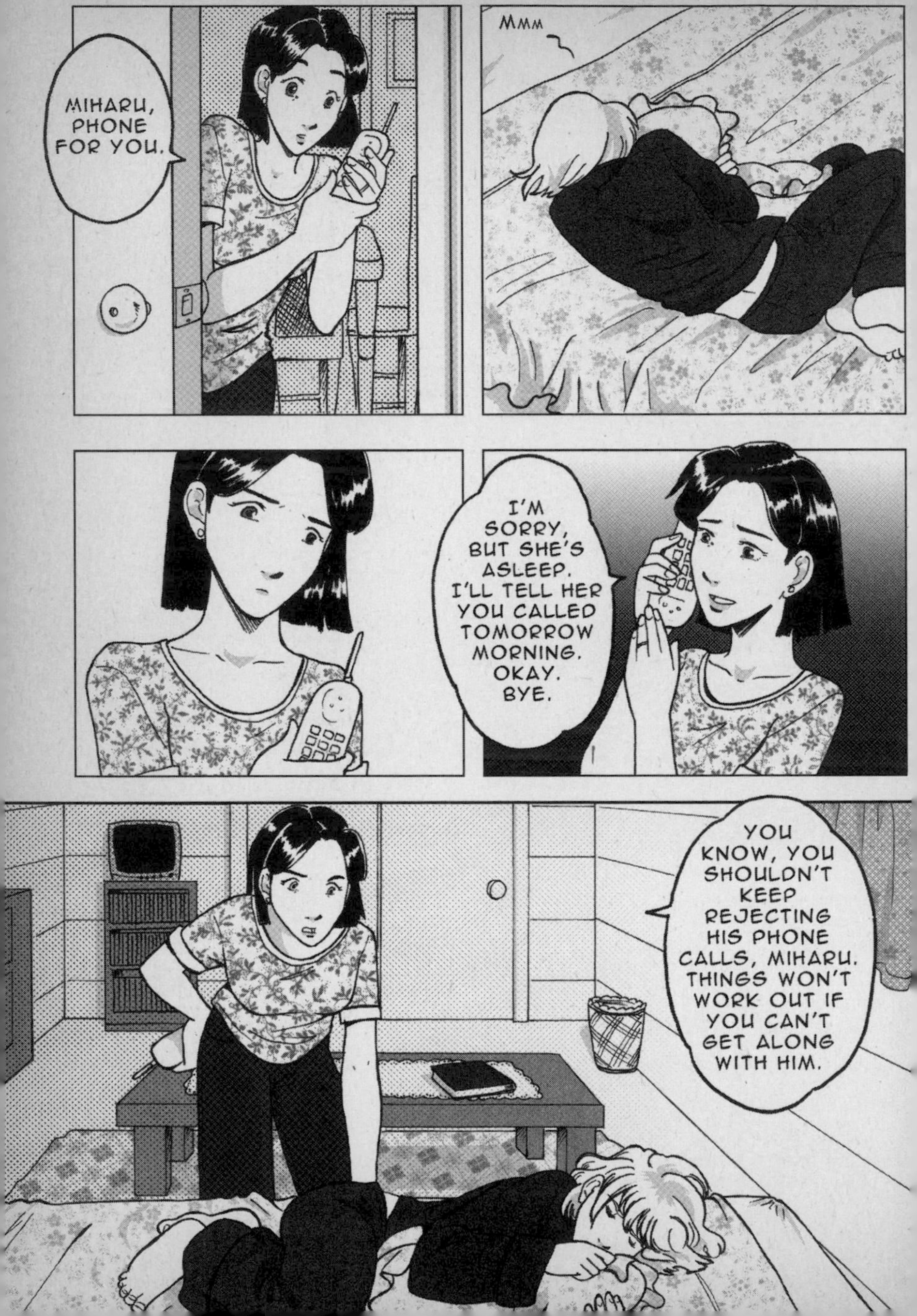
MIHARU, PHONE FOR YOU.
MMM
I'M SORRY, BUT SHE'S ASLEEP. I'LL TELL HER YOU CALLED TOMORROW MORNING. OKAY. BYE.
YOU KNOW, YOU SHOULDN'T KEEP REJECTING HIS PHONE CALLS, MIHARU. THINGS WON'T WORK OUT IF YOU CAN'T GET ALONG WITH HIM.

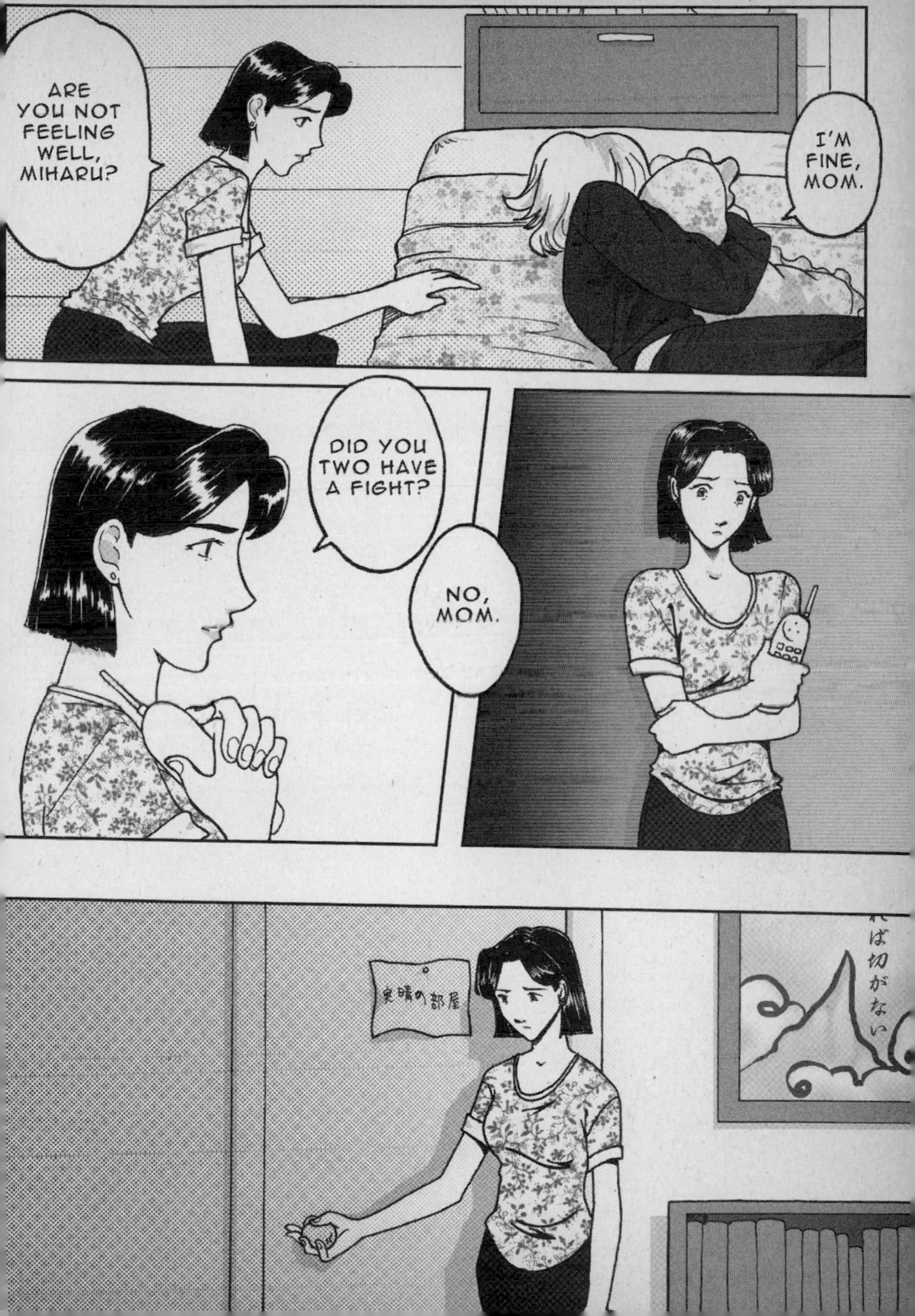
ARE YOU NOT FEELING WELL, MIHARU?
I'M FINE, MOM.
DID YOU TWO HAVE A FIGHT?
NO, MOM.
美晴の部屋

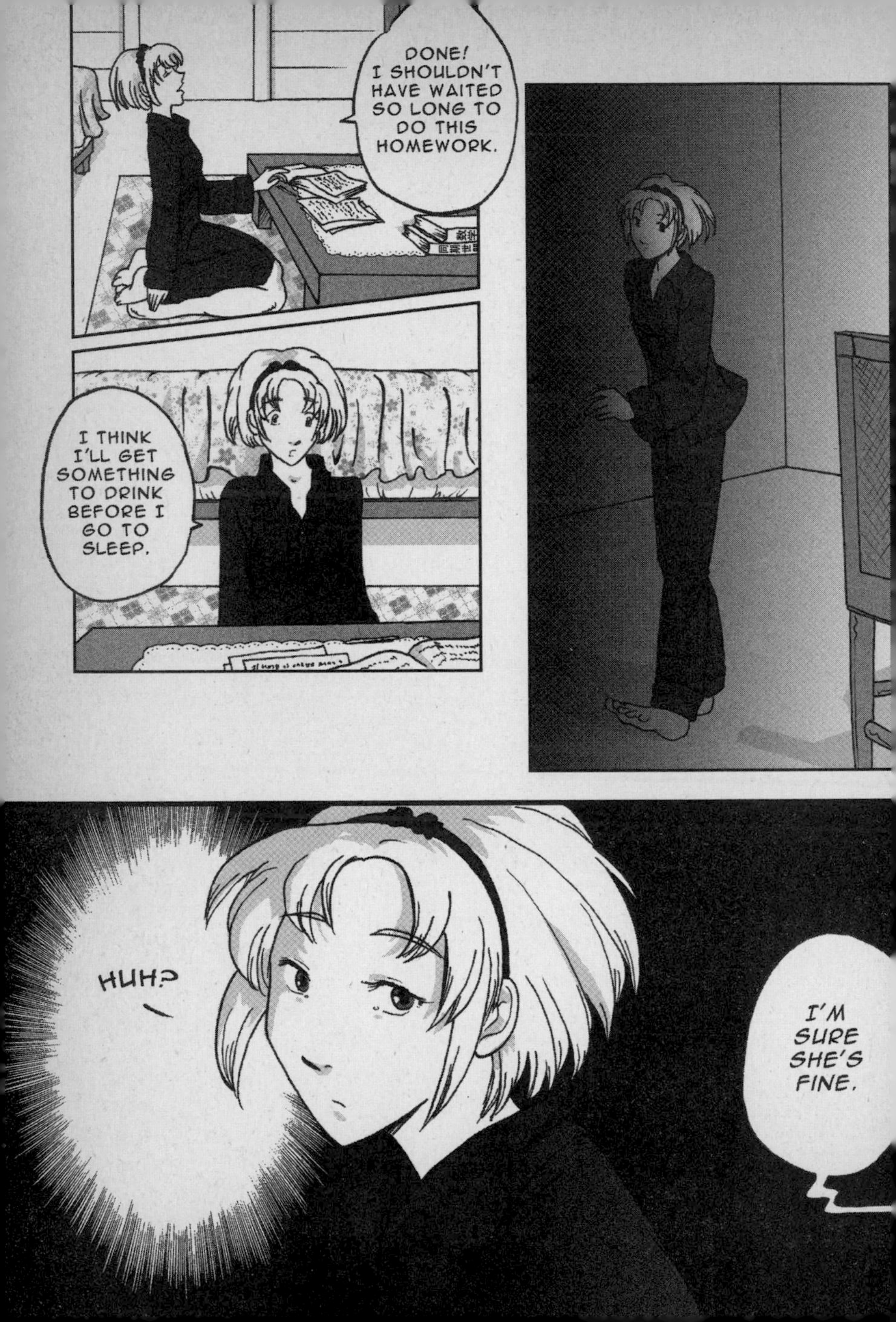
DONE! I SHOULDN'T HAVE WAITED SO LONG TO DO THIS HOMEWORK.
I THINK I'LL GET SOMETHING TO DRINK BEFORE I GO TO SLEEP.
HUH?
I'M SURE SHE'S FINE.

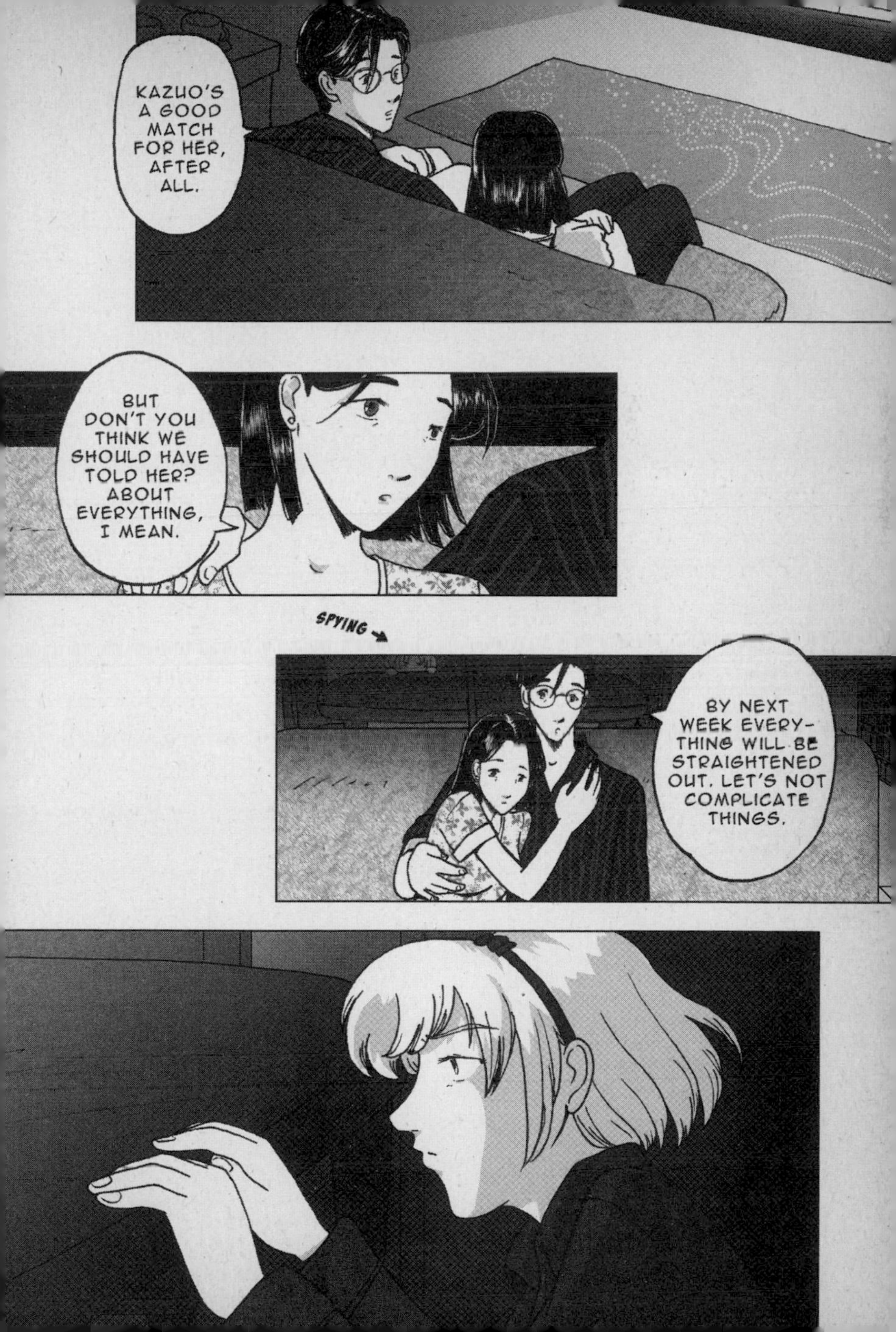
KAZUO'S A GOOD MATCH FOR HER, AFTER ALL.
BUT DON'T YOU THINK WE SHOULD HAVE TOLD HER? ABOUT EVERYTHING, I MEAN.
SPYING
BY NEXT WEEK EVERY-THING WILL BE STRAIGHTENED OUT. LET'S NOT COMPLICATE THINGS.

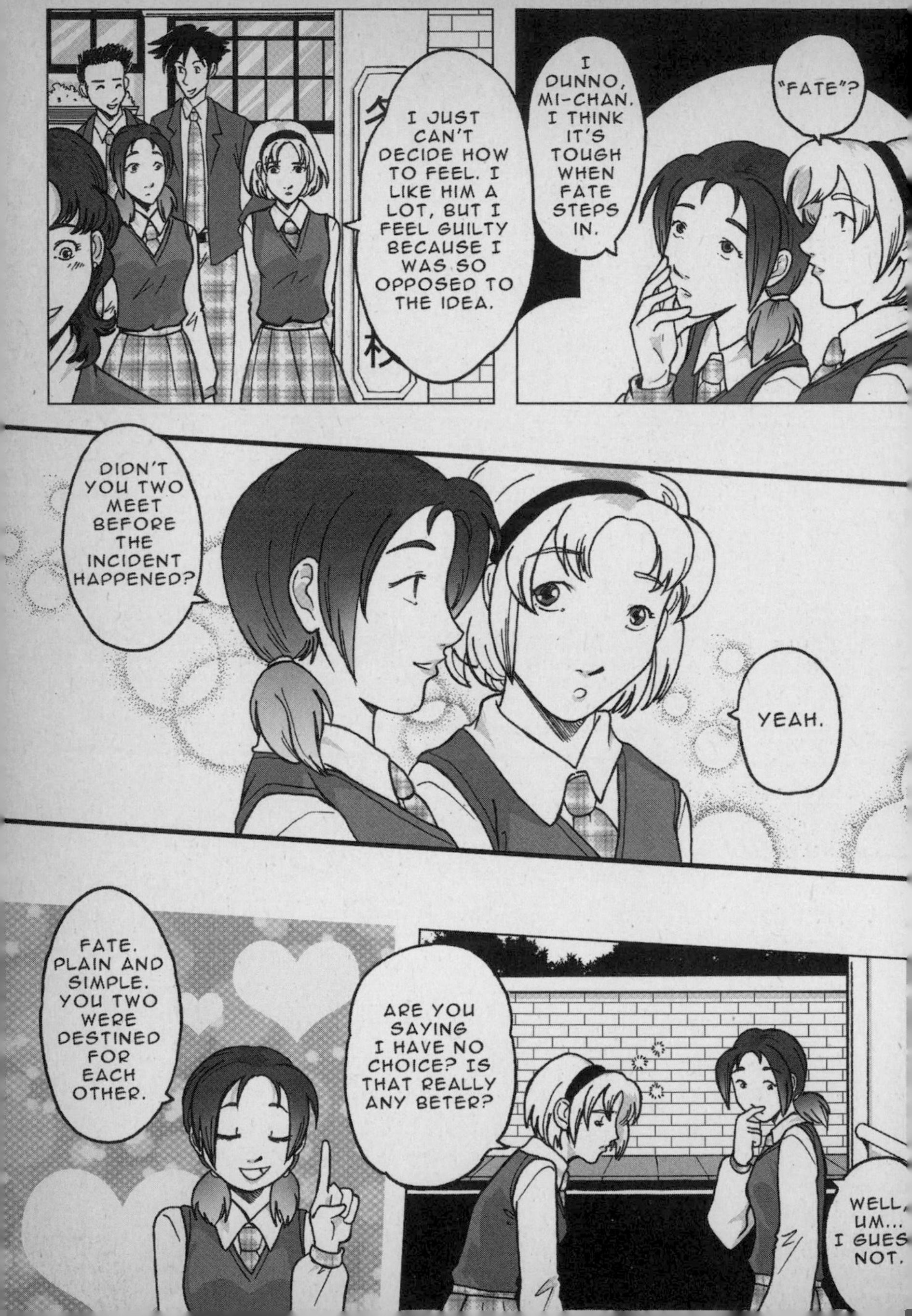
"FATE"?
I DUNNO, MI-CHAN. I THINK IT'S TOUGH WHEN FATE STEPS IN.
I JUST CAN'T DECIDE HOW TO FEEL. I LIKE HIM A LOT, BUT I FEEL GUILTY BECAUSE I WAS SO OPPOSED TO THE IDEA.
DIDN'T YOU TWO MEET BEFORE THE INCIDENT HAPPENED?
YEAH.
FATE. PLAIN AND SIMPLE. YOU TWO WERE DESTINED FOR EACH OTHER.
ARE YOU SAYING I HAVE NO CHOICE? IS THAT REALLY ANY BETER?
WELL, UM... I GUES NOT.

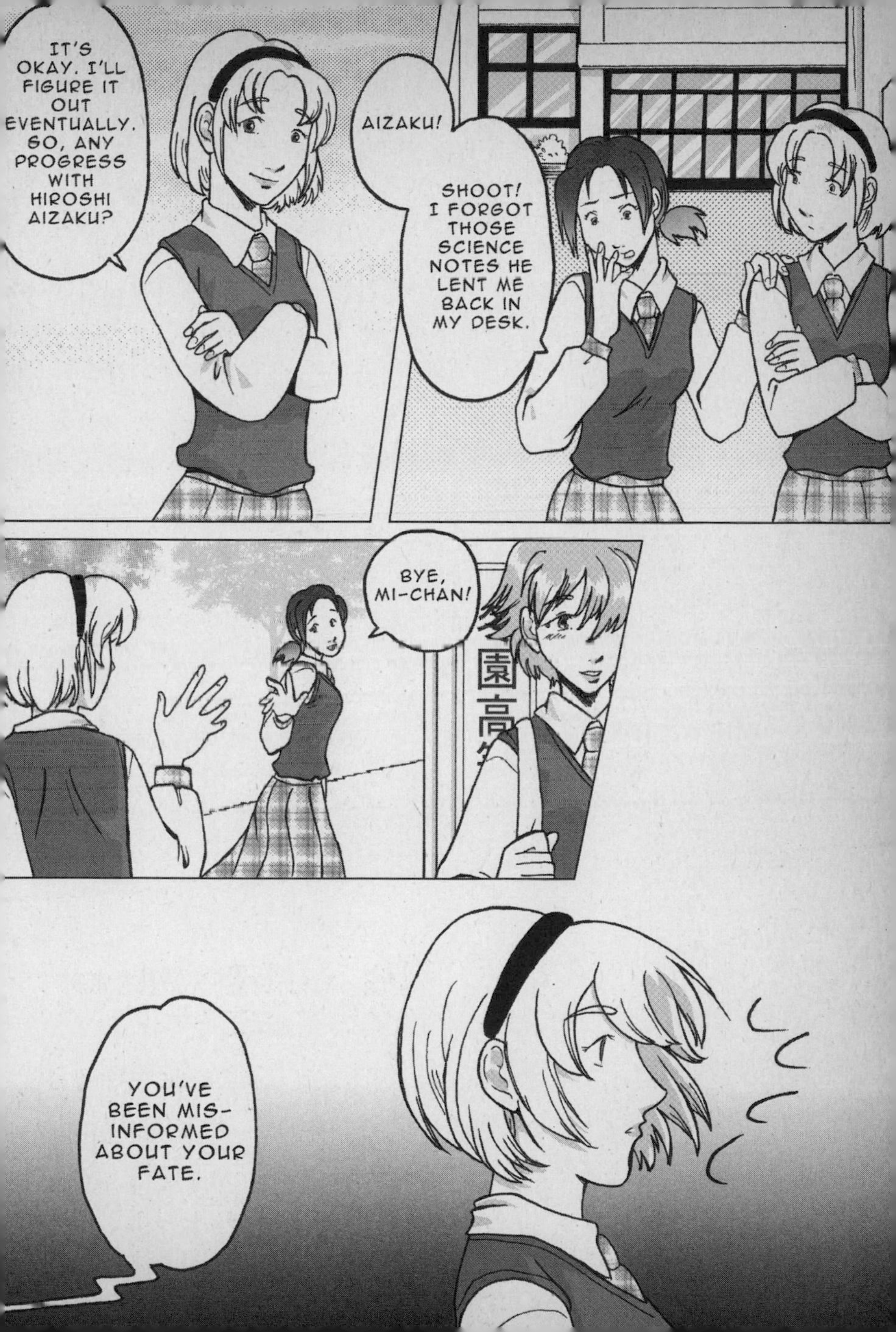
IT'S OKAY. I'LL FIGURE IT OUT EVENTUALLY. SO, ANY PROGRESS WITH HIROSHI AIZAKU?
AIZAKU!
SHOOT! I FORGOT THOSE SCIENCE NOTES HE LENT ME BACK IN MY DESK.
BYE, MI-CHAN!
YOU'VE BEEN MIS-INFORMED ABOUT YOUR FATE.

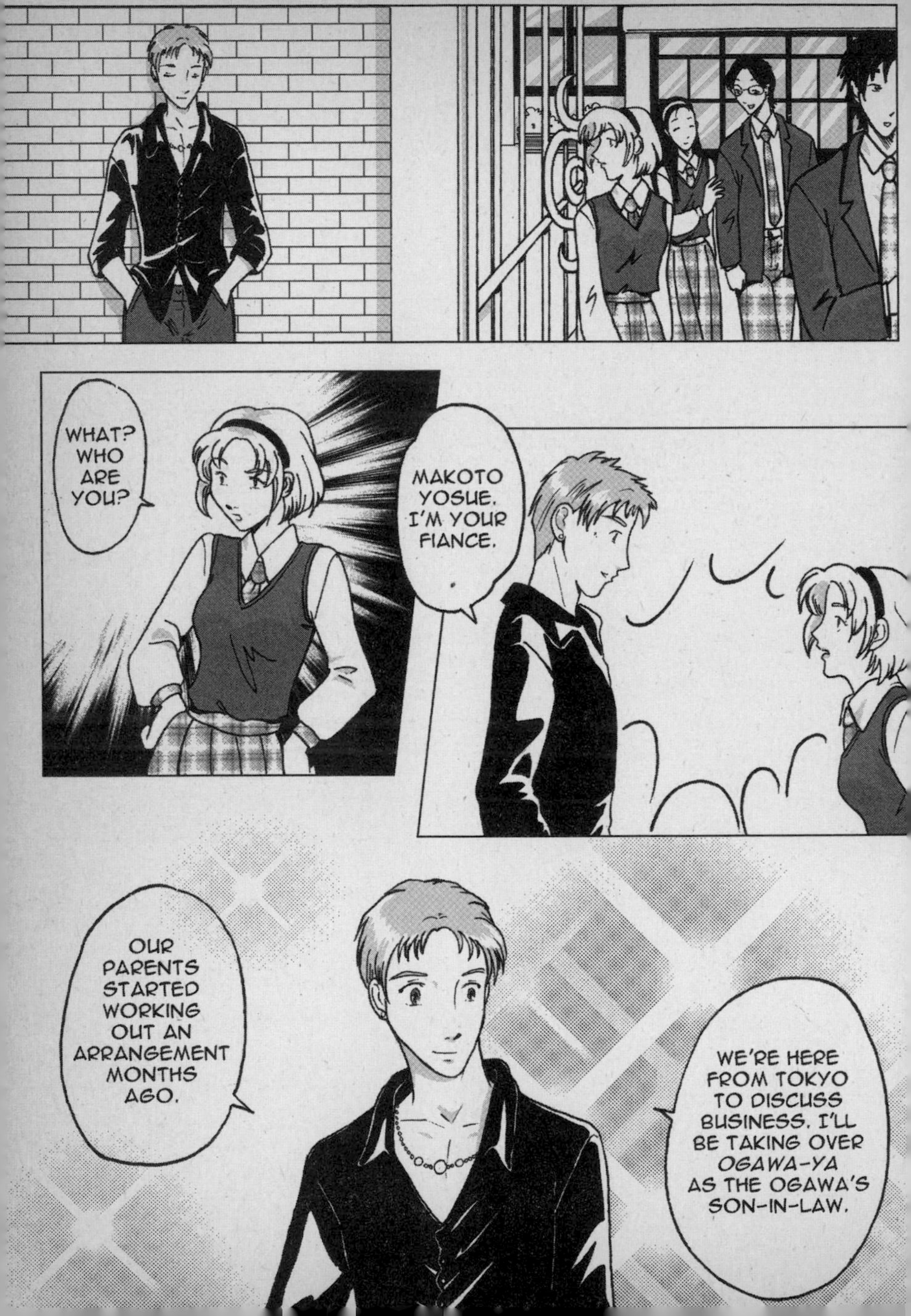
WHAT? WHO ARE YOU?
MAKOTO YOSUE. I'M YOUR FIANCE.
OUR PARENTS STARTED WORKING OUT AN ARRANGEMENT MONTHS AGO.
WE'RE HERE FROM TOKYO TO DISCUSS BUSINESS. I'LL BE TAKING OVER OGAWA-YA AS THE OGAWA'S SON-IN-LAW.

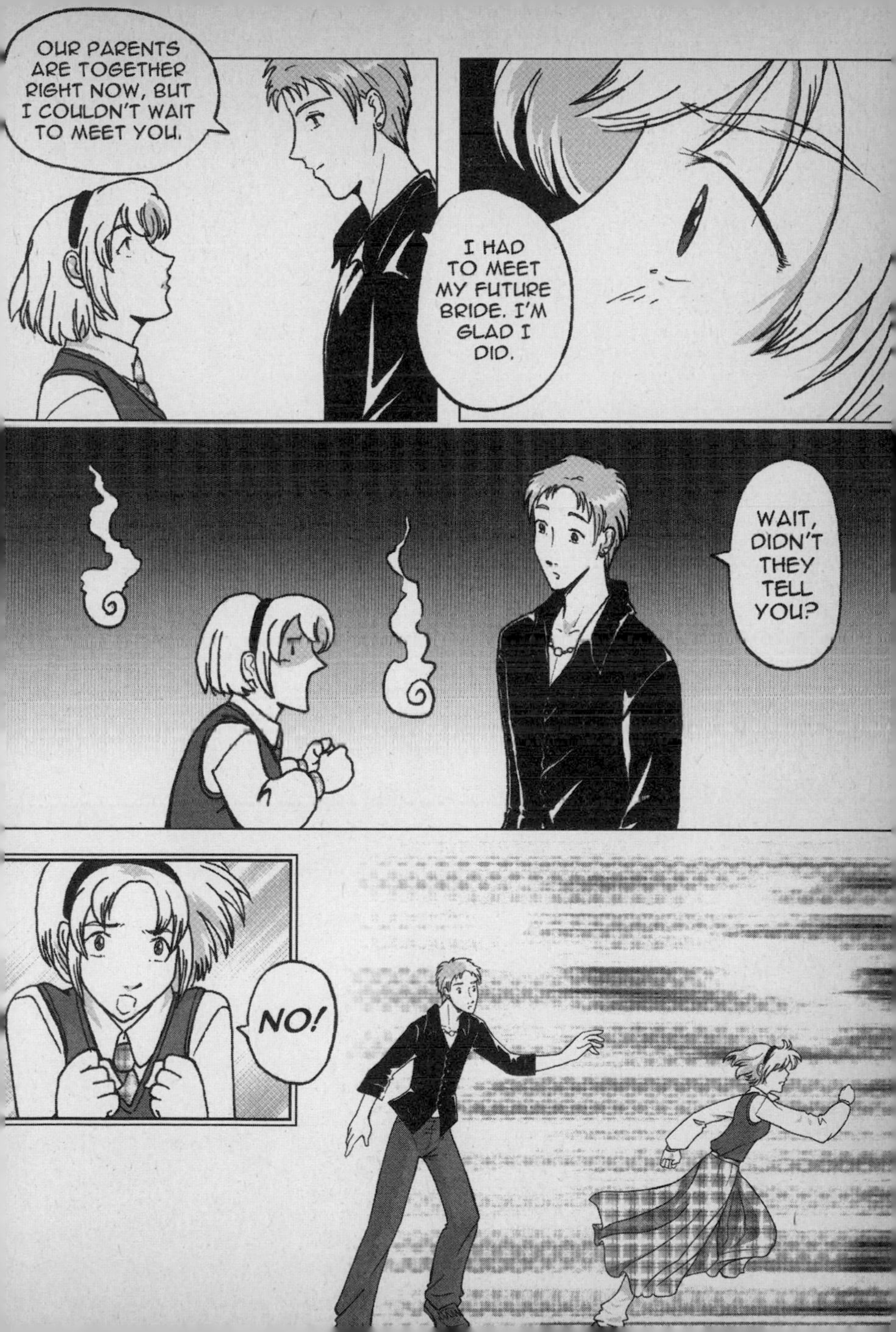
OUR PARENTS ARE TOGETHER RIGHT NOW, BUT I COULDN'T WAIT TO MEET YOU.
I HAD TO MEET MY FUTURE BRIDE. I'M GLAD I DID.
WAIT, DIDN'T THEY TELL YOU?
NO!

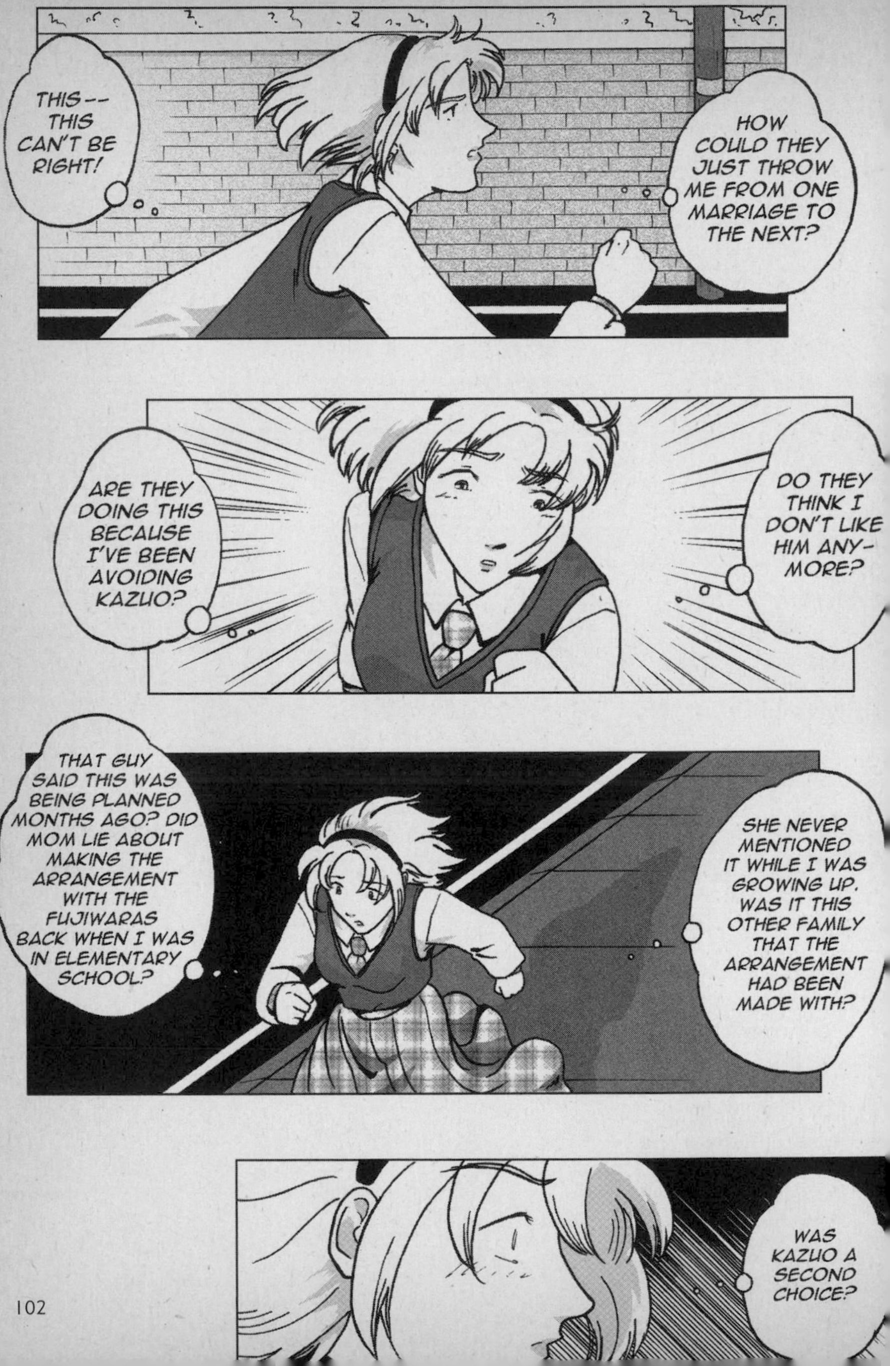

THIS-- THIS CAN'T BE RIGHT!
HOW COULD THEY JUST THROW ME FROM ONE MARRIAGE TO THE NEXT?
ARE THEY DOING THIS BECAUSE I'VE BEEN AVOIDING KAZUO?
DO THEY THINK I DON'T LIKE HIM ANY-MORE?
THAT GUY SAID THIS WAS BEING PLANNED MONTHS AGO? DID MOM LIE ABOUT MAKING THE ARRANGEMENT WITH THE FUJIWARAS BACK WHEN I WAS IN ELEMENTARY SCHOOL?
SHE NEVER MENTIONED IT WHILE I WAS GROWING UP. WAS IT THIS OTHER FAMILY THAT THE ARRANGEMENT HAD BEEN MADE WITH?
WAS KAZUO A SECOND CHOICE?

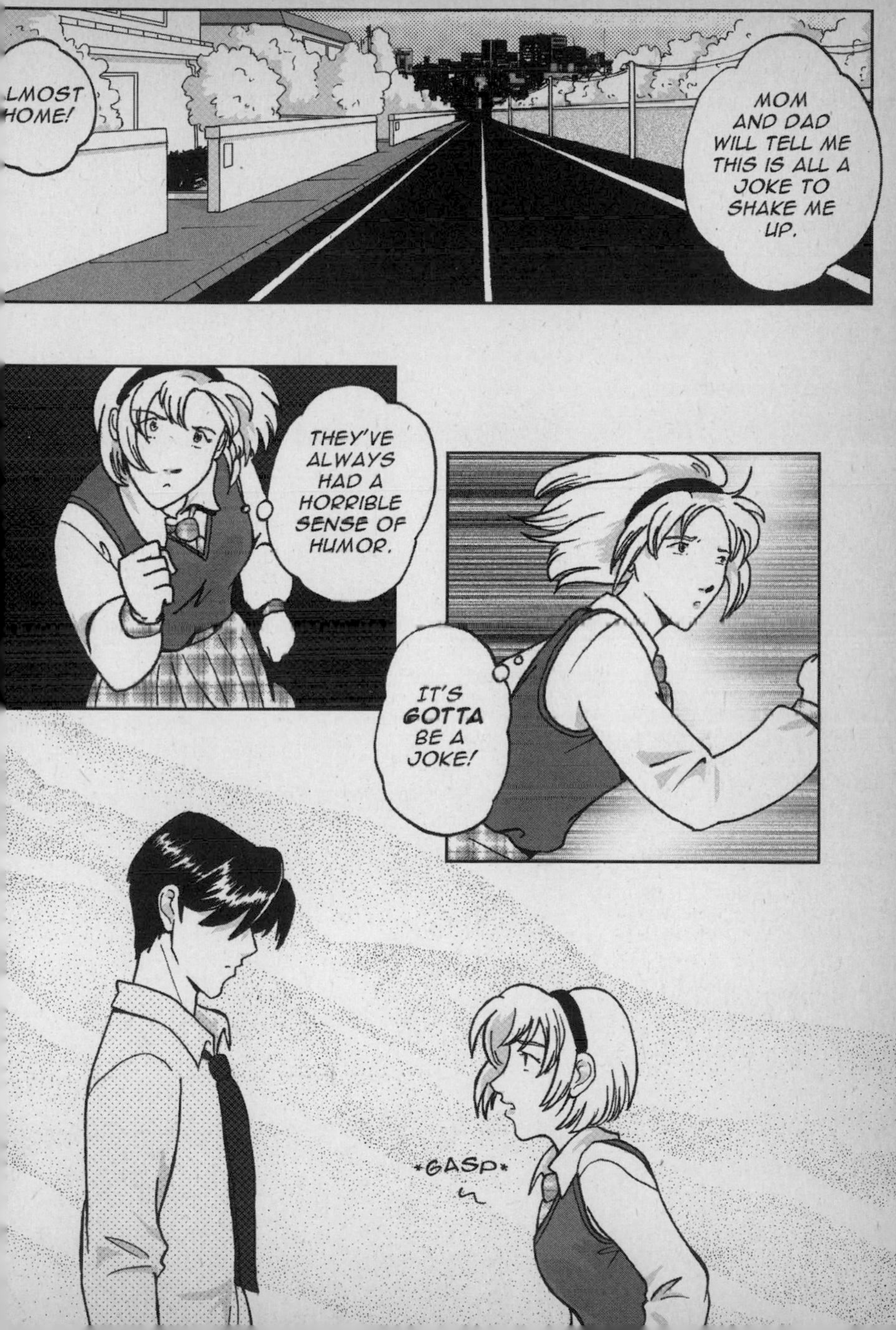
LMOST HOME!
MOM AND DAD WILL TELL ME THIS IS ALL A JOKE TO SHAKE ME UP.
THEY'VE ALWAYS HAD A HORRIBLE SENSE OF HUMOR.
IT'S GOTTA BE A JOKE!
GASP

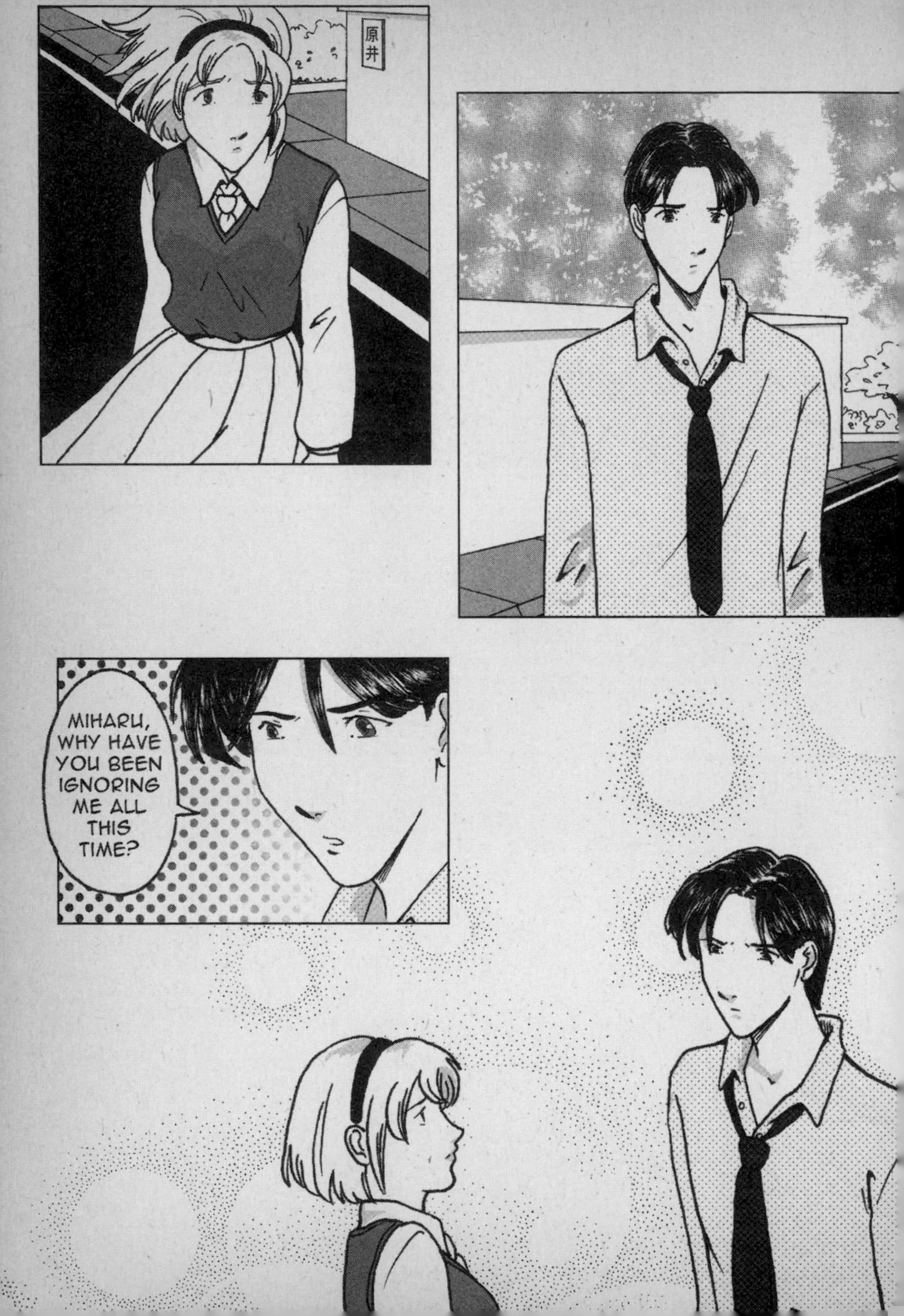
原井
MIHARU, WHY HAVE YOU BEEN IGNORING ME ALL THIS TIME?

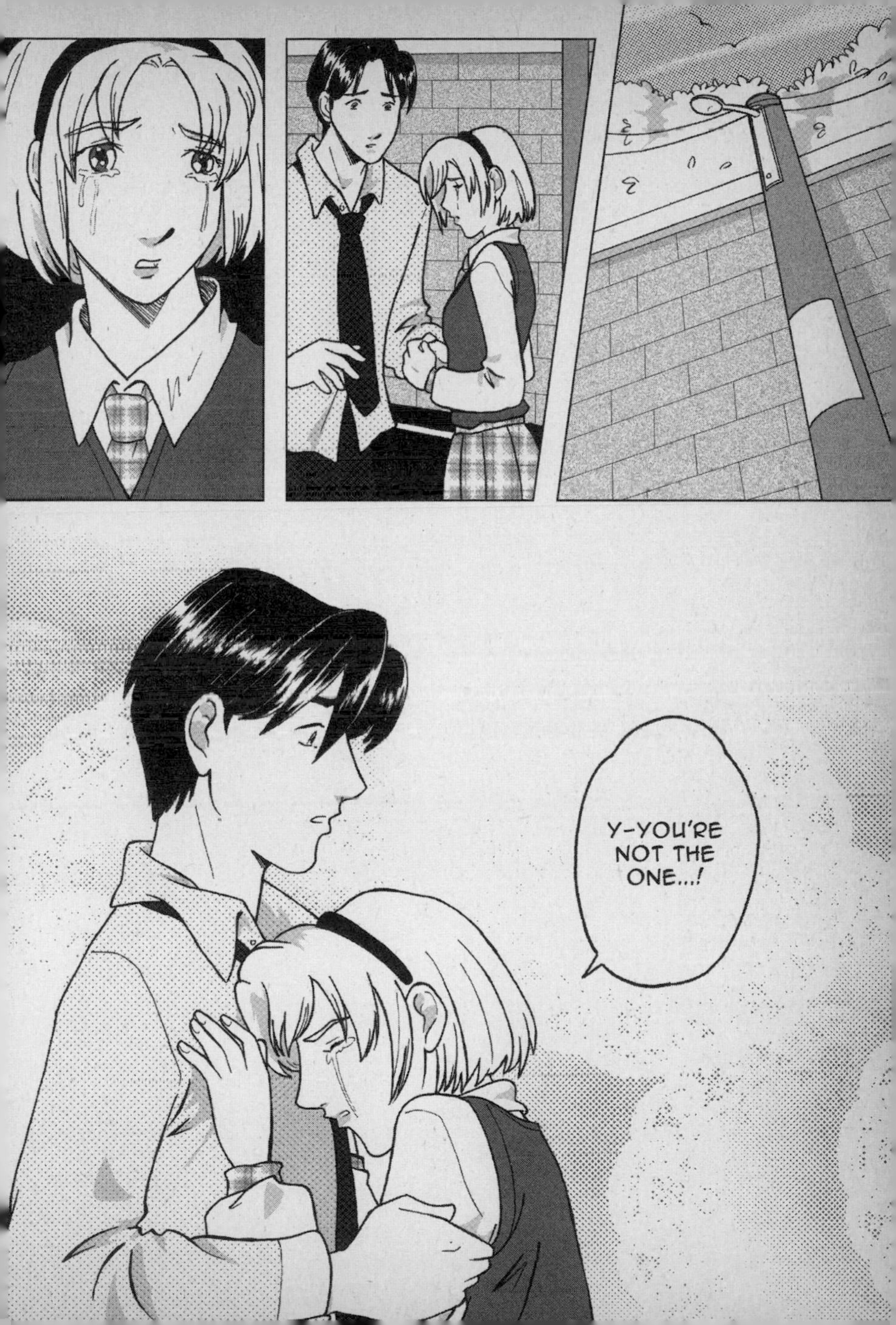
Y-YOU'RE NOT THE ONE...!

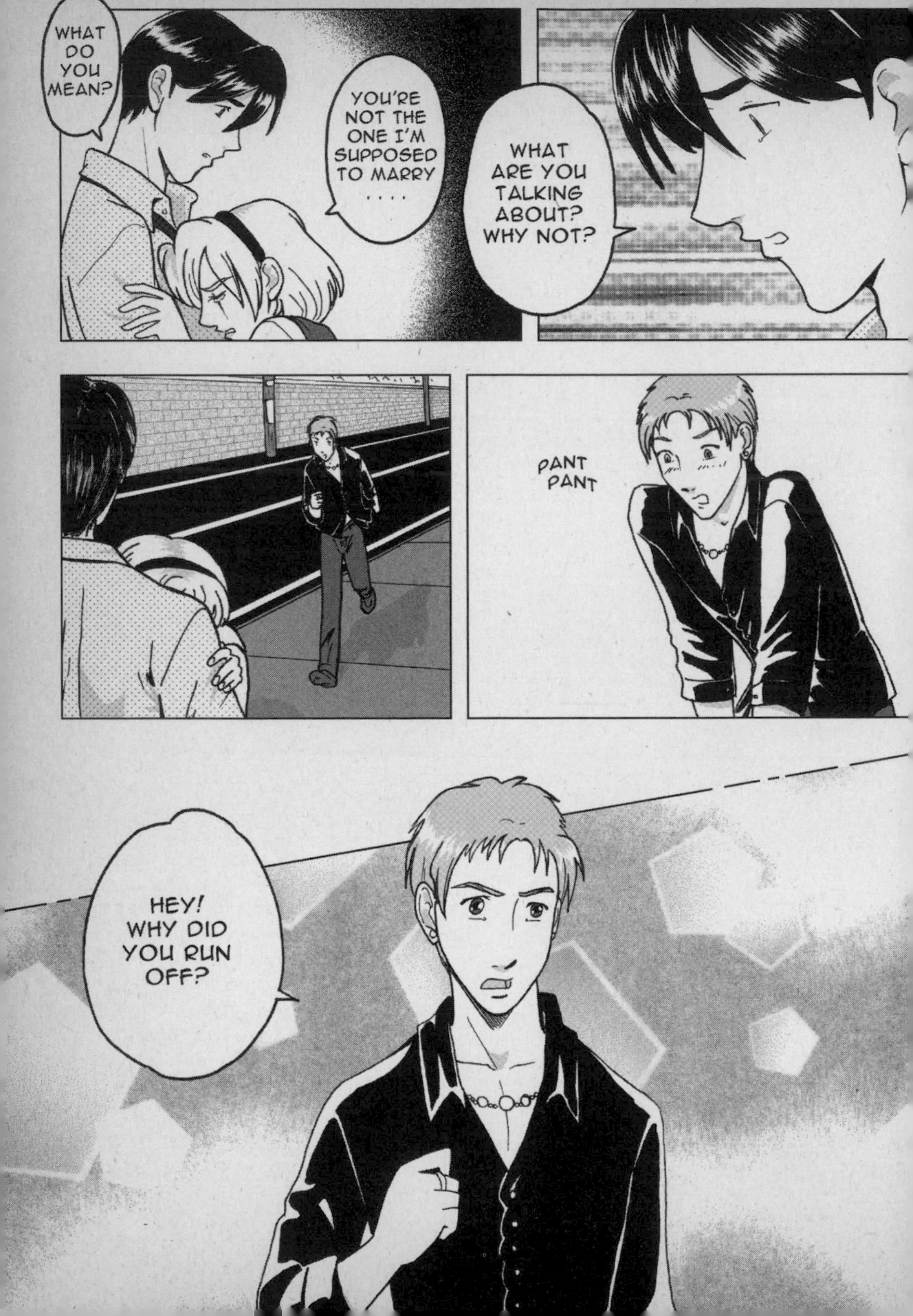
WHAT DO YOU MEAN?
YOU'RE NOT THE ONE I'M SUPPOSED TO MARRY . . . .
WHAT ARE YOU TALKING ABOUT? WHY NOT?
PANT PANT
HEY! WHY DID YOU RUN OFF?

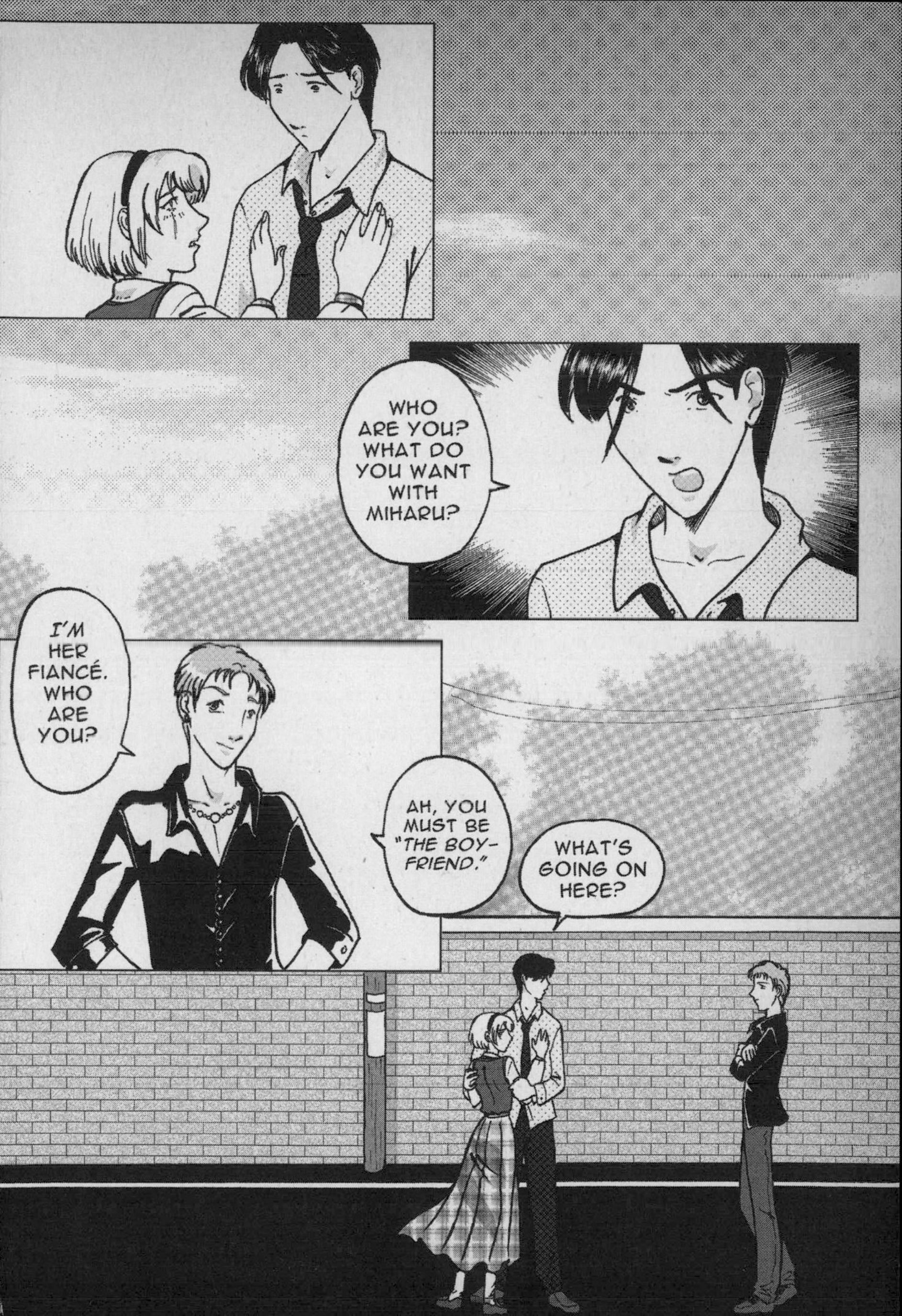
WHO ARE YOU? WHAT DO YOU WANT WITH MIHARU?
I'M HER FIANCÉ. WHO ARE YOU?
AH, YOU MUST BE *"THE BOY-FRIEND."*
WHAT'S GOING ON HERE?

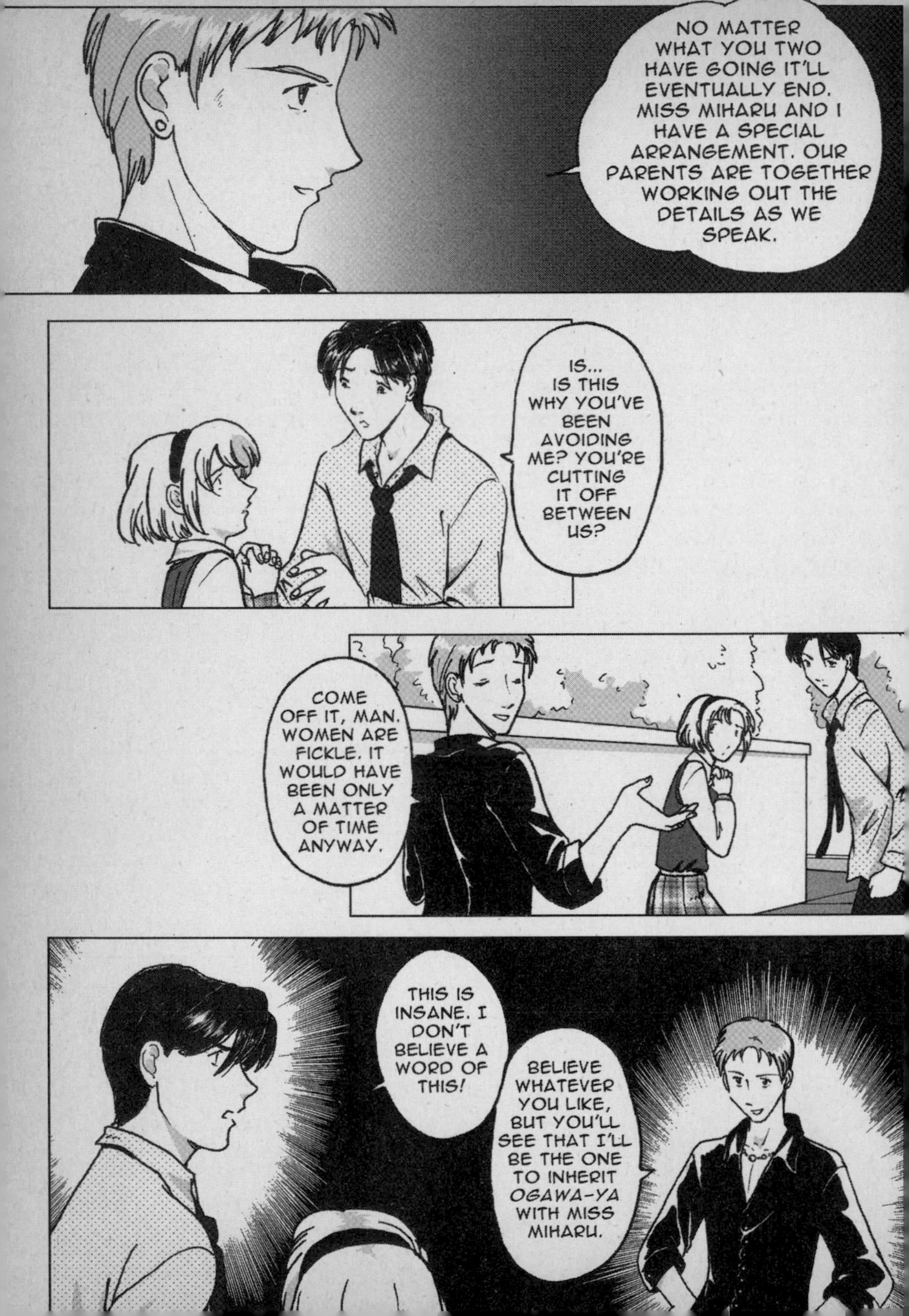
NO MATTER WHAT YOU TWO HAVE GOING IT'LL EVENTUALLY END. MISS MIHARU AND I HAVE A SPECIAL ARRANGEMENT. OUR PARENTS ARE TOGETHER WORKING OUT THE DETAILS AS WE SPEAK.
IS... IS THIS WHY YOU'VE BEEN AVOIDING ME? YOU'RE CUTTING IT OFF BETWEEN US?
COME OFF IT, MAN. WOMEN ARE FICKLE. IT WOULD HAVE BEEN ONLY A MATTER OF TIME ANYWAY.
THIS IS INSANE. I DON'T BELIEVE A WORD OF THIS!
BELIEVE WHATEVER YOU LIKE, BUT YOU'LL SEE THAT I'LL BE THE ONE TO INHERIT OGAWA-YA WITH MISS MIHARU.

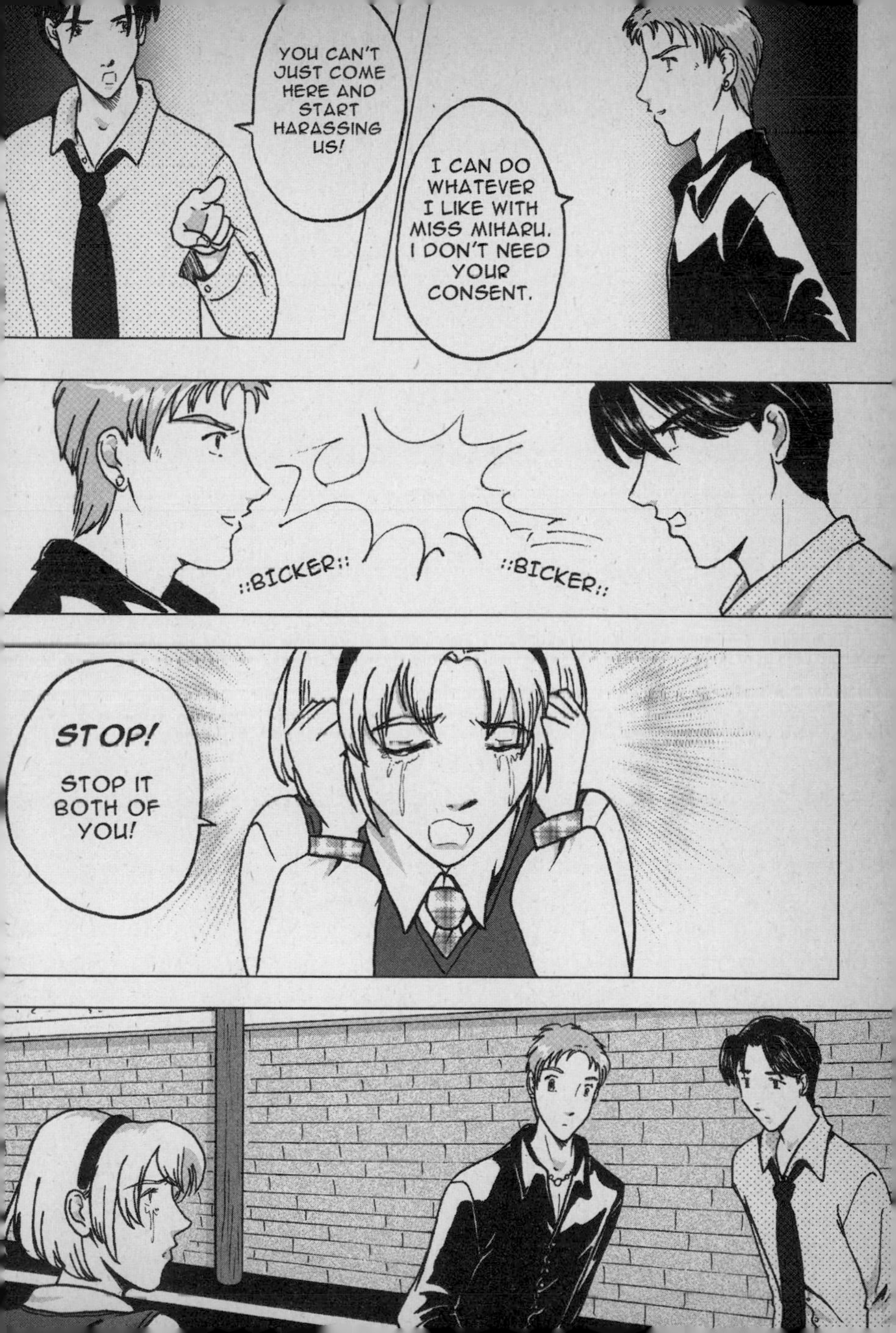
YOU CAN'T JUST COME HERE AND START HARASSING US!
I CAN DO WHATEVER I LIKE WITH MISS MIHARU. I DON'T NEED YOUR CONSENT.
::BICKER::
::BICKER::
STOP!
STOP IT BOTH OF YOU!

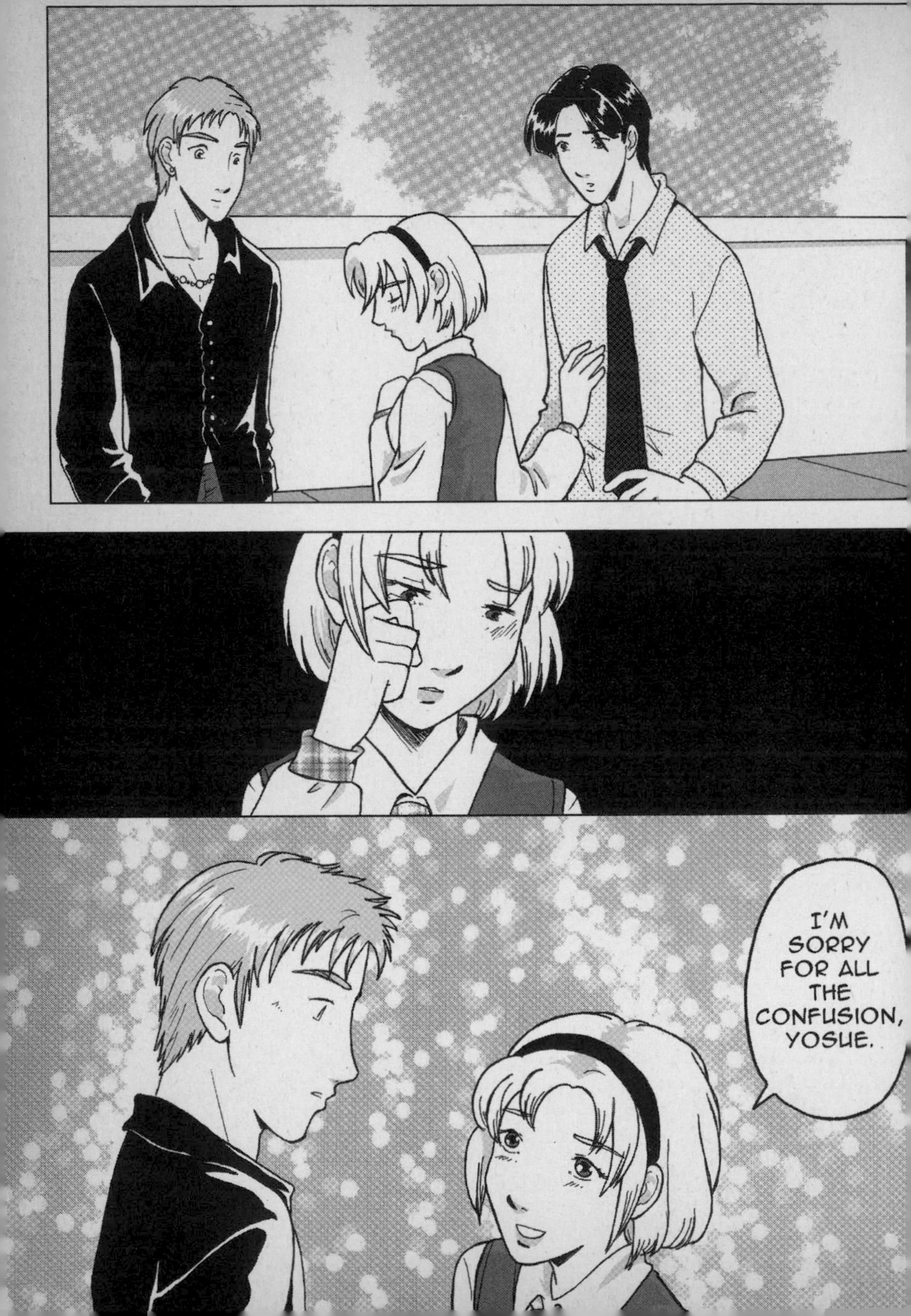
I'M SORRY FOR ALL THE CONFUSION, YOSUE.

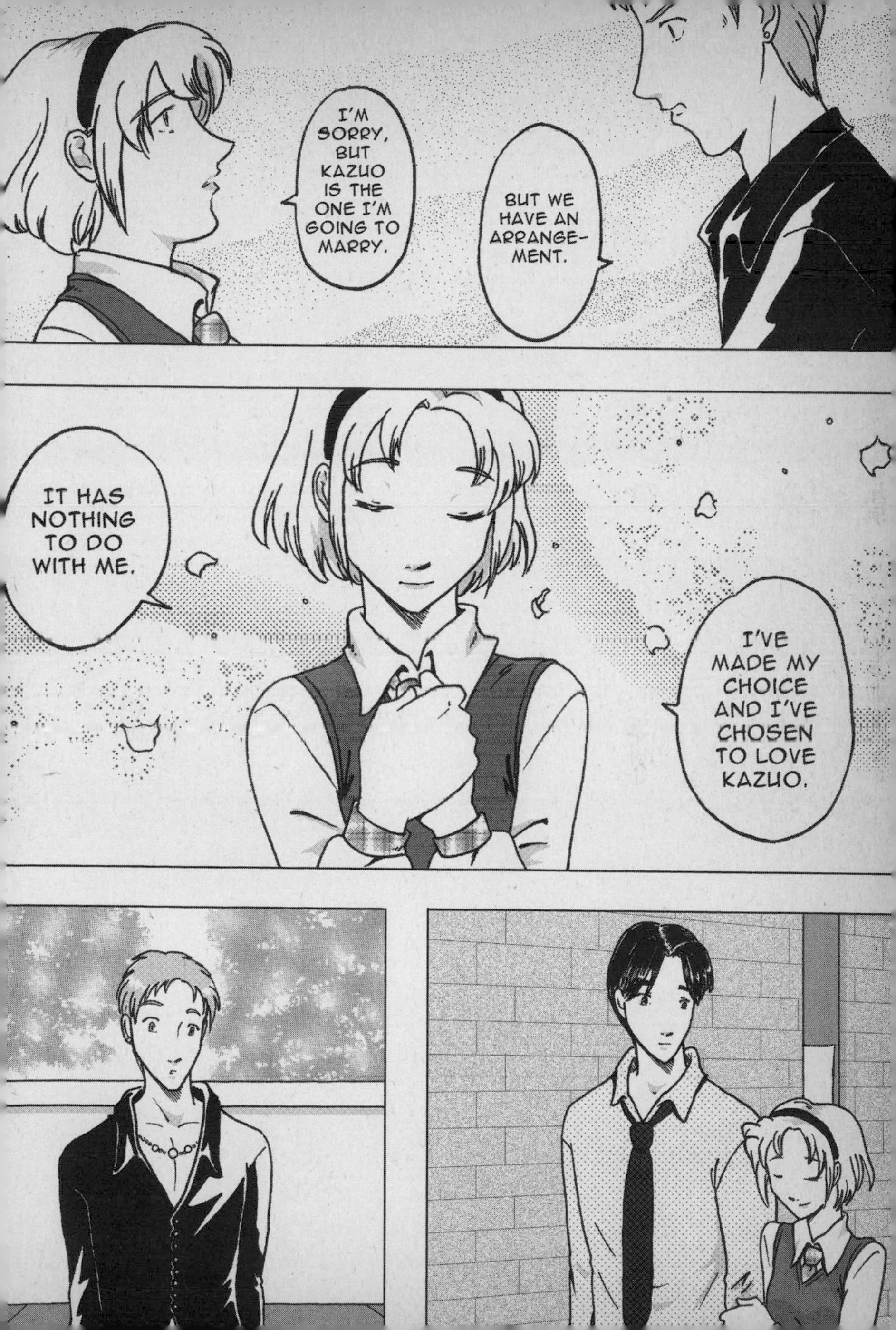

BUT WE HAVE AN ARRANGE-MENT.
I'M SORRY, BUT KAZUO IS THE ONE I'M GOING TO MARRY.
I'VE MADE MY CHOICE AND I'VE CHOSEN TO LOVE KAZUO.
IT HAS NOTHING TO DO WITH ME.

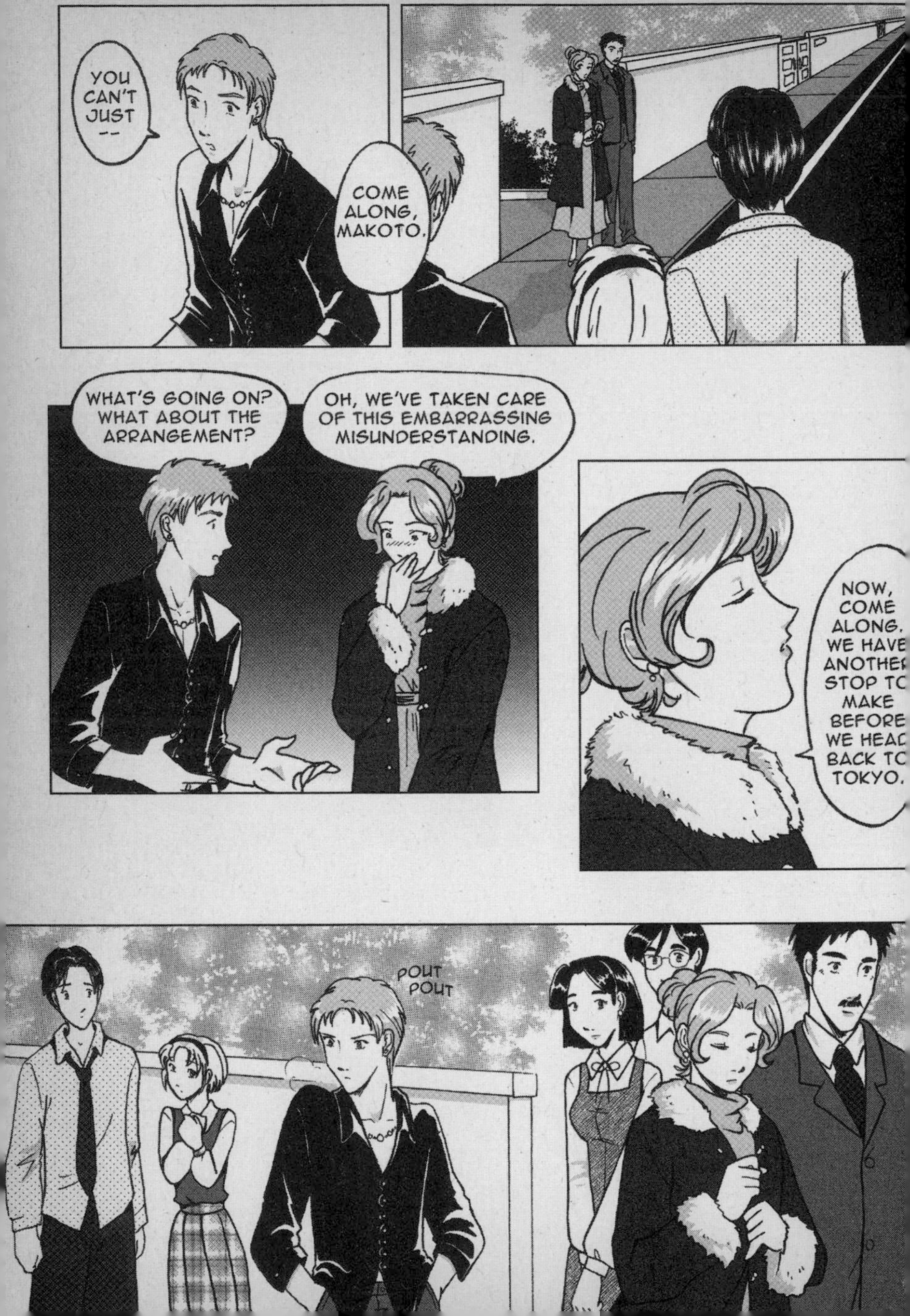
YOU CAN'T JUST --
COME ALONG, MAKOTO.
WHAT'S GOING ON? WHAT ABOUT THE ARRANGEMENT?
OH, WE'VE TAKEN CARE OF THIS EMBARRASSING MISUNDERSTANDING.
NOW, COME ALONG. WE HAVE ANOTHER STOP TO MAKE BEFORE WE HEAD BACK TO TOKYO.
POUT POUT

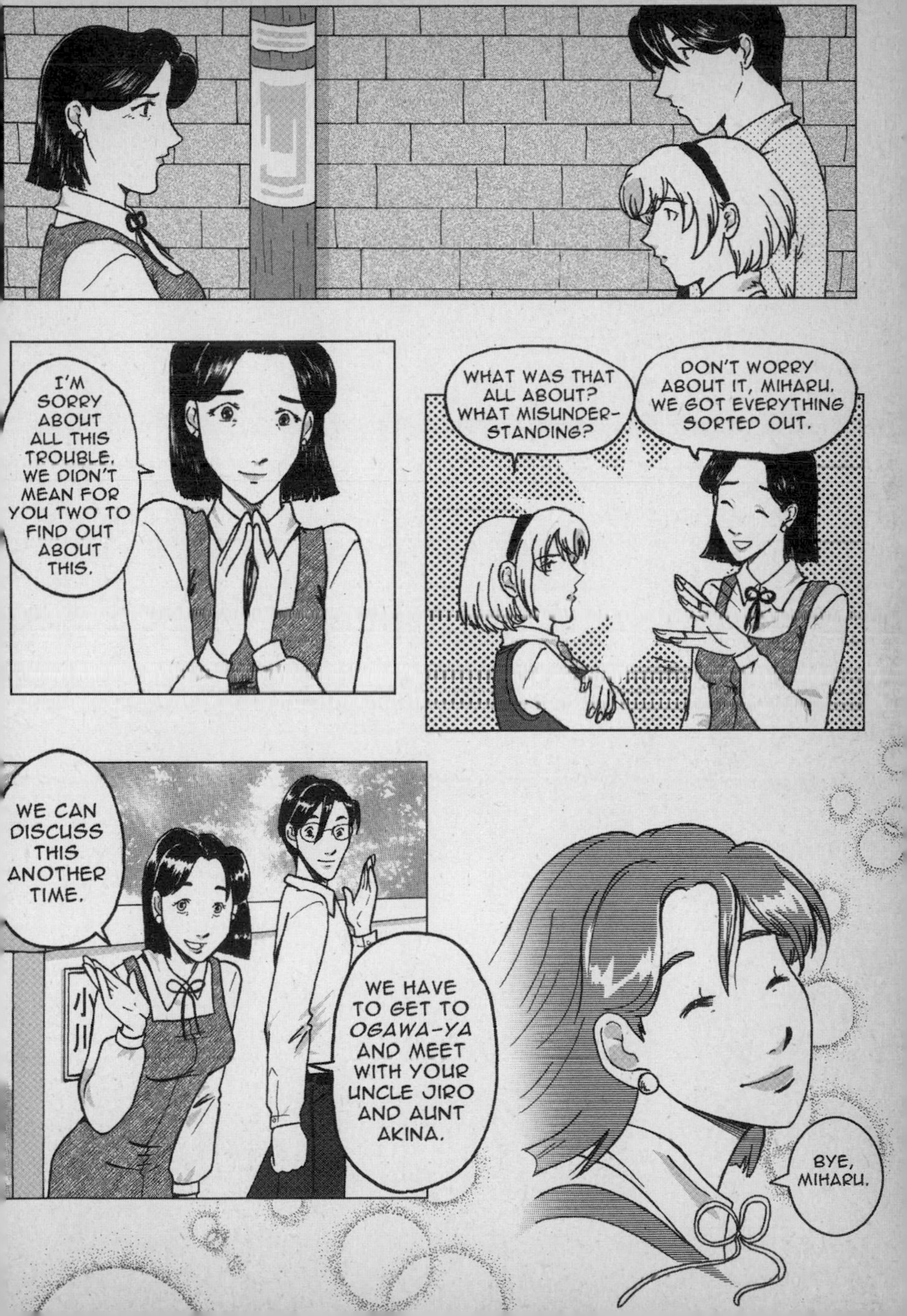

I'M SORRY ABOUT ALL THIS TROUBLE. WE DIDN'T MEAN FOR YOU TWO TO FIND OUT ABOUT THIS.
WHAT WAS THAT ALL ABOUT? WHAT MISUNDER-STANDING?
DON'T WORRY ABOUT IT, MIHARU. WE GOT EVERYTHING SORTED OUT.
WE CAN DISCUSS THIS ANOTHER TIME.
小川
WE HAVE TO GET TO *OGAWA-YA* AND MEET WITH YOUR UNCLE JIRO AND AUNT AKINA.
BYE, MIHARU.

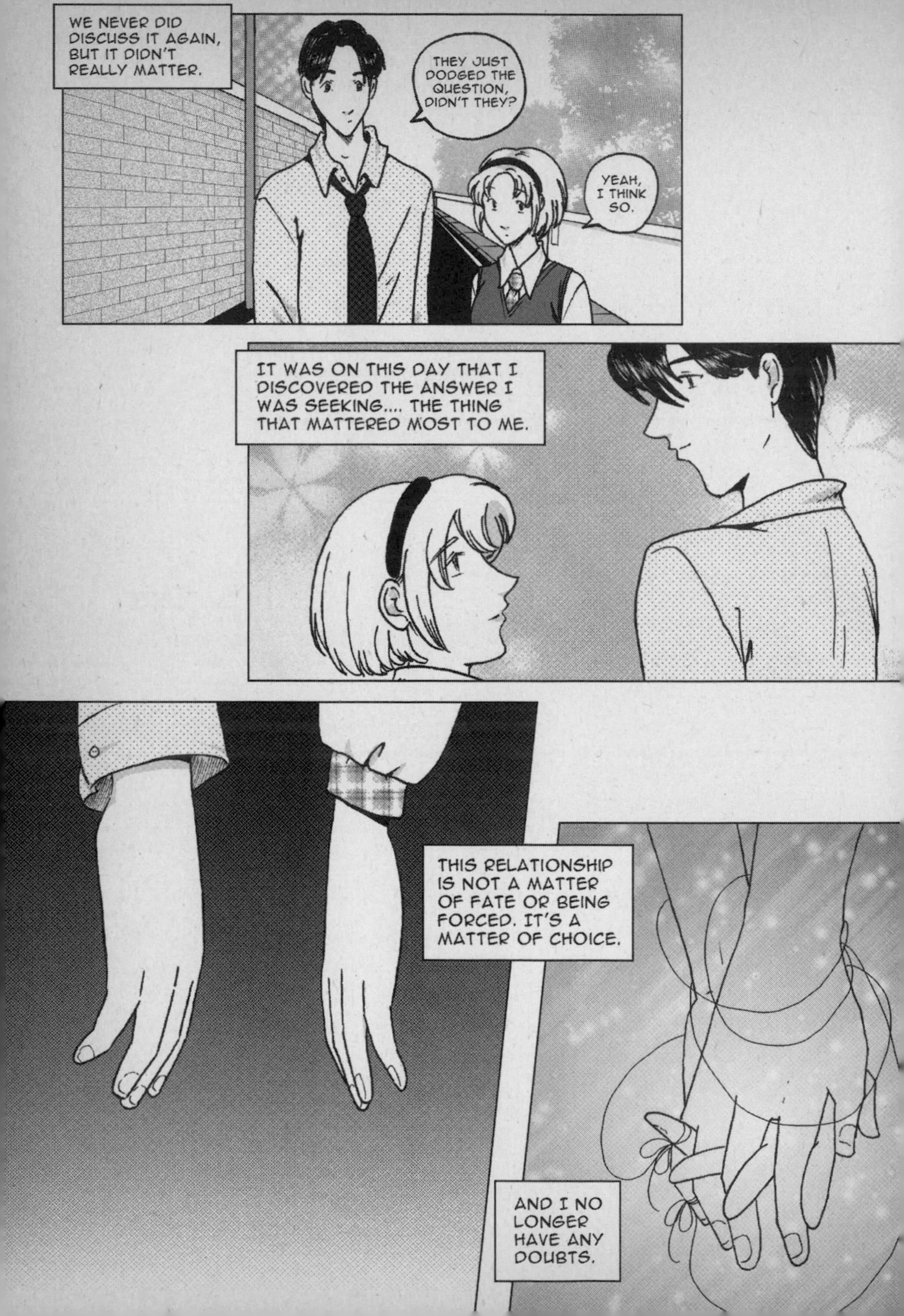
WE NEVER DID DISCUSS IT AGAIN, BUT IT DIDN'T REALLY MATTER.
THEY JUST DODGED THE QUESTION, DIDN'T THEY?
YEAH, I THINK SO.
IT WAS ON THIS DAY THAT I DISCOVERED THE ANSWER I WAS SEEKING.... THE THING THAT MATTERED MOST TO ME.
THIS RELATIONSHIP IS NOT A MATTER OF FATE OR BEING FORCED. IT'S A MATTER OF CHOICE.
AND I NO LONGER HAVE ANY DOUBTS.

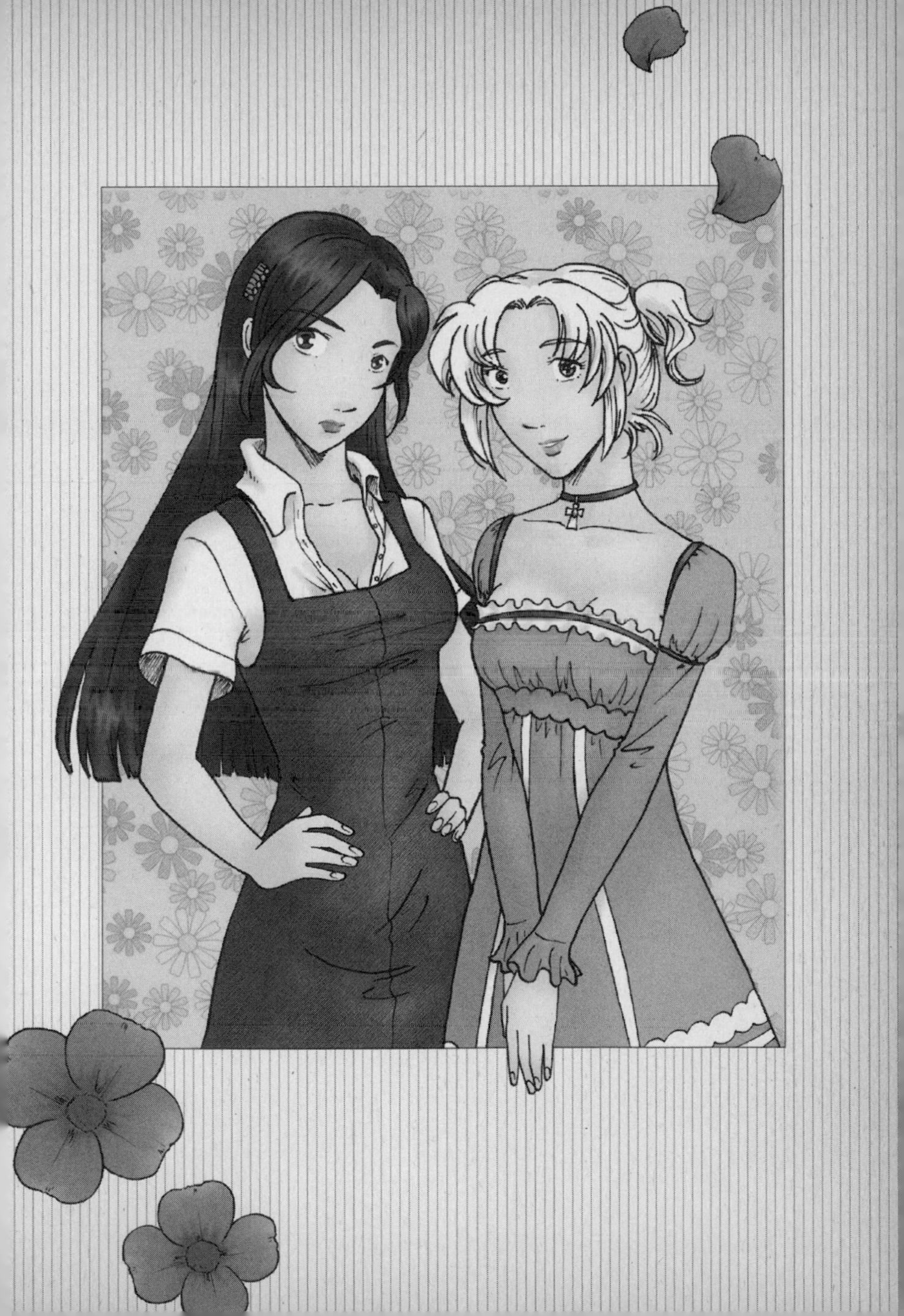

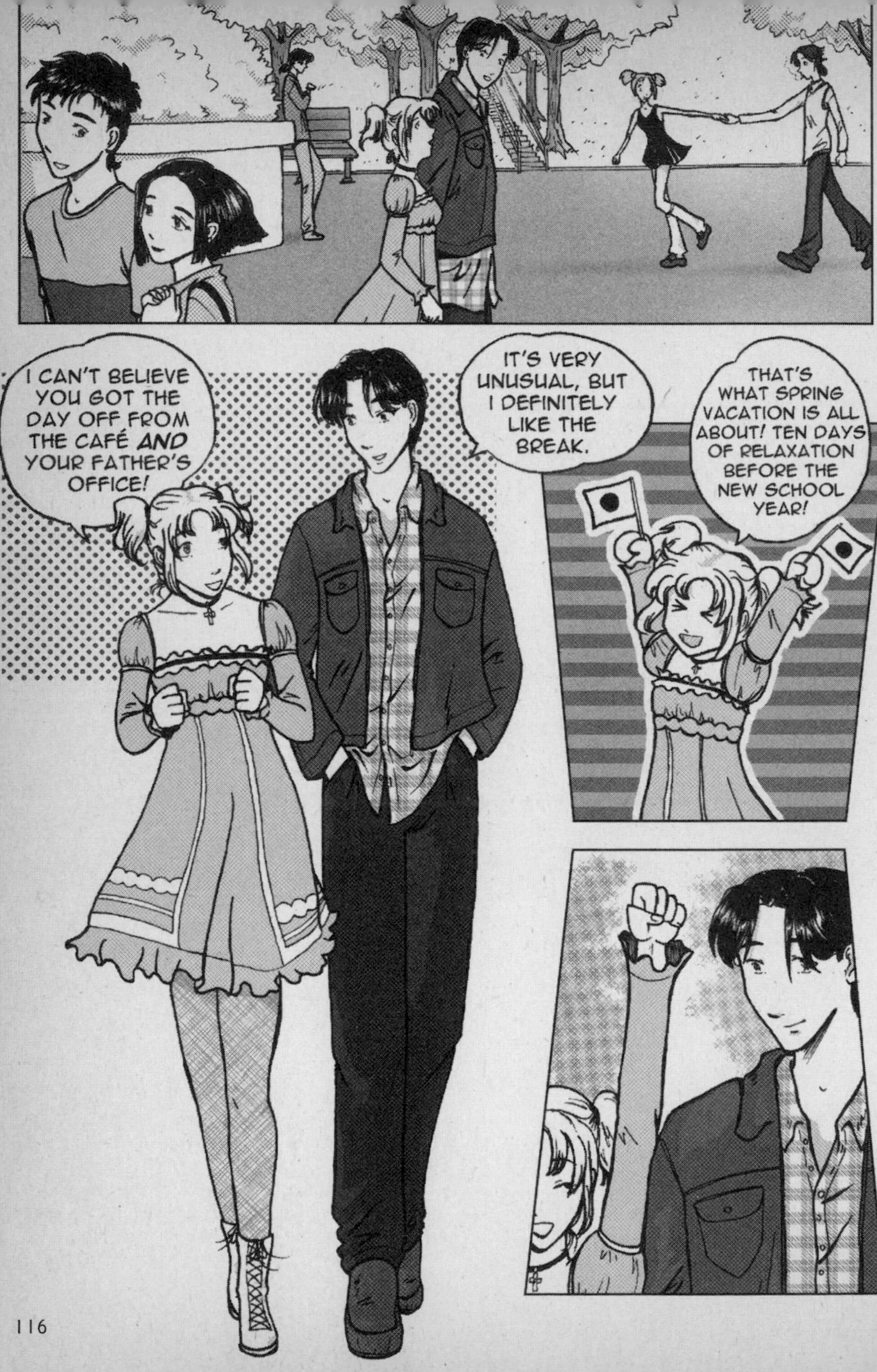
I CAN'T BELIEVE YOU GOT THE DAY OFF FROM THE CAFÉ AND YOUR FATHER'S OFFICE!
IT'S VERY UNUSUAL, BUT I DEFINITELY LIKE THE BREAK.
THAT'S WHAT SPRING VACATION IS ALL ABOUT! TEN DAYS OF RELAXATION BEFORE THE NEW SCHOOL YEAR!

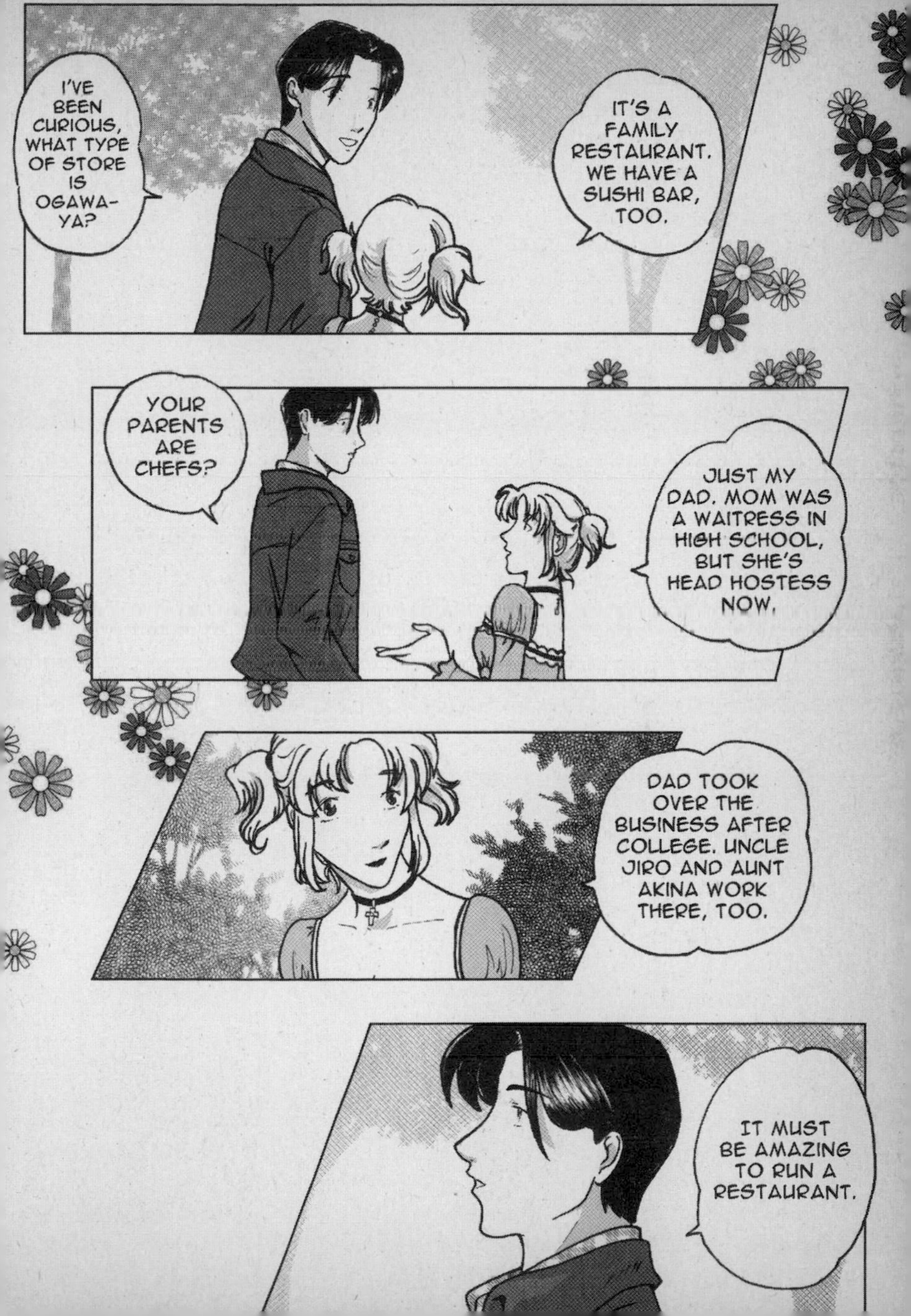
I'VE BEEN CURIOUS, WHAT TYPE OF STORE IS OGAWA-YA?
IT'S A FAMILY RESTAURANT. WE HAVE A SUSHI BAR, TOO.
YOUR PARENTS ARE CHEFS?
JUST MY DAD. MOM WAS A WAITRESS IN HIGH SCHOOL, BUT SHE'S HEAD HOSTESS NOW.
DAD TOOK OVER THE BUSINESS AFTER COLLEGE. UNCLE JIRO AND AUNT AKINA WORK THERE, TOO.
IT MUST BE AMAZING TO RUN A RESTAURANT.

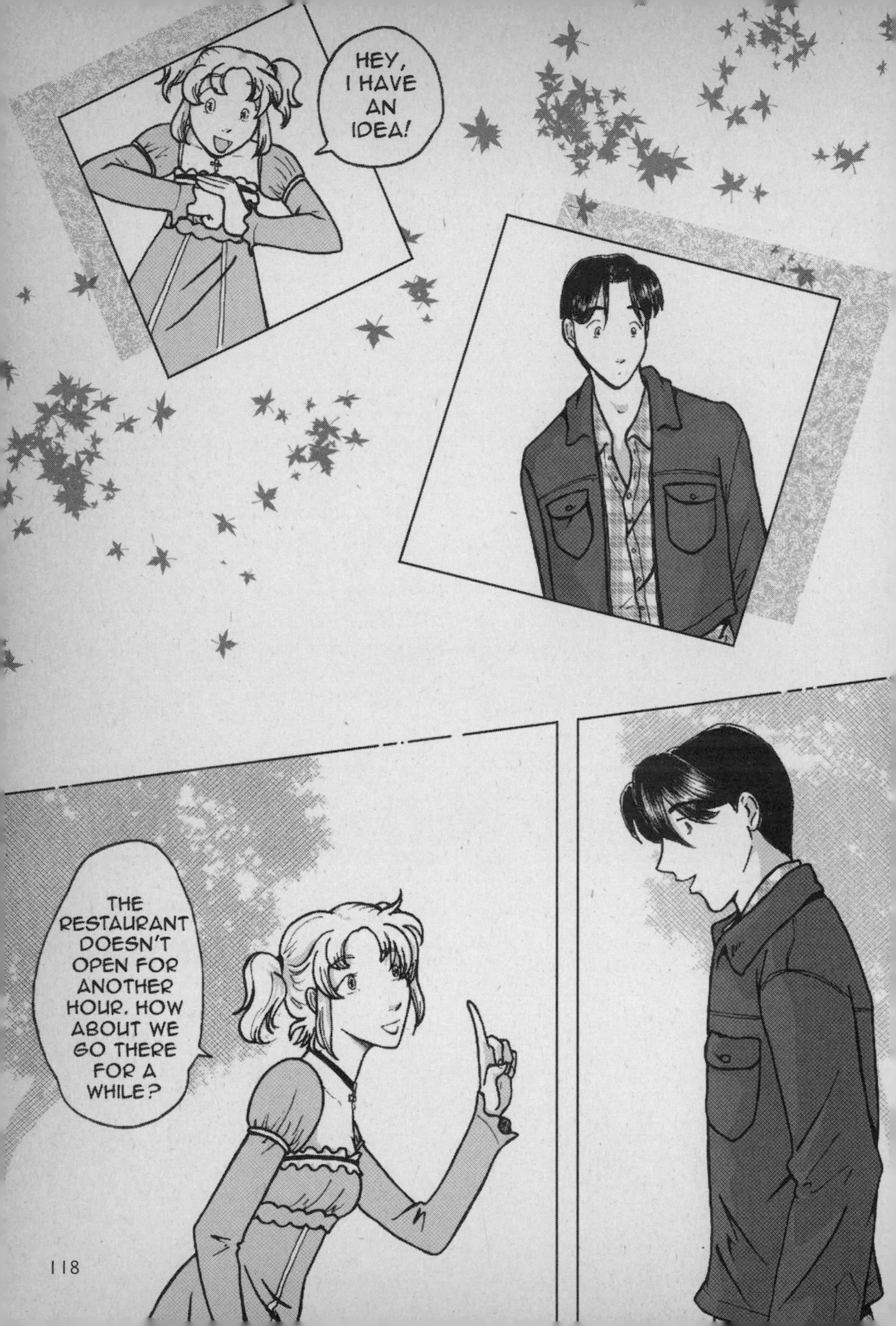
HEY, I HAVE AN IDEA!
THE RESTAURANT DOESN'T OPEN FOR ANOTHER HOUR. HOW ABOUT WE GO THERE FOR A WHILE?

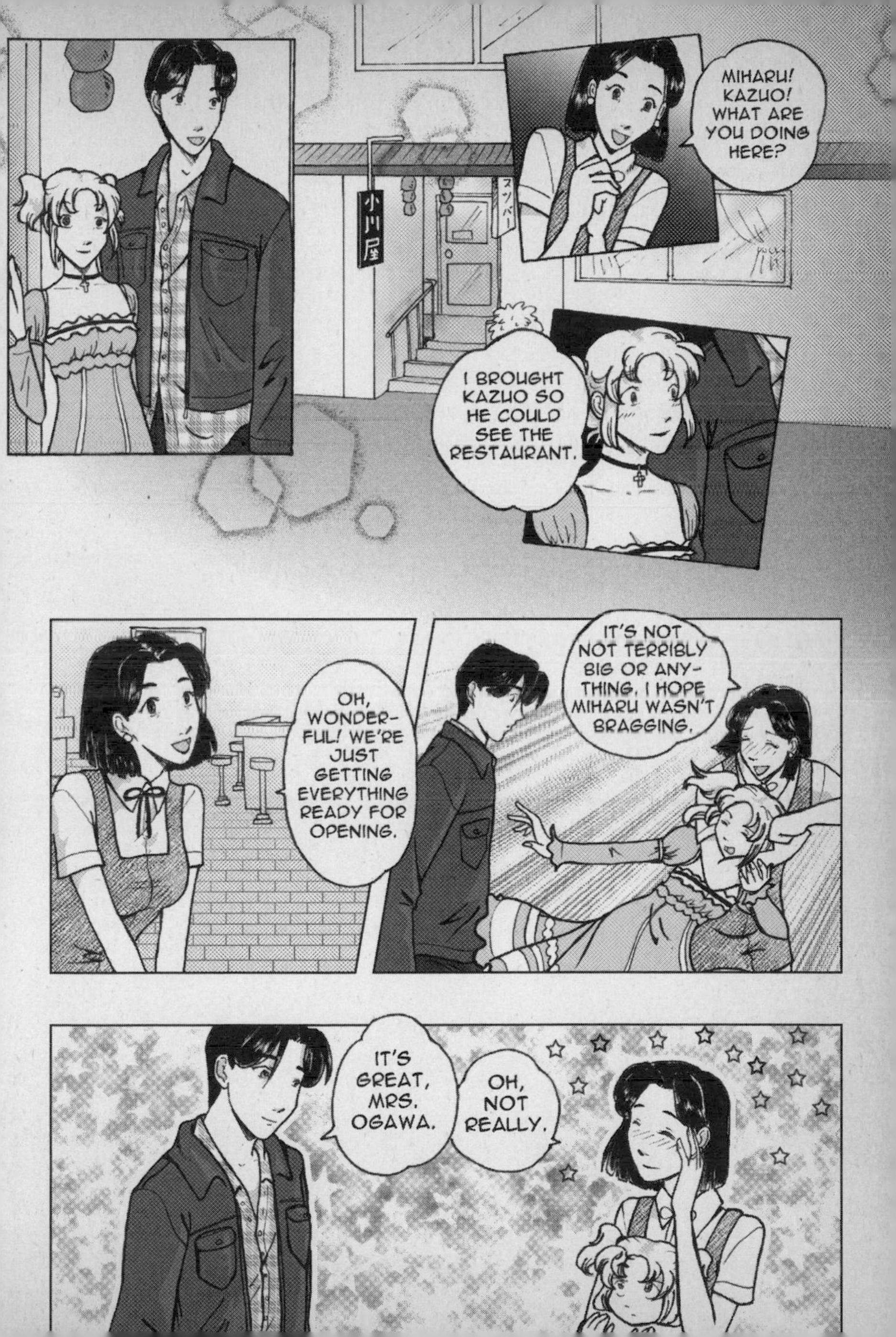
MIHARU! KAZUO! WHAT ARE YOU DOING HERE?
I BROUGHT KAZUO SO HE COULD SEE THE RESTAURANT.
小川屋
OH, WONDERFUL! WE'RE JUST GETTING EVERYTHING READY FOR OPENING.
IT'S NOT NOT TERRIBLY BIG OR ANYTHING. I HOPE MIHARU WASN'T BRAGGING.
IT'S GREAT, MRS. OGAWA.
OH, NOT REALLY.

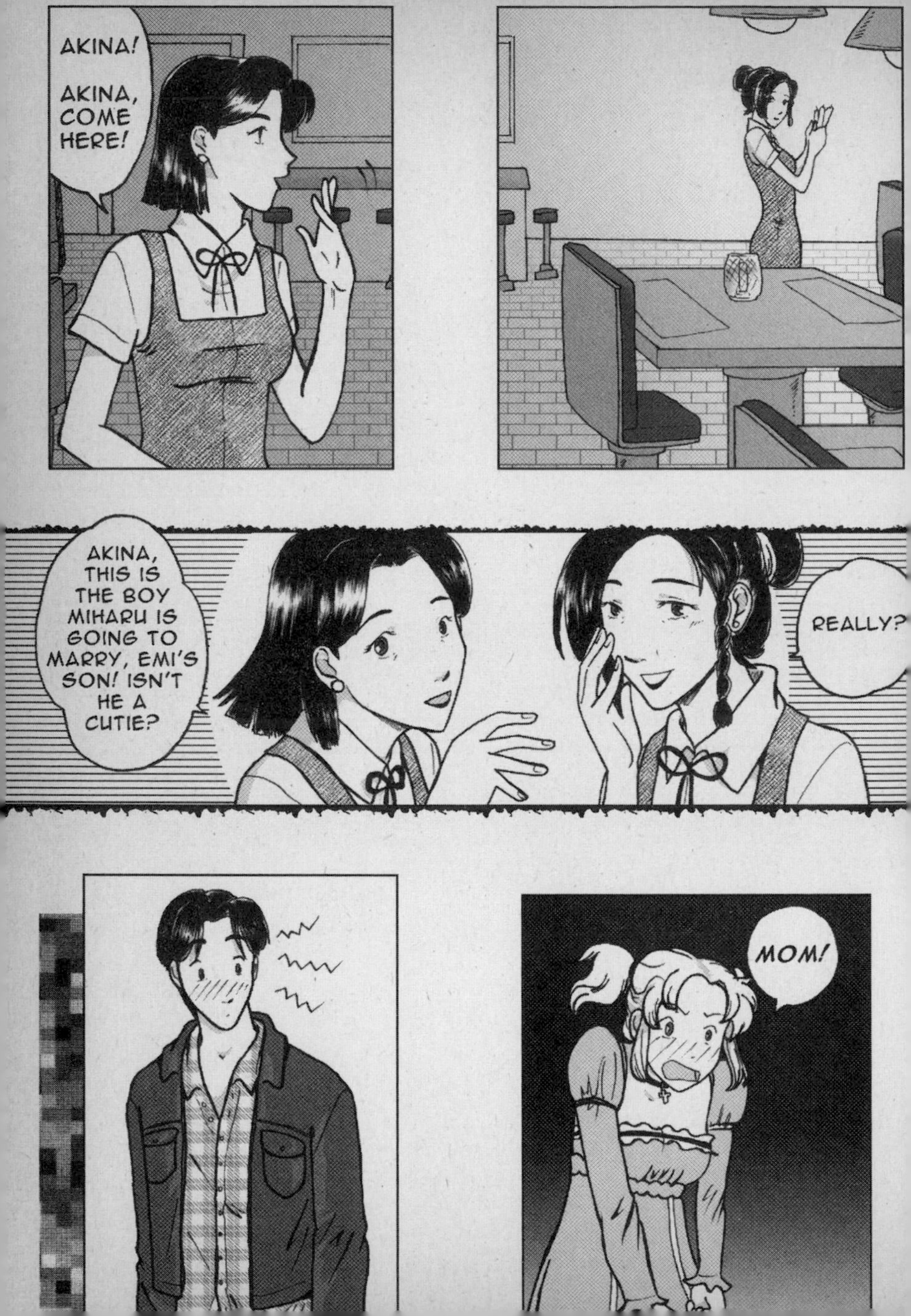
AKINA!
AKINA, COME HERE!
AKINA, THIS IS THE BOY MIHARU IS GOING TO MARRY, EMI'S SON! ISN'T HE A CUTIE?
REALLY?
MOM!

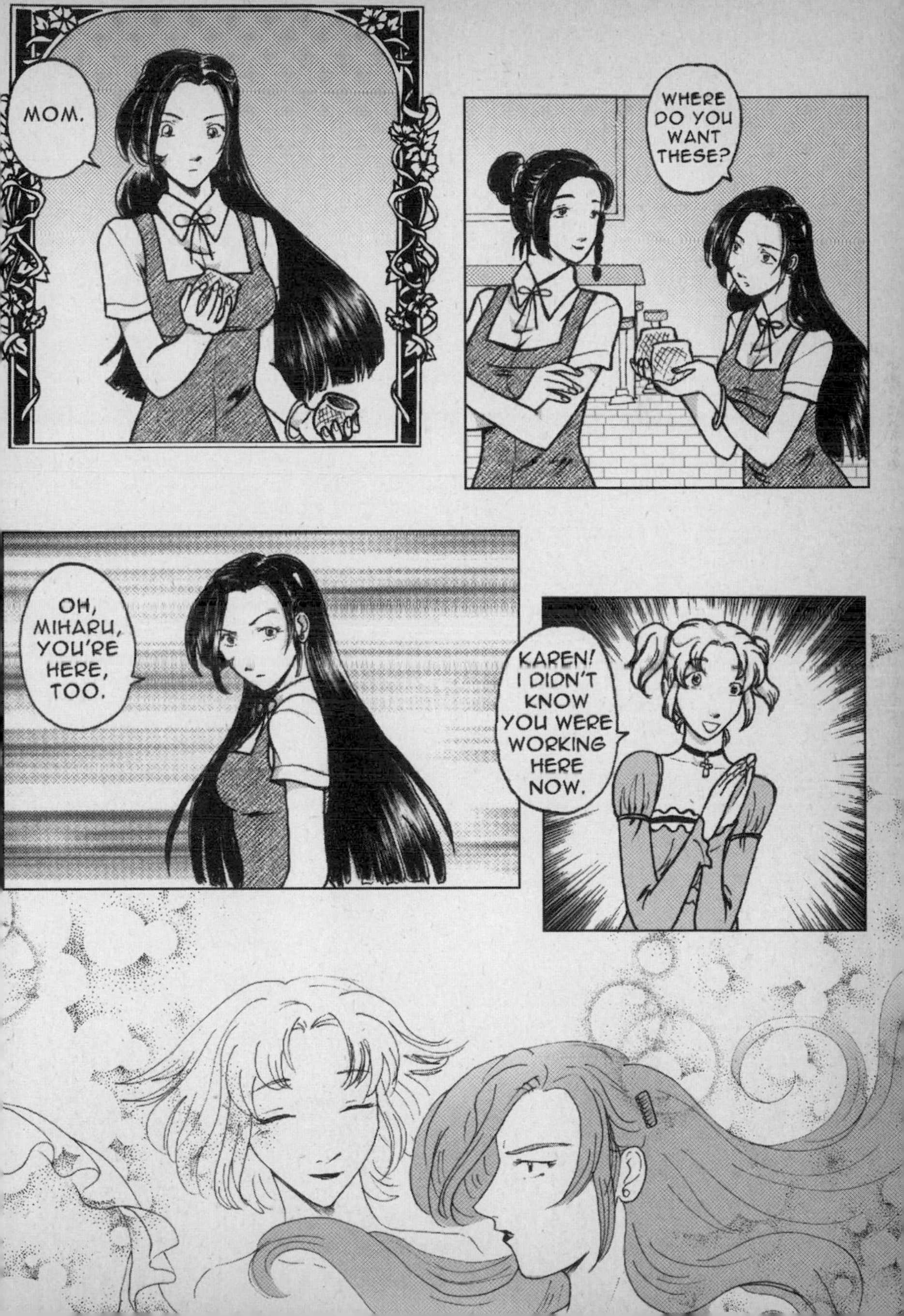
MOM.
WHERE DO YOU WANT THESE?
OH, MIHARU, YOU'RE HERE, TOO.
KAREN! I DIDN'T KNOW YOU WERE WORKING HERE NOW.

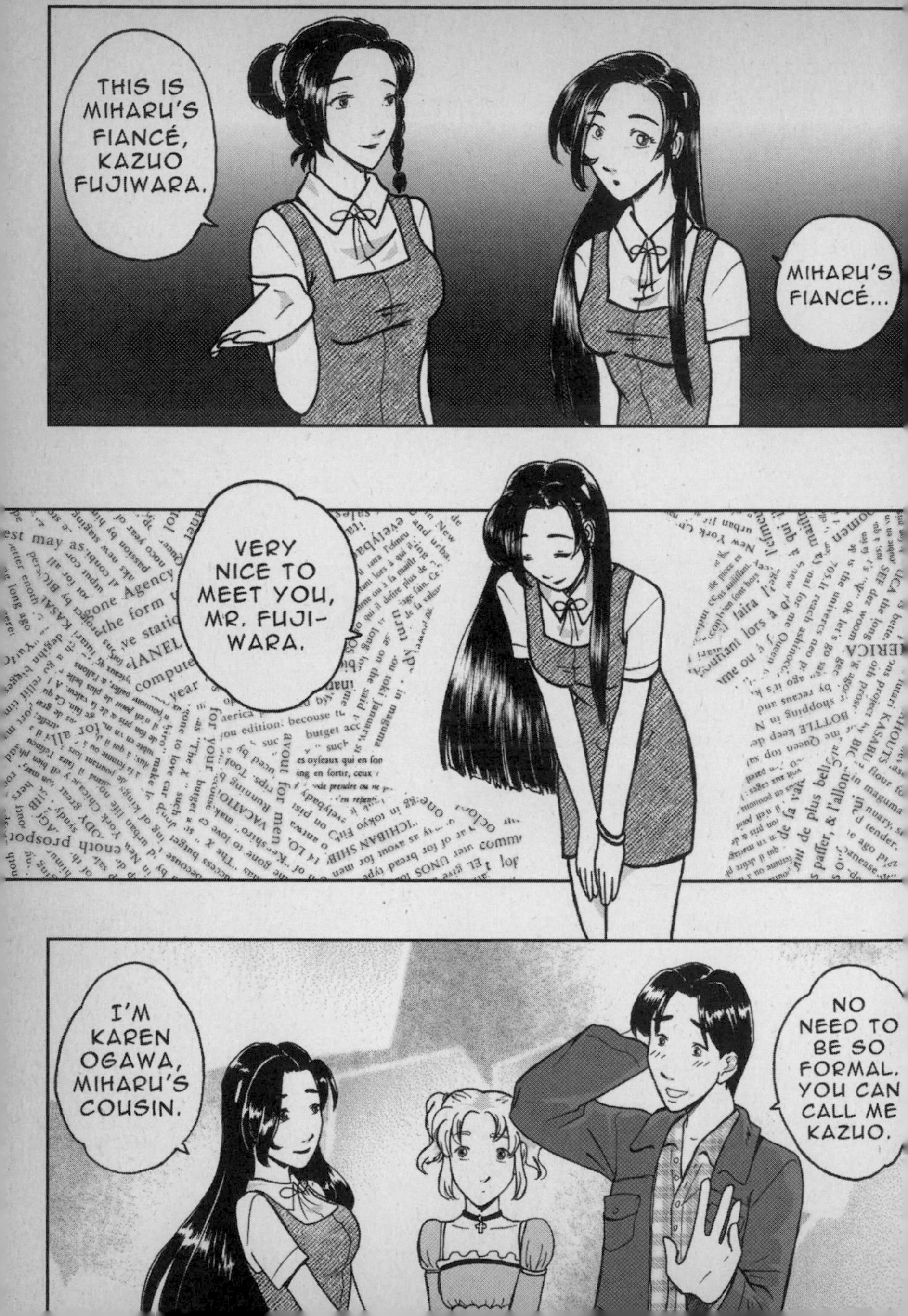
THIS IS MIHARU'S FIANCÉ, KAZUO FUJIWARA.
MIHARU'S FIANCÉ...
VERY NICE TO MEET YOU, MR. FUJI-WARA.
I'M KAREN OGAWA, MIHARU'S COUSIN.
NO NEED TO BE SO FORMAL. YOU CAN CALL ME KAZUO.

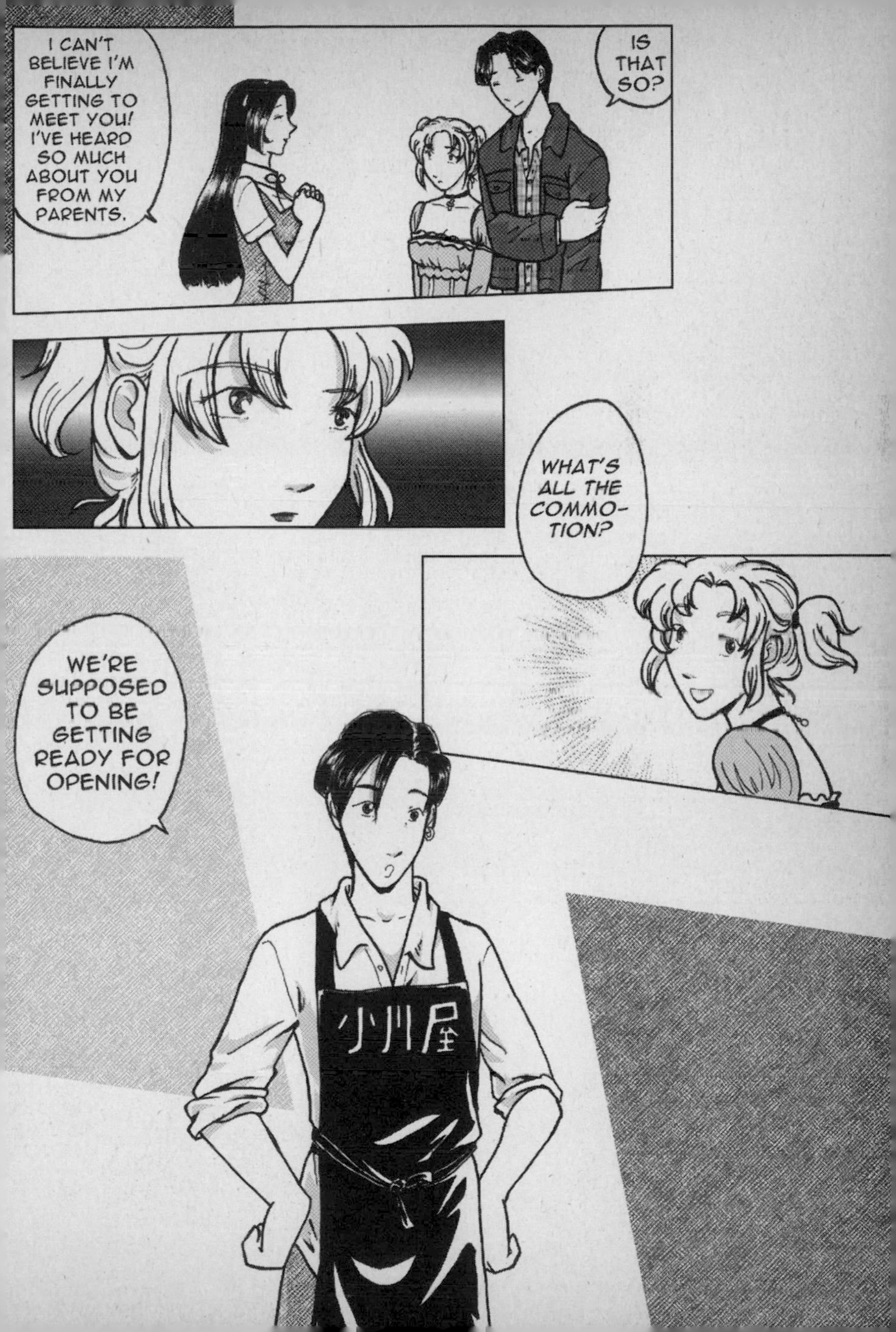

IS THAT SO?
I CAN'T BELIEVE I'M FINALLY GETTING TO MEET YOU! I'VE HEARD SO MUCH ABOUT YOU FROM MY PARENTS.
WHAT'S ALL THE COMMOTION?
WE'RE SUPPOSED TO BE GETTING READY FOR OPENING!
小川屋

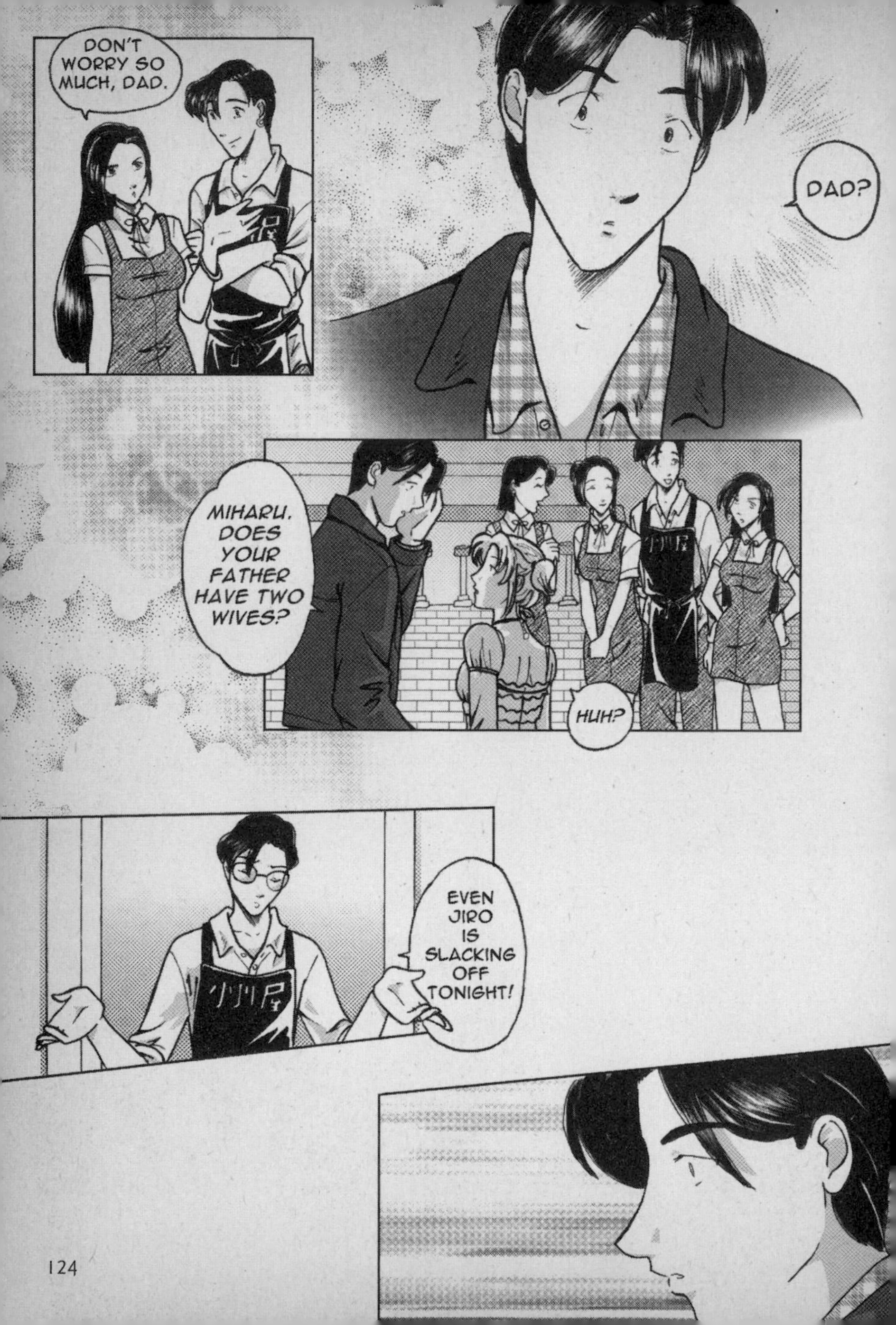
DON'T WORRY SO MUCH, DAD.
DAD?
MIHARU. DOES YOUR FATHER HAVE TWO WIVES?
HUH?
EVEN JIRO IS SLACKING OFF TONIGHT!

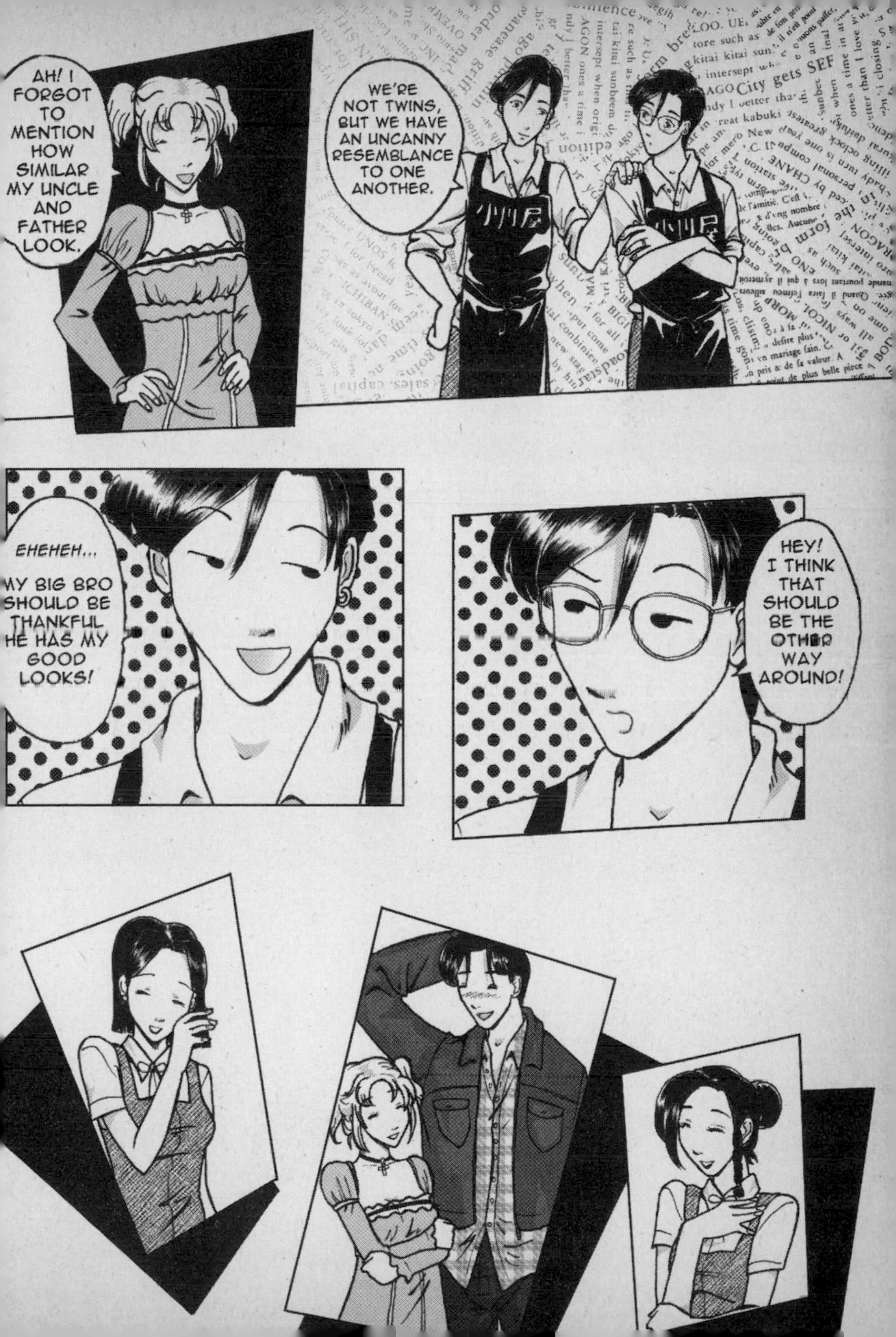
AH! I FORGOT TO MENTION HOW SIMILAR MY UNCLE AND FATHER LOOK.
WE'RE NOT TWINS, BUT WE HAVE AN UNCANNY RESEMBLANCE TO ONE ANOTHER.
EHEHEH...
MY BIG BRO SHOULD BE THANKFUL HE HAS MY GOOD LOOKS!
HEY! I THINK THAT SHOULD BE THE OTHER WAY AROUND!

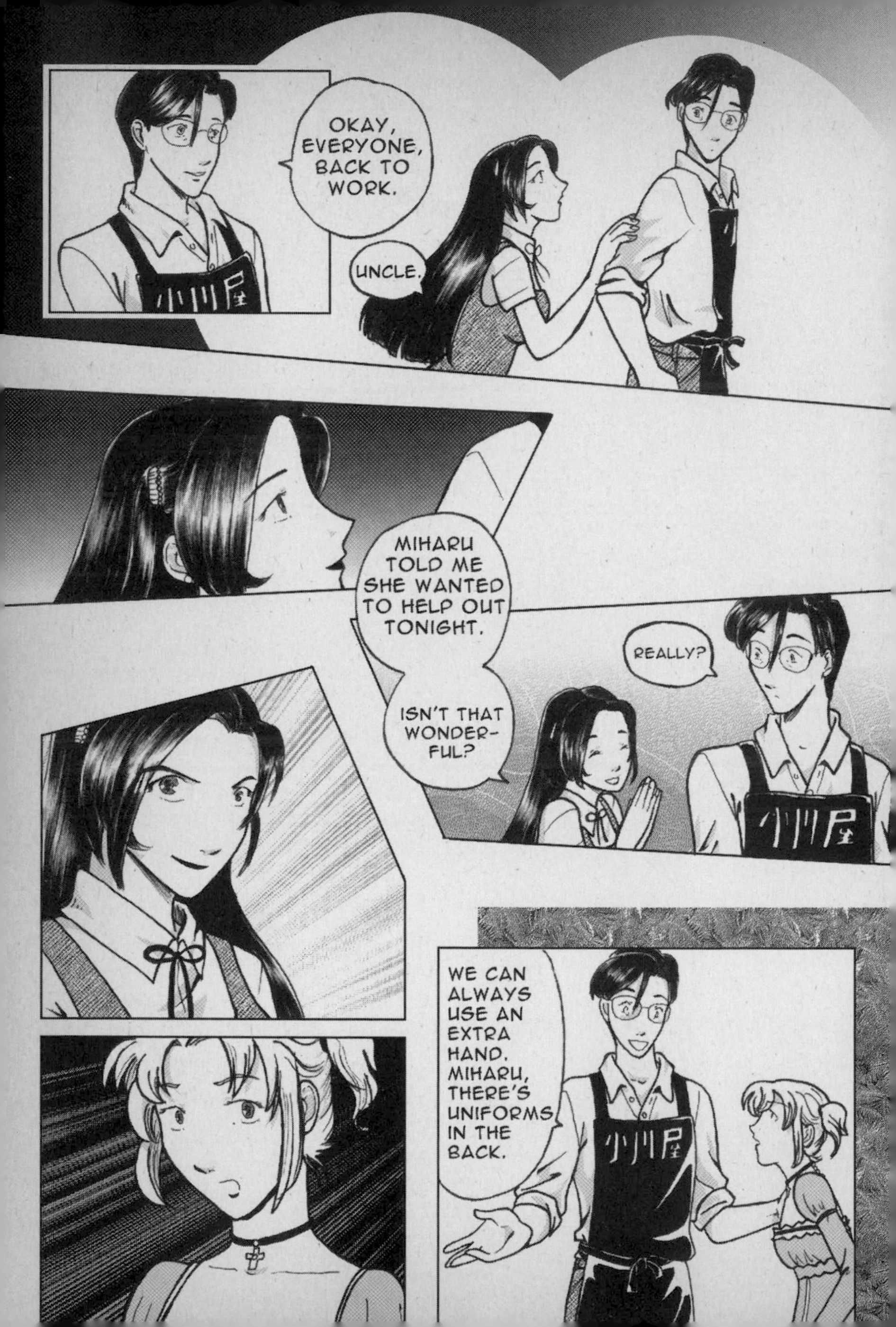
OKAY, EVERYONE, BACK TO WORK.
UNCLE.
MIHARU TOLD ME SHE WANTED TO HELP OUT TONIGHT.
ISN'T THAT WONDERFUL?
REALLY?
WE CAN ALWAYS USE AN EXTRA HAND. MIHARU, THERE'S UNIFORMS IN THE BACK.

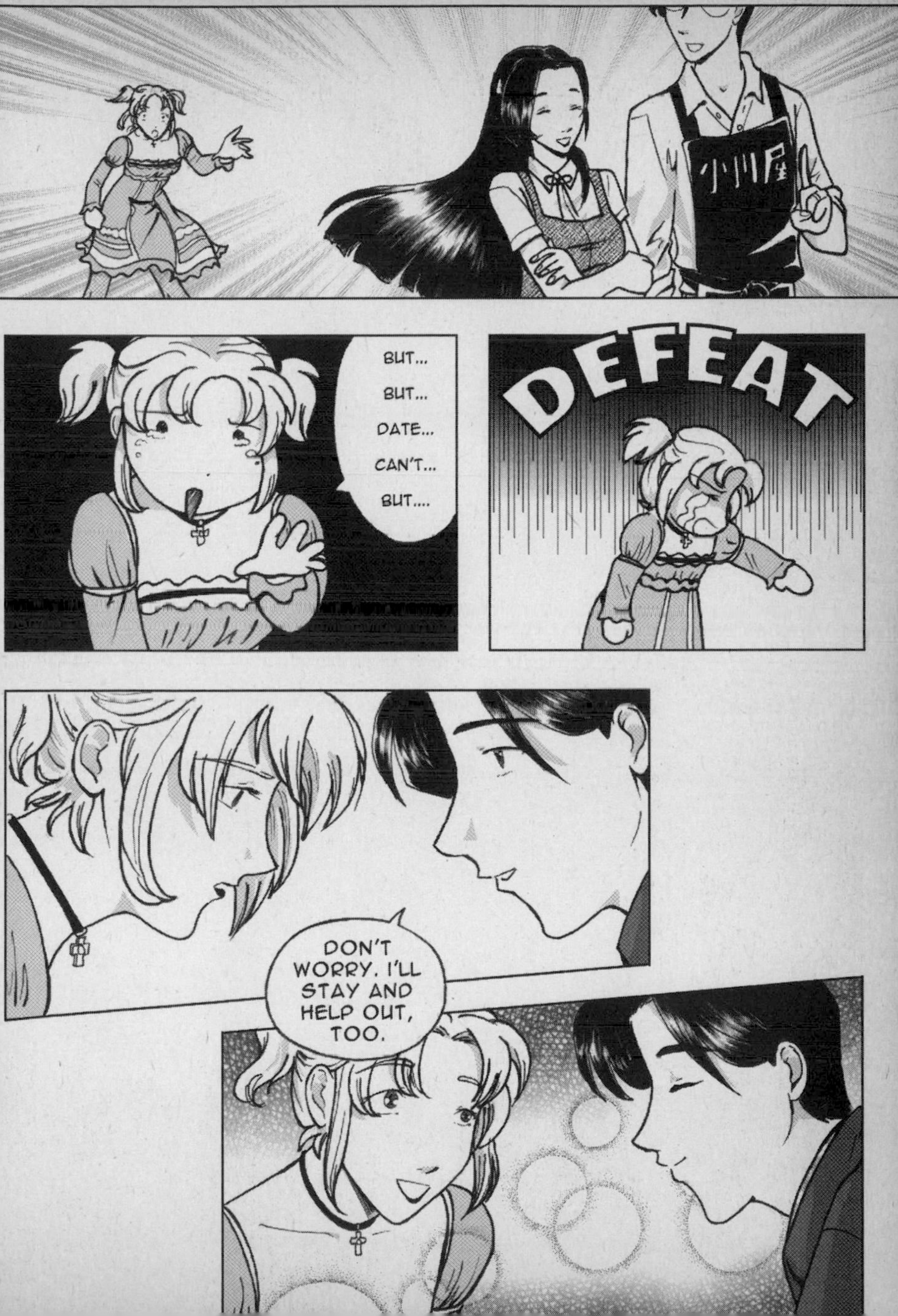
小川屋
BUT... BUT... DATE... CAN'T... BUT....
DEFEAT
DON'T WORRY. I'LL STAY AND HELP OUT, TOO.

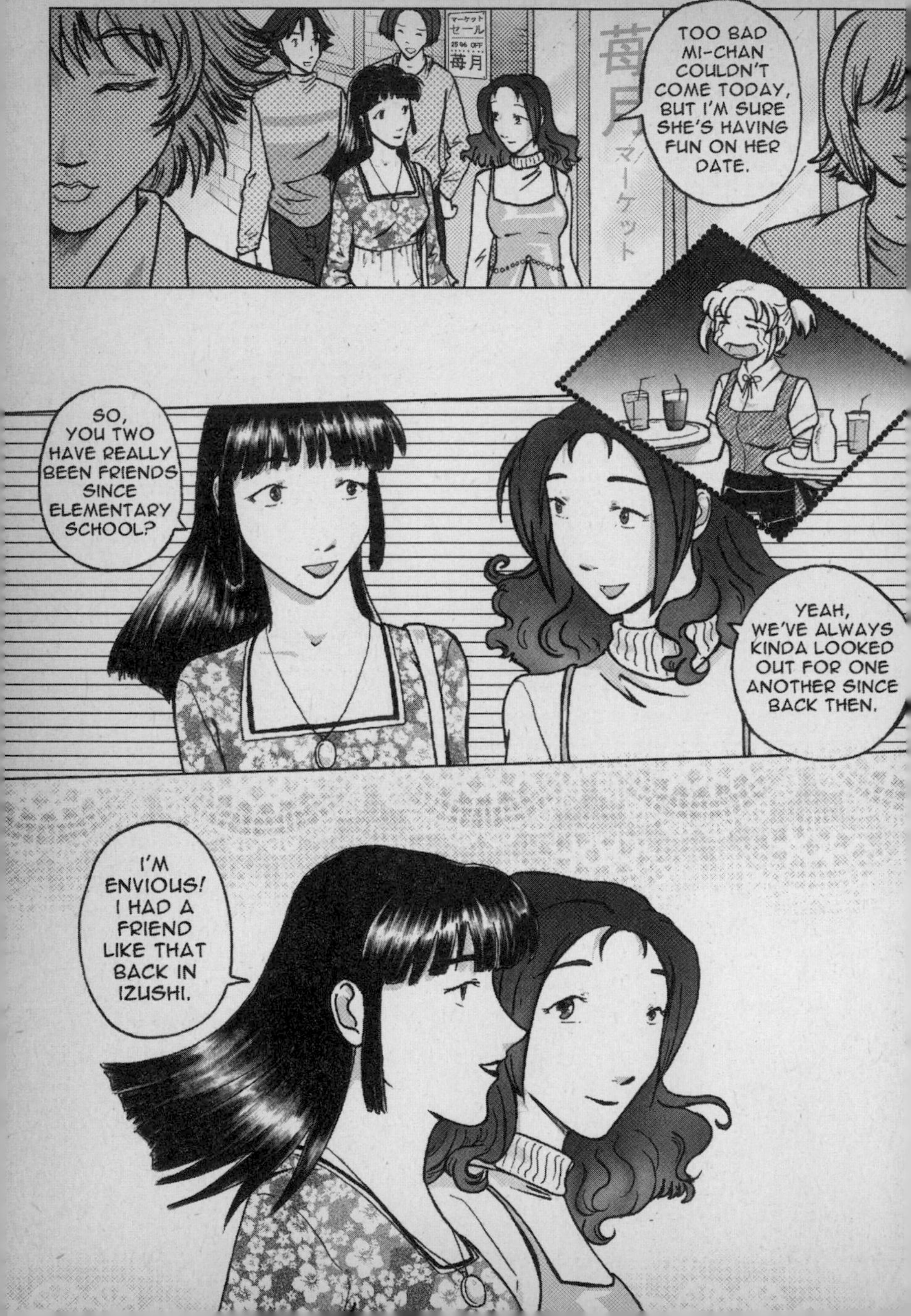
苺月
マーケット
TOO BAD MI-CHAN COULDN'T COME TODAY, BUT I'M SURE SHE'S HAVING FUN ON HER DATE.
SO, YOU TWO HAVE REALLY BEEN FRIENDS SINCE ELEMENTARY SCHOOL?
YEAH, WE'VE ALWAYS KINDA LOOKED OUT FOR ONE ANOTHER SINCE BACK THEN.
I'M ENVIOUS! I HAD A FRIEND LIKE THAT BACK IN IZUSHI.

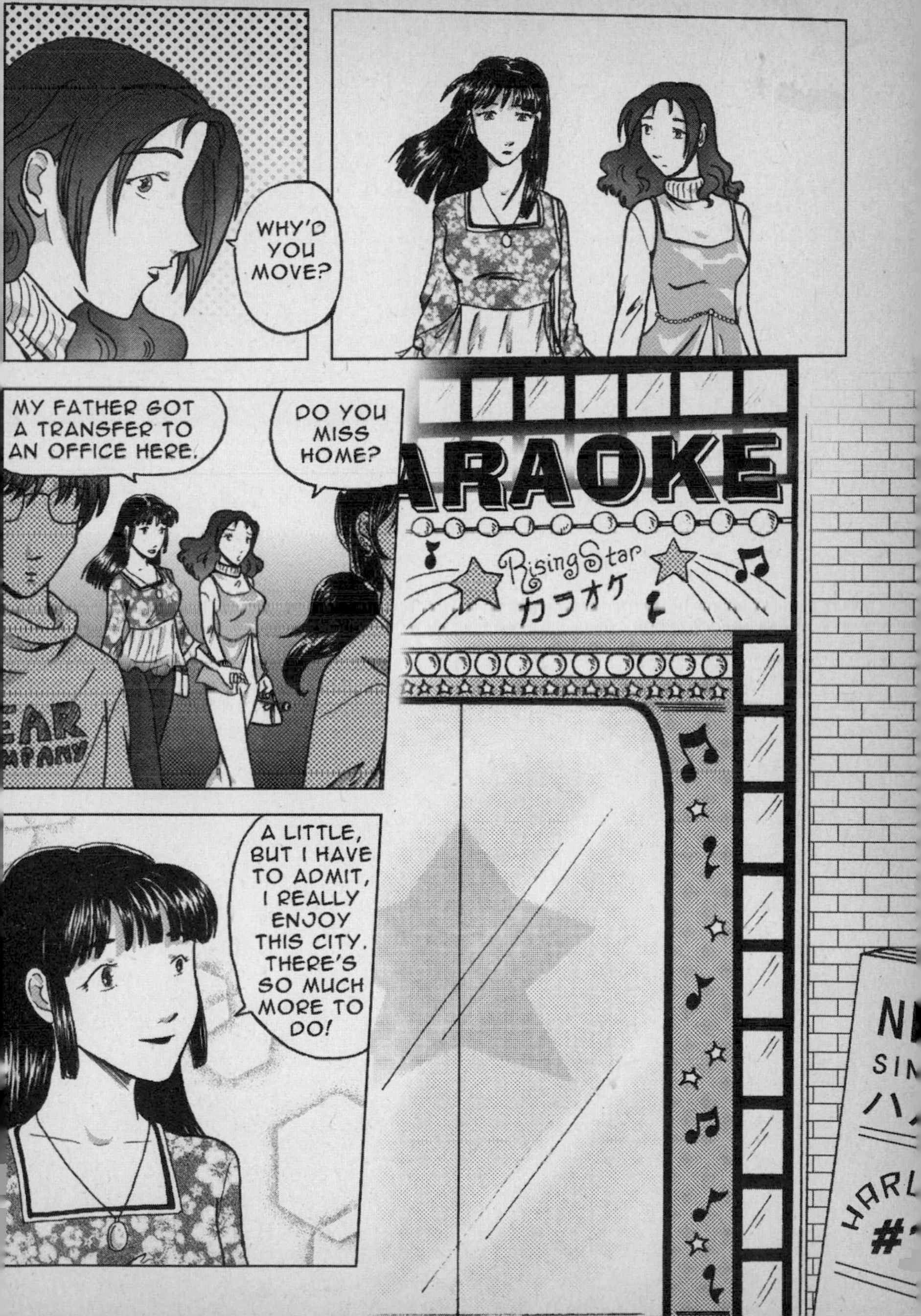
WHY'D YOU MOVE?
MY FATHER GOT A TRANSFER TO AN OFFICE HERE.
DO YOU MISS HOME?
ARAOKE
RisingStar
カラオケ
A LITTLE, BUT I HAVE TO ADMIT, I REALLY ENJOY THIS CITY. THERE'S SO MUCH MORE TO DO!

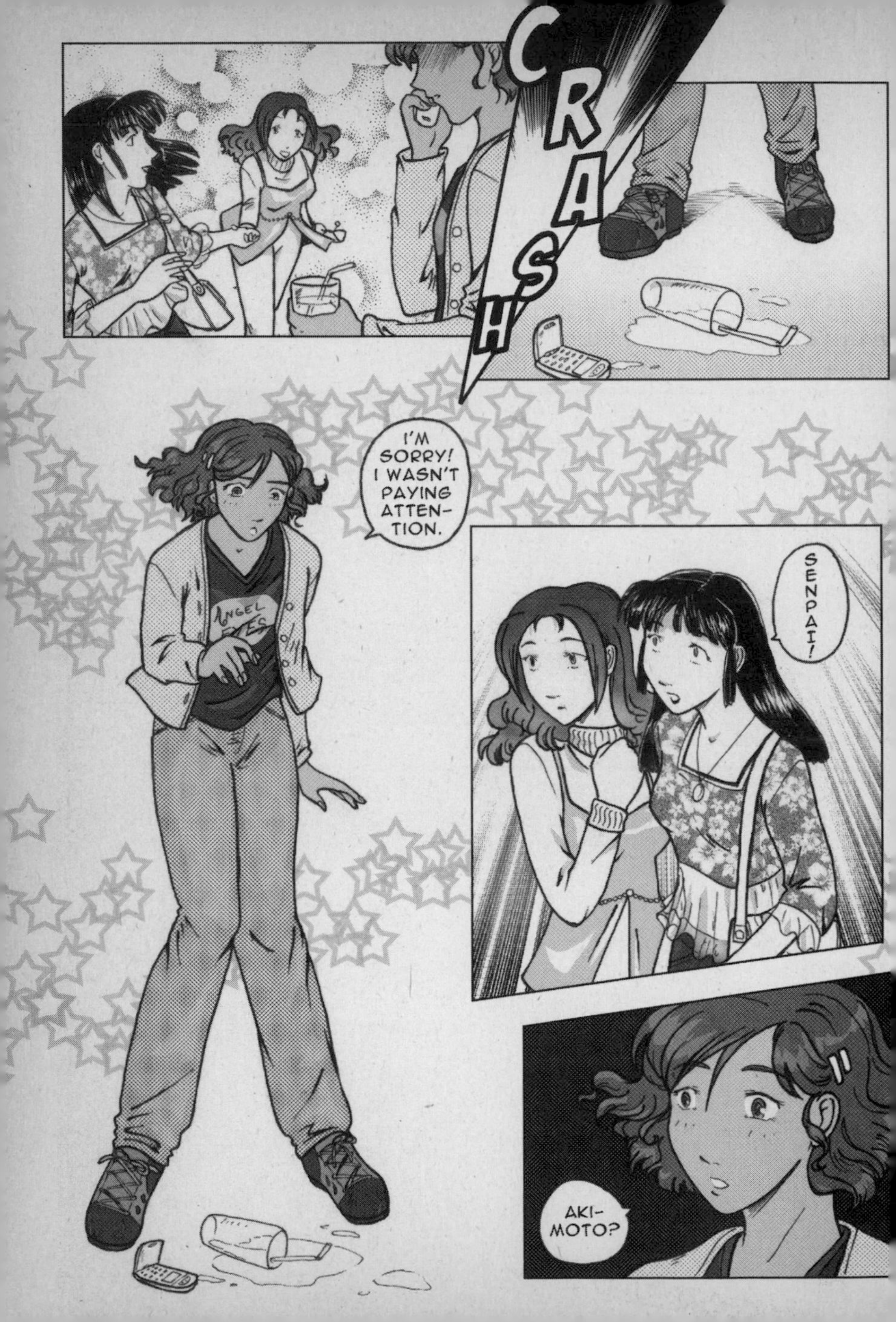
CRASH
I'M SORRY! I WASN'T PAYING ATTEN-TION.
ANGEL EYES
SENPAI!
AKI-MOTO?

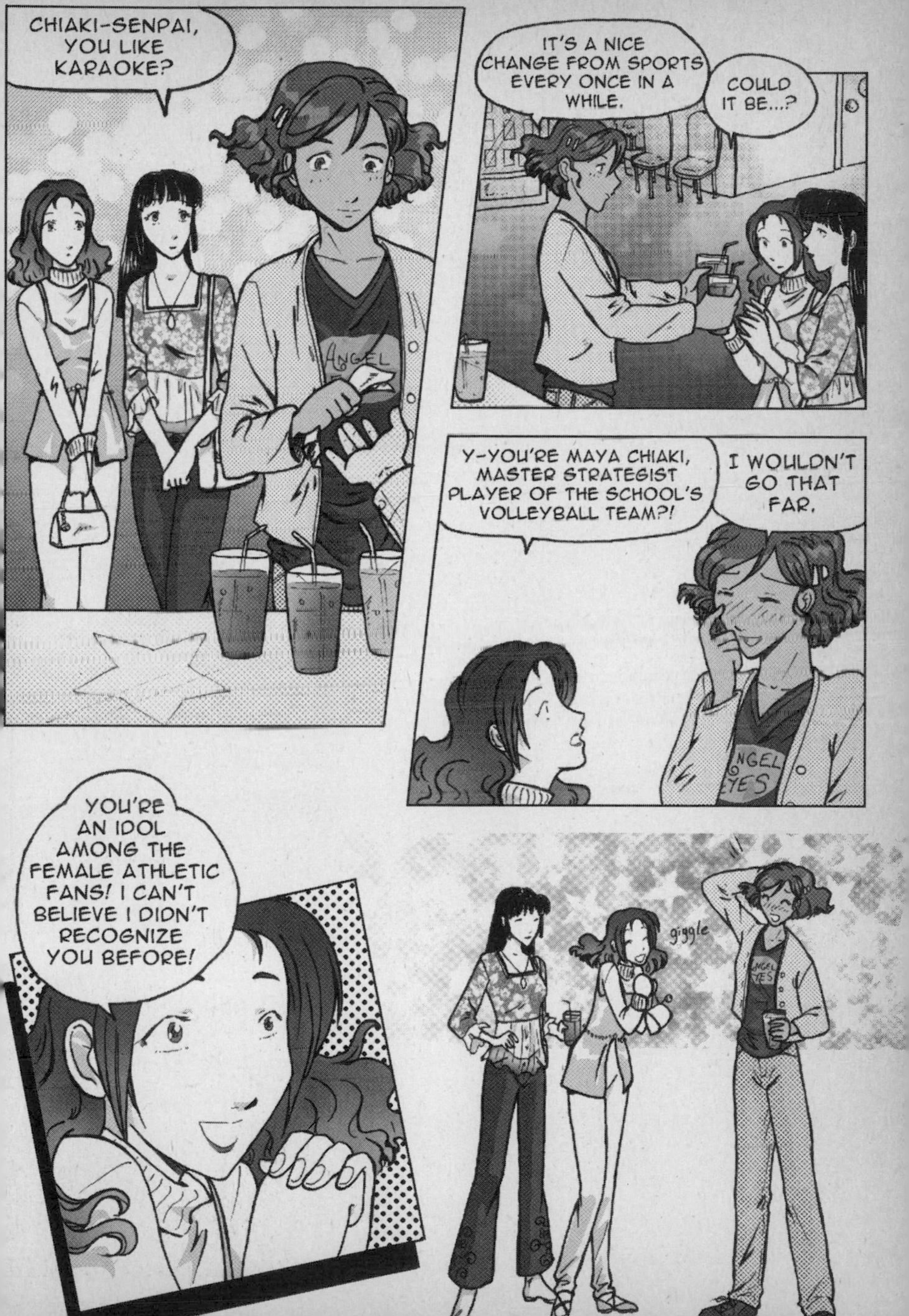
CHIAKI-SENPAI, YOU LIKE KARAOKE?
IT'S A NICE CHANGE FROM SPORTS EVERY ONCE IN A WHILE.
COULD IT BE...?
ANGEL
Y-YOU'RE MAYA CHIAKI, MASTER STRATEGIST PLAYER OF THE SCHOOL'S VOLLEYBALL TEAM?!
I WOULDN'T GO THAT FAR.
YOU'RE AN IDOL AMONG THE FEMALE ATHLETIC FANS! I CAN'T BELIEVE I DIDN'T RECOGNIZE YOU BEFORE!
giggle

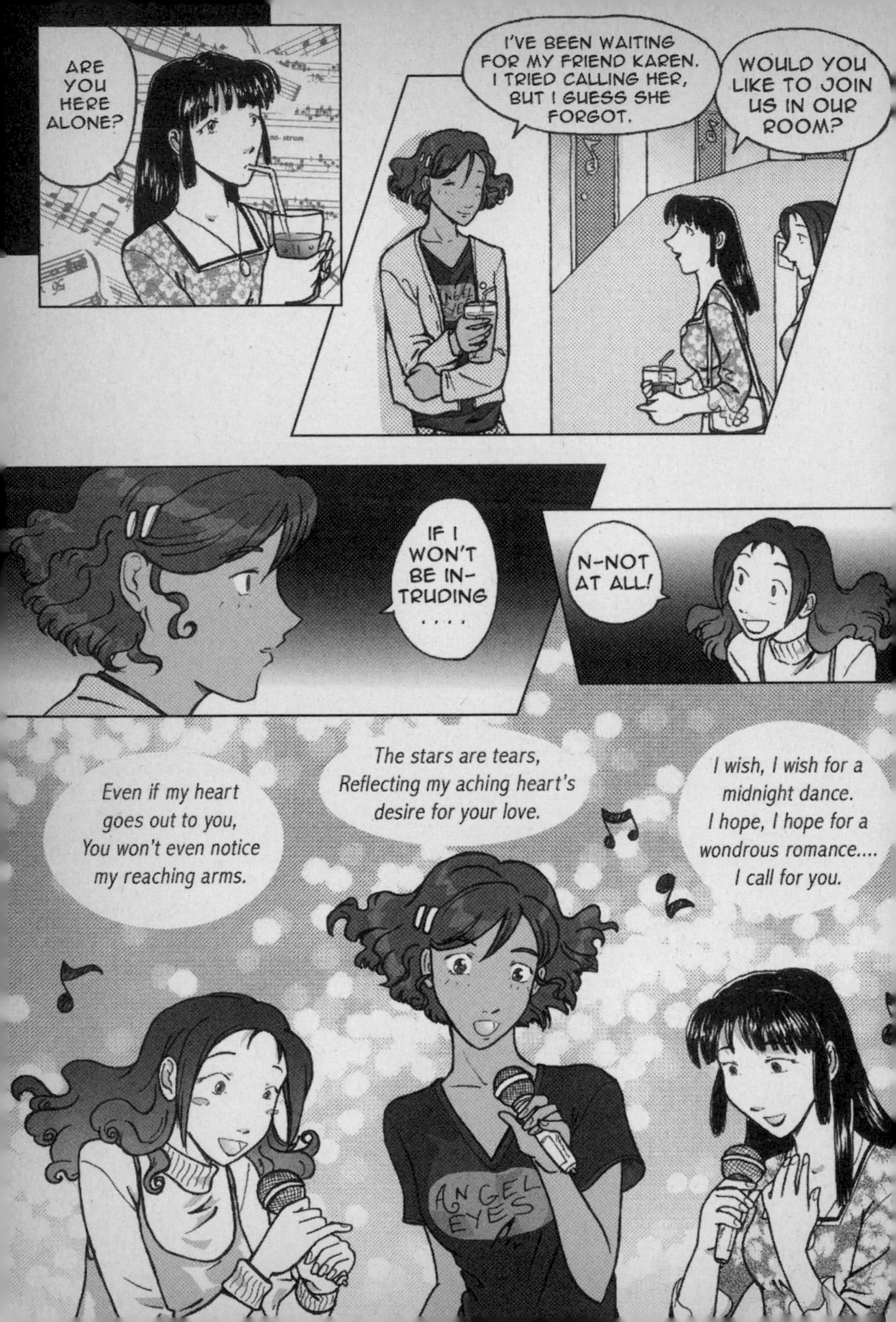
ARE YOU HERE ALONE?
I'VE BEEN WAITING FOR MY FRIEND KAREN. I TRIED CALLING HER, BUT I GUESS SHE FORGOT.
WOULD YOU LIKE TO JOIN US IN OUR ROOM?
IF I WON'T BE IN-TRUDING . . . .
N-NOT AT ALL!
Even if my heart goes out to you, You won't even notice my reaching arms.
The stars are tears, Reflecting my aching heart's desire for your love.
I wish, I wish for a midnight dance. I hope, I hope for a wondrous romance.... I call for you.
ANGEL EYES

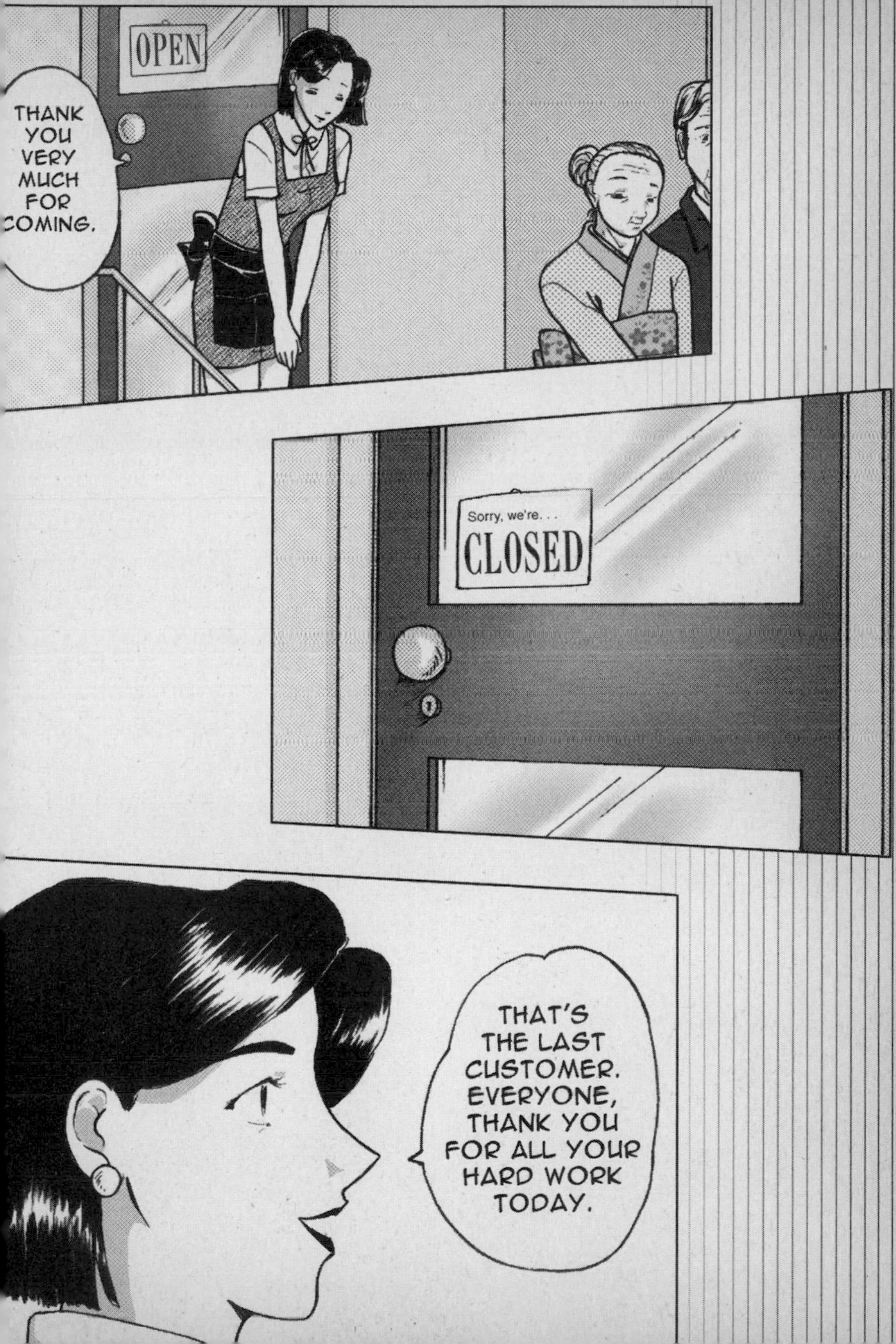
OPEN
THANK YOU VERY MUCH FOR COMING.
Sorry, we're. . .
CLOSED
THAT'S THE LAST CUSTOMER. EVERYONE, THANK YOU FOR ALL YOUR HARD WORK TODAY.

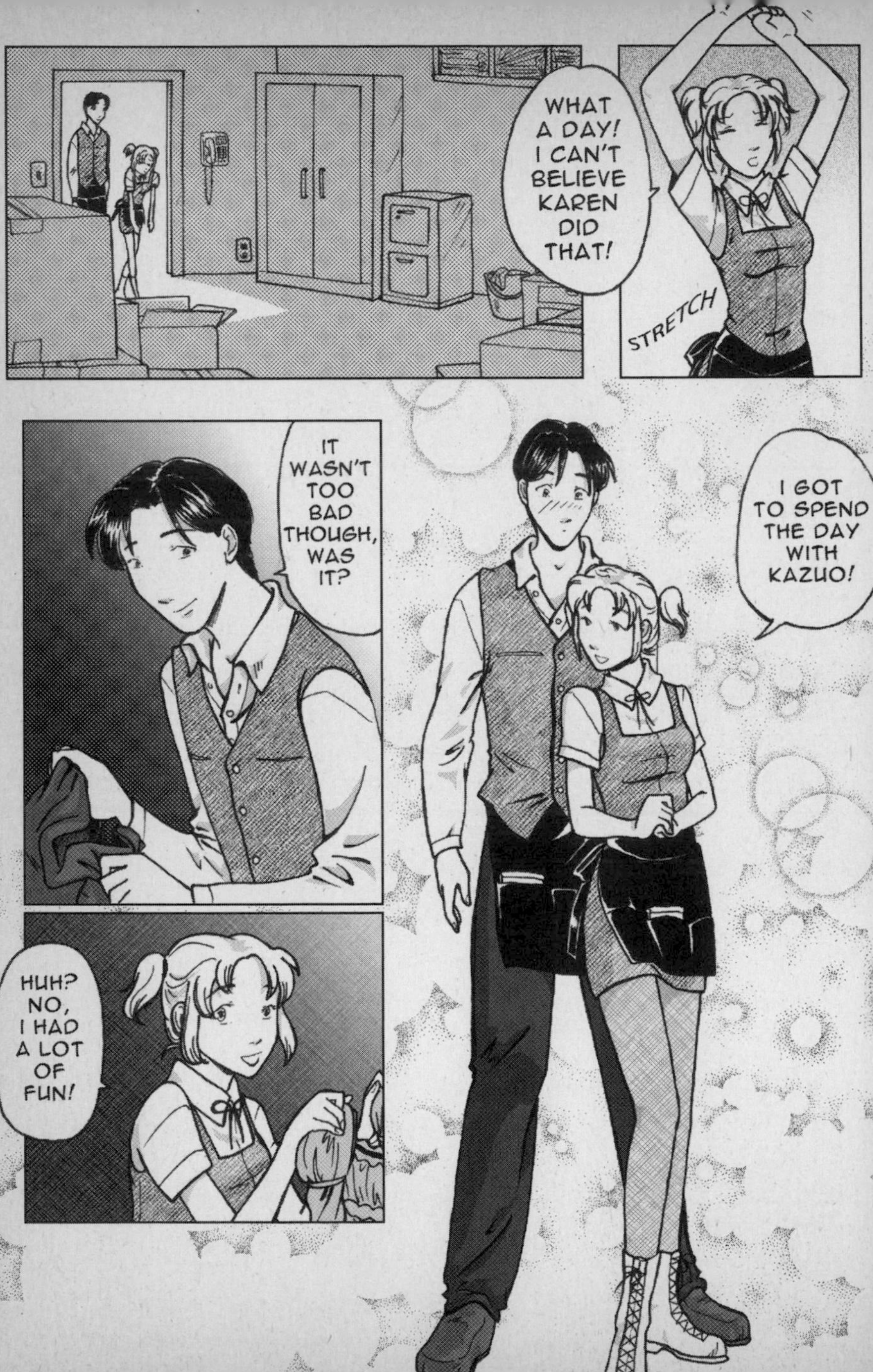
WHAT A DAY! I CAN'T BELIEVE KAREN DID THAT!
STRETCH
IT WASN'T TOO BAD THOUGH, WAS IT?
HUH? NO, I HAD A LOT OF FUN!
I GOT TO SPEND THE DAY WITH KAZUO!

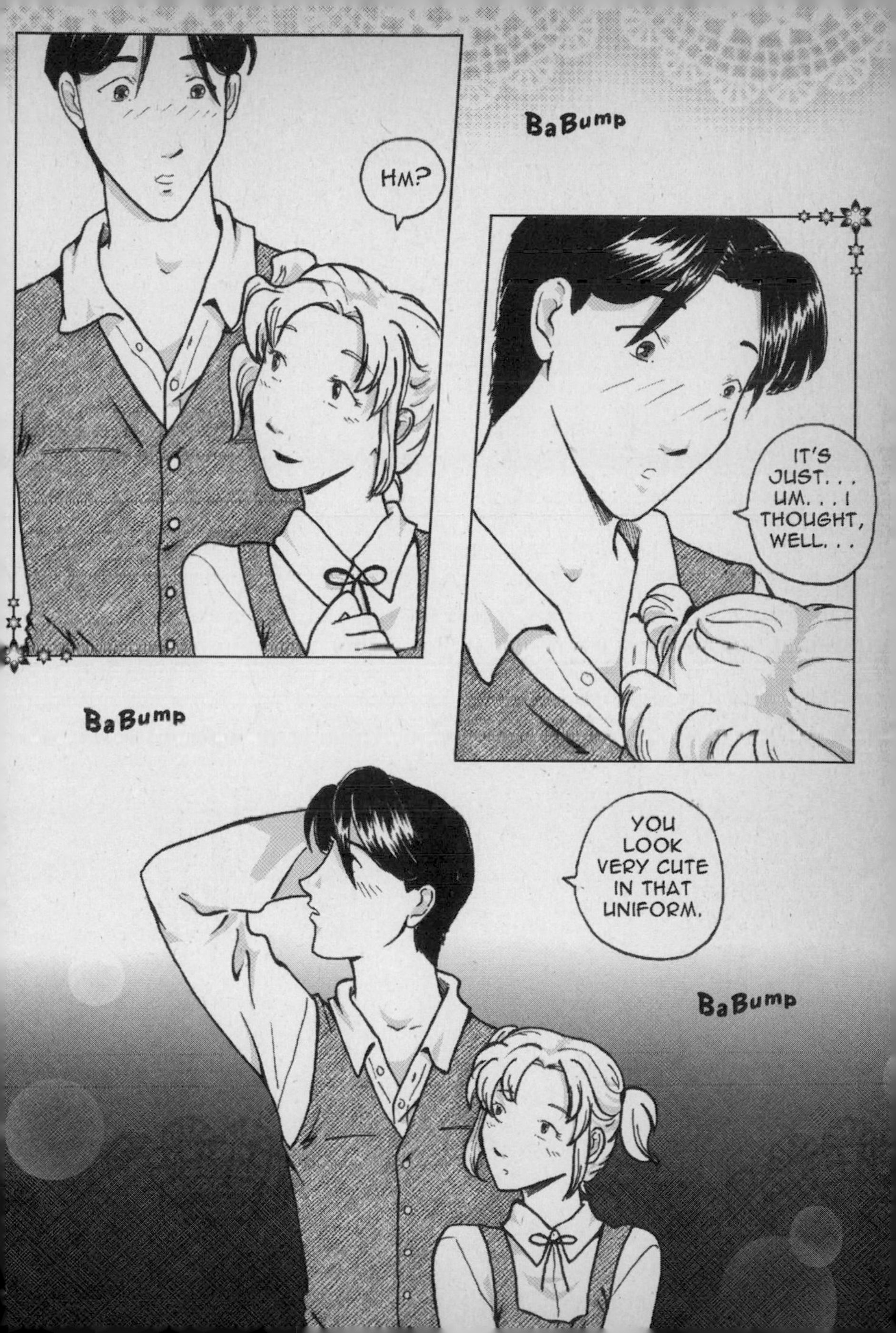
HM?
BaBump
IT'S JUST. . . UM. . . I THOUGHT, WELL. . .
BaBump
YOU LOOK VERY CUTE IN THAT UNIFORM.
BaBump

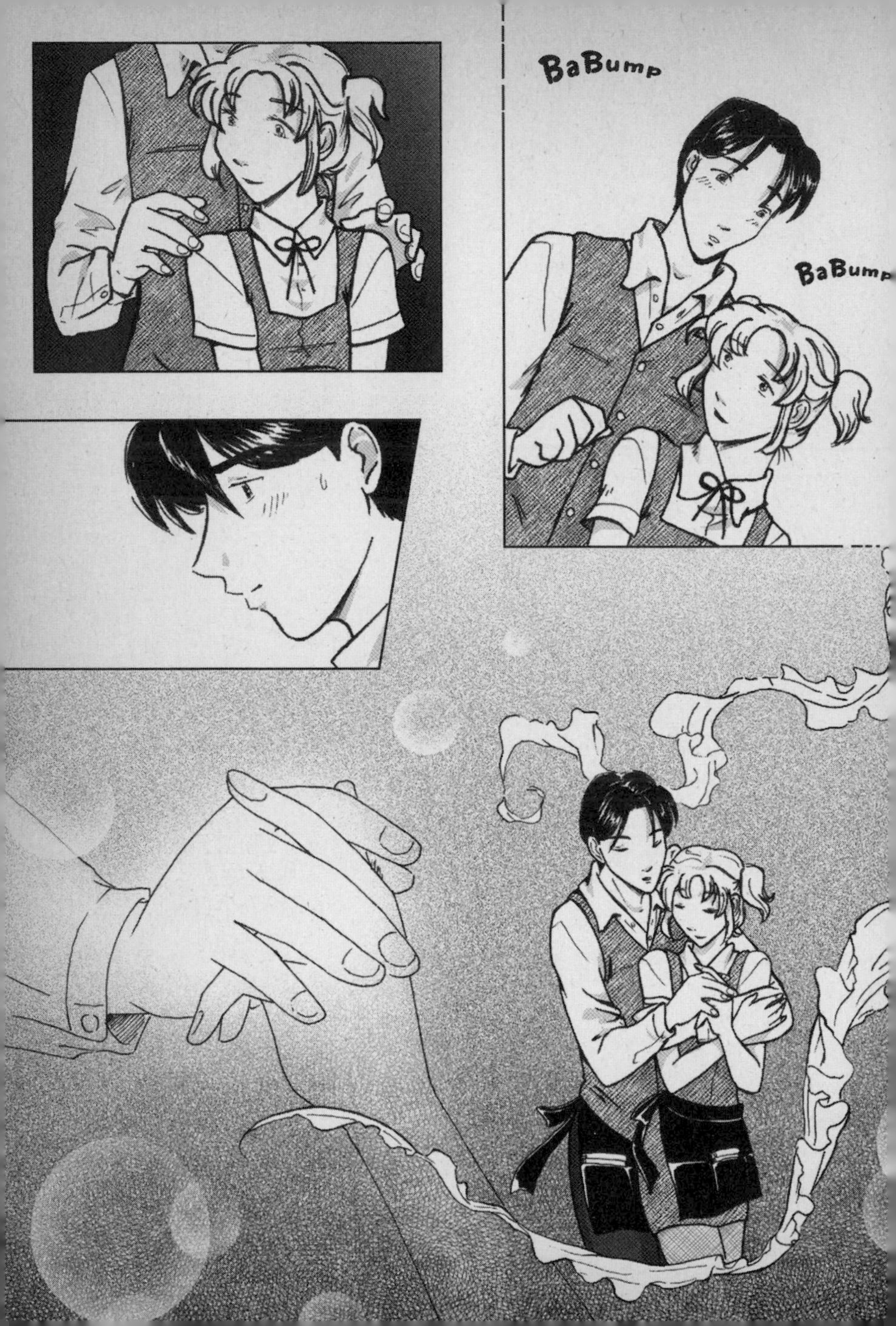
BaBump
BaBump

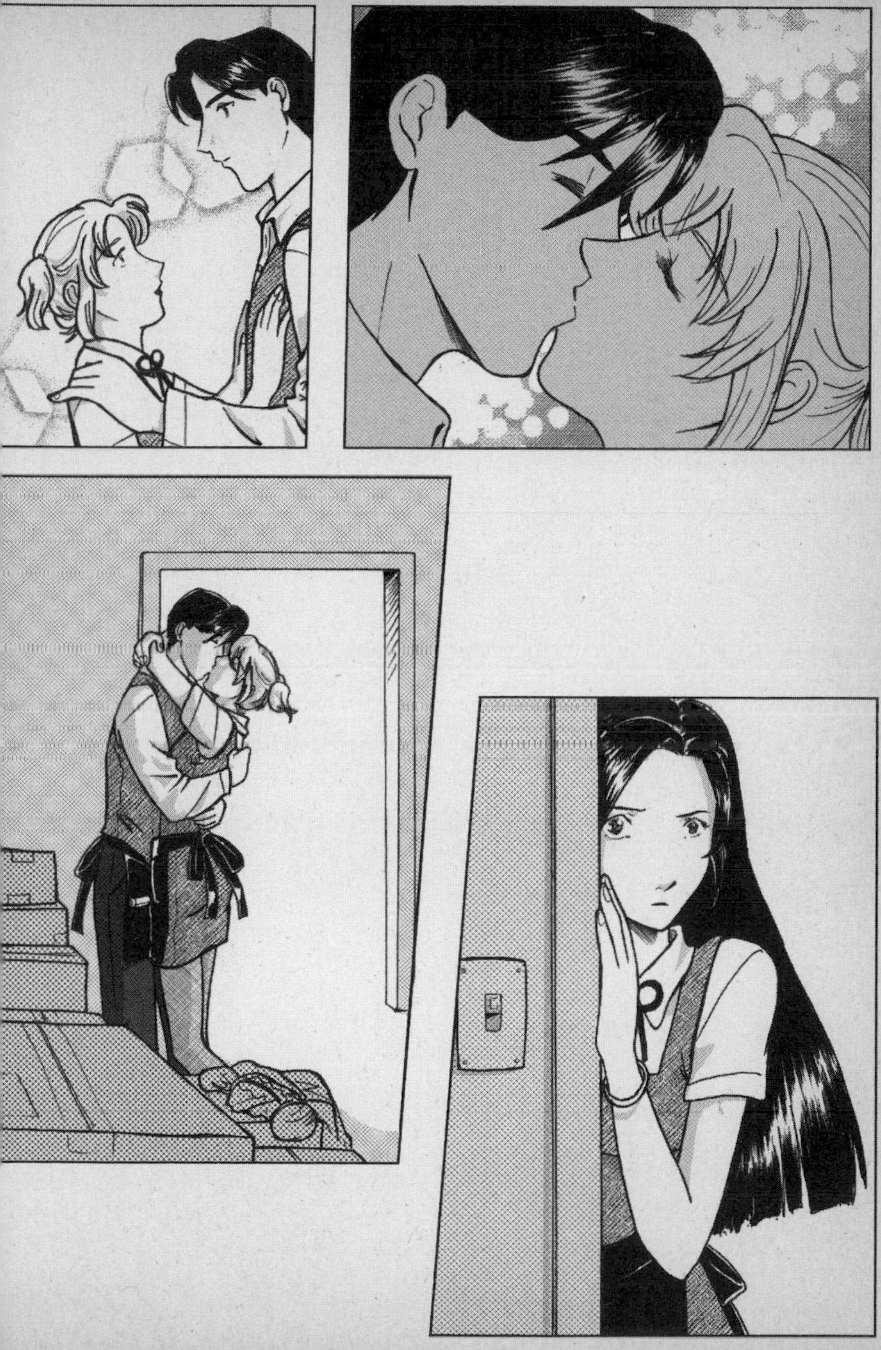

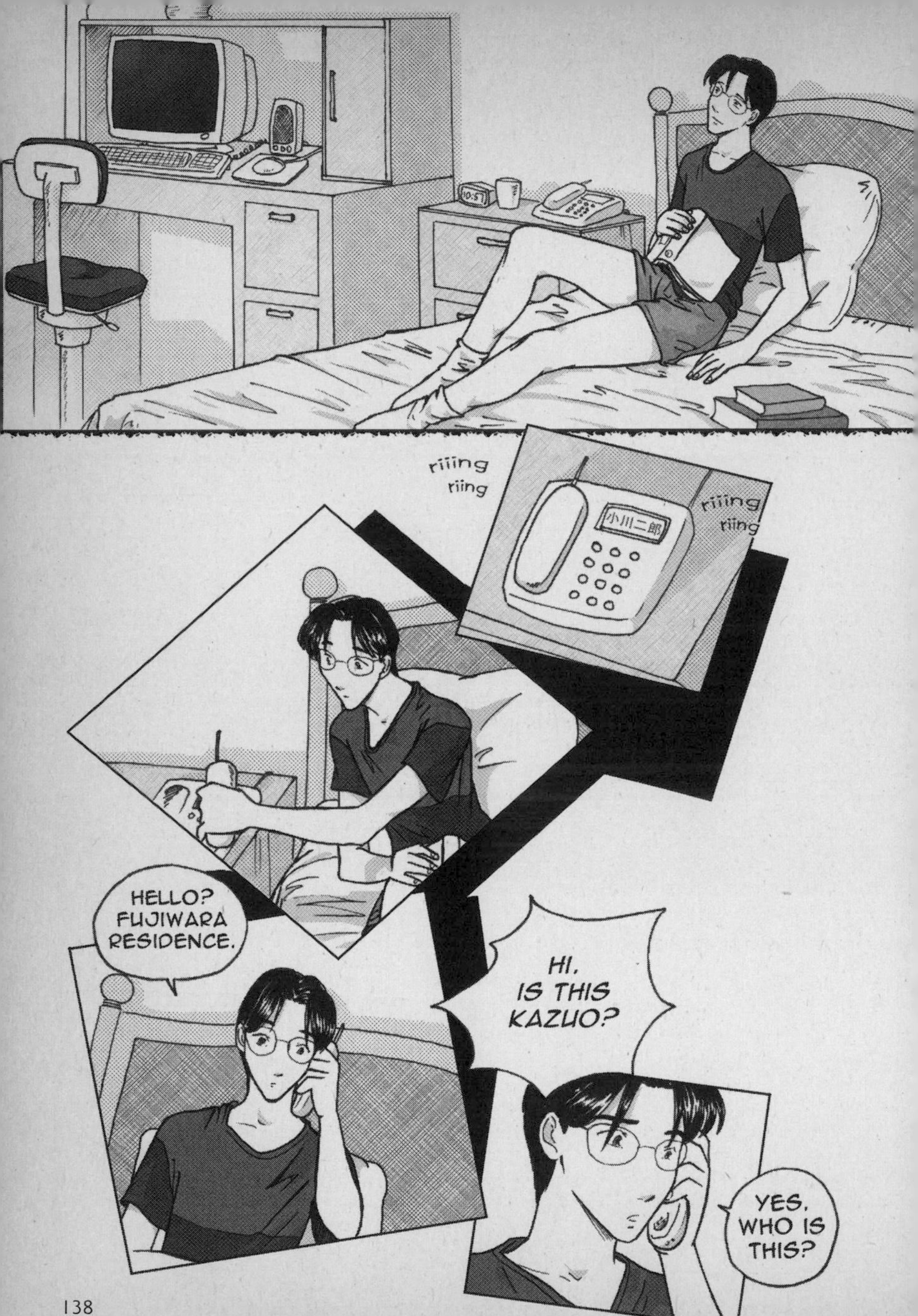
riiing
riing
小川二郎
riiing
riing
HELLO? FUJIWARA RESIDENCE.
HI. IS THIS KAZUO?
YES. WHO IS THIS?

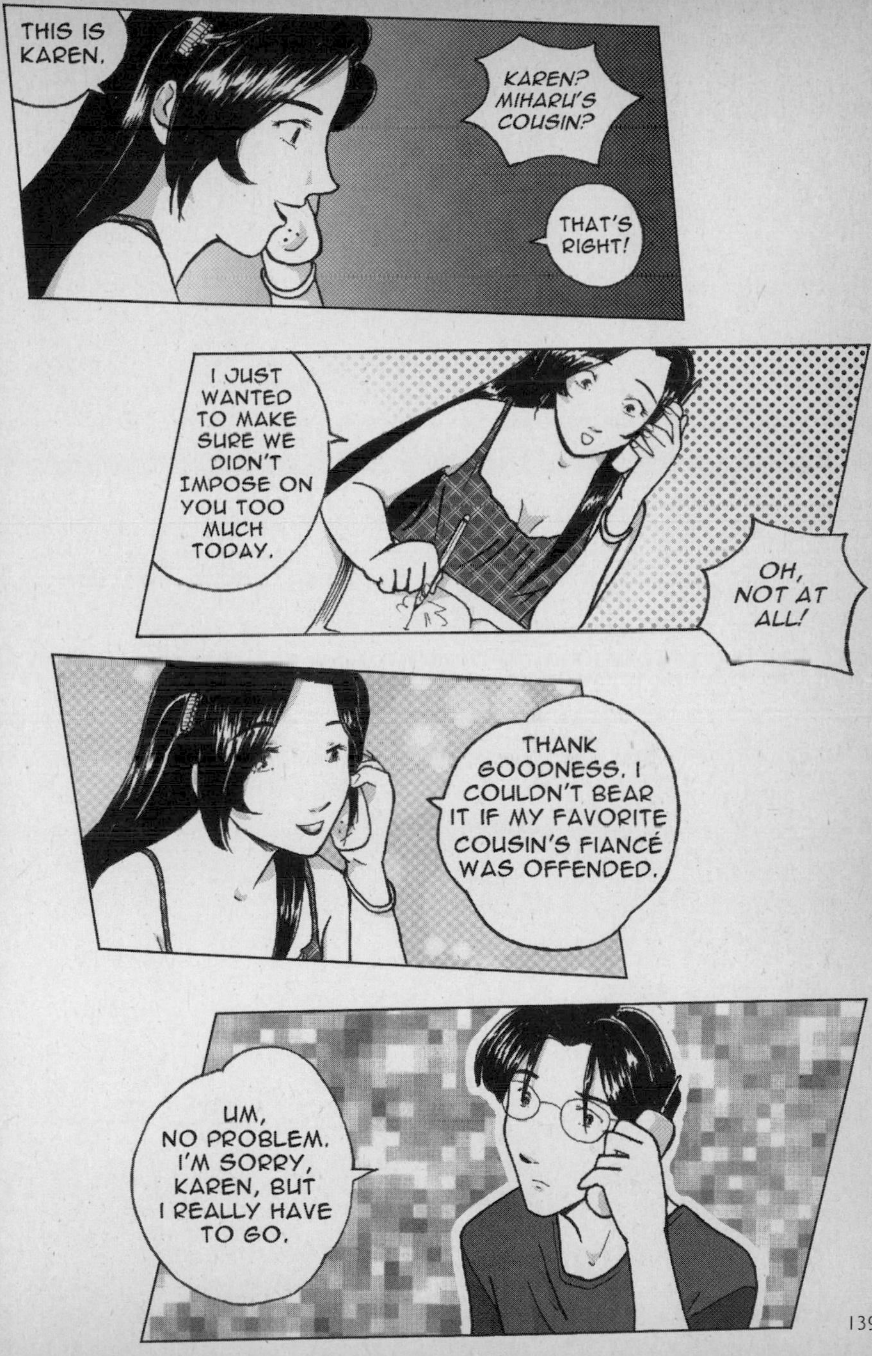
THIS IS KAREN.
KAREN? MIHARU'S COUSIN?
THAT'S RIGHT!
I JUST WANTED TO MAKE SURE WE DIDN'T IMPOSE ON YOU TOO MUCH TODAY.
OH, NOT AT ALL!
THANK GOODNESS. I COULDN'T BEAR IT IF MY FAVORITE COUSIN'S FIANCÉ WAS OFFENDED.
UM, NO PROBLEM. I'M SORRY, KAREN, BUT I REALLY HAVE TO GO.

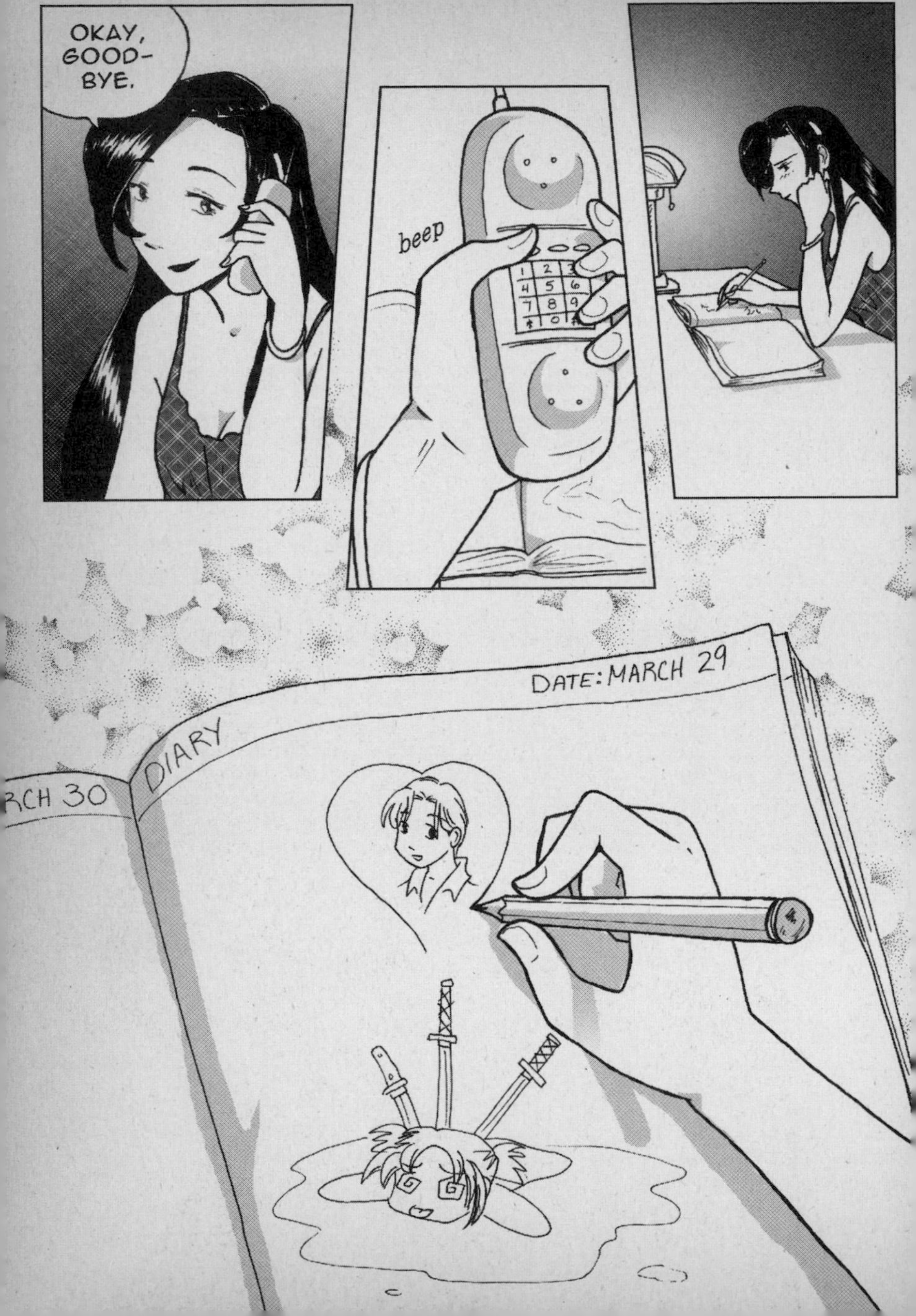
OKAY, GOOD-BYE.
beep
DATE: MARCH 29
DIARY
RCH 30

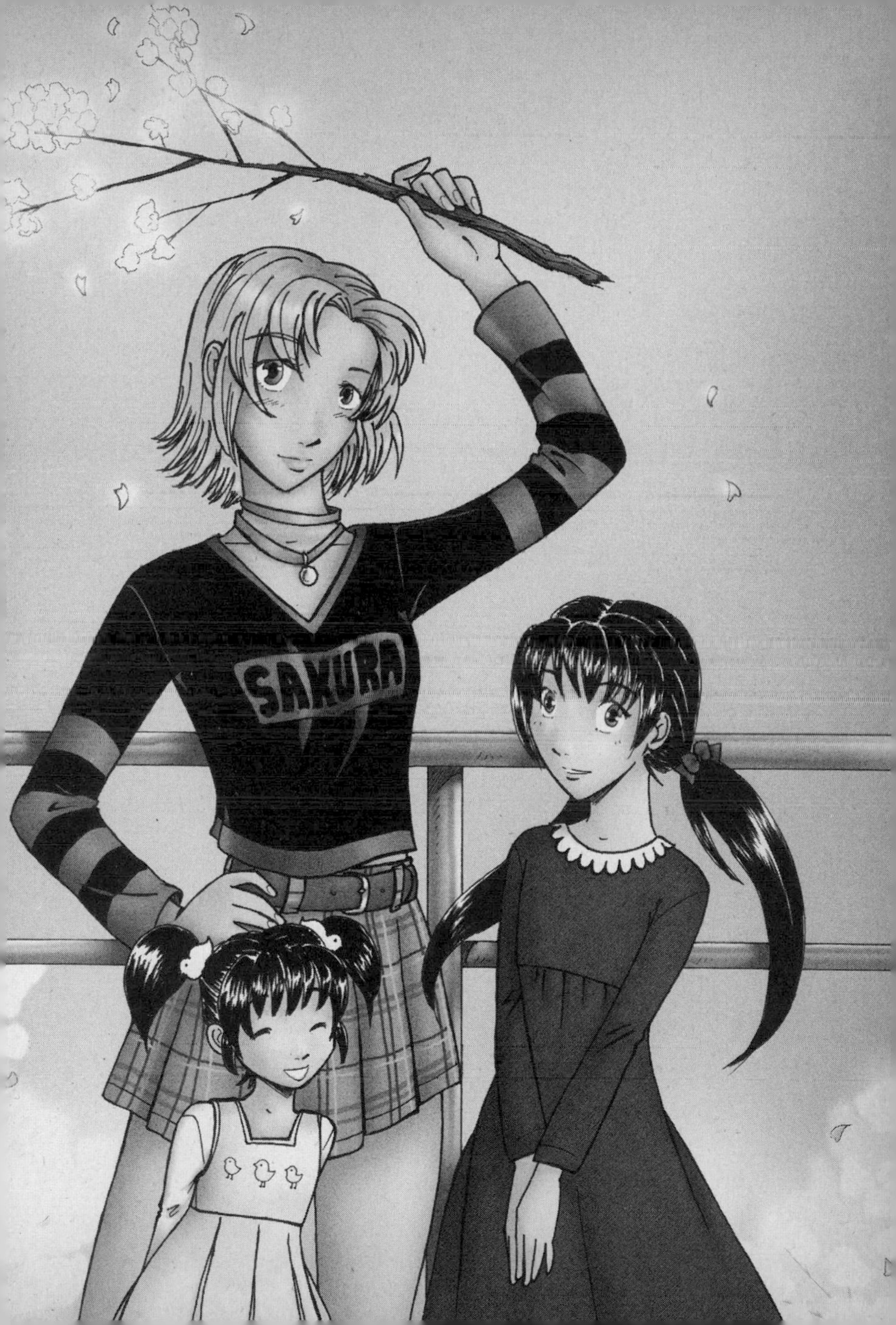
SAKURA

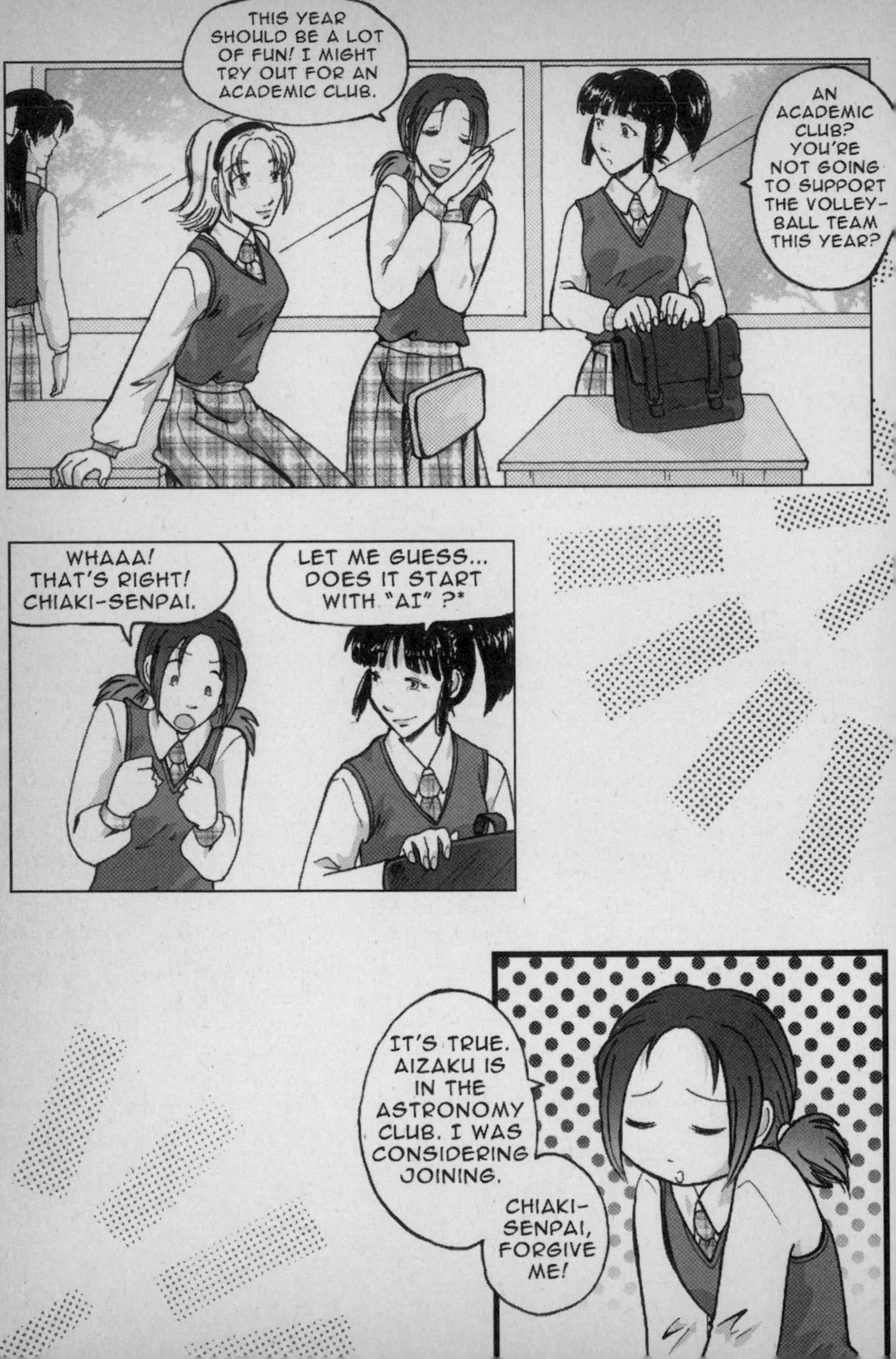
THIS YEAR SHOULD BE A LOT OF FUN! I MIGHT TRY OUT FOR AN ACADEMIC CLUB.
AN ACADEMIC CLUB? YOU'RE NOT GOING TO SUPPORT THE VOLLEY-BALL TEAM THIS YEAR?
WHAAA! THAT'S RIGHT! CHIAKI-SENPAI.
LET ME GUESS... DOES IT START WITH "AI" ?*
IT'S TRUE. AIZAKU IS IN THE ASTRONOMY CLUB. I WAS CONSIDERING JOINING.
CHIAKI-SENPAI, FORGIVE ME!

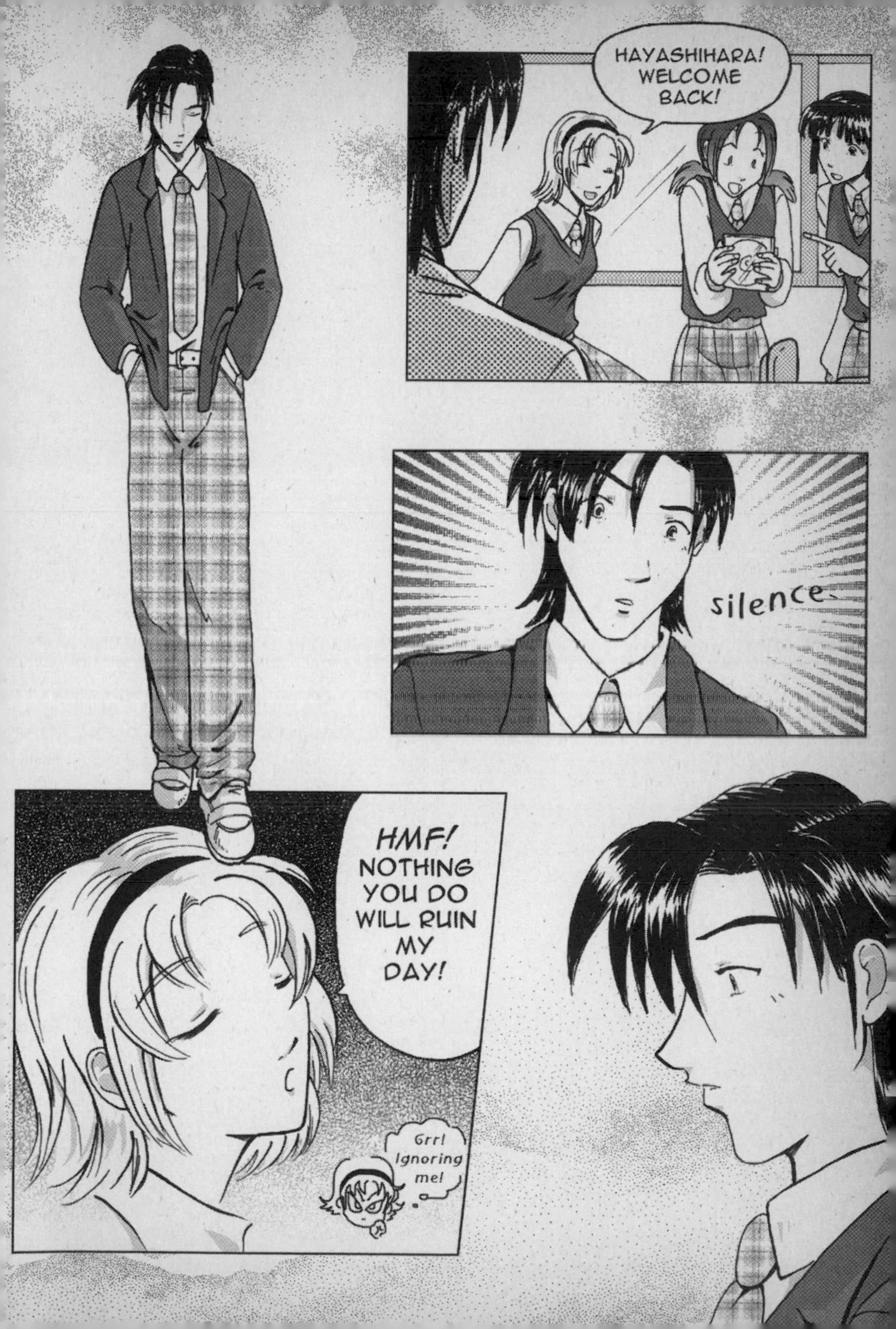
HAYASHIHARA! WELCOME BACK!
silence
HMF! NOTHING YOU DO WILL RUIN MY DAY!
Grr! Ignoring me!

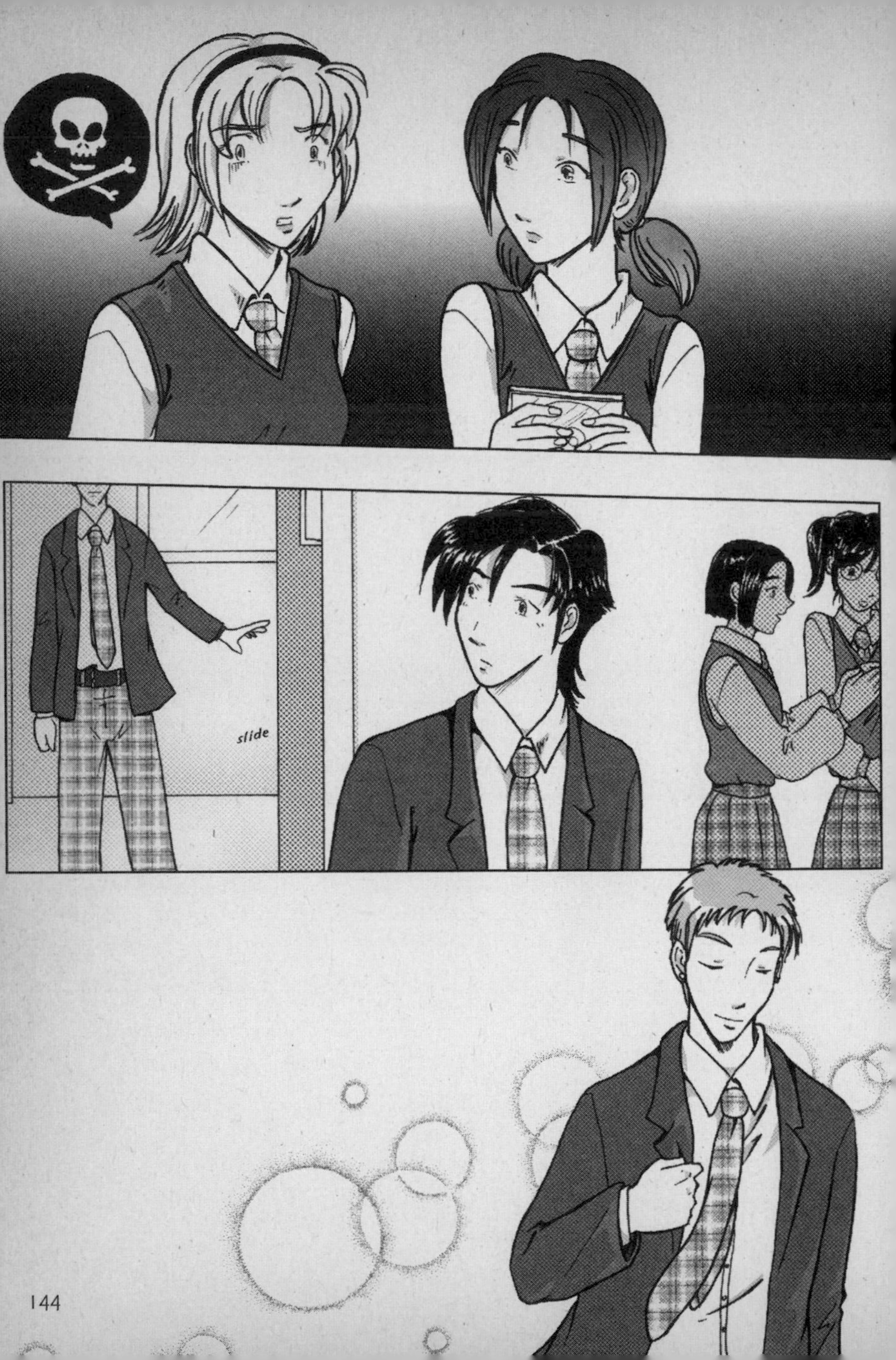
slide

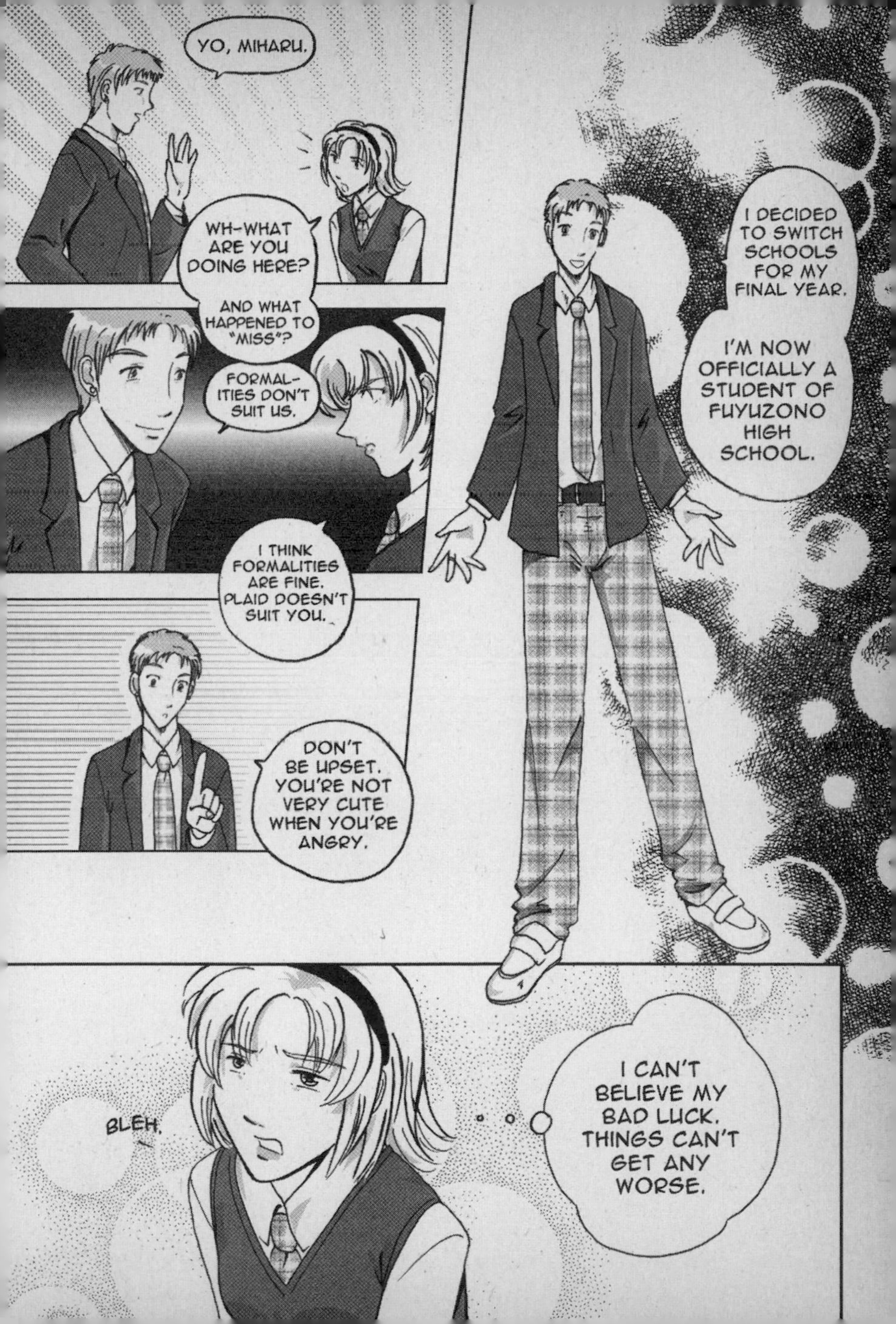
YO, MIHARU.
WH-WHAT ARE YOU DOING HERE?
AND WHAT HAPPENED TO "MISS"?
FORMAL-ITIES DON'T SUIT US.
I THINK FORMALITIES ARE FINE. PLAID DOESN'T SUIT YOU.
DON'T BE UPSET. YOU'RE NOT VERY CUTE WHEN YOU'RE ANGRY.
I DECIDED TO SWITCH SCHOOLS FOR MY FINAL YEAR.
I'M NOW OFFICIALLY A STUDENT OF FUYUZONO HIGH SCHOOL.
BLEH.
I CAN'T BELIEVE MY BAD LUCK. THINGS CAN'T GET ANY WORSE.

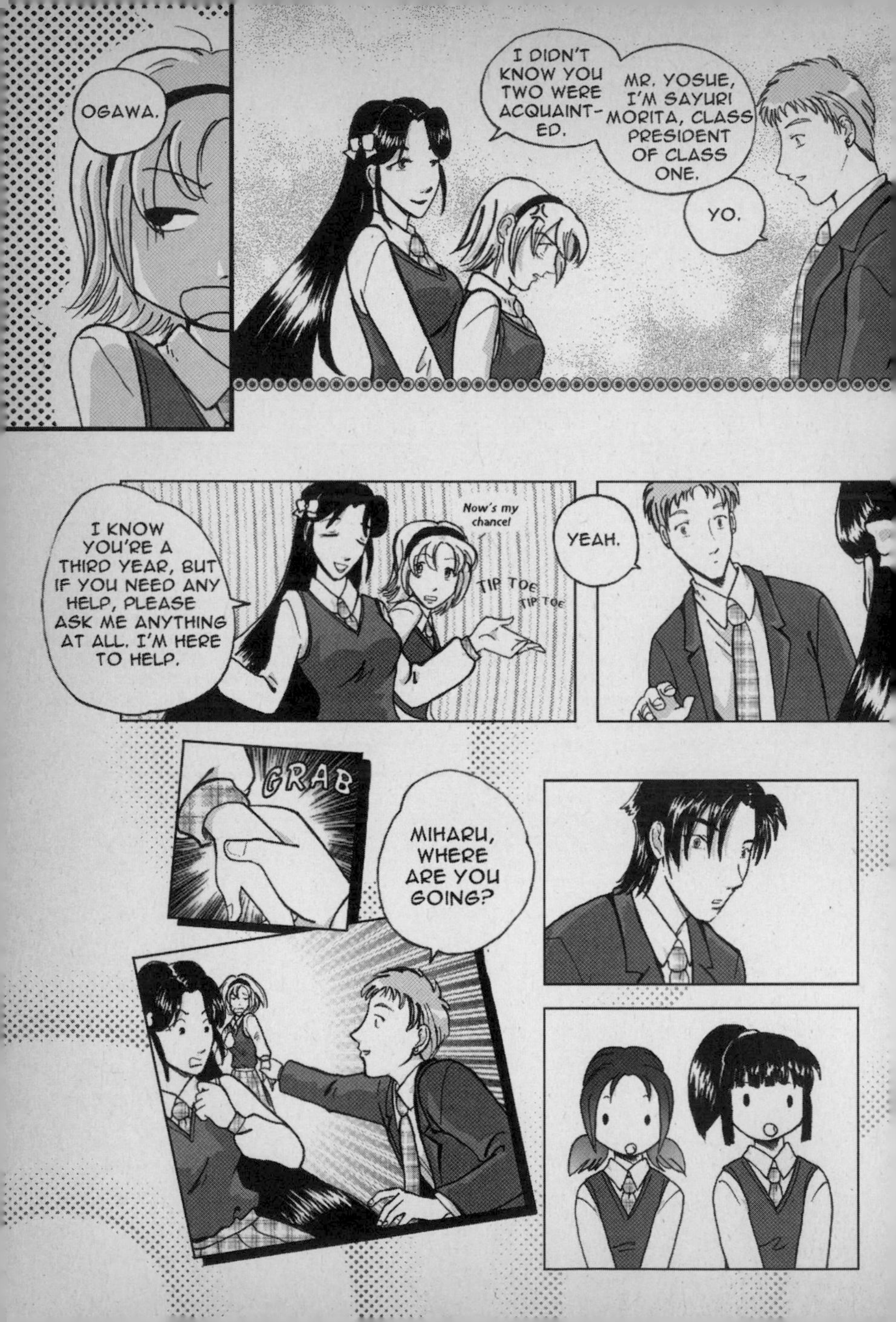
I DIDN'T KNOW YOU TWO WERE ACQUAINT-ED.
MR. YOSUE, I'M SAYURI MORITA, CLASS PRESIDENT OF CLASS ONE.
YO.
OGAWA.
I KNOW YOU'RE A THIRD YEAR, BUT IF YOU NEED ANY HELP, PLEASE ASK ME ANYTHING AT ALL. I'M HERE TO HELP.
Now's my chance!
TIP TOE
TIP TOE
YEAH.
GRAB
MIHARU, WHERE ARE YOU GOING?

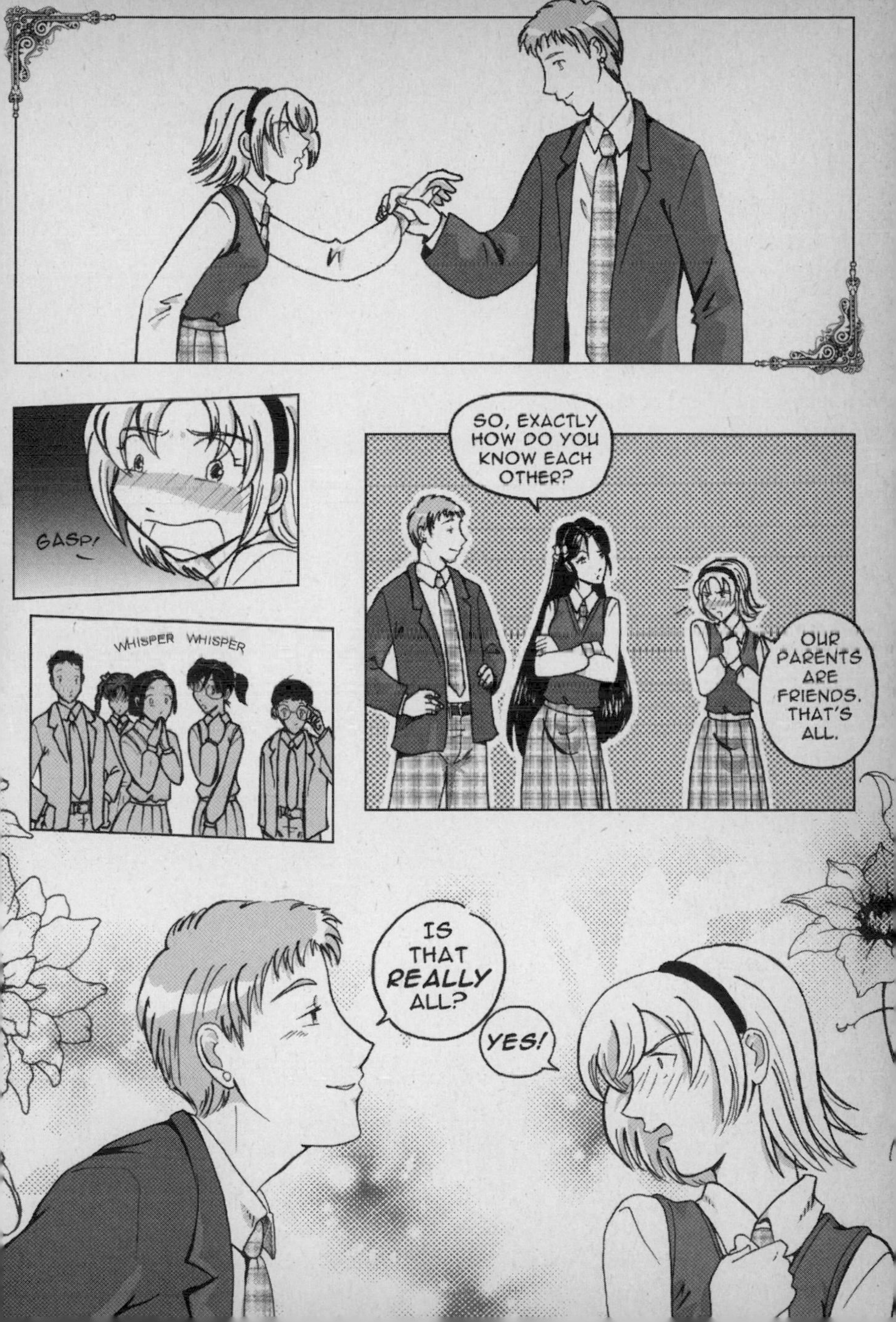
GASP!
WHISPER WHISPER
SO, EXACTLY HOW DO YOU KNOW EACH OTHER?
OUR PARENTS ARE FRIENDS. THAT'S ALL.
IS THAT REALLY ALL?
YES!

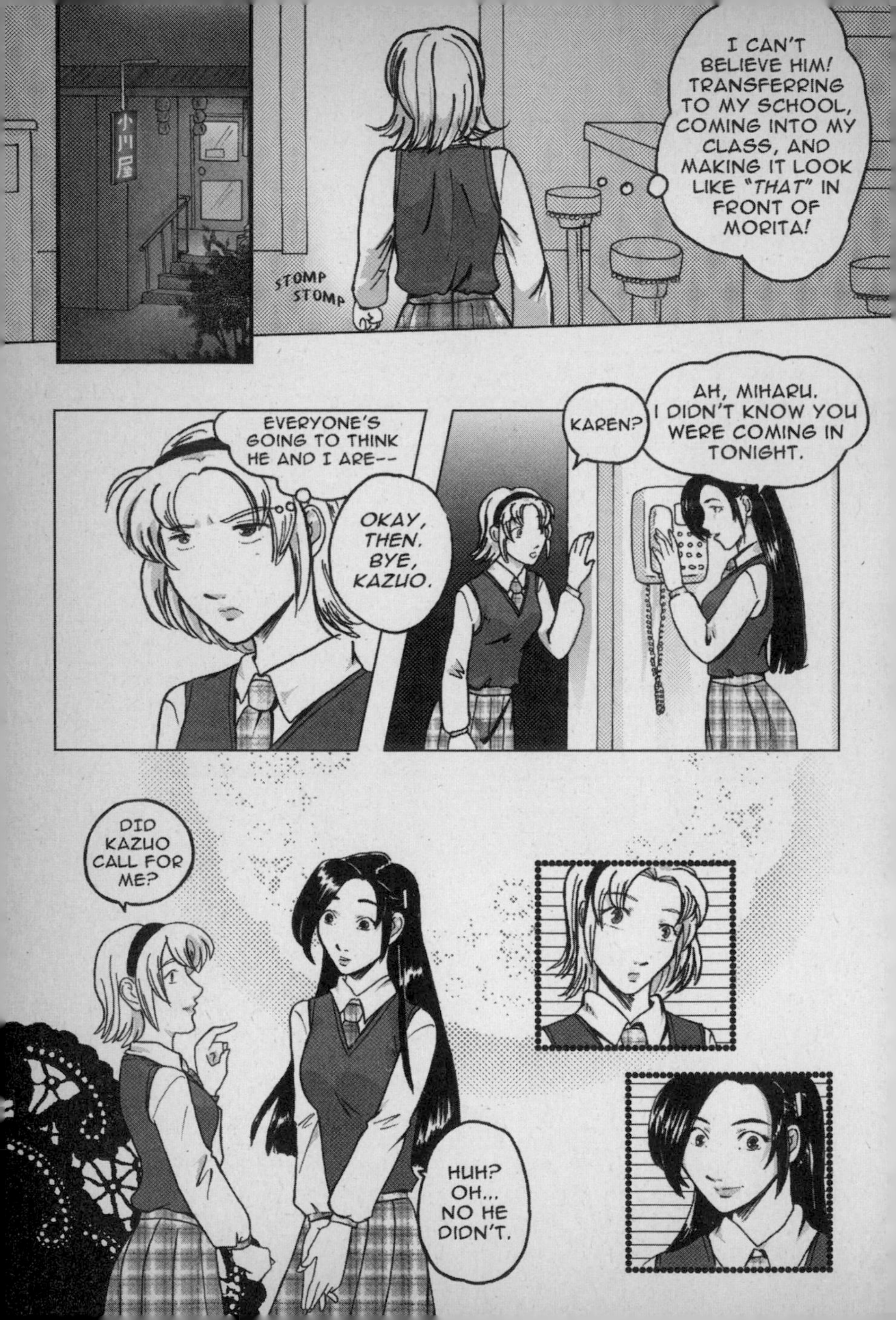
小川屋
STOMP STOMP
I CAN'T BELIEVE HIM! TRANSFERRING TO MY SCHOOL, COMING INTO MY CLASS, AND MAKING IT LOOK LIKE *"THAT"* IN FRONT OF MORITA!
EVERYONE'S GOING TO THINK HE AND I ARE--
OKAY, THEN. BYE, KAZUO.
KAREN?
AH, MIHARU. I DIDN'T KNOW YOU WERE COMING IN TONIGHT.
DID KAZUO CALL FOR ME?
HUH? OH... NO HE DIDN'T.

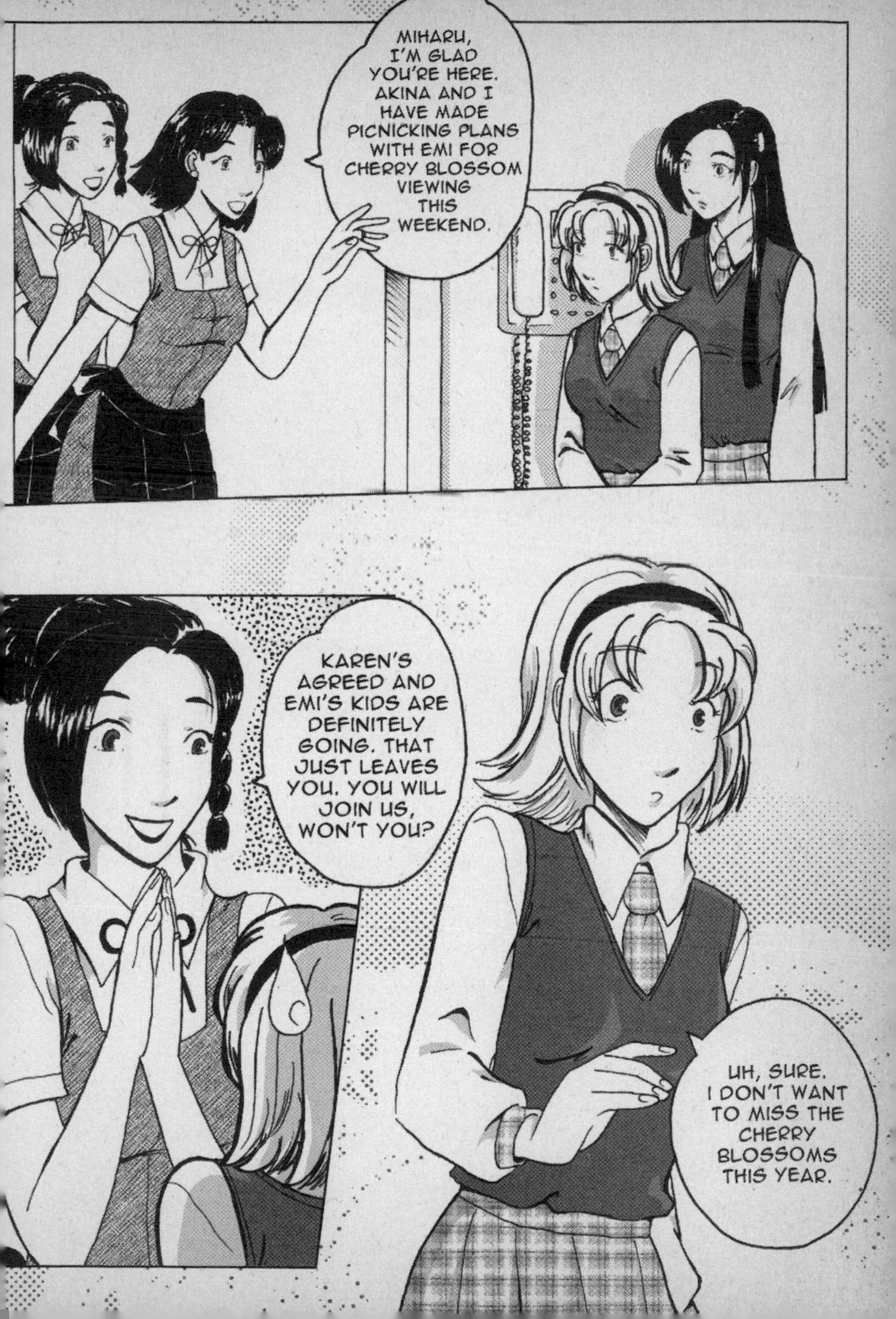
MIHARU, I'M GLAD YOU'RE HERE. AKINA AND I HAVE MADE PICNICKING PLANS WITH EMI FOR CHERRY BLOSSOM VIEWING THIS WEEKEND.
KAREN'S AGREED AND EMI'S KIDS ARE DEFINITELY GOING. THAT JUST LEAVES YOU. YOU WILL JOIN US, WON'T YOU?
UH, SURE. I DON'T WANT TO MISS THE CHERRY BLOSSOMS THIS YEAR.

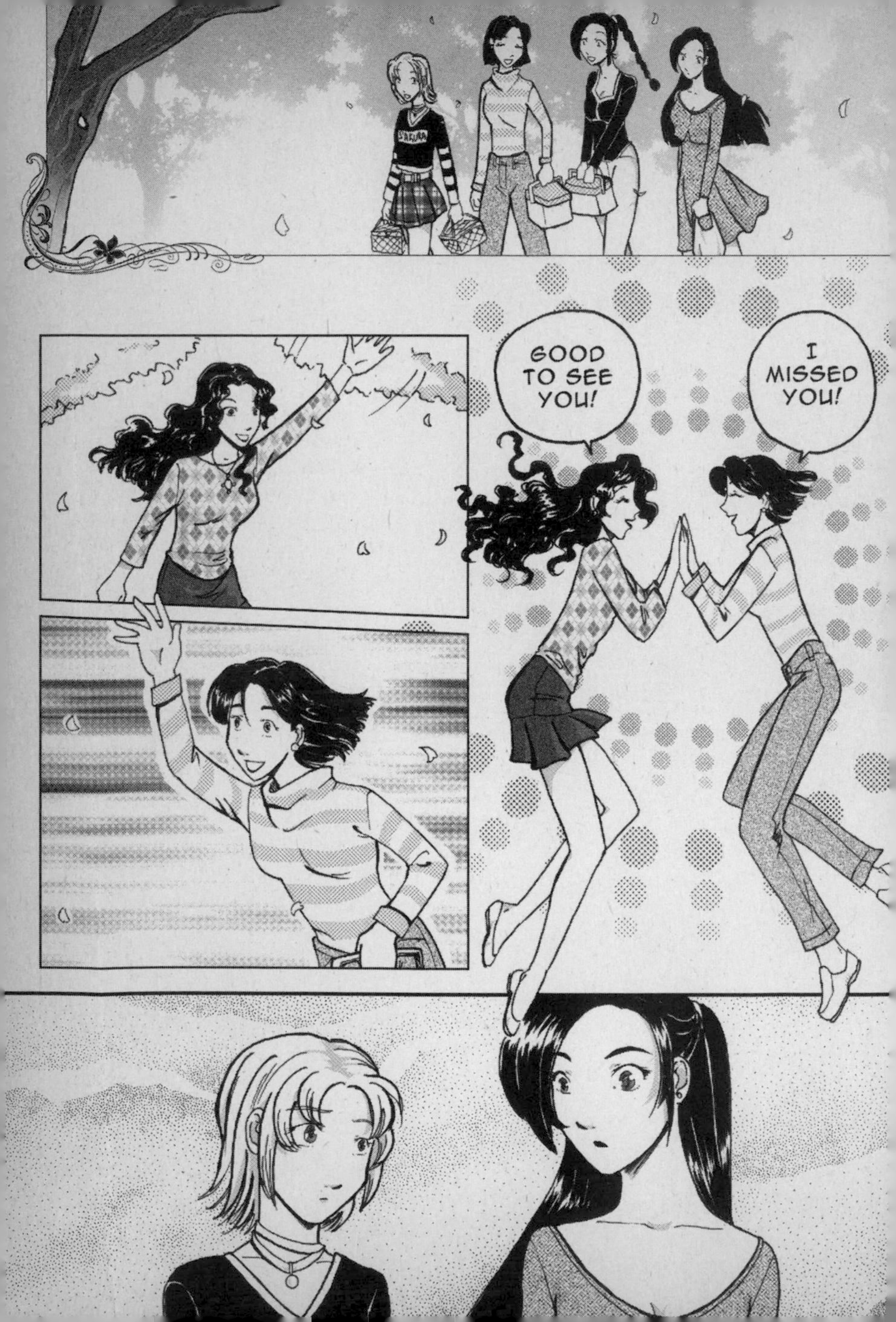
SAKURA
GOOD TO SEE YOU!
I MISSED YOU!

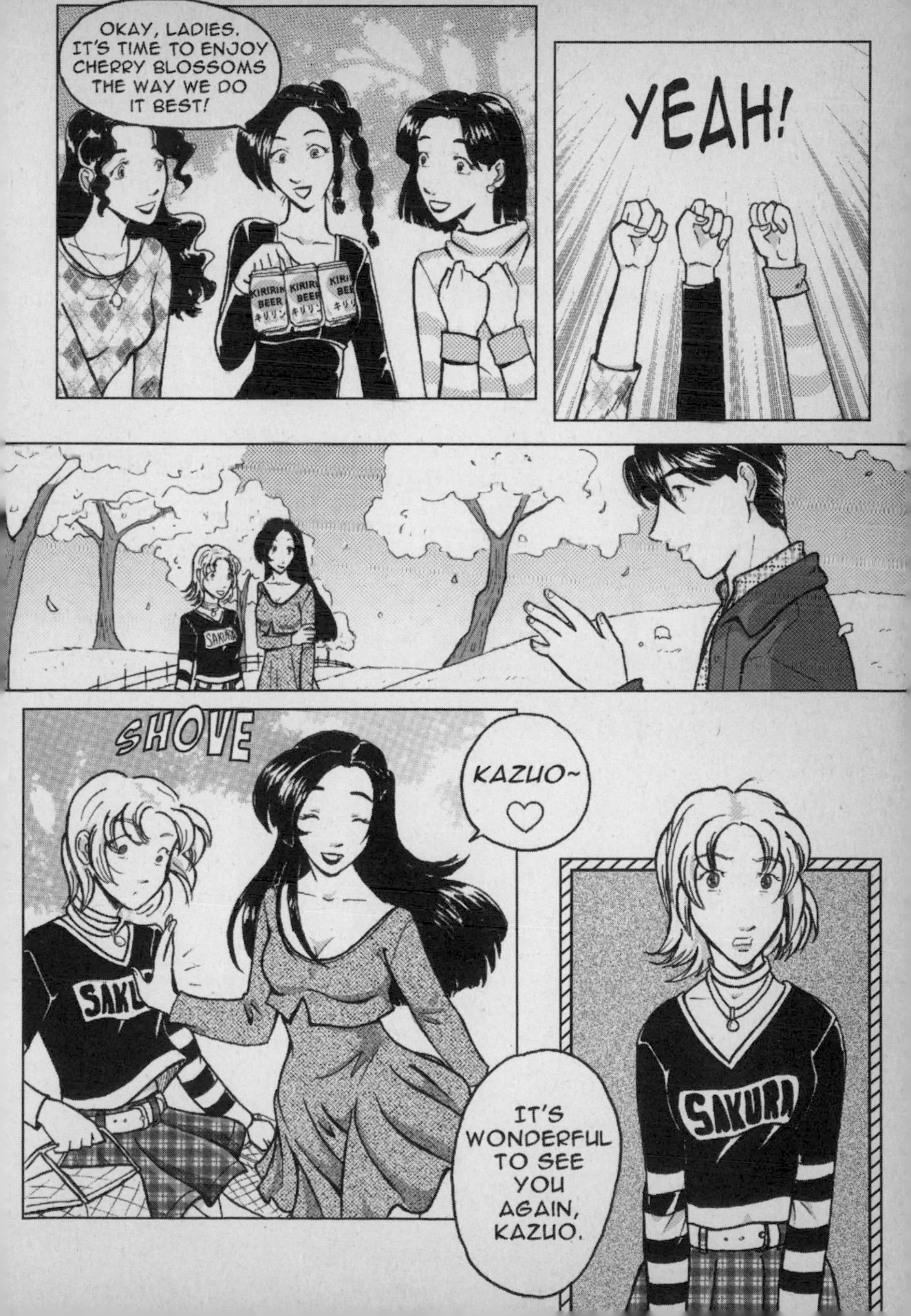
OKAY, LADIES. IT'S TIME TO ENJOY CHERRY BLOSSOMS THE WAY WE DO IT BEST!
KIRIRIN BEER キリリン
YEAH!
SAKURA
SHOVE
KAZUO~ ♡
IT'S WONDERFUL TO SEE YOU AGAIN, KAZUO.
SAKURA

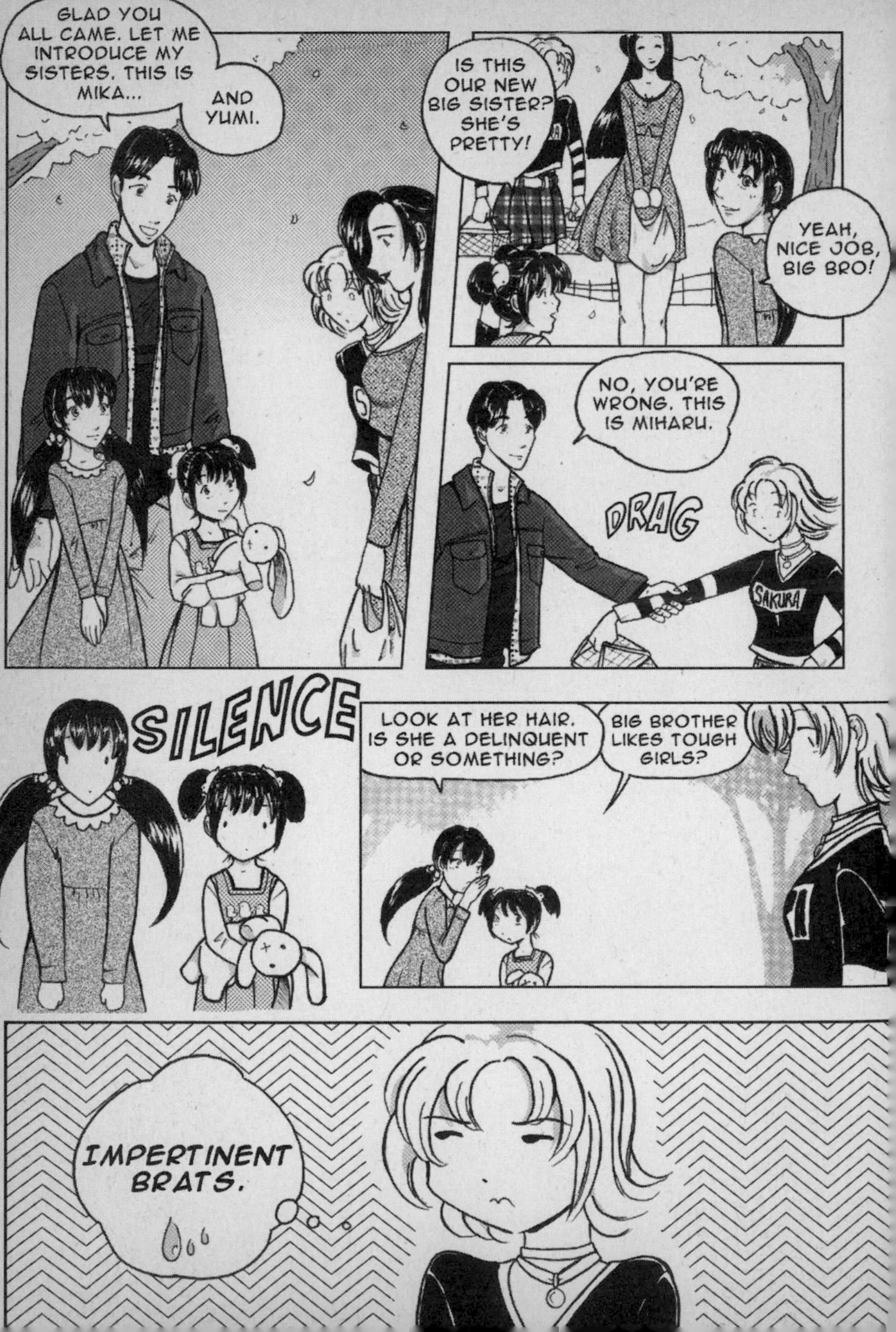

GLAD YOU ALL CAME. LET ME INTRODUCE MY SISTERS. THIS IS MIKA...
AND YUMI.
IS THIS OUR NEW BIG SISTER? SHE'S PRETTY!
YEAH, NICE JOB, BIG BRO!
NO, YOU'RE WRONG. THIS IS MIHARU.
DRAG
SAKURA
SILENCE
LOOK AT HER HAIR. IS SHE A DELINQUENT OR SOMETHING?
BIG BROTHER LIKES TOUGH GIRLS?
IMPERTINENT BRATS.

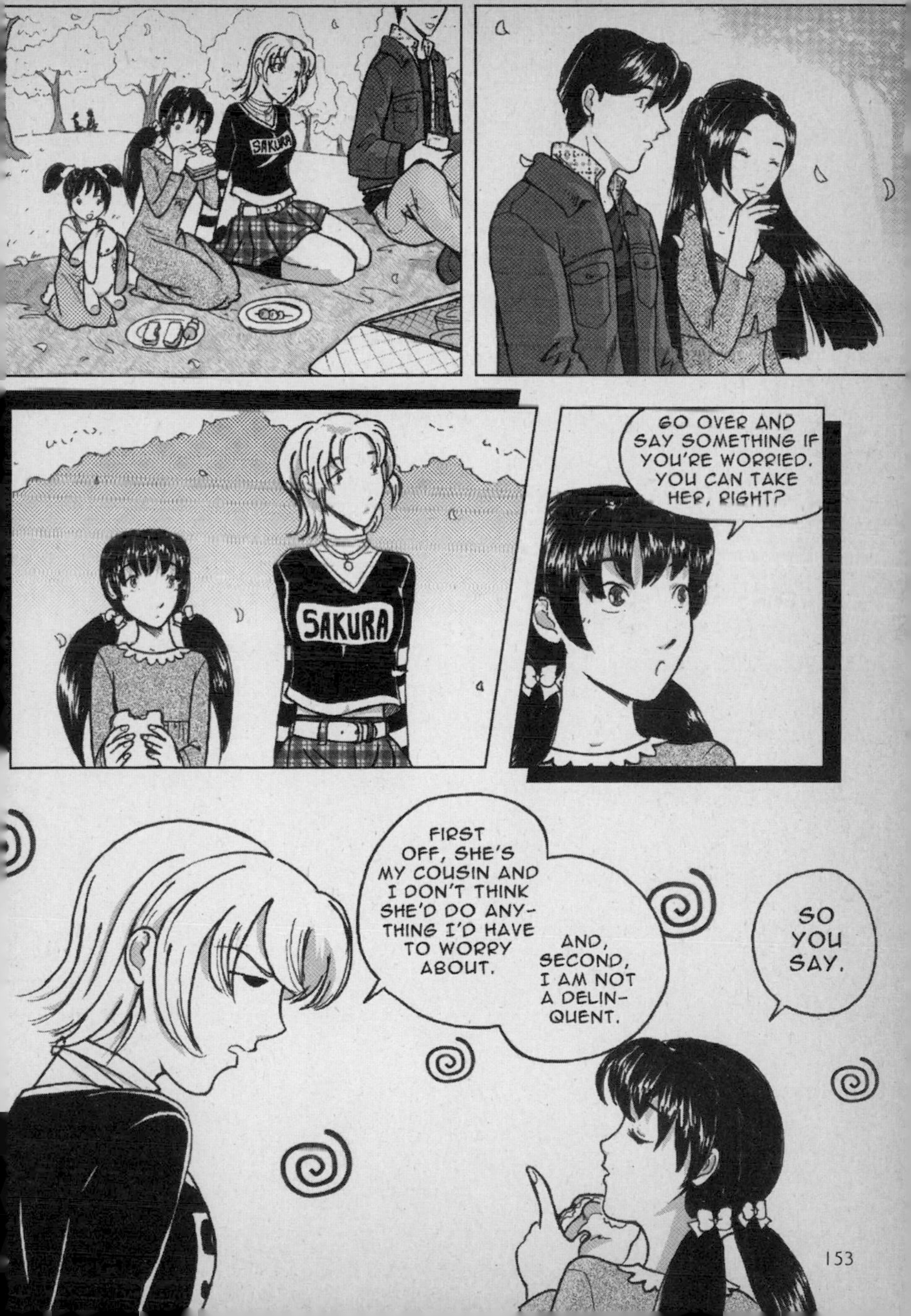
GO OVER AND SAY SOMETHING IF YOU'RE WORRIED. YOU CAN TAKE HER, RIGHT?
FIRST OFF, SHE'S MY COUSIN AND I DON'T THINK SHE'D DO ANY-THING I'D HAVE TO WORRY ABOUT.
AND, SECOND, I AM NOT A DELIN-QUENT.
SO YOU SAY.

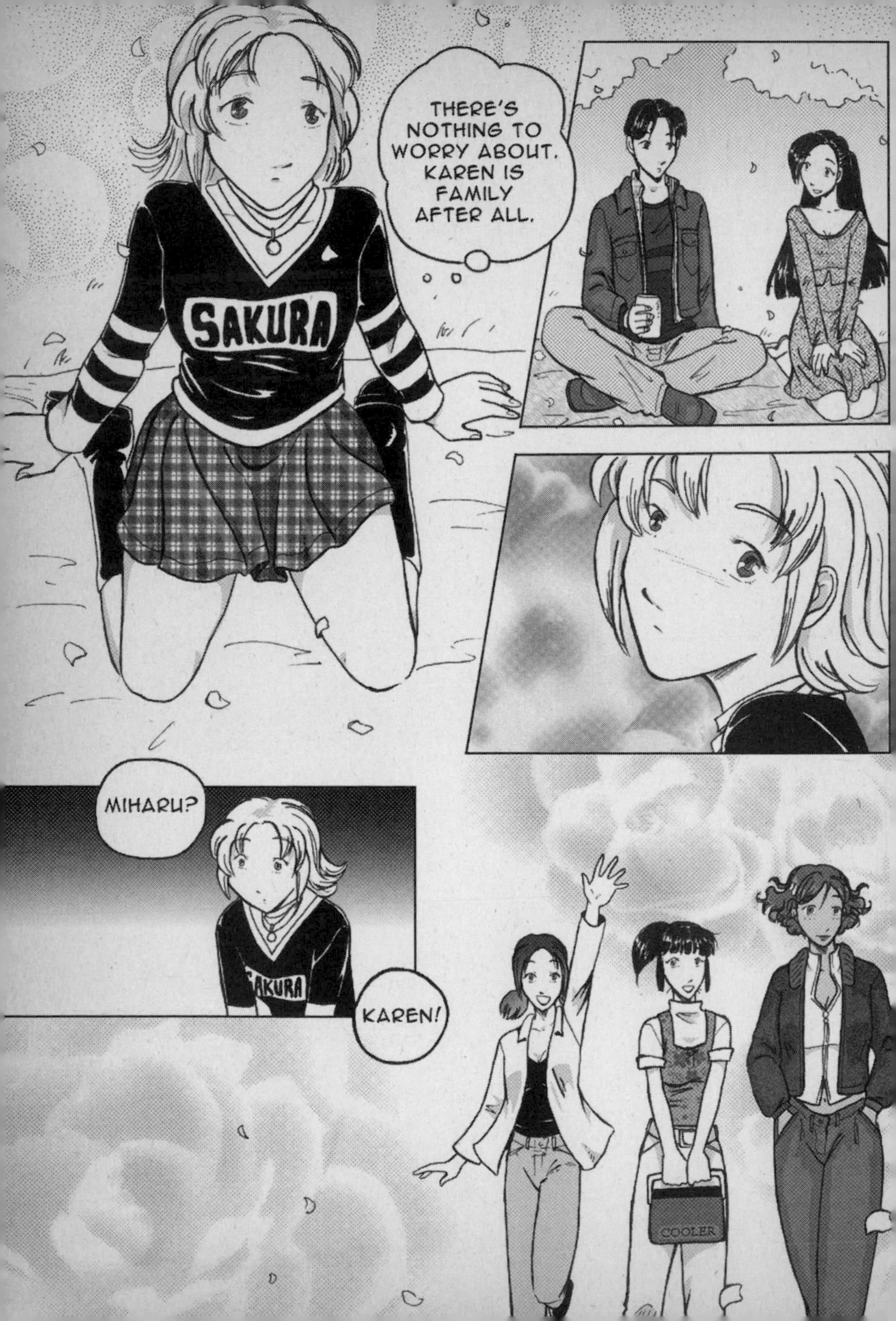
SAKURA
THERE'S NOTHING TO WORRY ABOUT. KAREN IS FAMILY AFTER ALL.
MIHARU?
SAKURA
KAREN!
COOLER

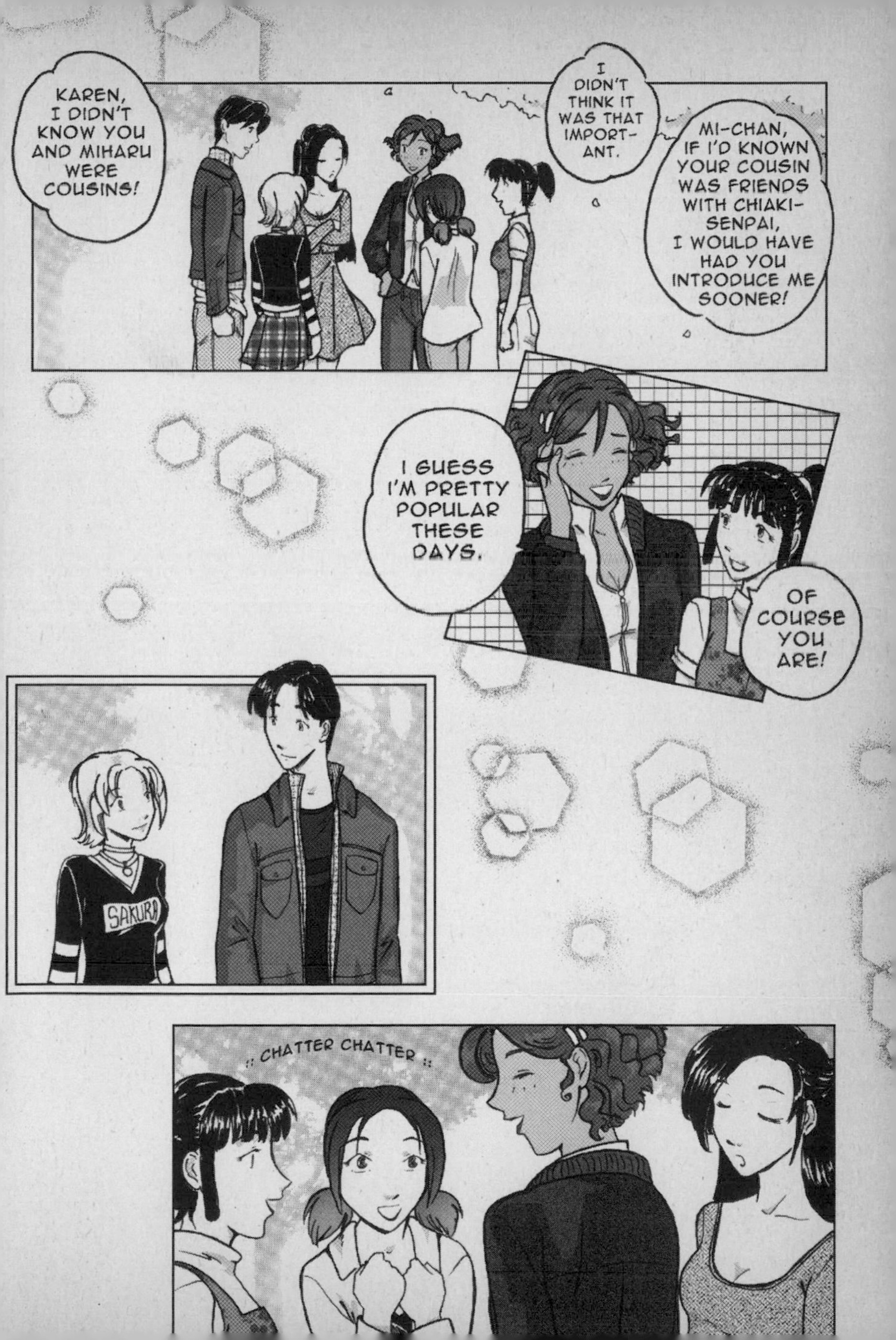
KAREN, I DIDN'T KNOW YOU AND MIHARU WERE COUSINS!
I DIDN'T THINK IT WAS THAT IMPORT- ANT.
MI-CHAN, IF I'D KNOWN YOUR COUSIN WAS FRIENDS WITH CHIAKI-SENPAI, I WOULD HAVE HAD YOU INTRODUCE ME SOONER!
I GUESS I'M PRETTY POPULAR THESE DAYS.
OF COURSE YOU ARE!
SAKURA
:: CHATTER CHATTER ::

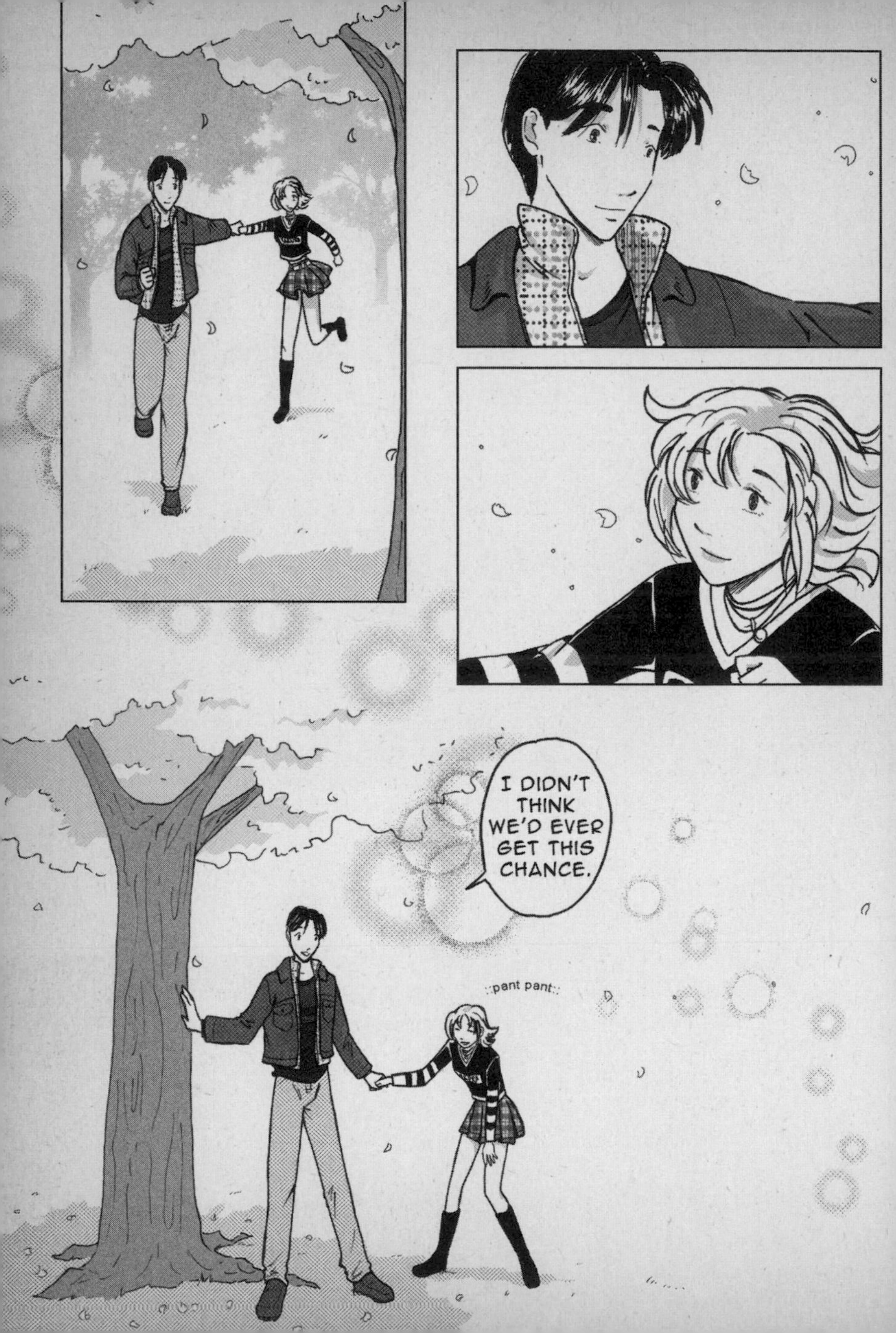
I DIDN'T THINK WE'D EVER GET THIS CHANCE.
::pant pant::

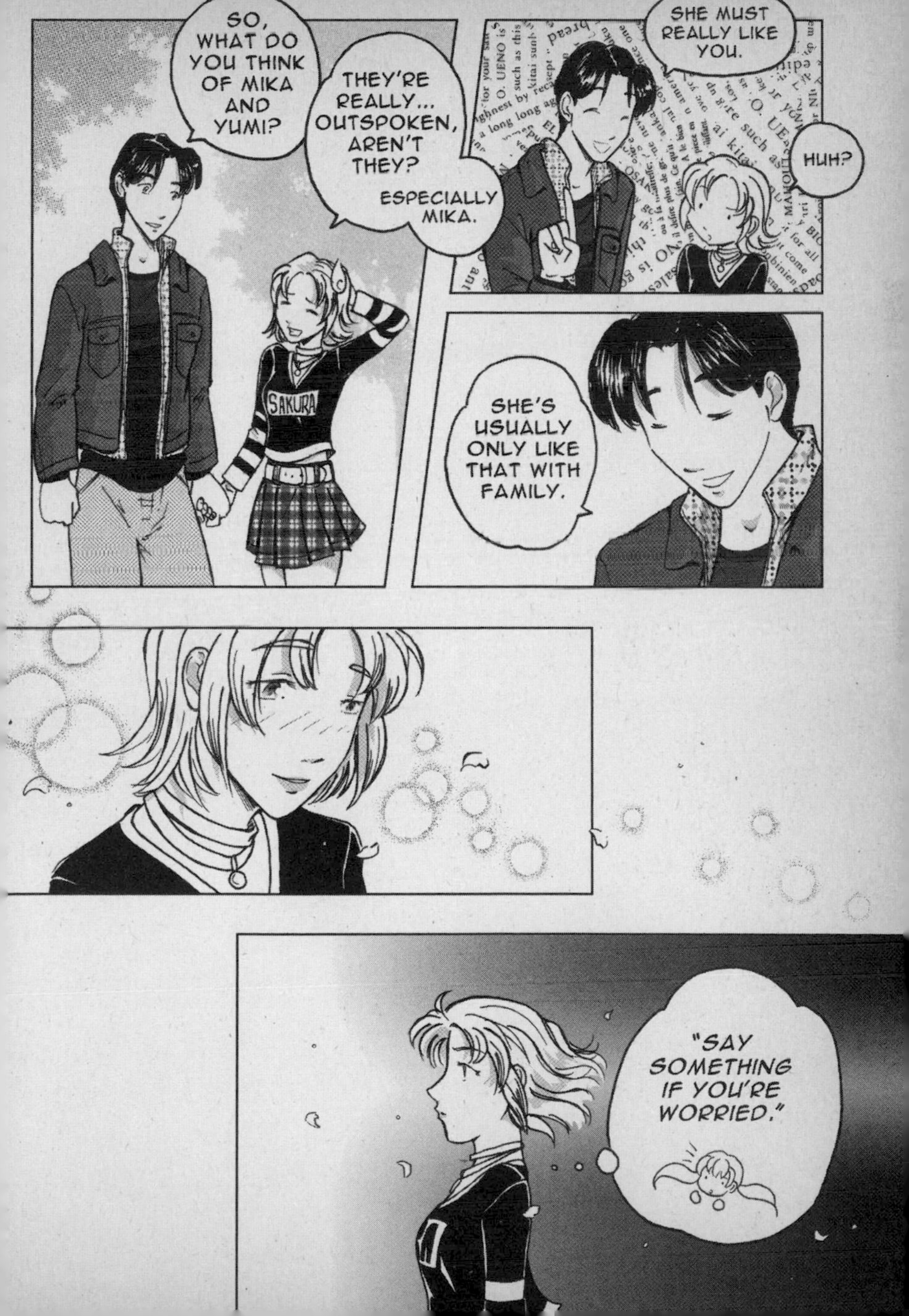
SO, WHAT DO YOU THINK OF MIKA AND YUMI?
THEY'RE REALLY... OUTSPOKEN, AREN'T THEY?
ESPECIALLY MIKA.
SHE MUST REALLY LIKE YOU.
HUH?
SAKURA
SHE'S USUALLY ONLY LIKE THAT WITH FAMILY.
"SAY SOMETHING IF YOU'RE WORRIED."

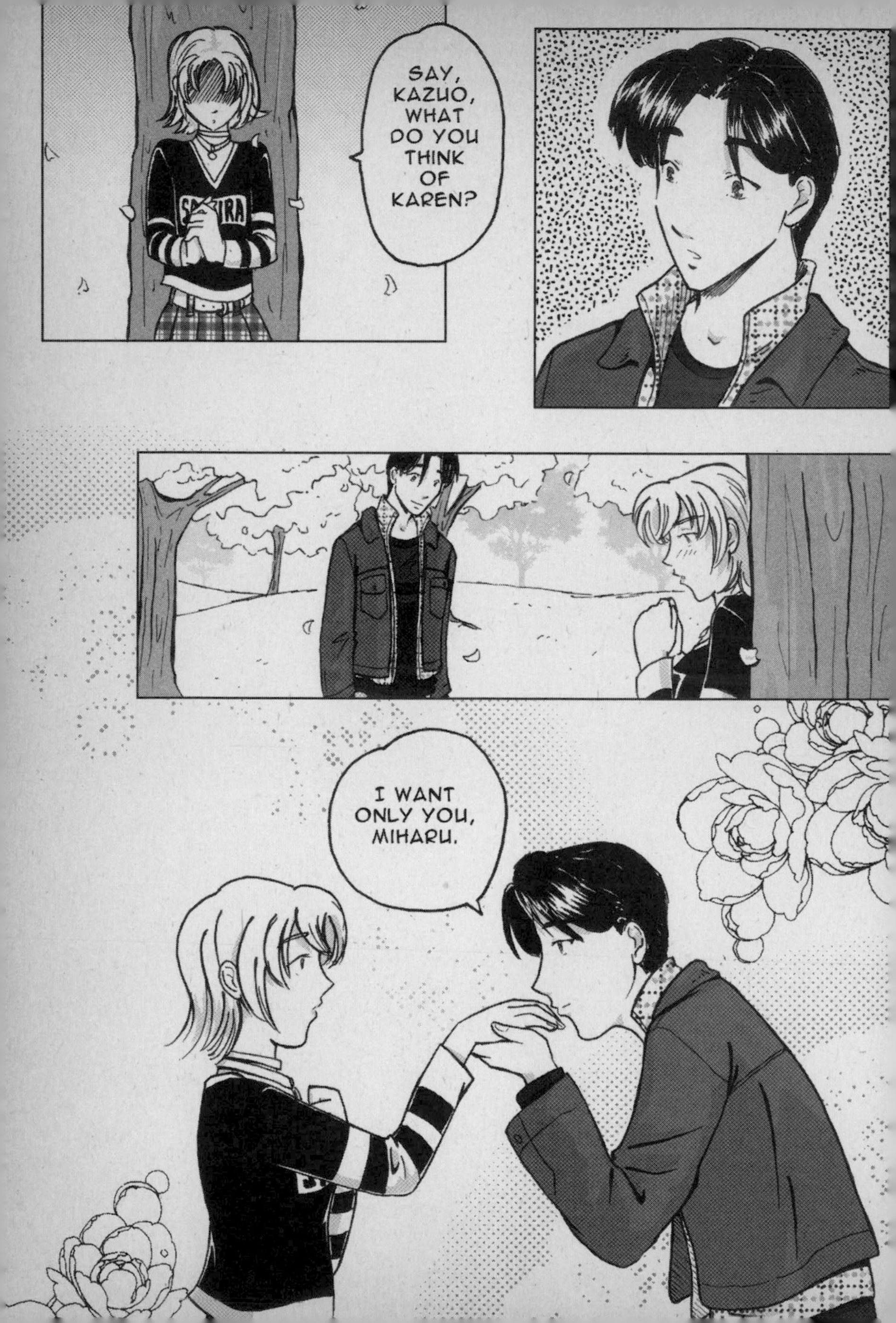
SAY, KAZUO, WHAT DO YOU THINK OF KAREN?
I WANT ONLY YOU, MIHARU.

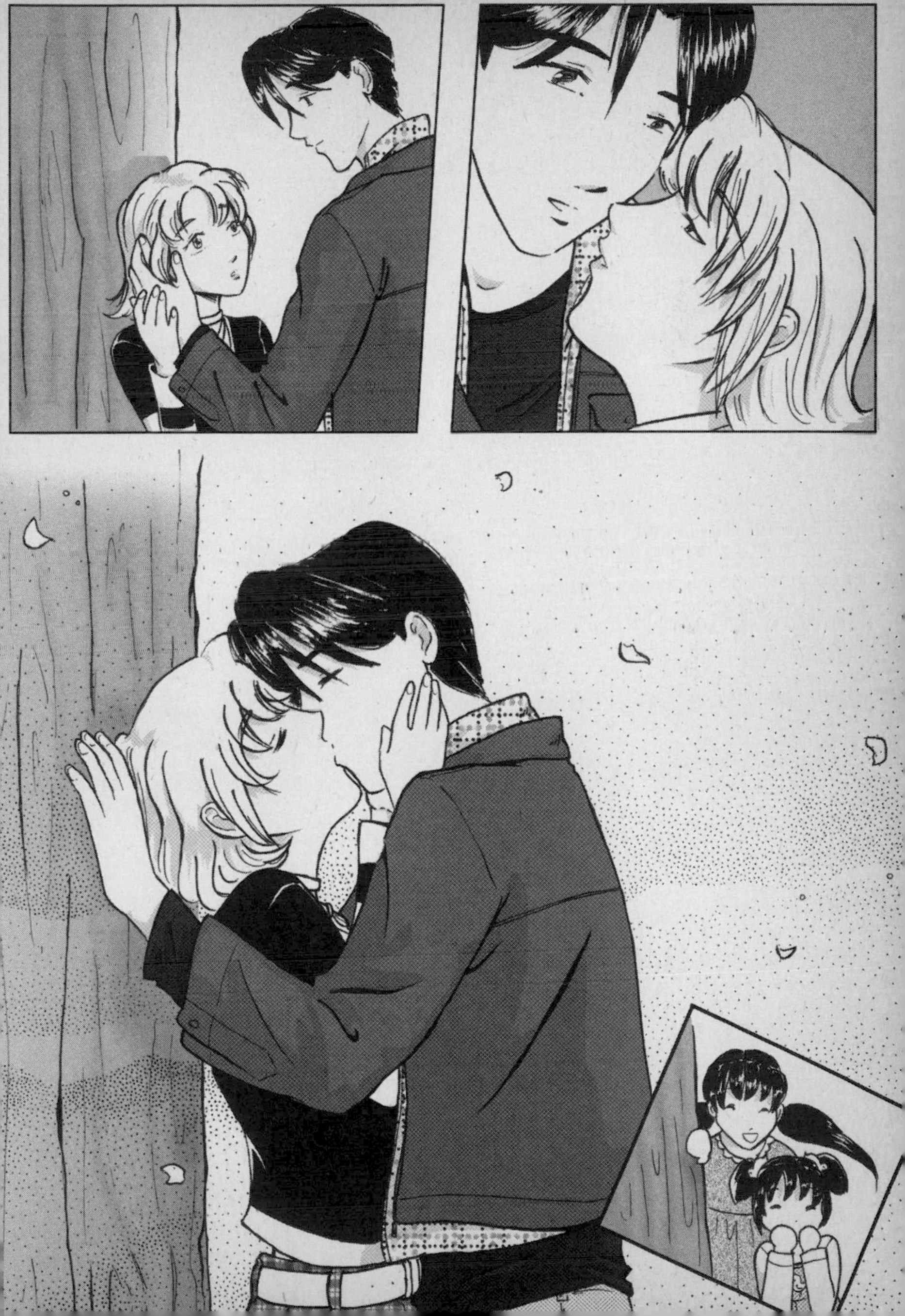

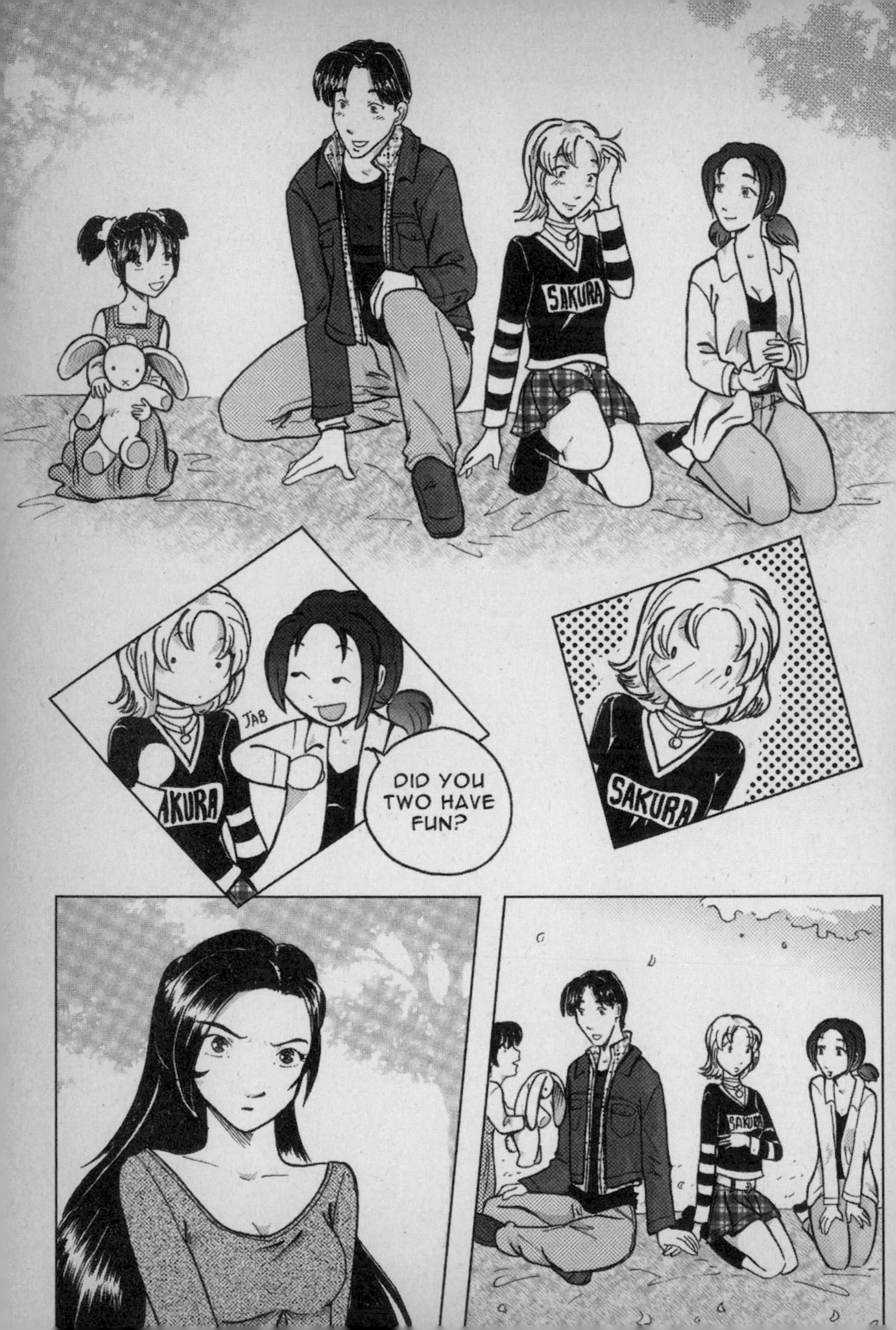
SAKURA
JAB
SAKURA
DID YOU TWO HAVE FUN?
SAKURA
SAKURA

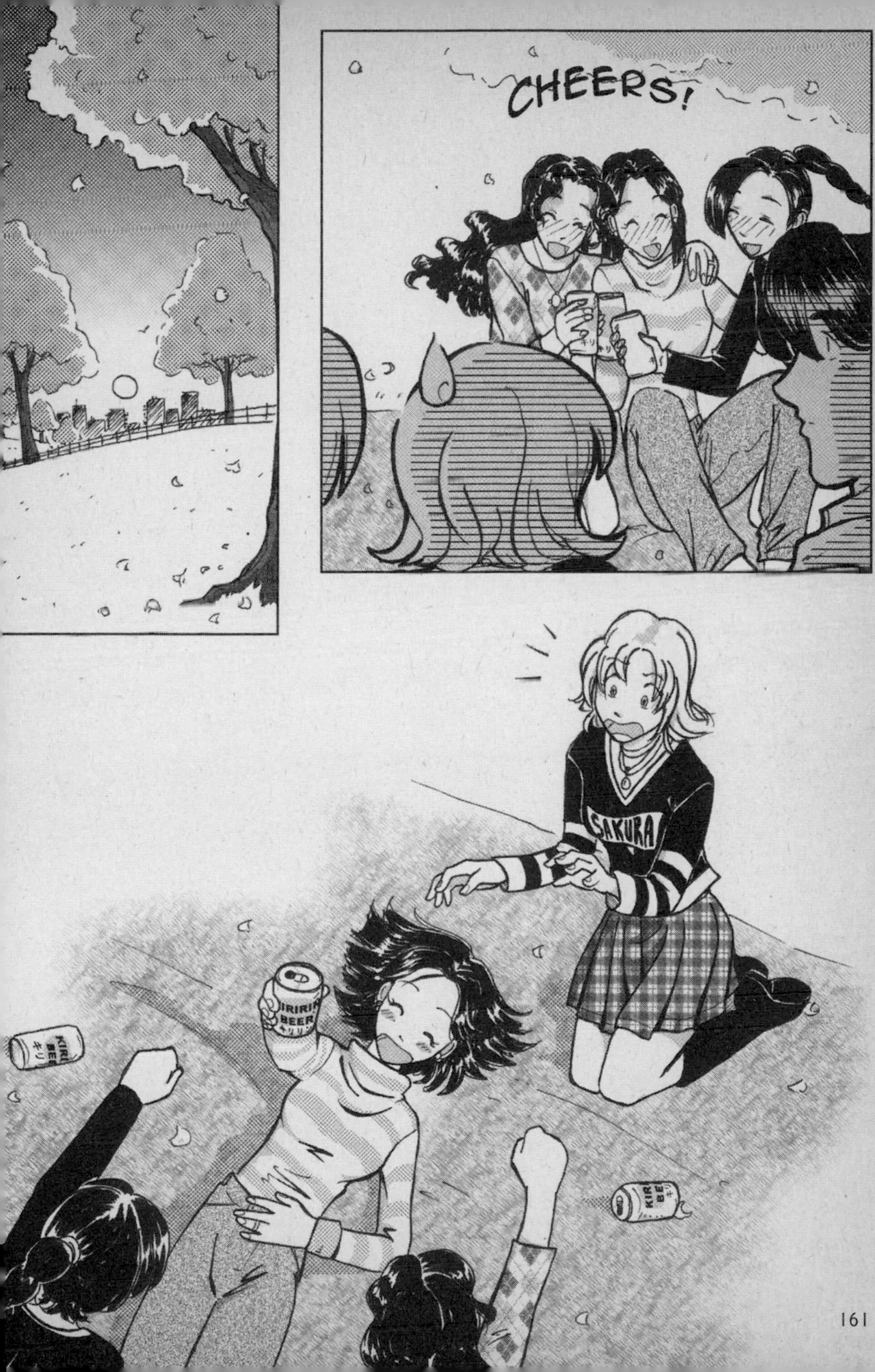

CHEERS!
SAKURA
KIRIRIN BEER

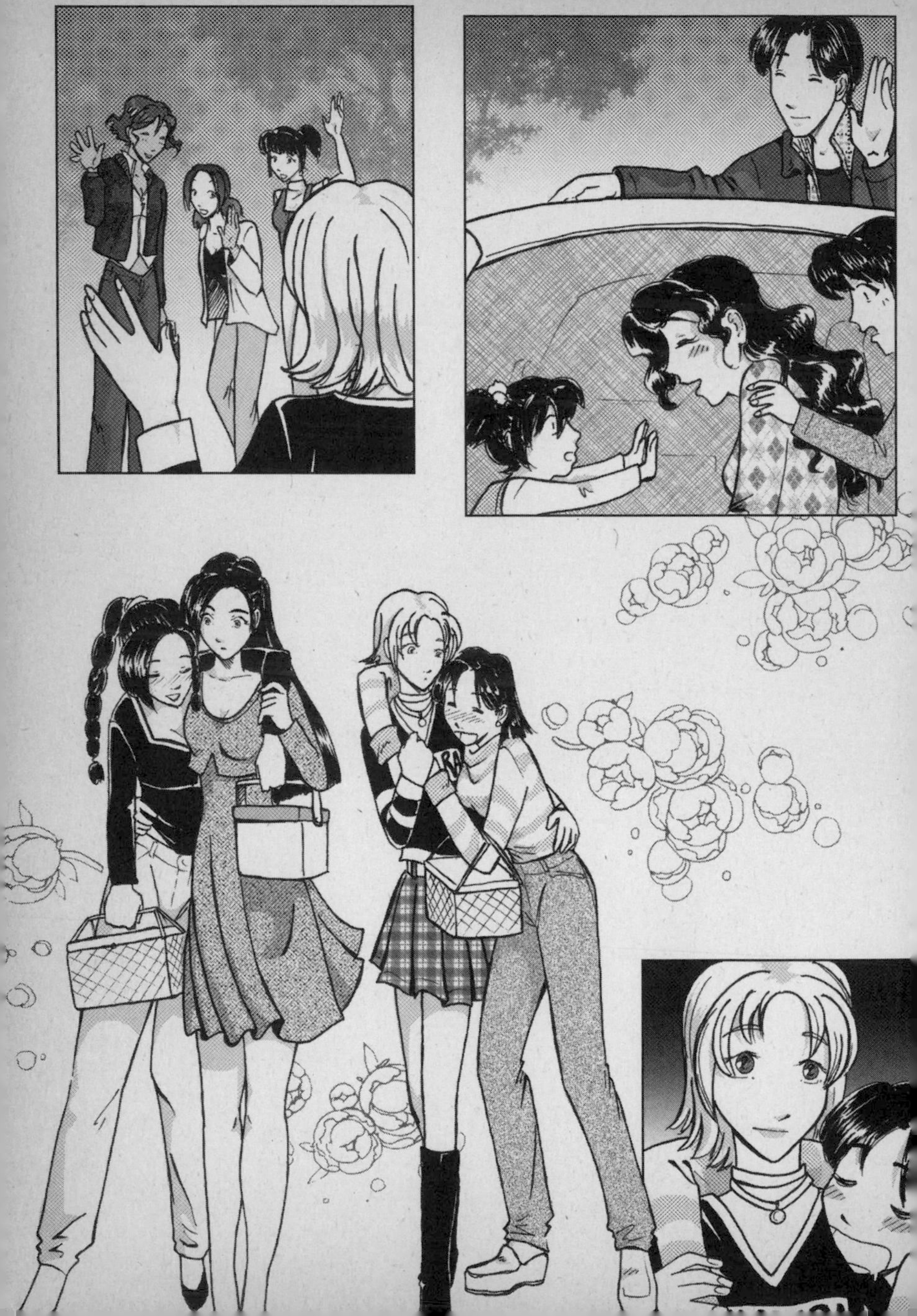

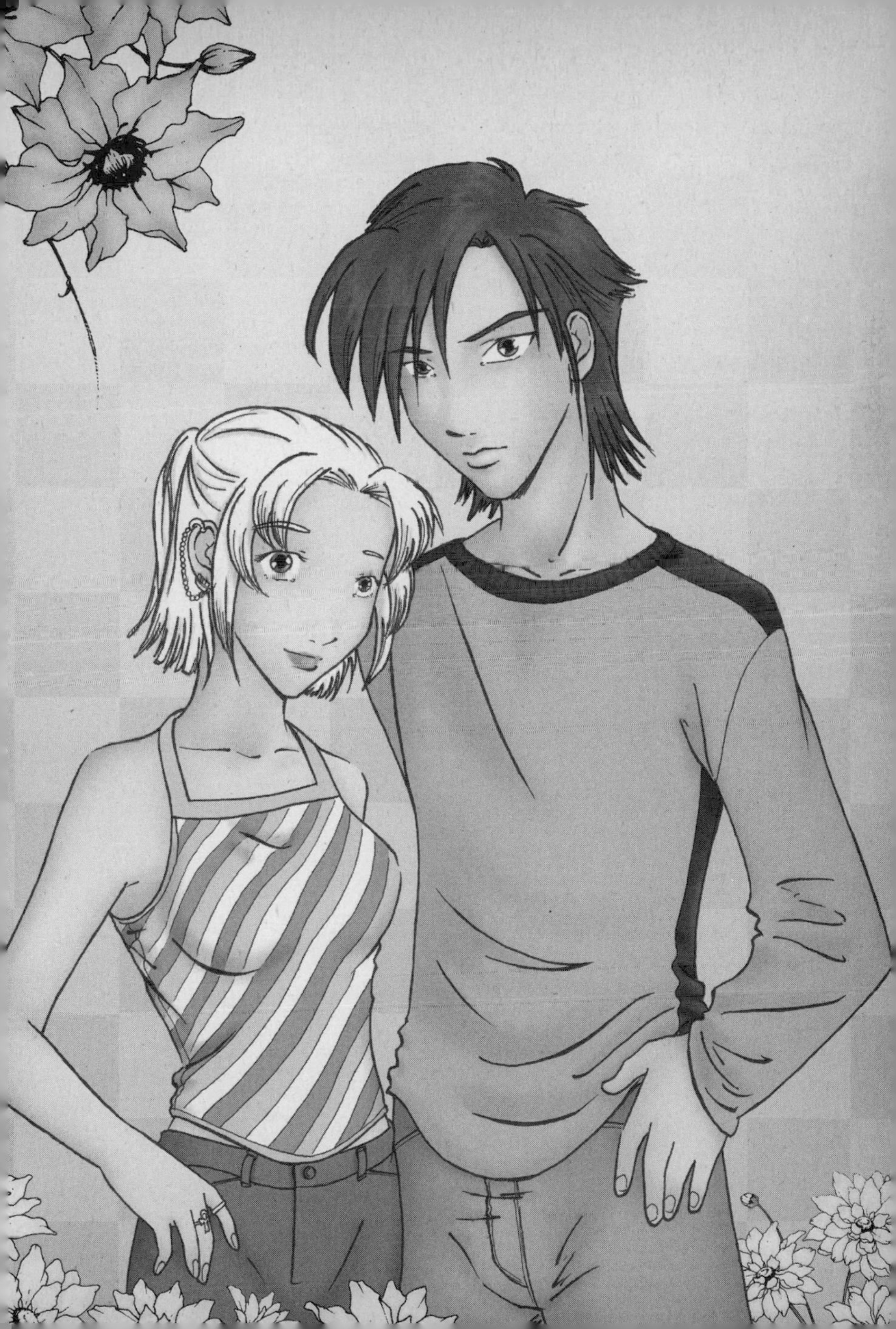

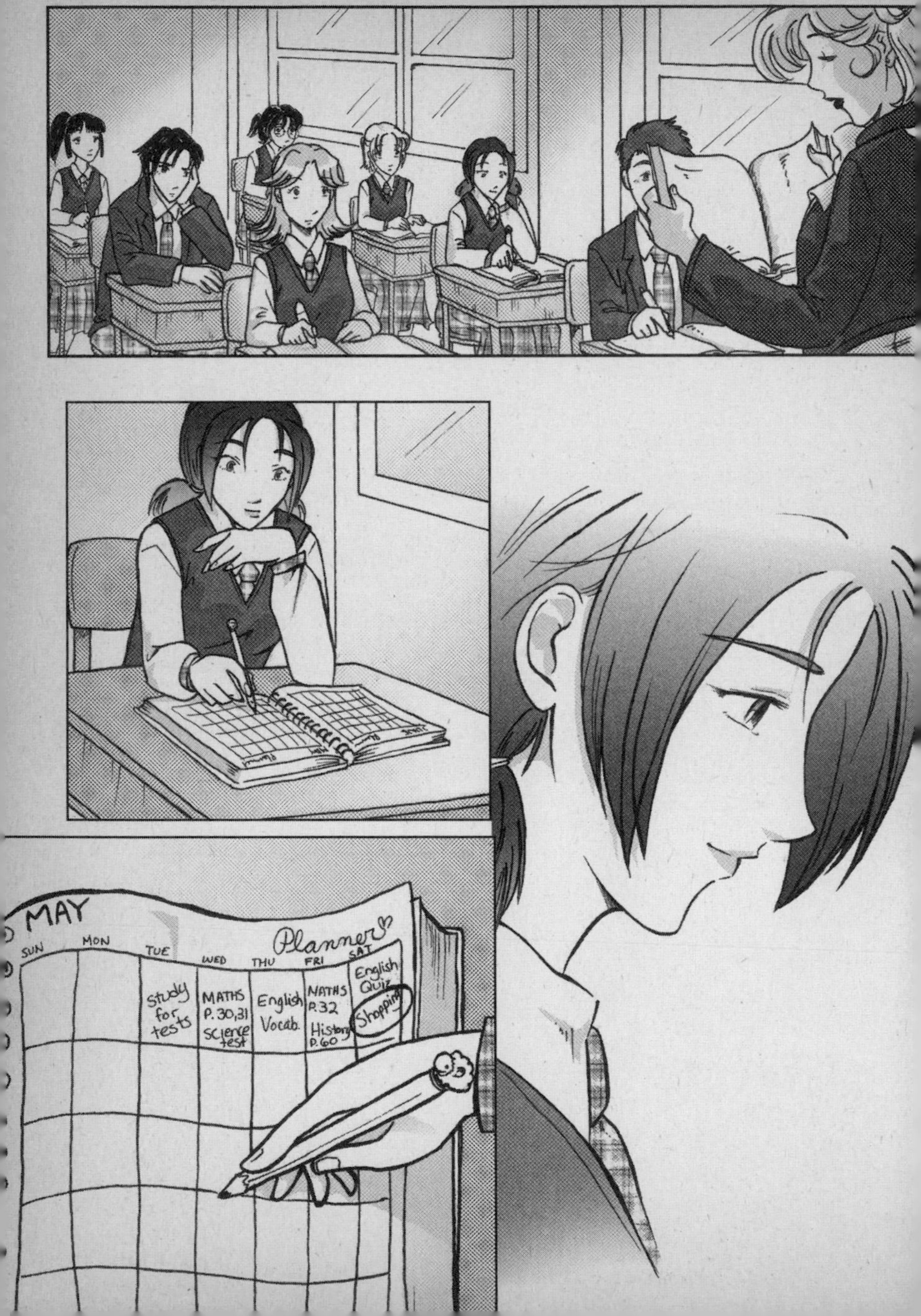
MAY
Planner
SUN
MON
TUE
WED
THU
FRI
SAT
study for tests
MATHS P. 30,31 science test
English Vocab.
MATHS P.32 History P.60
English Quiz
Shopping

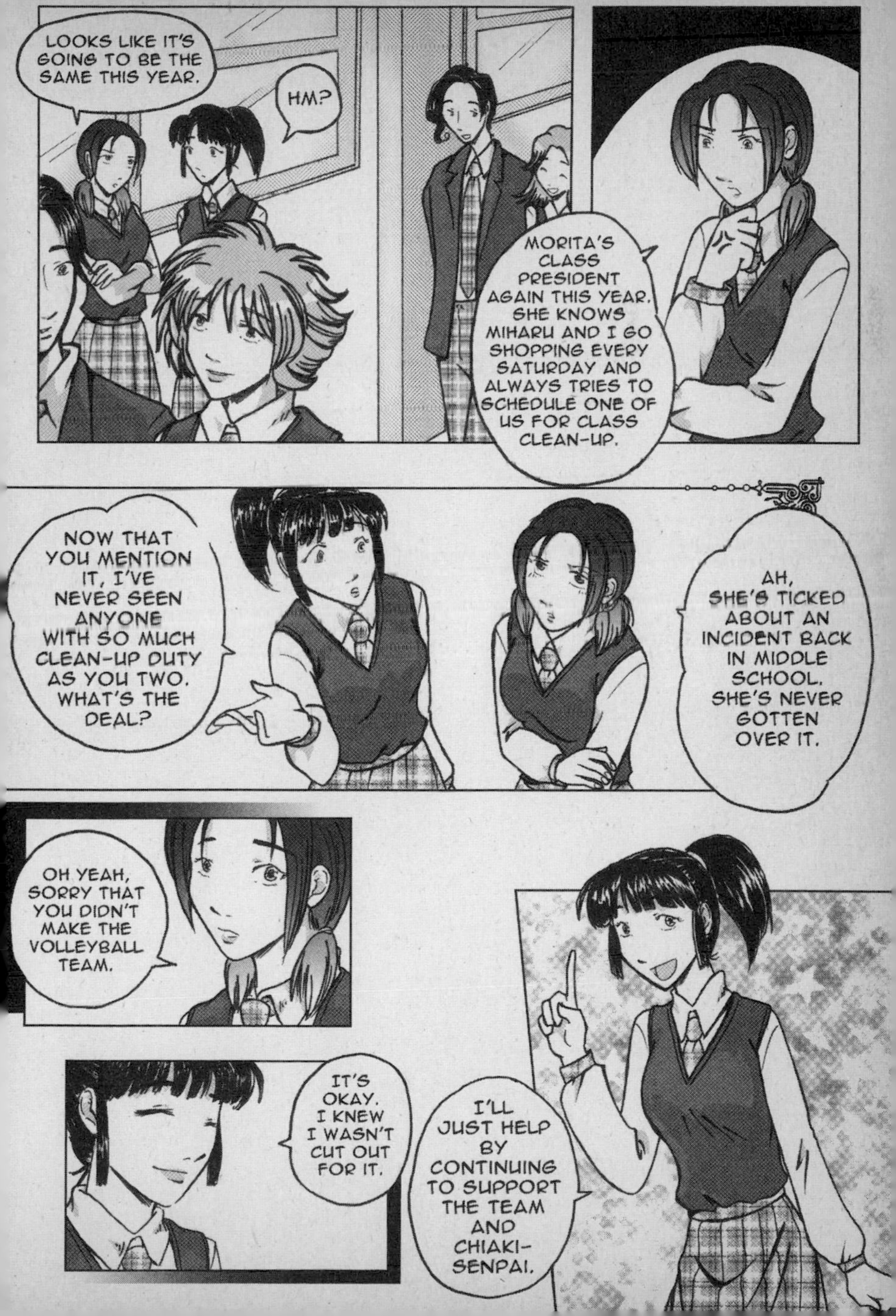

LOOKS LIKE IT'S GOING TO BE THE SAME THIS YEAR.
HM?
MORITA'S CLASS PRESIDENT AGAIN THIS YEAR. SHE KNOWS MIHARU AND I GO SHOPPING EVERY SATURDAY AND ALWAYS TRIES TO SCHEDULE ONE OF US FOR CLASS CLEAN-UP.
NOW THAT YOU MENTION IT, I'VE NEVER SEEN ANYONE WITH SO MUCH CLEAN-UP DUTY AS YOU TWO. WHAT'S THE DEAL?
AH, SHE'S TICKED ABOUT AN INCIDENT BACK IN MIDDLE SCHOOL. SHE'S NEVER GOTTEN OVER IT.
OH YEAH, SORRY THAT YOU DIDN'T MAKE THE VOLLEYBALL TEAM.
IT'S OKAY. I KNEW I WASN'T CUT OUT FOR IT.
I'LL JUST HELP BY CONTINUING TO SUPPORT THE TEAM AND CHIAKI-SENPAI.

YOU REALLY ADMIRE CHIAKI-SENPAI, HUH?

I DO. SHE IS SUCH A PASSIONATE PERSON!

SHE SURE IS!

MATSUO, I HEARD YOU JOINED THE ASTRONOMY CLUB.

BABUMP BABUMP BABUMP BABUMP BABUMP BABUMP BABUMP B

I DIDN'T KNOW YOU WERE INTO THAT SORT OF THING.

I'LL BE LOOKING FORWARD TO THE NEXT MEETING.

M-ME TOO!

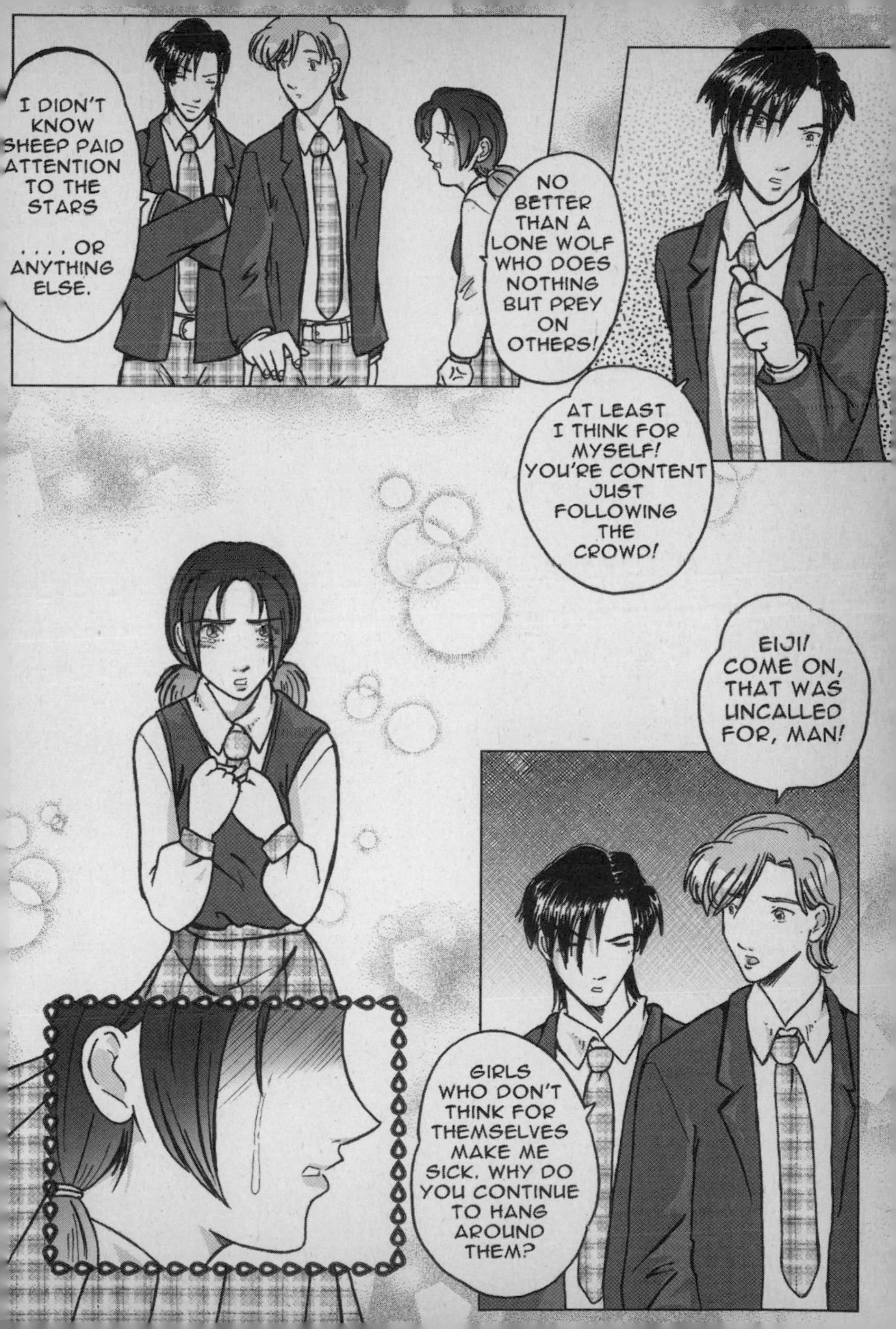
I DIDN'T KNOW SHEEP PAID ATTENTION TO THE STARS
. . . . OR ANYTHING ELSE.
NO BETTER THAN A LONE WOLF WHO DOES NOTHING BUT PREY ON OTHERS!
AT LEAST I THINK FOR MYSELF! YOU'RE CONTENT JUST FOLLOWING THE CROWD!
EIJI! COME ON, THAT WAS UNCALLED FOR, MAN!
GIRLS WHO DON'T THINK FOR THEMSELVES MAKE ME SICK. WHY DO YOU CONTINUE TO HANG AROUND THEM?

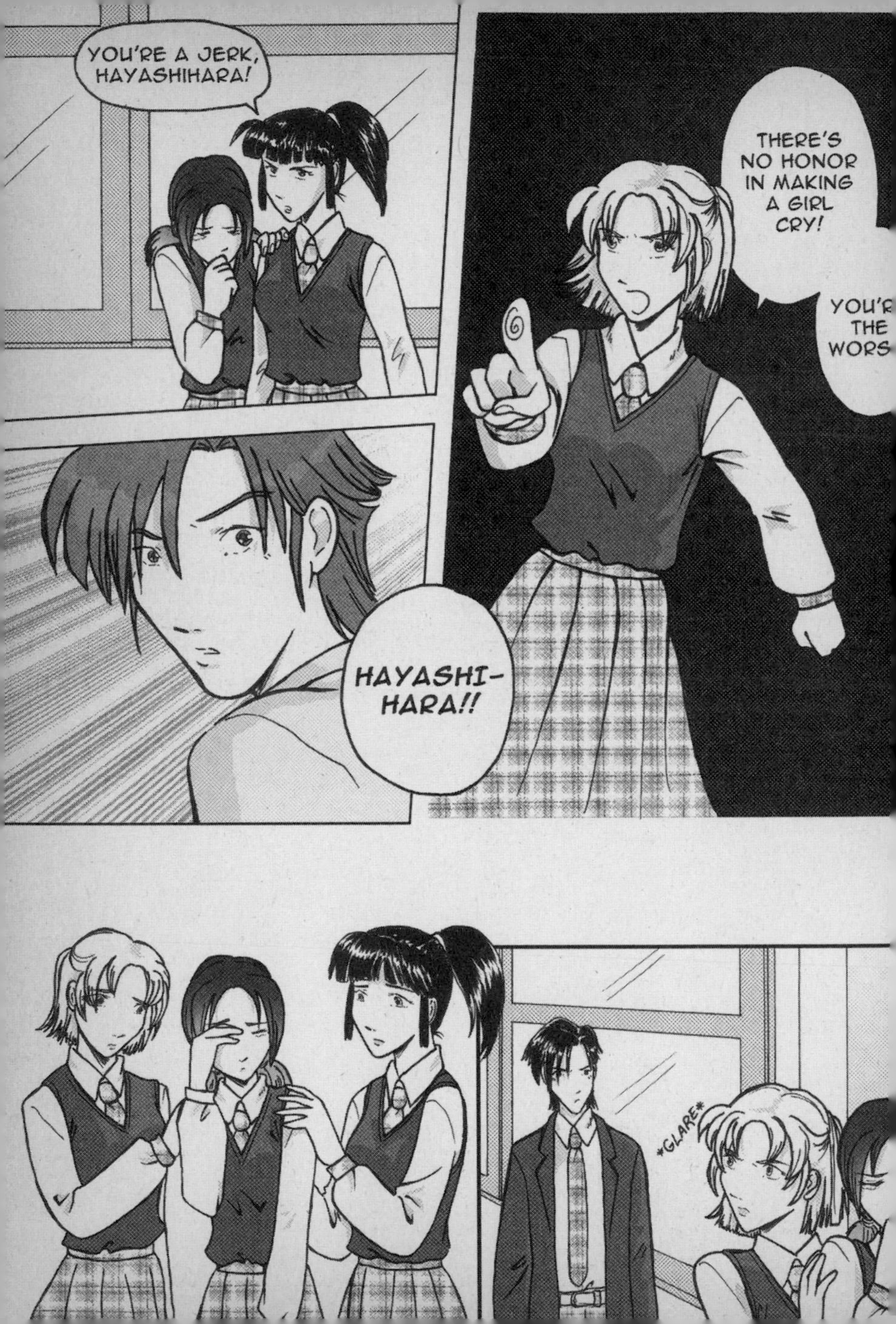
YOU'RE A JERK, HAYASHIHARA!
THERE'S NO HONOR IN MAKING A GIRL CRY!
YOU'R THE WORS
HAYASHI-HARA!!
GLARE

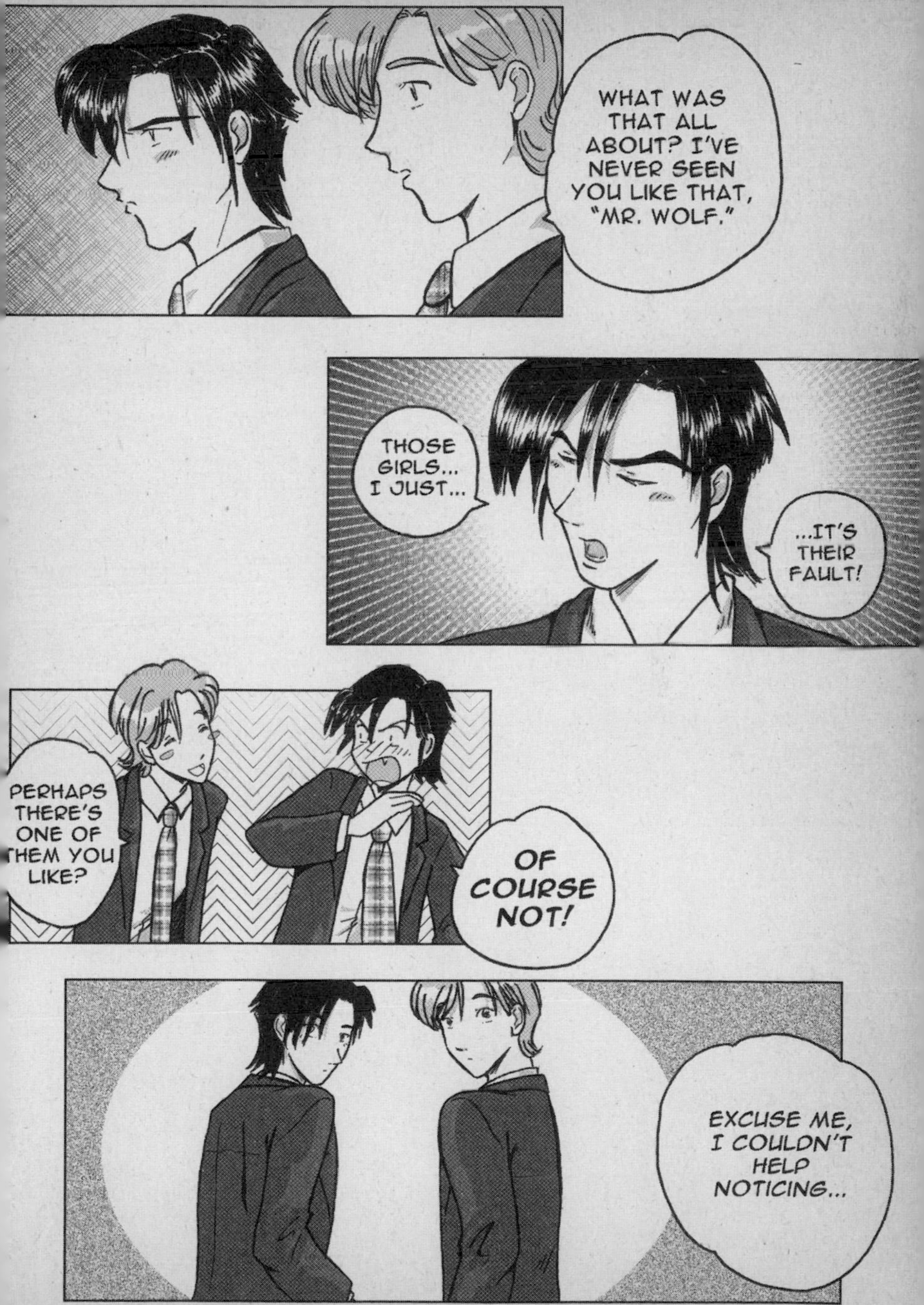
WHAT WAS THAT ALL ABOUT? I'VE NEVER SEEN YOU LIKE THAT, "MR. WOLF."
THOSE GIRLS... I JUST...
...IT'S THEIR FAULT!
PERHAPS THERE'S ONE OF THEM YOU LIKE?
OF COURSE NOT!
EXCUSE ME, I COULDN'T HELP NOTICING...

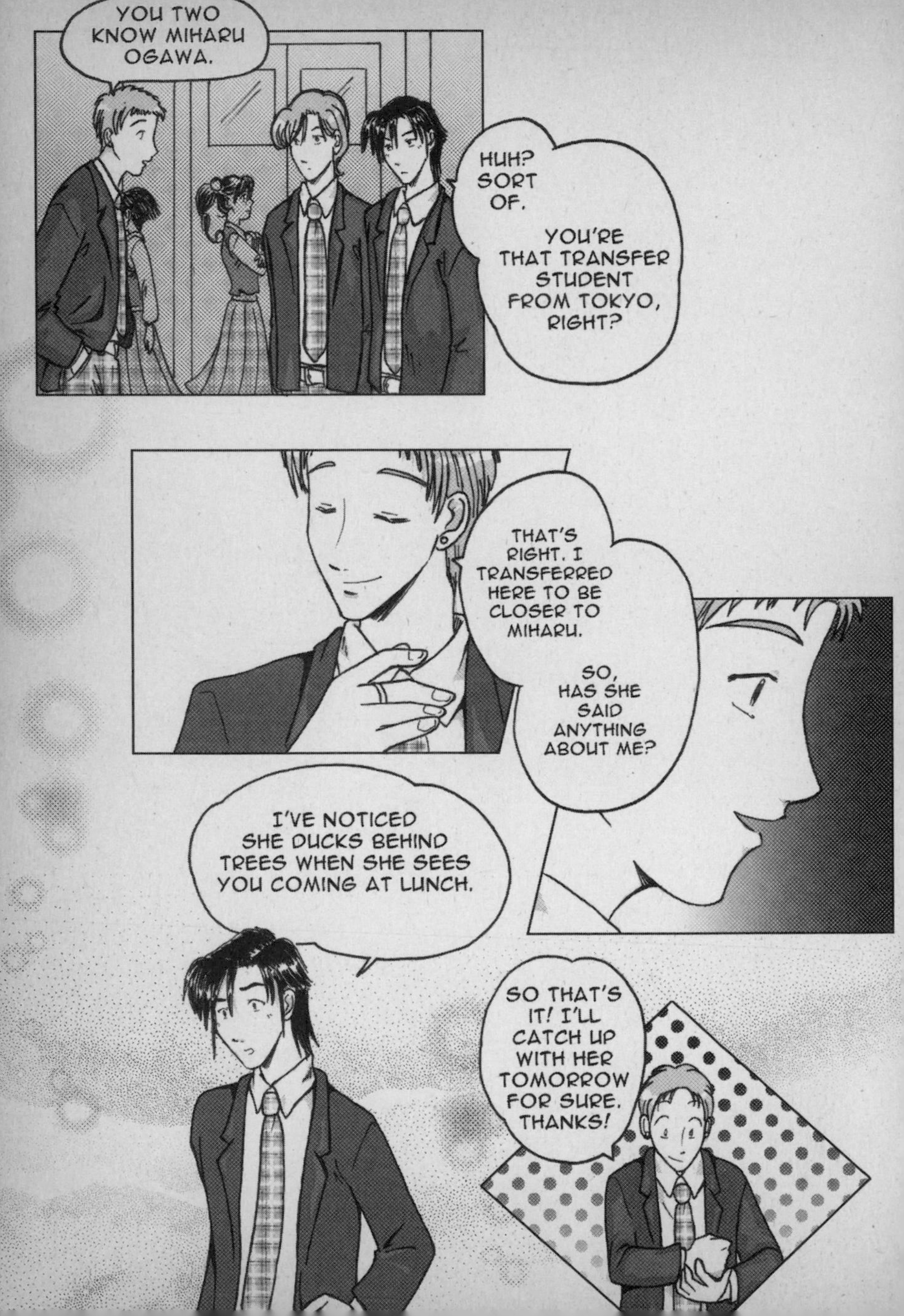
YOU TWO KNOW MIHARU OGAWA.
HUH? SORT OF.
YOU'RE THAT TRANSFER STUDENT FROM TOKYO, RIGHT?
THAT'S RIGHT. I TRANSFERRED HERE TO BE CLOSER TO MIHARU.
SO, HAS SHE SAID ANYTHING ABOUT ME?
I'VE NOTICED SHE DUCKS BEHIND TREES WHEN SHE SEES YOU COMING AT LUNCH.
SO THAT'S IT! I'LL CATCH UP WITH HER TOMORROW FOR SURE. THANKS!

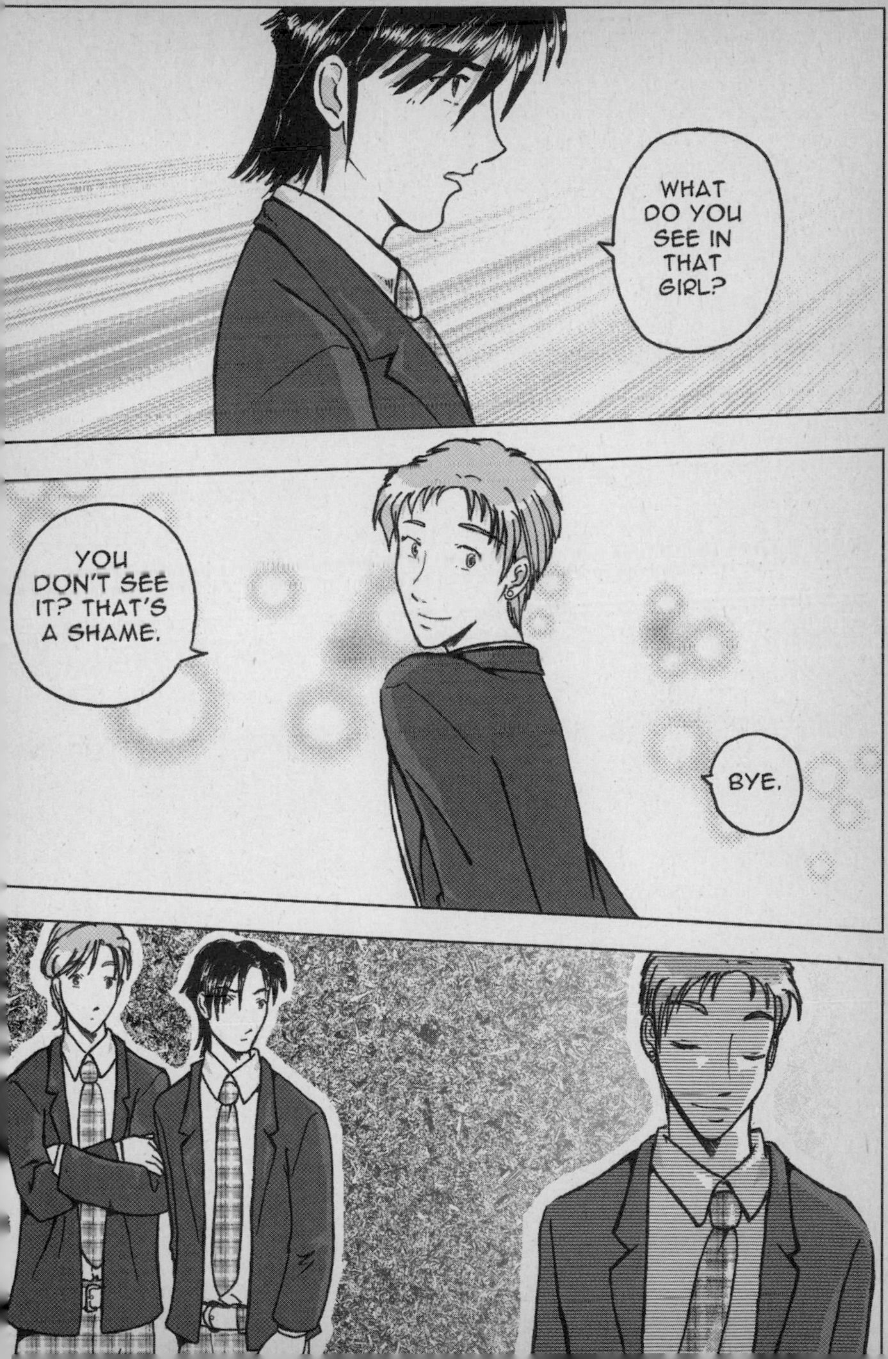
WHAT DO YOU SEE IN THAT GIRL?
YOU DON'T SEE IT? THAT'S A SHAME.
BYE.

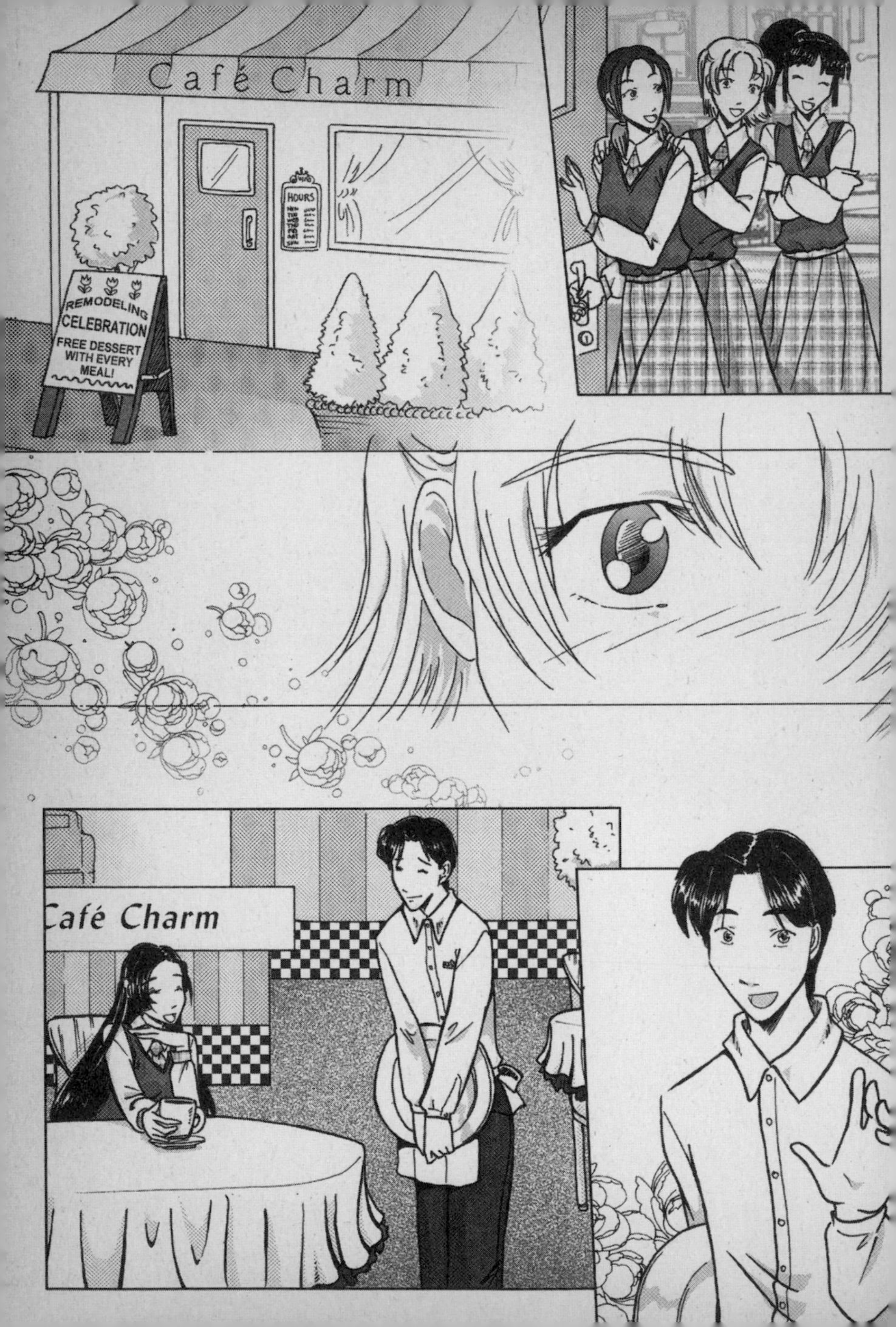
Café Charm
HOURS
REMODELING
CELEBRATION
FREE DESSERT
WITH EVERY
MEAL!
Café Charm

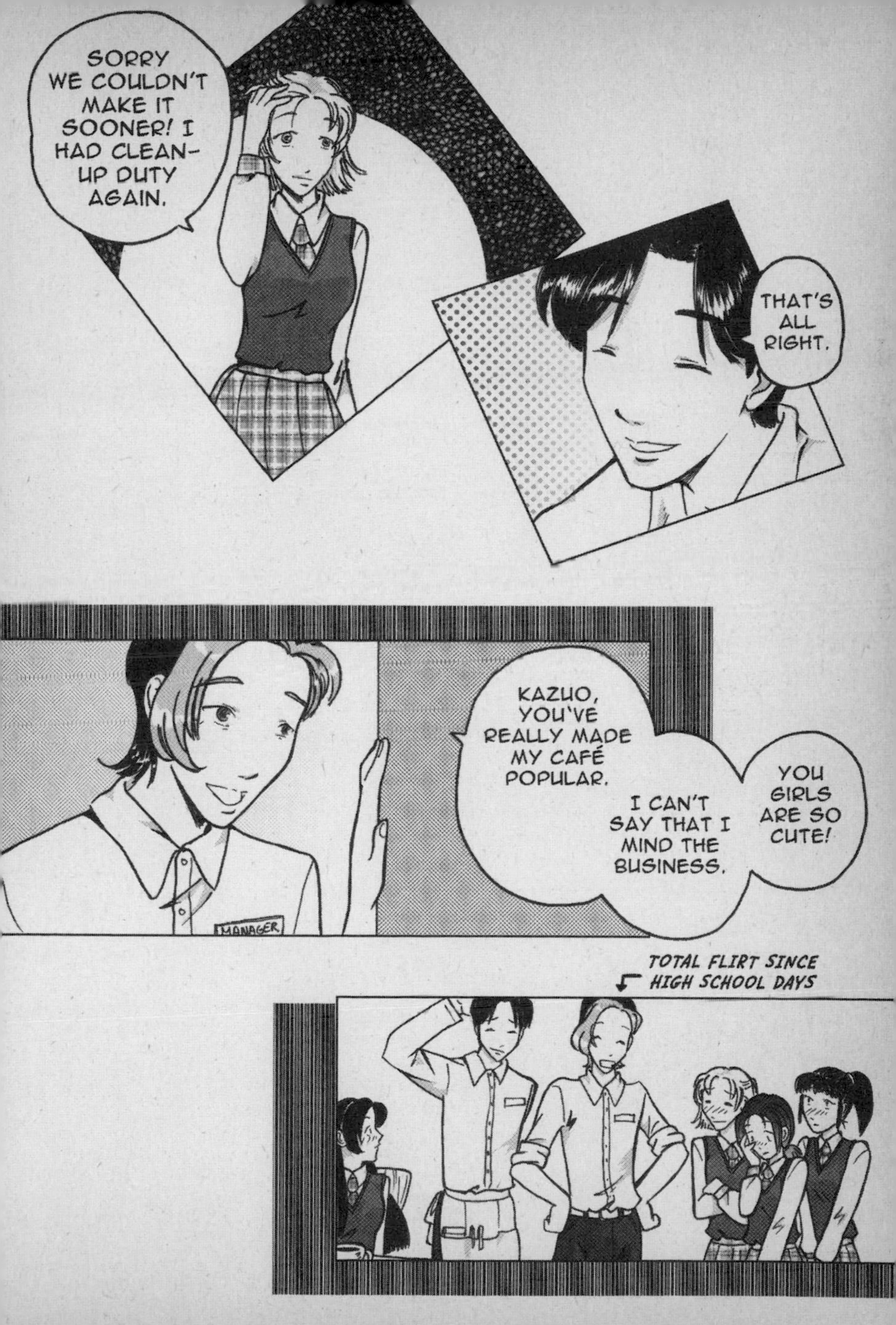
SORRY WE COULDN'T MAKE IT SOONER! I HAD CLEAN-UP DUTY AGAIN.
THAT'S ALL RIGHT.
KAZUO, YOU'VE REALLY MADE MY CAFÉ POPULAR.
I CAN'T SAY THAT I MIND THE BUSINESS.
YOU GIRLS ARE SO CUTE!
MANAGER
TOTAL FLIRT SINCE HIGH SCHOOL DAYS

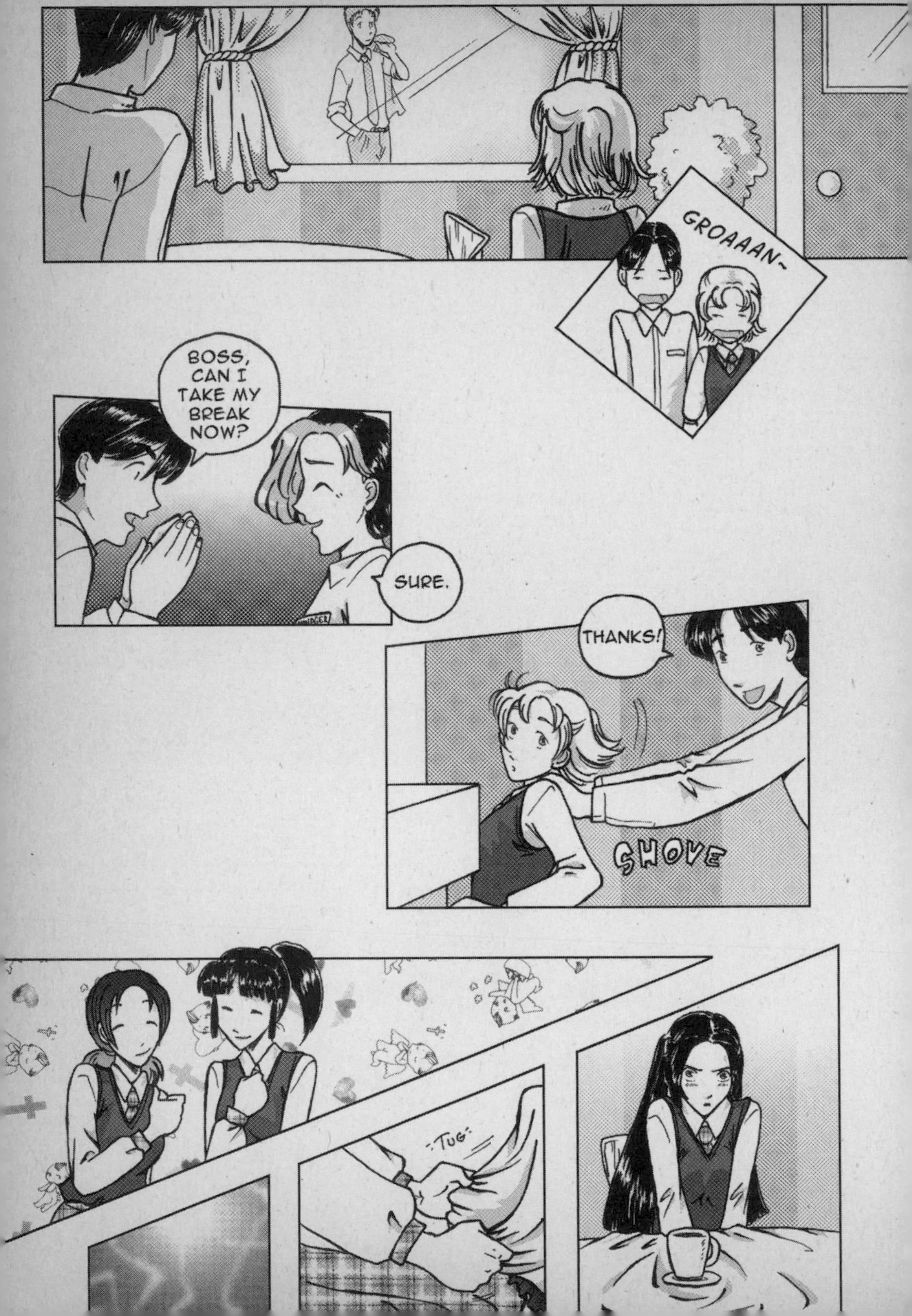
GROAAAN~
BOSS, CAN I TAKE MY BREAK NOW?
SURE.
THANKS!
SHOVE
TUG

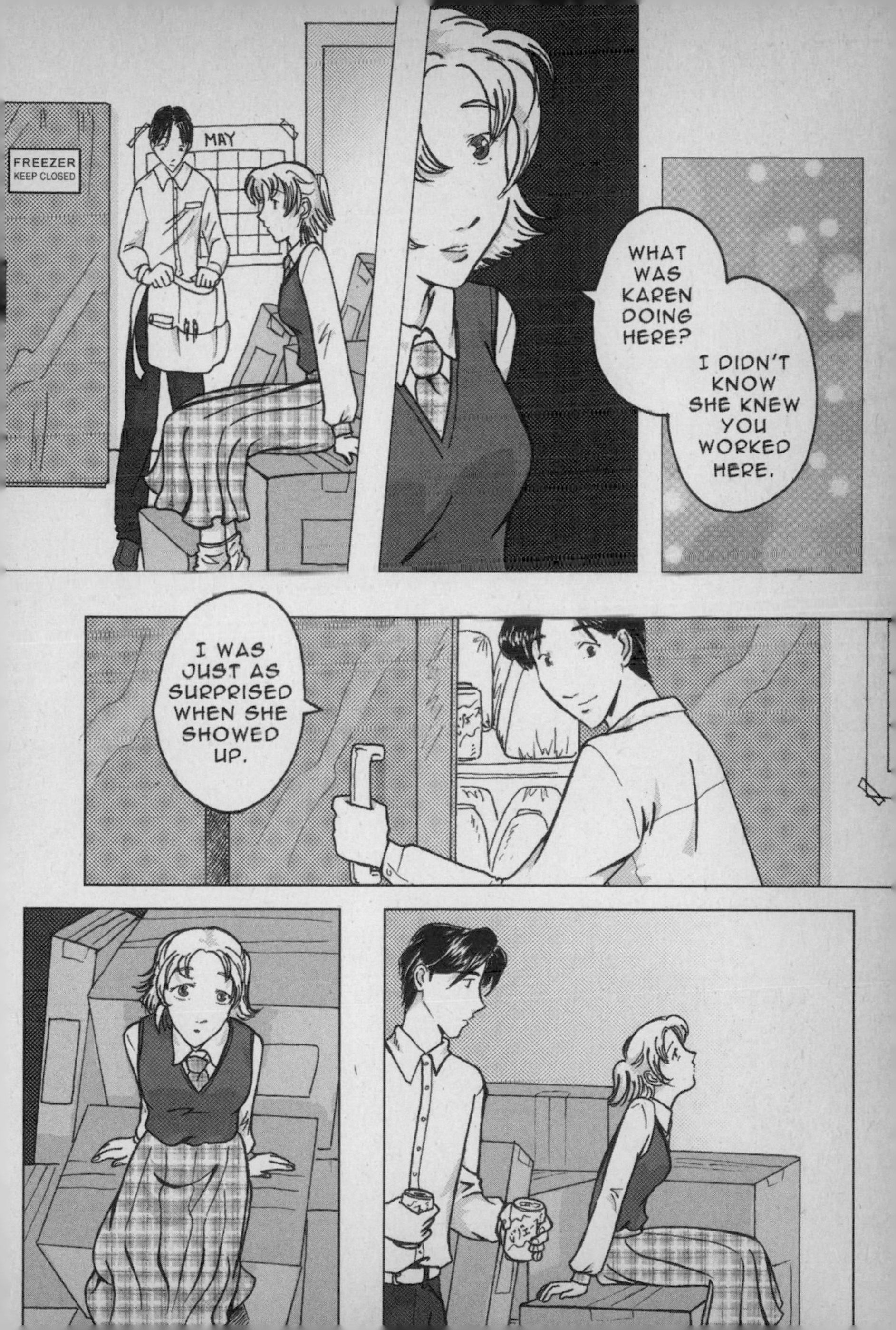
FREEZER
KEEP CLOSED
MAY
WHAT WAS KAREN DOING HERE?
I DIDN'T KNOW SHE KNEW YOU WORKED HERE.
I WAS JUST AS SURPRISED WHEN SHE SHOWED UP.

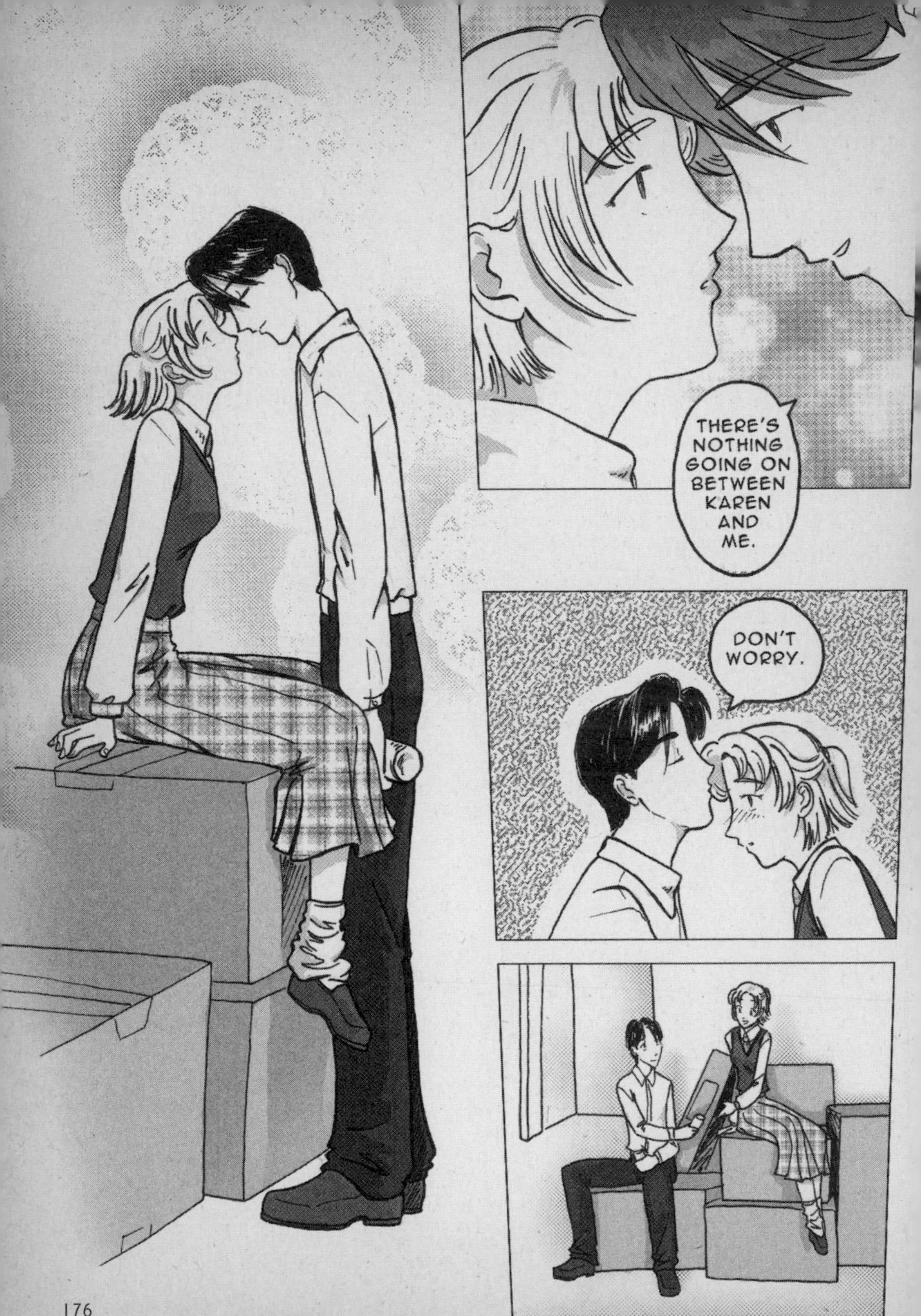
THERE'S NOTHING GOING ON BETWEEN KAREN AND ME.
DON'T WORRY.

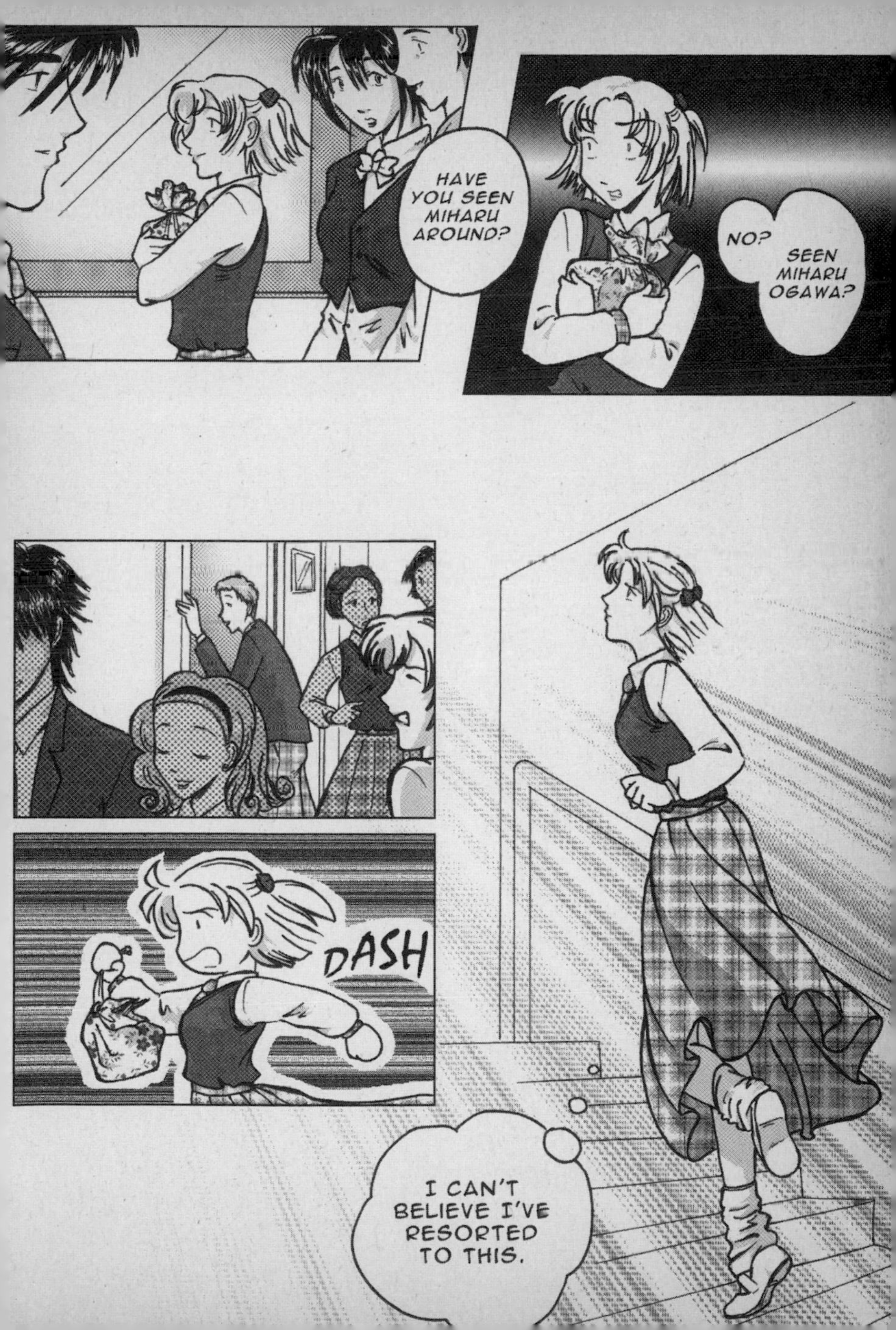
HAVE YOU SEEN MIHARU AROUND?
NO?
SEEN MIHARU OGAWA?
DASH
I CAN'T BELIEVE I'VE RESORTED TO THIS.

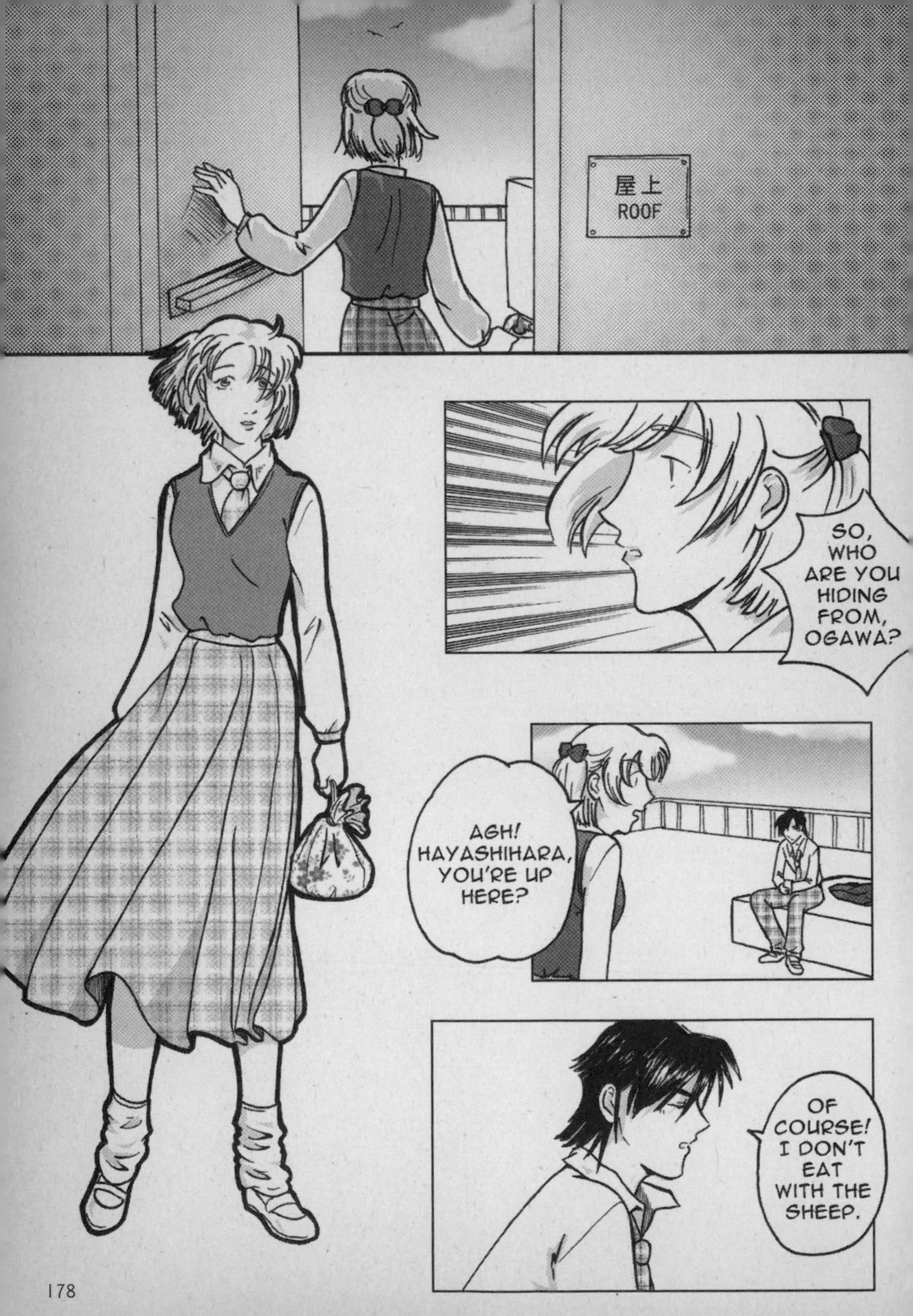
屋上
ROOF
SO, WHO ARE YOU HIDING FROM, OGAWA?
AGH! HAYASHIHARA, YOU'RE UP HERE?
OF COURSE! I DON'T EAT WITH THE SHEEP.

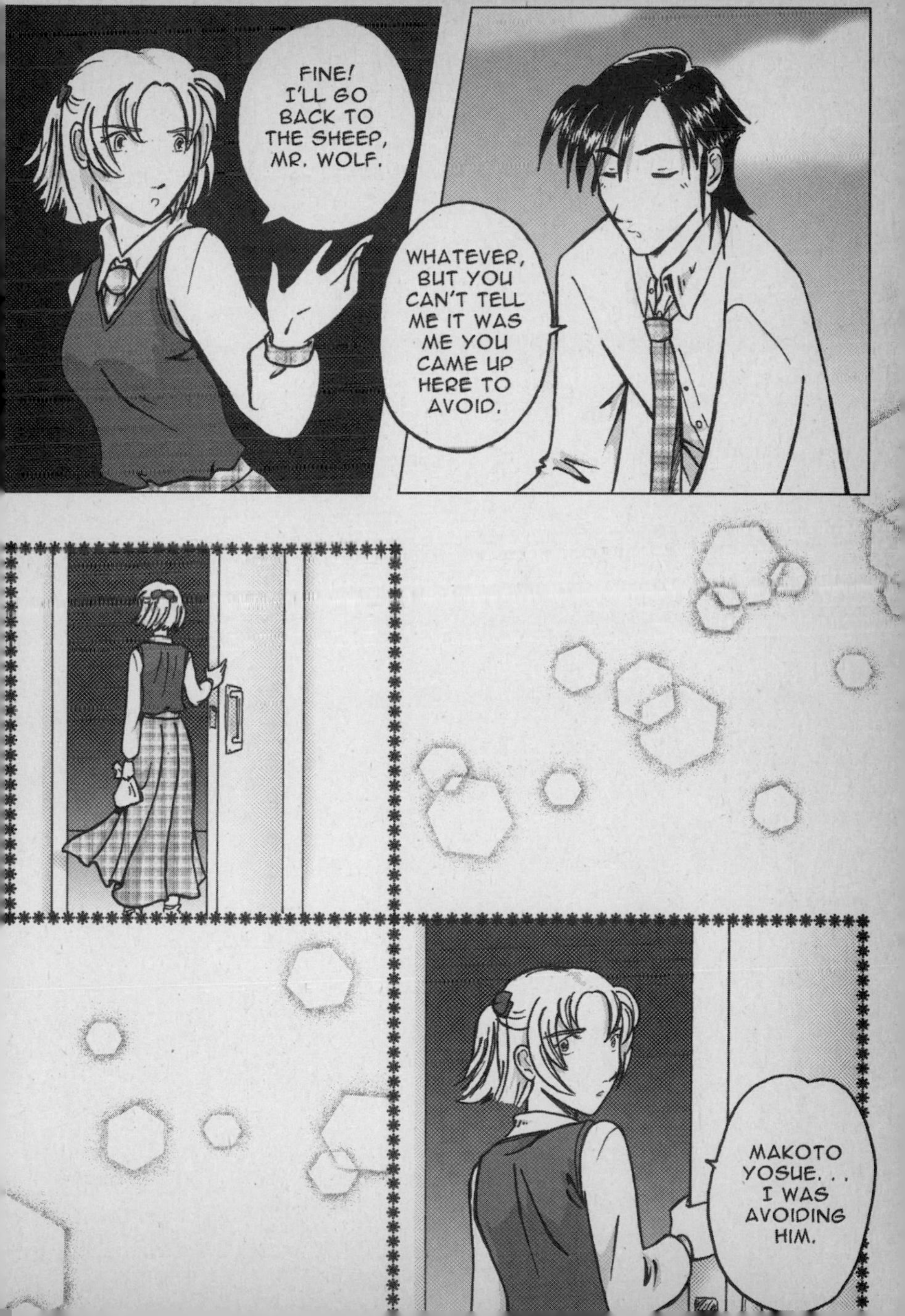
FINE! I'LL GO BACK TO THE SHEEP, MR. WOLF.
WHATEVER, BUT YOU CAN'T TELL ME IT WAS ME YOU CAME UP HERE TO AVOID.
MAKOTO YOSUE. . . I WAS AVOIDING HIM.

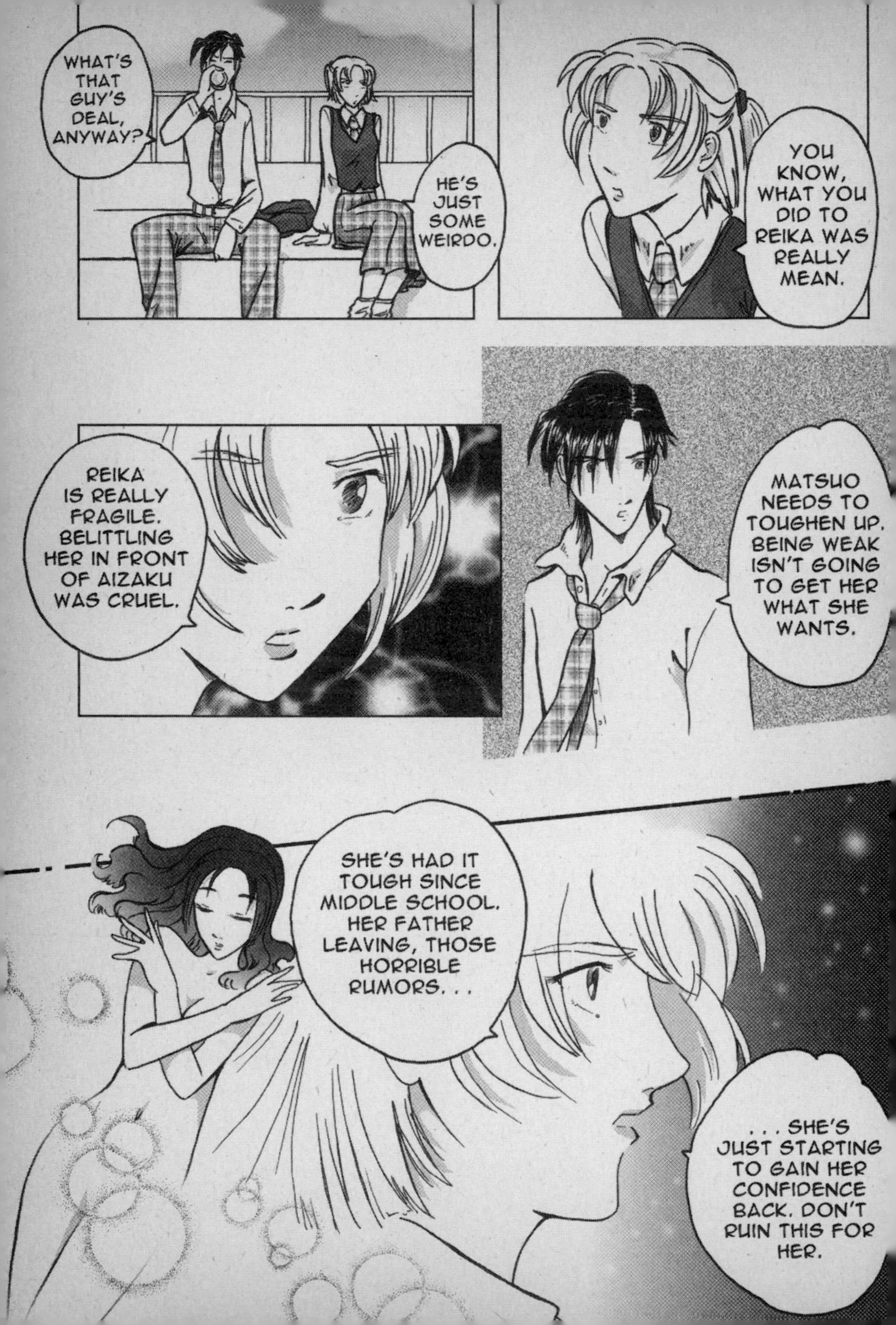
WHAT'S THAT GUY'S DEAL, ANYWAY?
HE'S JUST SOME WEIRDO.
YOU KNOW, WHAT YOU DID TO REIKA WAS REALLY MEAN.
MATSUO NEEDS TO TOUGHEN UP. BEING WEAK ISN'T GOING TO GET HER WHAT SHE WANTS.
REIKA IS REALLY FRAGILE. BELITTLING HER IN FRONT OF AIZAKU WAS CRUEL.
SHE'S HAD IT TOUGH SINCE MIDDLE SCHOOL. HER FATHER LEAVING, THOSE HORRIBLE RUMORS. . .
. . . SHE'S JUST STARTING TO GAIN HER CONFIDENCE BACK. DON'T RUIN THIS FOR HER.

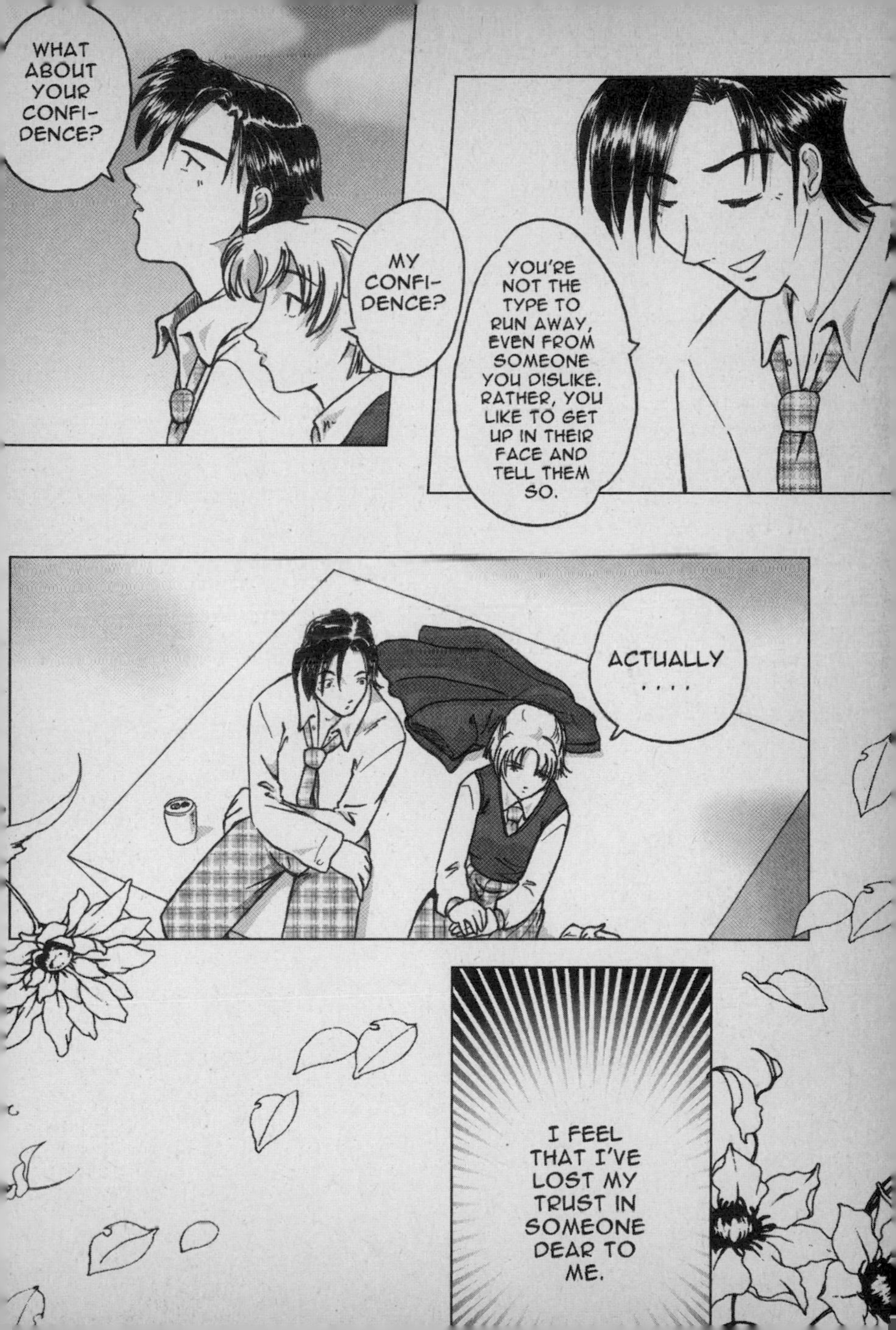
WHAT ABOUT YOUR CONFI-DENCE?
MY CONFI-DENCE?
YOU'RE NOT THE TYPE TO RUN AWAY, EVEN FROM SOMEONE YOU DISLIKE. RATHER, YOU LIKE TO GET UP IN THEIR FACE AND TELL THEM SO.
ACTUALLY ....
I FEEL THAT I'VE LOST MY TRUST IN SOMEONE DEAR TO ME.

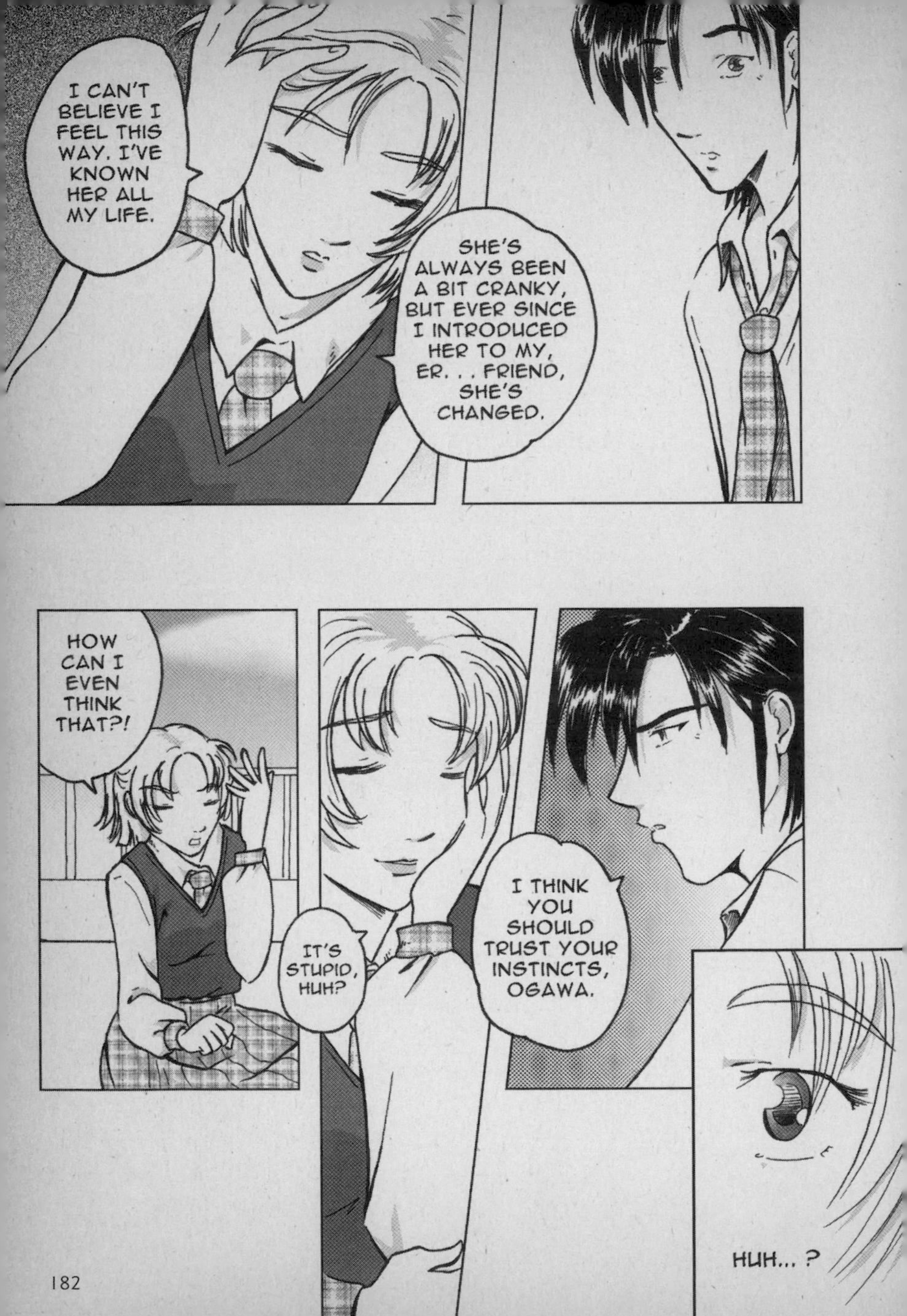
I CAN'T BELIEVE I FEEL THIS WAY. I'VE KNOWN HER ALL MY LIFE.
SHE'S ALWAYS BEEN A BIT CRANKY, BUT EVER SINCE I INTRODUCED HER TO MY, ER. . . FRIEND, SHE'S CHANGED.
HOW CAN I EVEN THINK THAT?!
IT'S STUPID, HUH?
I THINK YOU SHOULD TRUST YOUR INSTINCTS, OGAWA.
HUH... ?

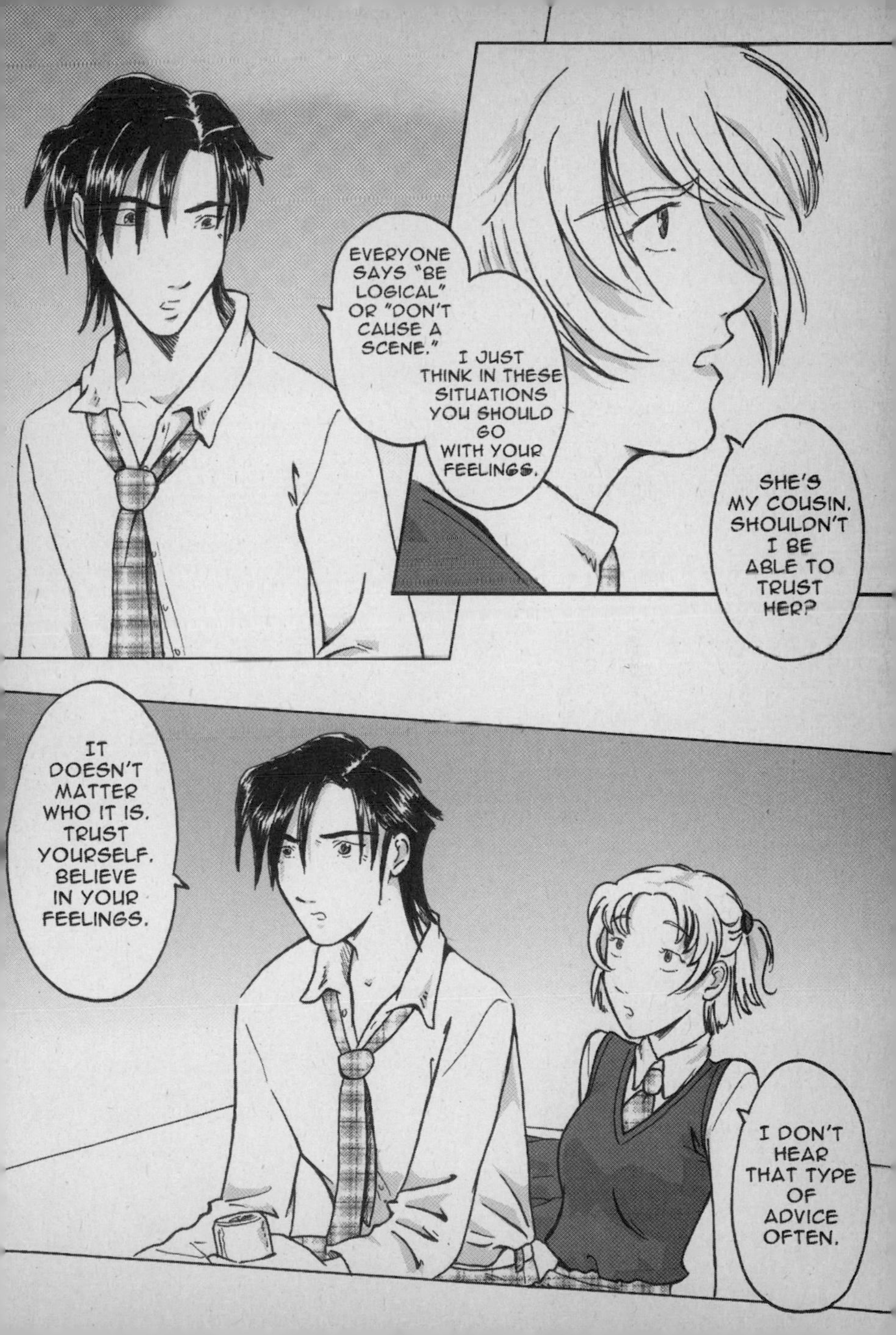
SHE'S MY COUSIN. SHOULDN'T I BE ABLE TO TRUST HER?
EVERYONE SAYS "BE LOGICAL" OR "DON'T CAUSE A SCENE."
I JUST THINK IN THESE SITUATIONS YOU SHOULD GO WITH YOUR FEELINGS.
IT DOESN'T MATTER WHO IT IS. TRUST YOURSELF. BELIEVE IN YOUR FEELINGS.
I DON'T HEAR THAT TYPE OF ADVICE OFTEN.

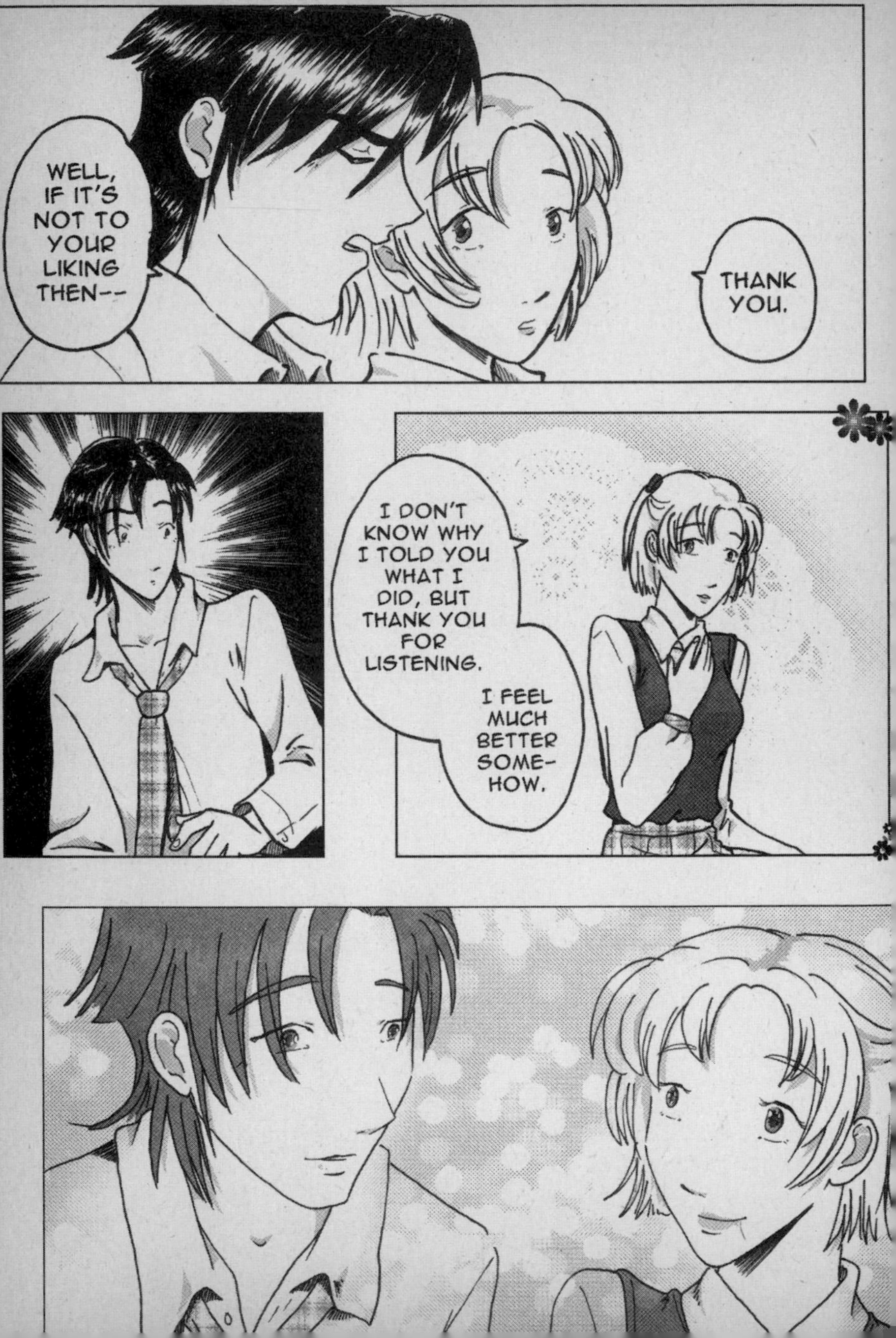
THANK YOU.
WELL, IF IT'S NOT TO YOUR LIKING THEN--
I DON'T KNOW WHY I TOLD YOU WHAT I DID, BUT THANK YOU FOR LISTENING.
I FEEL MUCH BETTER SOME-HOW.

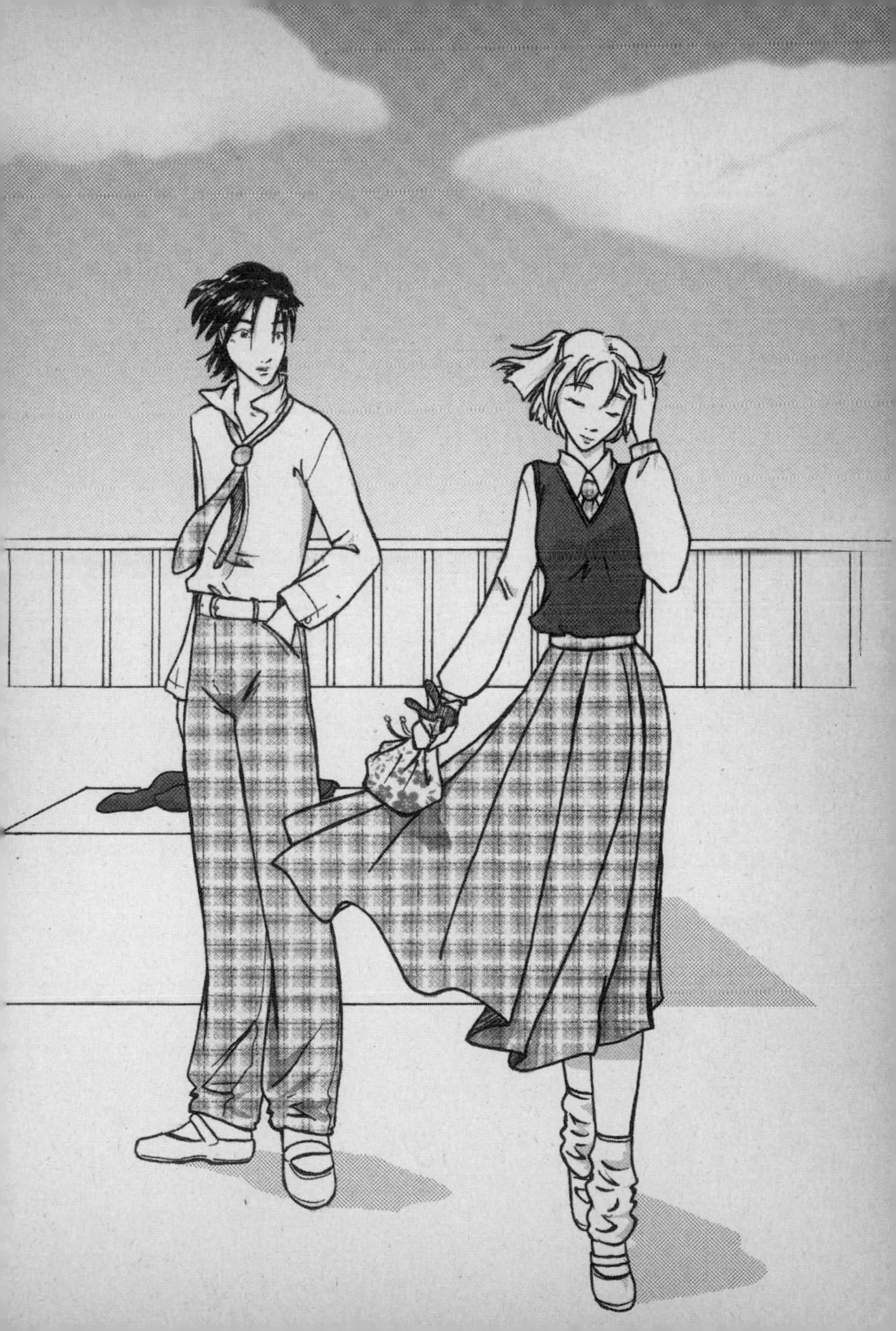

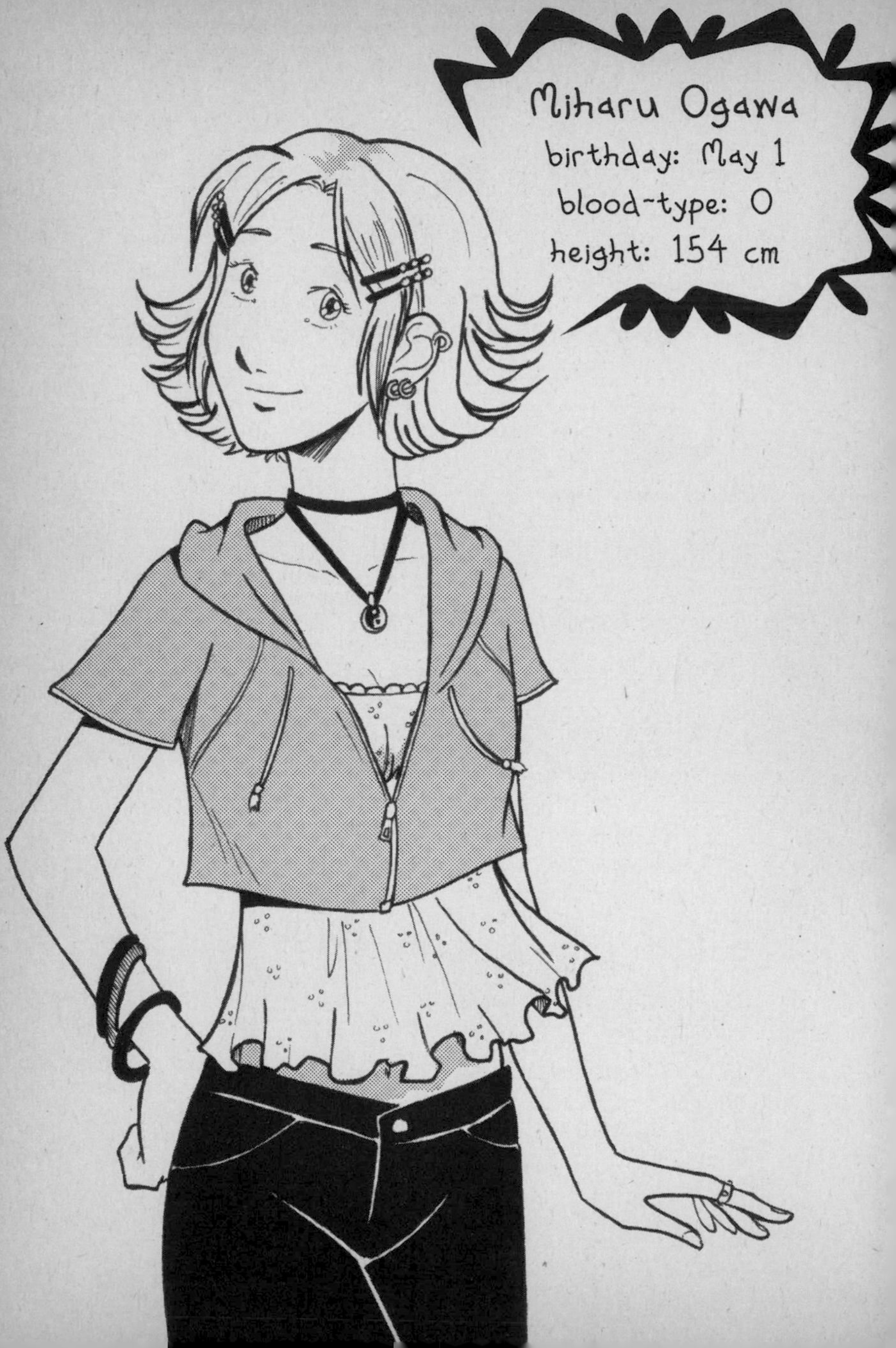
Miharu Ogawa
birthday: May 1
blood-type: O
height: 154 cm

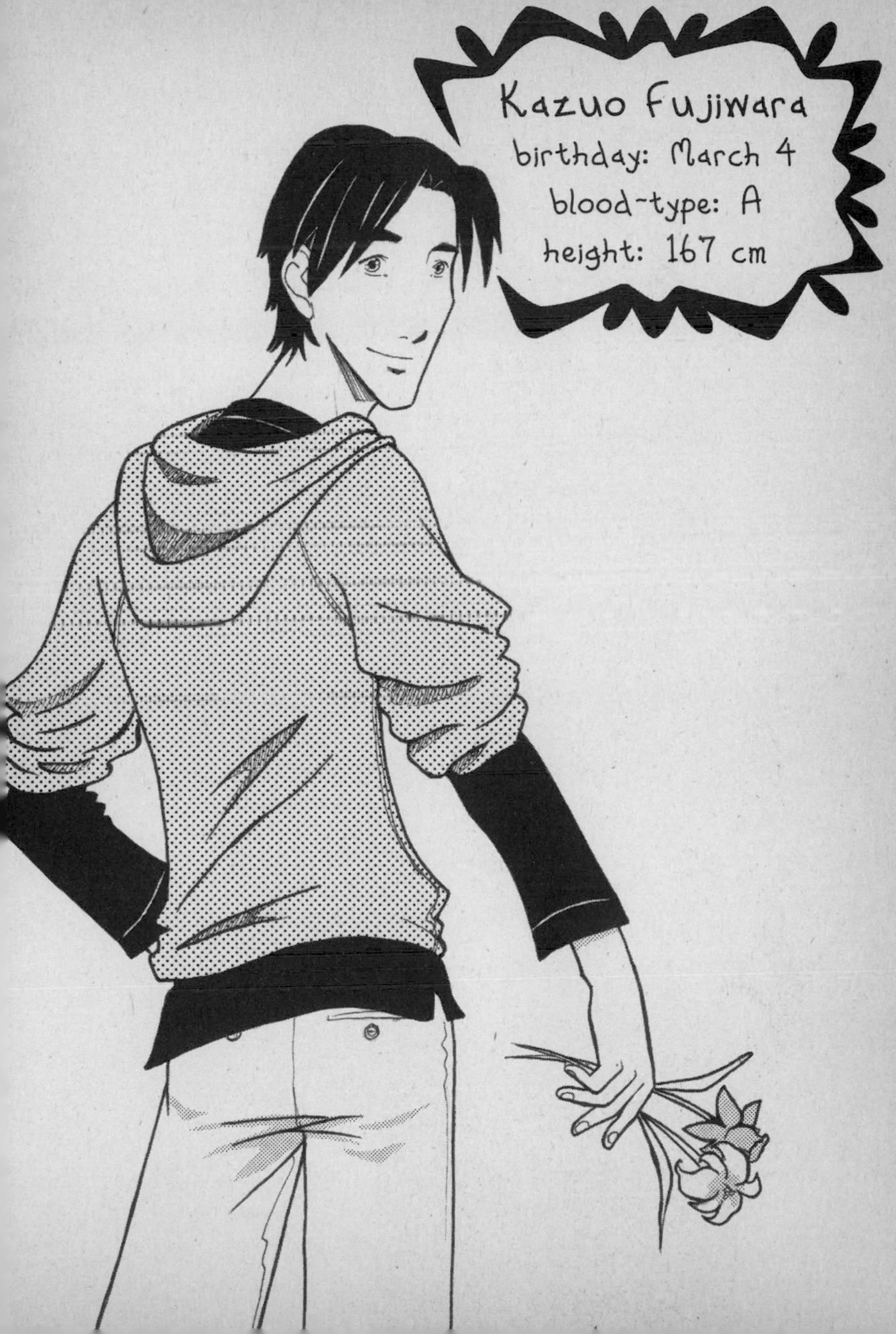
Kazuo Fujiwara
birthday: March 4
blood-type: A
height: 167 cm

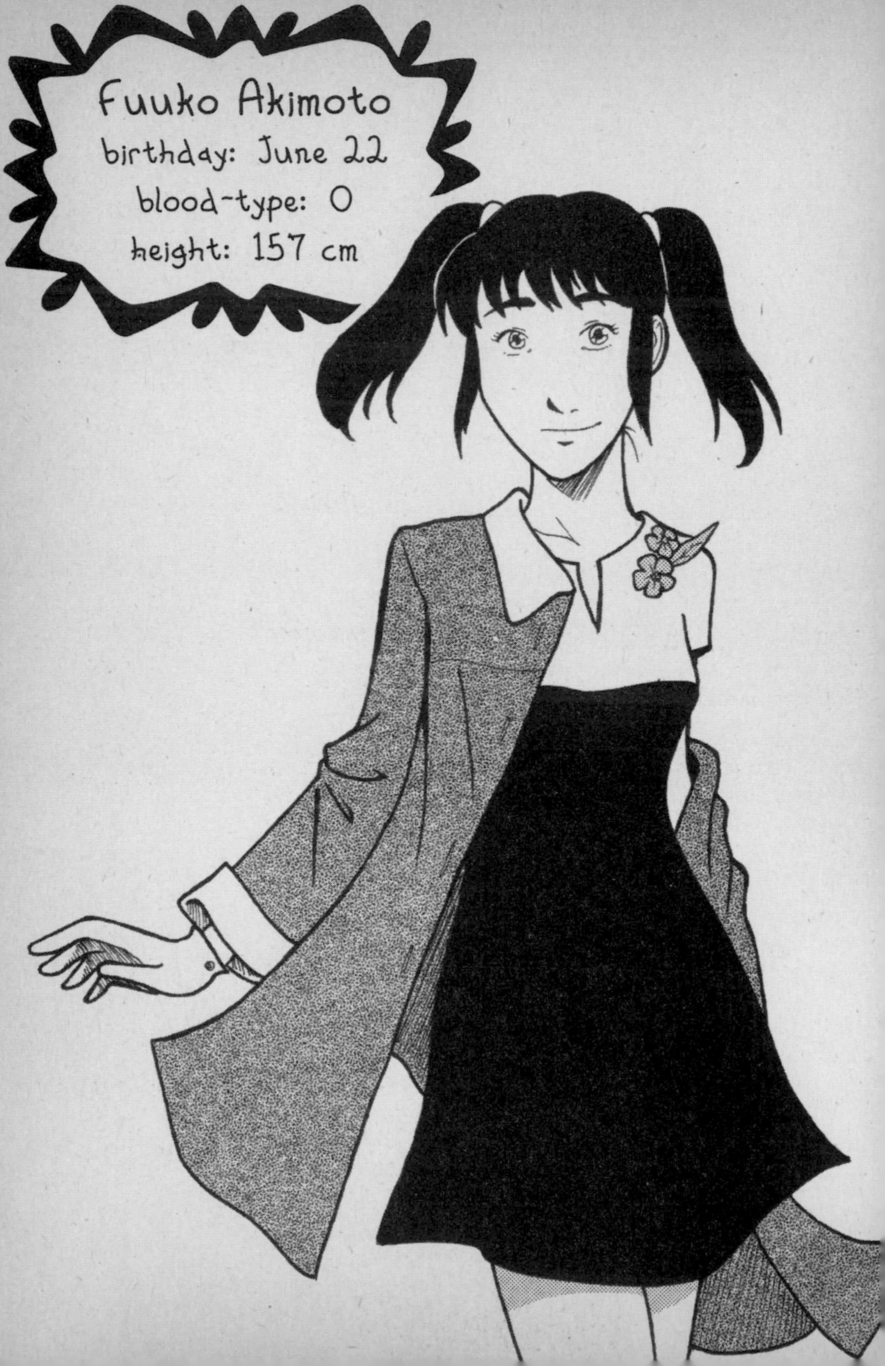
Fuuko Akimoto
birthday: June 22
blood-type: O
height: 157 cm

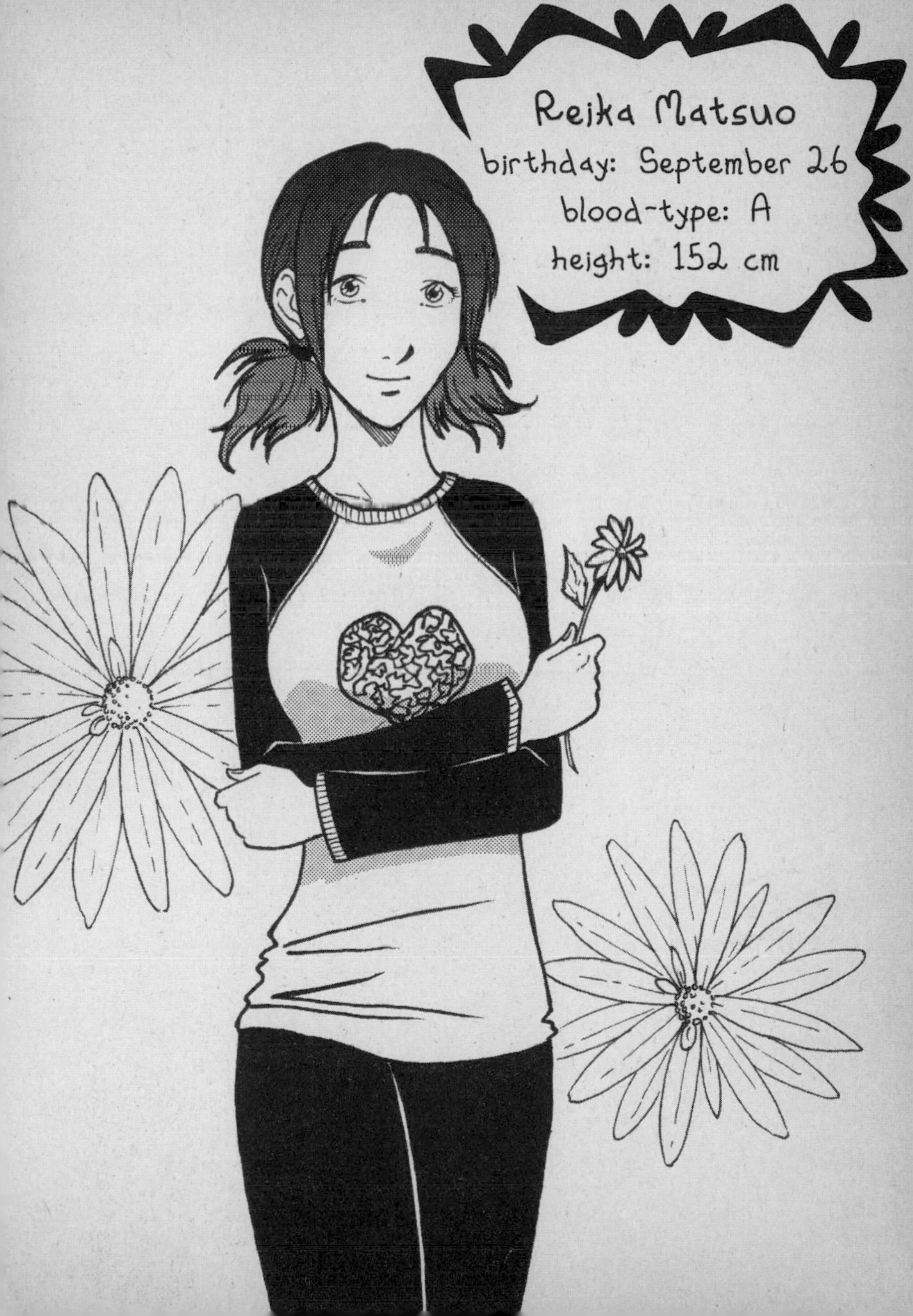
Reika Matsuo
birthday: September 26
blood-type: A
height: 152 cm

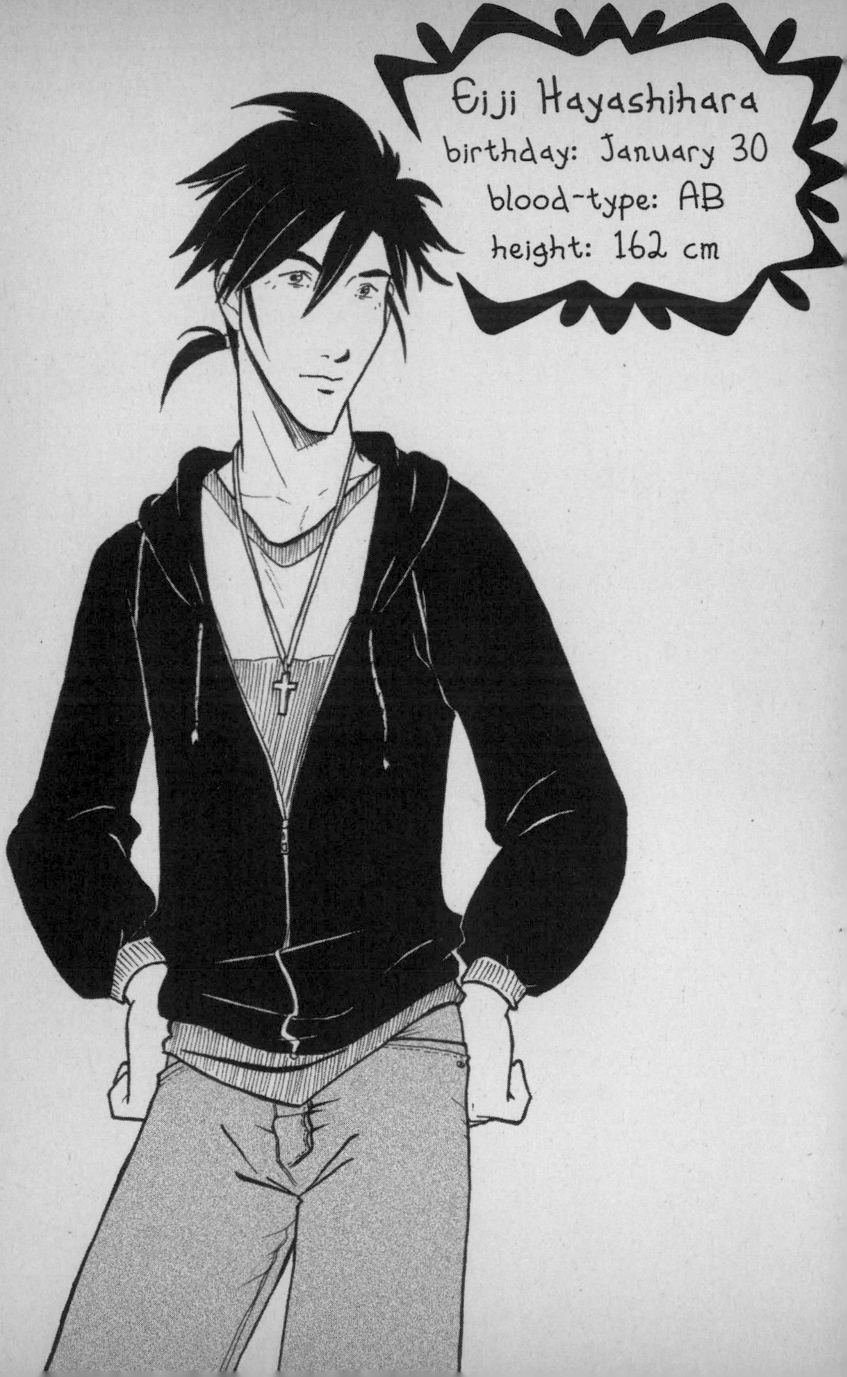
Eiji Hayashihara
birthday: January 30
blood-type: AB
height: 162 cm

About the Author

Gina Biggs has been creating comics for over six years. Her previous works include *Prophesy of Destiny* and various short stories in the *Fractured Kisses* anthology. *Red String* and Gina's latest work, titled *Love of Sausage*, can be found online at StrawberryComics.com.